Austria and the Papacy
in the Age of Metternich

Austria and the Papacy
in the Age of Metternich

I

Between Conflict and Cooperation
1809-1830

Alan J. Reinerman

The Catholic University of America Press
Washington, D.C.

Library of Congress Cataloging in Publication Data

Reinerman, Alan J.   1935–
  Austria and the papacy in the age of Metternich.

  Bibliography: v. 1, p.
  CONTENTS: 1. Between conflict and cooperation, 1809–1830.
  1. Catholic Church—Relations (diplomatic) with Austria. 2. Austria—Foreign relations—
Catholic Church. 3. Church and state in Austria. 4. Austria—History—Francis I.,
1792–1835. 5. Catholic Church in Austria—History. I. Title.
BX1517.R44   327.436'045'6   79-774
ISBN 0-8132-0548-4

TO FLORENCE
FOR INSPIRATION AND TOLERANCE

Table of Contents

Preface

Metternich has never ceased to interest historians. His forty-year ascendancy in the Habsburg Empire, his rarely paralleled mastery of international affairs, his controversial role as champion and symbol of the conservative order, his many-faceted personality—all these have combined to make him a subject of continuing fascination to scholars and the general public from his day to our own. In the liberal heyday of the nineteenth century, when he was seen as the supreme embodiment of Restoration conservatism, this interest had something of the Romantic fascination with Mephistopheles, and he was usually viewed as a wicked but glamorous figure. In our own century, reaction set in—a reaction fundamentally well justified, but at times carried to extremes, creating the danger that a new romanticization might emerge—Metternich as the omniscient prophet warning against the perils of radicalism and totalitarianism, or as the infallible guide to the dilemmas of diplomacy in a revolutionary age, whose words we would do well to heed today.

It is, I think, possible to reject both the old romanticization of Metternich and the new without detracting from the genuine interest of his career, whose immense significance for his age few historians, admiring or otherwise, would venture to deny. Certainly, the study of the past may help to illuminate the problems of the present, and in studying Metternich we may well uncover useful insights into certain persistent problems of the international order or of domestic policy—may even find alarming parallels to contemporary situations; yet historical parallels are notoriously tricky, and when I embarked upon this study, it was not with any particular intention of drawing lessons for our time, but only to clarify an important yet neglected and misunderstood aspect of the Age of Metternich.

As the title indicates, the study of which this book forms the first of two volumes deals with the relationship between Austria and the Papacy during the four decades when Metternich guided Habsburg foreign policy. In view of the continuing interest in Metternich's career, it is surprising that the present work should provide the first systematic study of a major aspect of his policy, yet his relationship with the Papacy has hitherto only been treated in either of two equally unsatisfactory ways: as an incidental and usually misinterpreted ingredient in his diplomacy, to be dismissed with a brief mention, or in the fragmentary form of isolated monographs on unrelated incidents, never drawn together to form a coherent whole. That the subject deserves better at the hands of historians is revealed by even a brief consideration of its importance. For Metternich, relations with Rome were of major significance for his lifelong struggle to defend the Austrian Empire and the Restoration Order against the revolutionary challenge, as well as for his Italian policy and for his involvement in the domestic affairs of the Empire, while its importance for his personal career can be seen in the simple reflection that his downfall in 1848 was the end result of the sequence of events that began with the election of Pope Pius IX in 1846—that is, of the ultimate failure of his Papal policy. For the Papacy, the relationship with Austria was important, often decisively so, for the formation during this crucial period not only of its foreign policy, but of its domestic policy in the Papal State, and of its attitude to the rising currents of liberalism and nationalism; it was thus intimately linked with the fate of the Temporal Power, and indeed with the whole question of the proper role of the Papacy and the Catholic Church in the modern world. For Italy, Austro-Papal relations were of great consequence for their intersection at several key points with the course of the Risorgimento, whose development they thus helped to shape. Nor was that relationship without significance for the overall course of Restoration Europe, with whose fate it was closely tied and whose overthrow in 1848 it helped indirectly to precipitate. A thorough study of Austro-Papal relations, making use of the relevant literature, but based essentially—and, indeed, necessarily, given the wide gaps that exist in that literature—upon archival research, can thus make a significant contribution to our understanding of nineteenth century Europe. The present work was written with that aim in mind; whether it has been attained, I must leave the reader to judge.

Since the dearth of scholarly studies and printed sources has compelled me to rely primarily upon archival materials, I would like to express my gratitude to the many archivists without whose assistance I could not have written this work, and in particular to: Dr. Richard Blaas, Director of the Austrian State Archives at the time when I worked there, and his staff; Monsignor M. Giusti, Prefect of the Vatican Archives, and his staff; Professor Emilia Morelli, Director of the Istituto per la Storia del Risorgimento, Rome; and the archivists of the Congregazione De Propaganda Fide; the Archivio Arcivescovile di Bologna; the Országos Széchenyi Könyvtár, Budapest; the Archives Diplomatiques of the Ministère des Affaires Étrangeres, Paris; the Geheimes Staatsarchiv, Munich; the Deutsches Zentralarchiv, Historisches Abteilung II, Merseburg; the Public Record Office, London; the Archivo General of the Ministerio de Asuntos Exteriores; Madrid; the Central State Archives, Prague; and the State Archives in Turin, Florence, Parma, Lucca, and Naples. My gratitude is also due for the Fulbright grant which enabled me to begin my research in Rome. I am likewise grateful to Professor Margaret O'Dwyer, who first aroused my interest in this area, and to Professor Enno Kraehe and Professor Raymond Schmandt for their perceptive comments on my work at various stages. My final but most important thanks are to my wife and daughter for their constant support, and for their understanding tolerance of my frequent disappearances into distant archives or into the almost equally inaccessible depths of my study.

I

Austria and the
Papacy to 1815

1. Legacy of Conflict

Down to the late eighteenth century, Austro-Papal relations were characterized in general by a *de facto* alliance against common enemies.[1] At both Rome and Vienna, Austria was regarded as the champion of Catholicism in Central Europe, the bulwark of the Church against Moslem Turks, Protestant Germans, and Orthodox Russians. Although Austria's struggles against these foes might owe more to political calculation than to religious zeal, the zeal was not lacking, and, whatever her motives, Vienna was indeed fighting the Church's battle. Appreciating this service, the Papacy offered moral and material support to the Habsburgs, who in turn endeavored to protect and spread Catholicism. All was not perfect harmony: questions of religious jurisdiction led to prolonged controversies, while Austrian power in Italy aroused the apprehensions of Rome, anxious as ever to safeguard the political independence that it considered essential for its spiritual freedom.[2] Yet these quarrels did not upset the basic understanding and community of interest between the two courts, and their *de facto* alliance endured into the second half of the eighteenth century. Only then, with the accession to the throne of Joseph II (1780–1790), did a controversy over fundamental interests arise, beginning a deterioration in Austro-Papal relations that continued virtually unchecked until Metternich's day. The source of the conflict was Josephism, the Emperor's religious policy aimed at subordinating the church in Austria to the state and severing its ties with Rome. Despite bitter Papal opposition, Joseph pushed his policy through, and by the end of his reign the state church was firmly established and Papal authority had become largely nominal. Thereafter, with the Papacy working ceaselessly to overthrow Josephism while the bureaucracy at Vienna sought its ever-greater extension, distrust and conflict came to characterize Austro-Papal relations.[3]

The wars of the 1790's brought political conflict to disrupt those relations further. At stake were the Legations, the northern Papal provinces of Bologna, Ferrara, and Ravenna (or the Romagna), which Napoleon had forced the Papacy to cede in 1797. Austria expelled the French from the Legations in 1799, but instead of returning them to the Pope, began a determined effort to annex them. At the conclave of 1800, Austria sought the election of a pope who would consent to this annexation. When, despite her efforts, Pius VII (1800–1823) was elected, she attempted to bully him into

1

yielding the coveted provinces. Only Napoleon's victory over Austria in 1801
brought this pressure to an end. The distrust of Austrian designs on Papal
territory which had thus been aroused at Rome would remain for decades an
obstacle to good Austro-Papal relations.[4]

Nothing was done after 1801 to efface the impression left by these events.
Down to 1809, Austria's dealings with Rome were largely confined to efforts
to eliminate the last vestiges of Papal jurisdiction over her religious affairs,
and to use the Papacy for her political advantage.[5] Vienna did her best to
prevent a Papal rapprochement with France, opposing the Concordat of 1801
and criticizing Pius's coronation of Napoleon. While at war with France in
1805, Austria sought to stir up the Papacy against Napoleon; then, after her
defeat, she courted French good will by advising Rome to grant the religious
and political concessions that Napoleon was demanding.[6] As Napoleon's
pressure on the Holy See grew, the latter found little sympathy at Vienna:
Austrian diplomats were more inclined to criticize Pius VII for his "obstinate
resistance" than to sympathize with his efforts to defend his political and
spiritual freedom.[7] When the French occupied the Papal State in 1808,
Austria ignored Papal appeals for aid: the Pope's predicament was "unfortunate," but Austria had no intention of risking a quarrel with Napoleon on
his behalf.[8]

Only when in 1809 Austria again prepared to challenge France did she
begin to express support for the Papacy. Now she denounced in ringing terms
the "exorbitant pretensions" of Napoleon and assured Pius that the Emperor
Francis I would do everything possible to alleviate his plight; in fact, the pontiff was given to understand that Austria was about to go to war at least
partly in order to come to his rescue.[9] Vienna ceaselessly exhorted Pius to
stand firm in his resistance to Napoleon, and no doubt Austrian exhortations
and assurances played a part in his increasingly firm opposition to French
demands. But Austria hoped for more from the Pope than mere verbal resistance. Plans were laid for a popular uprising against the French, to begin at
Rome in May, 1809, and spread throughout the peninsula. The rebellion was
to be launched as a holy war in the name of the persecuted Pope. Despite the
efforts of the Austrian chargé, Chevalier Lebzeltern, Pius refused his active
cooperation, partly because he considered such a role contrary to his spiritual
character, partly because he feared it might provoke bloody reprisals against
his subjects. Yet he admitted that he "considered the Austrian cause in this
war as his own," and would pray for her victory.[10] Lebzeltern carried on with
the plan, but the rising proved abortive. An English fleet that was to give the
signal for the revolt by seizing Civitavecchia failed to appear; an Austrian
army that was to invade northern Italy was halted by the French; finally, in
June, the French expelled Lebzeltern from Rome, and the project collapsed.[11]

But Lebzeltern departed from Rome with the consolation that Pius's attitude towards Austria had begun to change. Austria's past efforts to annex
the Legations now seemed minor in comparison with Napoleon's seizure of
the entire Papal State, and Josephism less dangerous than Napoleon's gran-
diose assumption of the authority of Charlemagne or Constantine over the
universal Church. Moreover, Austria had at least tried to drive the French
from Italy. In consequence, Pius was more favorably disposed towards Aus-

tria than he had ever been. At his farewell audience with Lebzeltern, he praised Francis I lavishly for his effort to liberate Europe, expressed confidence in his good will towards the Papacy, and promised to support him with what means he still possessed. As the chargé left, Pius gave him a bull of excommunication against Napoleon, asking him to smuggle it to Austria so that it might be published there.[12]

The rebirth of the old *de facto* alliance between Austria and Rome seemed at hand; but before Lebzeltern could reach Vienna, Napoleon, infuriated by Papal resistance, had arrested and imprisoned Pius VII.[13] Soon afterward, Austria, defeated at Wagram, signed the disastrous Peace of Schönbrunn. Hereafter, the exhausted Empire would have to devote all its energies to the task of surviving in a Napoleonic Europe, with little time to spare for other questions.

Nonetheless, the potential importance of Austro-Papal relations was not forgotten by all at Vienna. When Lebzeltern finally managed to reach the Imperial court in October, 1809, he found that his August Master had chosen a new Foreign Minister, the man with whom Austria's fate was to be linked for the next forty years.[14] Even in the midst of his preoccupation with ensuring Austria's survival, Metternich found time for a lengthy discussion of the Papal situation with Lebzeltern, for he felt that "even now, the affairs of the Holy Father...merit the particular interest" of Austria. Regretting the ill-will and distrust that recent Austrian policy had produced at Rome, Metternich hoped by adopting a new and more conciliatory attitude to erase the legacy of the past, win back Papal good will, and pave the way for a close and cooperative relationship that would be mutually beneficial. Though present circumstances hardly seemed propitious, he was determined to seize the first opportunity to launch this new initiative.[15]

Metternich soon decided that his most promising line of approach was to work for the Pope's liberation. He would have liked to work for the restoration of the Temporal Power as well, for he shared the contemporary opinion that the Papacy could hardly preserve its freedom of action and impartiality without it; but he saw that this was at present impossible in the face of Napoleon's obvious determination to make Rome the second city of his empire.[16] There seemed, however, some hope that Napoleon might be persuaded to release the pontiff, and Austria certainly had good cause to desire his liberation, even aside from the considerations of humanity and piety which were of some weight with the devout Francis I. Pius's captivity was creating numerous difficulties in the administration of the Austrian Church, for example by making it virtually impossible to obtain the required Papal confirmation of Imperial appointments to bishoprics and certain dispensations which only the Pope could grant. There would be worse to come, however, if Napoleon could break his captive's will and impose his domination upon the Papacy: the threat of a new Avignon Papacy, with all that implied for Papal impartiality and the interests of other Catholic states. Metternich was resolved that Austria, even at the cost of schism, would never accept the authority of a French-controlled Papacy.[17]

At present, direct contact between Austria and the Pope had been cut off: Pius was virtually incommunicado, Rome a French city from which the Curia had been expelled. Metternich was therefore anxious to preserve his last link with the Papacy, the Vienna Nunciature, whose suppression both Napoleon and the Josephists were urging. At length, Metternich secured an arrangement by which the current Nuncio, Monsignor Severoli, would remain in Vienna as a private person without formal diplomatic character.[18]

The Papal captivity, Metternich had to admit, did have one major advantage: it helped him overcome the doubts that Francis I and the Archbishop of Vienna felt about the validity of the annulment of Napoleon's first marriage, thus making possible the marriage with Marie Louise that Metternich regarded as vital. The annulment of a sovereign's marriage had always been reserved to the judgment of the Pope himself, and Pius, had he been free, would certainly have refused his consent in this case, to the great detriment of Metternich's plans for a Franco-Austrian alliance.[19] With Pius imprisoned, however, it was easy to brush aside the protests of the Nuncio and the Archbishop, and to persuade Francis to accept the French position on the annulment.[20] The marriage was duly celebrated in April, 1810, to the immense satisfaction of the Foreign Minister and the great annoyance of the Nuncio, who had made heroic efforts to enlighten Metternich on the grave doubts existing as to the validity of the marriage—doubts about which Metternich preferred to remain in happy ignorance.[21]

Metternich hoped that this marriage would give Austria had gained influence over Napoleon which might be used to persuade him to free the Pope. When he visited Paris for the wedding, he did so with the intention of undertaking this task.[22] He found Napoleon apparently prepared to accept his father-in-law's mediation of his quarrel with the Pope, and they agreed to send Lebzeltern to sound out Pius VII.[23]

Metternich had several motives for undertaking the mediation. Fundamentally, it was the first move in his long campaign to regain Papal good will for Austria and erase the distrust created by thirty years of conflict. If he could arrange a settlement that would restore Pius's freedom and spiritual authority, the Papacy might once again come to regard Austria as its natural protector and ally. The resulting revival of Austria's influence over the Papacy and her prestige in the Catholic world would in turn contribute to that revival of her international position for which Metternich was working. Nor would it be without value in the Habsburg Empire itself, where popular loyalties, shaken by the unending stream of disasters in recent years, could be rallied to a ruler who had demonstrated his devotion to the Head of the Church. Such a demonstration was particularly desirable now that the marriage of Marie Louise to the jailor of Pius VII had irritated Catholic sensibilities. Moreover, Metternich hoped to win the gratitude of Napoleon by arranging a satisfactory settlement of an embarrassing dispute. Finally, a settlement would end the difficulties which the Pope's imprisonment had created in Austrian religious affairs, eliminate both the threat of a new Avignon Papacy should Pius be driven to yield to French pressure and the danger of a schism if Pius died in captivity and Napoleon tried to create his own pope, and extricate Austria from her present difficult position as middleman in the Franco-Papal quarrel, thus making possible better relations with both parties.[24]

Foreseeing these advantages, Metternich gladly undertook the mediation, even though he was not sanguine as to his chances of success. Only after a lengthy argument with Napoleon was Metternich able to secure a few grudging concessions: provided the Pope would withdraw his excommunication of Napoleon and, if not renounce his claim to the Temporal Power, at least refrain from pressing it, he would be set at liberty, allowed to establish a center of government for the Church anywhere except in Rome, given full freedom to exercise his religious authority, and provided with an independent revenue.[26] Metternich considered these terms acceptable, since they would give the Pope the minimum conditions necessary to carry out his spiritual office. However, he was doubtful whether Pius, after his recent experiences, would have enough trust in Napoleon to be willing to negotiate on these or any terms. Even more fundamental was the question of Napoleon's sincerity. Metternich suspected that Napoleon aimed only at improving his position in Catholic eyes by offering a settlement that he expected Pius to reject, and at commiting Austria to support the French position in the quarrel. These dangers the Foreign Minister was determined to avert by keeping the negotiations secret and by maintaining a scrupulous neutrality.[27]

Metternich's caution was evident in his instructions to Lebzeltern.[28] The envoy's ostensible mission was to secure from Pius certain spiritual faculties for Austrian bishops; his real mission, to be kept secret, was to explain to Pius the conditions on which Napoleon seemed willing to reach a settlement, urge him to accept those conditions as a basis for negotiations, and deduce from his reaction whether a formal mediation had some chance of success.

Lebzeltern reached Savona, where Pius was imprisoned, on May 15, 1810.[29] Pius, touched by this effort to free him, welcomed him cordially, but felt compelled to express his indignation at Austria's "strange daring" in allying itself to an excommunicate by a marriage of dubious validity. Passing quickly over the delicate religious aspect of the marriage, Lebzeltern stressed that it had been politically necessary for Austria's survival; moreover, he declared, Francis I had agreed to it partly in the hope that it would enable him to help the Pope. Pius was impressed by these arguments, for he had come to believe that "it is of the greatest importance for us all that Austria survive strong and independent," since in her lay the only hope for the liberation of the Church and of Europe. He therefore admitted that the marriage had been politically justified, and promised to make no public criticism of it.[30]

Lebzeltern next explained the conditions proposed for a settlement. Pius was reluctant to consider them, for he feared that if he made concessions, Napoleon would accept and publicize them, then renege on his side of the bargain, as had happened before. By refusing to negotiate, the Papacy would lose nothing, and would gain in moral stature. Lebzeltern could not deny Napoleon's unreliability, but he pointed out that, though the Pope's resistance had indeed enhanced his moral prestige, his captivity had done great harm to the Church, and might even lead to schism. Pius would do best to accept the offer of mediation and discover whether Napoleon might not be sincere; Napoleon would surely seize upon a refusal as proof of the Pope's intransigence which justified his imprisonment.[31]

After several days of discussion, Pius was persuaded to agree to the mediation and to make the chief concessions that Napoleon demanded.[32] Metternich, delighted at the Pope's agreement, felt that a settlement was within reach.[33] But when he informed Napoleon of the mission's outcome, the Emperor responded with a tirade against the Pope, whom he charged with plotting secretly against him. Metternich had no difficulty in refuting the flimsy charges, but soon realized that they had been only pretexts to break off the negotiation. After listening to his account of the Pope's willingness to reach a settlement, Napoleon merely replied that he felt the time was not yet ripe to negotiate.[34] It was apparent that the Emperor had never seriously intended to reach a compromise settlement, for he was confident that in due course Pius would have to accept whatever terms he might wish to dictate; he had only agreed to the mediation in order to put himself in a stronger moral position by making an offer which he expected the Pope to reject.[35]

Metternich's first initiative in Papal policy thus ended in failure. Yet it had not been without value. Pius had been favorably impressed by the Austrian effort to aid him, which had done much to cancel the prejudicial effects of past Austrian policy.[36] Metternich had thus won Papal good will for Austria for the first time in decades, paving the way for a more cordial relationship to develop between the two courts when Pius at last regained his freedom.[37]

For the present, however, Metternich could do little either to help the Pope or to work for better Austro-Papal relations. He continued to hope for the Pope's liberation, and from time to time over the next few years he urged Napoleon to set him free; but he was not surprised to receive a negative response.[38] Despite his interest in the French alliance, he consistently rejected Napoleon's hints that Austria should join in breaking down the Pope's continued resistance—a stand of considerable importance, if Napoleon and the Nuncio were correct in believing that only the continued sympathy and passive support of Austria gave Pius the courage to resist his captor's demands.[39]

But in general Austro-Papal relations stagnated until the power of Napoleon began at last to wane. In July, 1813, Pius learned that an armistice had been arranged between France and her enemies, and that a congress would meet at Prague, under Austrian mediation, to attempt to settle the conflict. The news stirred him to action: here at last was an opportunity to present to the Powers his claim for freedom and the restoration of his states. He was particularly encouraged to learn that Austria would conduct the mediation, regarding her as the Power most favorable to the Papacy.[40] He quickly appealed to Francis I to act on his behalf at the Congress.[41] His letter had no immediate effect: the Congress of Prague proved abortive, and Francis, though willing, had no opportunity to present the Pope's case.[42] However, Metternich did set the restoration of the Papal State as one of Austria's goals for the final peace settlement,[43] and for the rest of the war Austria was the most outspoken champion of liberating the Pope and restoring the Temporal Power.[44]

An opportunity to work for these objectives came at the Congress of Chatillon, where Metternich set the Pope's liberation and return to Rome as a condition of the peace negotiations. The Congress ended in failure, but not before the Allies, at Austria's urging, drafted a note on March 19, 1814, asking Napoleon to free Pius.[45] Napoleon, warned in advance of this demand and reluctant to allow the Allies credit for freeing the pontiff, had already given orders that he be released and allowed to return to Rome.[46] On March 25, the Pope was passed through the Austrian lines in Italy, where he was received with all possible honors. A few days later, escorted by Austrian troops, he returned in triumph to his states.[47]

Soon afterwards Napoleon's power collapsed, and a new age dawned for Europe. For Metternich, the new era offered encouraging prospects, not least that of a new relationship with Rome. By his moves since 1809, he had laid the foundation for an alliance with the Papacy: his attempted mediation in 1810, his support in subsequent years for the Pope's liberation, and his role in securing Pius's release in 1814 had gone far towards winning him the Pope's trust and good will.[48] The coming peace settlement would provide him with the opportunity to build upon that foundation; but it would also be the occasion of disputes that for a time threatened to undo all that Metternich had thus far accomplished.

2. Metternich, Consalvi and the Peace Settlement

Immediately upon learning of the Pope's release, Metternich sent Lebzeltern to him as envoy extraordinary.[49] "Your instructions will be found in your heart," Lebzeltern was informed. He was to "say all that you can of congratulation, of filial respect, of devotion" to Pius—but "do not speak to him of any political arrangement."[50]

What lay behind this reluctance to discuss political questions? In part, it merely reflected the general intention of the Powers to reserve the major decisions on the peace settlement to themselves; but beyond this lay certain embarrassing facts, which cast a shadow on the apparently bright future of Austro-Papal relations. As we have seen, Metternich was determined to restore the Temporal Power; but the extent of that restoration had yet to be decided. Should the Pope receive all his former Italian possessions, or would certain subtractions have to be made? The old plan to annex the Legations was again under discussion at Vienna.[51] Having driven out the French, Austria now held the coveted provinces by right of conquest, and her troops were in effective possession; it would be easy to convert this hold into permanent control. Moreover, it was already clear that there was widespread antipathy to the return of Papal rule in the Legations: two decades of French administration had accustomed the educated classes to efficient secular rule, so that many would prefer Austrian rule to the return of the inefficient ecclesiastical regime. Finally, the Allies, in particular the Tsar, were not merely willing, but even eager for Austria to annex the Legations, so that she would be more inclined to acquiesce in their own territorial ambitions. Metternich, it is true, was not impressed by these arguments, and wished to set the Po as the Austrian frontier; but many in the Austrian government disagreed with him.[52]

Whether Metternich would in the end annex the Legations remained to be seen; but he had already signed, albeit reluctantly, a treaty with King Joachim Murat of Naples that was equally threatening to Papal interests.[53] In 1813 Austria had sought Murat's alliance against Napoleon. Metternich had offered to guarantee Murat's possession of Naples against the claims of his rival, the Bourbon King Ferdinand IV, who was in exile in Sicily; but Murat, ambitious to unite all Italy under his rule, had demanded extensive gains. In the end, Metternich, under pressure from the Austrian military to secure Murat's alliance,[54] agreed by a treaty of January 14, 1814, that the King would receive "an acquisition, calculated on the basis of 400,000 souls, to be taken from the Roman State." Austria would "lend its good offices to have this concession admitted and sanctioned by the Holy Father."[55] In return, Murat entered the war, though his campaign seemed largely directed towards occupying as large an area of central Italy as possible so as to ensure the promised compensation. His particular attention was fixed on the Marches of Ancona, the Papal territory closest to Naples and hence his most likely gain. Though Murat felt he had driven a good bargain, he had over-reached himself. Metternich had accepted his demands only under the pressure of military necessity; once that necessity had passed, he would have good cause not to fulfill a commitment that threatened both his policy towards the Papacy and his plans for Austrian predominance in Italy, which would be jeopardized by any expansion of the ambitious Murat's power. Both Metternich's later conduct and the logic of his policy indicate that he never seriously intended to fulfill this agreement—if he could avoid doing so.[56] Nonetheless, the pledge had been given. It remained to be seen whether circumstances would compel Metternich to honor it.

The fate of the Legations and Marches, then, was still unsettled when Pius returned to Italy; and it was not long before he learned of the threat to his State. The Austrian occupation of the Legations, reports of pro-Austrian demonstrations there, and moves by Austrian officials apparently aimed at creating a basis for permanent Habsburg rule there—all was too reminiscent of 1799–1800 not to revive the Pope's fears.[57] As for the Marches, Murat himself soon revealed the situation. At Austrian urging, he had reluctantly turned over the area around Rome to Papal administration, but continued to occupy the rest of the Papal State. Suspecting his aims, Pius at once turned to the Power in which he had greatest confidence. On April 1, he wrote to inform Francis I of the King's questionable conduct and to ask Austrian intervention to bring it to an end.[58]

On April 28, Lebzeltern reached Pius VII at Cesena in the Legations. The envoy was uneasy at the ambiguous role he had to play, well aware how much the "complications" of Austrian policy were in "contrast with the friendly overtures which our August Court makes to the Holy Father."[59] Nonetheless the first meeting went well, for Pius was deeply grateful to Austria for its efforts towards his liberation. Soon, however, Pius raised the question of the Marches and expressed his hope that Austria would compel Murat to evacuate them. Lebzeltern, seeing that the Pope's anger might lead to an open break with Murat, which would place Austria in a difficult position between their rival claims, decided to propose a temporary compromise: Murat would evacuate Papal territory, while the Pope would refrain from public criticism of him, leaving the fundamental question to be settled at the peace conference. Unfortunately, the meeting Lebzeltern arranged to discuss his proposal ended disastrously: not only did both parties refuse to compromise, but Murat blurted out the truth about the secret treaty of January 1814.[60]

Pius was deeply shocked. Austria, the "first protector of the Church,"[61] had agreed to the usurpation of Papal territory! He at once demanded an explanation from Lebzeltern, who, forbidden by his instructions even to admit the existence of the treaty, could only reply that he was too unfamiliar with Austro-Neapolitan relations to describe any treaty that might exist.[62]

Such a reply only encouraged the Pope's suspicions, and his manner towards Lebzeltern became guarded.[63] Though his faith in Austria was not completely destroyed,[64] he decided that he could not simply rely on Francis I to secure the return of his lands, as he had imagined. He would have to send a representative to argue his case at Paris, where the Allies were now arranging a peace settlement. Since the cardinals in whom he had greatest trust had not yet rejoined him, he sent Monsignor Della Genga, a prelate with extensive diplomatic experience.[65]

The Pope instructed Della Genga to demand the return of all pre-revolutionary Papal lands as a matter of simple justice, as well as a necessity for the interests of the whole Catholic world. He was in particular to reject any suggestion that the Legations not be returned, for these were the most productive part of the Papal State and essential to its economic stability. Della Genga was to denounce Murat's occupation of the Marches and his obvious annexationist ambitions. He was to appeal for support to all the Allies, but in particular to ask the aid of Francis I, whom Pius still considered his most likely champion.[66] Della Genga was given a personal letter from Pius to the Emperor, which explained that Murat was still occupying the Marches, on the "unconvincing pretext that such is the agreement with Your Majesty." Surely the Emperor would take the lead in restoring all Papal territory to its rightful ruler.[67]

Yet as reports continued to arrive of Austrian designs on the Legations and the existence of the secret treaty became undeniable, Papal faith in Austria inevitably declined. If Pius continued to send Francis I appeals for support, their tone became increasingly distant.[68] He did not try to hide from Lebzeltern that "he expects the same fatal complications with Austria over the Legations" as in 1800, but he was "determined never to yield." His indignation was "stronger than one could believe possible."[69] Lebzeltern did his best to convince him that, despite appearances, Austria was his friend and would protect his interests, and the envoy's tireless efforts kept the situation from deteriorating into open hostility.[70] Yet he knew that he was only fighting a delaying action, for an open break was in the long run inevitable unless Austria altered her course; and he filled his reports to Metternich with appeals to change Austrian policy while there was still time.[71]

It was against this background of deteriorating Austro-Papal relations that Pius was at last rejoined by the trusted adviser whom he had been impatiently awaiting: Cardinal Consalvi, his former Secretary of State and the most skillful Papal diplomat of the nineteenth century.[72]

Consalvi, whom Metternich soon came to consider "the only man at Rome of enlightened views,. . .capable of saving the State,"[73] was indeed the only Papal statesman with whom he had to deal whose outlook was compatible with his own, and who approached him in diplomatic skill and understanding of the post-revolutionary world. Typical statesmen of the Restoration both, they agreed on its fundamental principle: the need to build a stable social order based on a middle course between reaction and revolution. Both felt that church and state should cooperate in this process, and they agreed that the Temporal Power should be preserved as a necessary part of the Restoration order. Along with this similarity of outlook went a similarity of temperament, for both were diplomatic virtuosi, pragmatic realists who dealt with the world as it was and not as they would have wished it to be. These similarities were to become the basis of a mutual respect and understanding that would endure, despite numerous controversies, until the end of the Cardinal's life.[74]

In 1814 Consalvi was at the height of his career. Born in 1757, he rose rapidly in the Papal service under Pius VI. As Secretary of the conclave of 1800, he had promoted the compromise that led to the election of Pius VII. The new pontiff promptly demonstrated his gratitude and trust by appointing him Secretary of State. Thereafter, Consalvi was Pius's most trusted adviser and closest friend, and increasingly the true directing force in Papal policy.

As Secretary of State, Consalvi conducted the domestic and foreign policies of the Papacy with great skill until in 1806 Napoleon, angered by his defense of Papal independence, forcing him to resign. Much to Napoleon's annoyance, he remained the dominant influence on the Pope, and when Pius was carried into captivity, Consalvi too was imprisoned in France. Released upon the fall of Napoleon, he hastened to rejoin Pius, whom he found at Cesena on May 7, 1814. Reappointed Secretary of State, Consalvi decided that the chief immediate problem facing the Papacy was to secure the restoration of the Papal State. Rightly doubting that Della Genga was equal to this task, Consalvi took it upon himself and set out for Paris on May 21, leaving Cardinal Pacca as Prosecretary of State during his absence.[75]

The instructions which Consalvi had drawn up for his mission were brief, intended to leave him maximum freedom of action. He was to attend the Allied deliberations at Paris in order to secure the restoration of all pre-revolutionary Papal territory; if necessary, he might follow the Allied leaders to London or Vienna for the same purpose.[76] Travelling day and night, he reached Paris on June 2, only to find that, though a general settlement had not been reached, a treaty with France had been signed on May 30—and signed without Papal participation, for Della Genga had reached Paris only the day before. Consalvi exploded with wrath at Della Genga, for his dilatory pace had allowed the treaty-makers to ignore Papal interests: not only had they awarded Avignon to France—Consalvi had been resigned to this loss, but had hoped to secure reciprocal compensation—but they had set the Po as Austria's frontier, thus implicitly granting her part of the Legation of Ferrara, and passed over in silence the question of the Marches.[77]

Consalvi resolved that the Papal territories in Italy would not go as had

Avignon, undefended and uncompensated. Having learned that the Allied leaders were now in London, whence they would travel to Vienna for the Congress that would devise the final peace settlement, he at once set out for England.[78]

Since Consalvi realized that the fate of the Papal State was largely in Austria's hands, his first concern upon arriving in London was to see Metternich. The Foreign Minister explained that Austria did not want the Legations and hoped for their return to the Pope. However, the Legations were a "European affair" that Austria could not settle alone: since they had been ceded to France by a formal treaty, they fell within the category of French conquests whose fate the Allies would decide at the Congress as they saw fit. As for the Marches, he "advised the Holy Father to have patience, since this affair would have to be negotiated, and he would urge King Joachim to evacuate these provinces." Despite this encouragement, Consalvi remained skeptical of Austrian intentions, "inclined to believe Austria wants the Legations." He knew that Russia was encouraging Austria to annex the Legations as compensation for her own proposed gains in Poland, and he feared Austria would yield. On the other hand, if Austria resisted Russia, the Marches would be in danger, since war would be likely and Austria would need to barter them for Murat's military support.[79]

But Consalvi was unduly pessimistic. Metternich was in fact more sympathetic to Papal claims than Consalvi or Lebzeltern feared. However, he had to take many factors besides the Papacy into consideration in formulating his policy. His basic aim at the Congress was to re-establish the power of Austria on a stable basis. This involved, first, regaining for her a size and population roughly comparable to those of the other Powers; second, gaining a predominant influence over Central Europe, from the Baltic to the Mediterranean; and third, preventing other Powers—notably Russia, France, and Prussia—from endangering Austrian interests in Central Europe, or reviving over all Europe the overwhelming predominance that Napoleon had held. These considerations involved him in the well-known confrontation with Russia and Prussia over the Poland-Saxony question, which nearly led to war, and in complicated dealings with such states as France, Spain, and Naples, whose support or acquiescence in his plans he might need to buy. These factors complicated his policy towards the Papacy, so that he could not act in the straightforward way he would have preferred, but had instead to pursue a devious course, marked by delay and secrecy, which was to cause Consalvi frequent anxiety.

In essence, however, Metternich's policy on the Papal claims was simple: he intended to support the restoration, not merely of Rome, but of virtually all the former Papal State, provided he could do so without injury to vital Austrian interests. This policy did not derive from any conviction that the Pope *ex officio* deserved special treatment: "in the matter of temporal property, His Holiness can only be treated as a temporal Power."[80] Rather, it was based on two sound political arguments. First, if he opposed Papal claims, failed to give them effective support, or, worst of all, annexed the Legations, he would arouse a distrust and resentment at Rome that would be fatal to his plans for Austro-Papal cooperation. Second, Metternich wished to restore central Italy to the Pope because the other claimants to it were less likely to be susceptible to Austrian influence and more likely to be hostile—to the detriment of Austrian hegemony in Italy. "Austria is lucky to have the Pope as a neighbor," he confided to Consalvi.[81] Thus, he was fundamentally hostile to the schemes much discussed at the Congress for establishing, for example, Maria Louisa of Bourbon-Parma—certain to be under French influence—or Eugene Beauharnais—probably under Russian influence—in the Legations.

Nor did Metternich want to annex the Legations. Their annexation would alienate the Papacy, and would also alarm the other Italian princes, thus weakening Austria's influence in the peninsula. Moreover, he did not consider the Legations as very desirable acquisitions: given the political ferment prevailing there, they could be a source of weakness rather than strength to Austria. Finally, if Austria annexed the Legations, she would have to allow Russia and Prussia appropriate compensation in Poland and Saxony—a prospect Metternich was determined to avert.[82] There were, however, many advocates of annexation in the Imperial government, especially among the military, who argued that possession of at least Ferrara, the northernmost Legation, would improve Austria's defensive line along the Po frontier. To placate these critics, whose arguments were strategically sound, Metternich eventually agreed to two concessions: first, to annex the small section of the Legation of Ferrara that lay on the left bank of the Po—this taken, Austria would hold the entire left bank and would have a much stronger defensive line for its Italian possessions; second, to insist that Austria have the right to garrison the citadels of the strategic towns of Ferrara and Comacchio. These concessions would satisfy the fundamental objections of his critics, with minimal loss to the Papacy.[83]

Metternich realized, of course, that circumstances could arise that might compel him to alter his stand on the Legations. For example, Austria might prove unable to prevent Russia and Prussia from annexing Poland and Saxony. She would then need a corresponding increment of territory in order to maintain her relative strength, and it might then be necessary to consider the Legations as compensation. Partly to keep this option open, Metternich was unwilling to allow the fate of the Legations to be settled until the Poland-Saxony question was resolved. But he saw annexation as a last desperate measure, only to be adopted in the unlikely event that Austria suffered total defeat over Poland and Saxony.[84]

Metternich also planned to secure the restoration of the Marches to the Pope. He had not yet decided whether Austria would best serve her interests by supporting Murat as King of Naples, or by taking the lead in his overthrow; but he was resolved that the King should not have the Marches. In this decision, Metternich's wish to please the Papacy was a factor, but so was his unwillingness to strengthen with new territory so ambitious and untrustworthy a ruler as Murat.[85] Yet he had to proceed with caution: tension over Poland and Saxony was growing, and Murat's army could be invaluable to Austria if war came.[86] Therefore, though he frequently urged Murat to evacuate the Marches, Metternich refused to exert pressure upon him until the Poland-Saxony question had been settled; instead, he followed a policy of procrastination, coupled with repeated assurances to Consalvi that the Pope would have the Marches if he would only be patient.[87]

It was thus a reasonably honest statement of Austrian intentions that Metternich had given Consalvi at their first meeting, rather than a "mere form of politeness" veiling hidden amibitions as the Cardinal had feared.[88] At their second meeting a few days later, Metternich was evidently in better form, for though he made essentially the same points as before, he now managed to convince Consalvi of his sincerity.[89]

Reassured, Consalvi left London for Vienna, where he arrived on September 2.[90] Metternich received him with great cordiality, stressing Austria's continued support for the Papal claims. He expressed confidence that the Legations would be returned to the Pope, but only at the end of the Congress, for Italian affairs were the last item on the agenda. As for the Marches, he had long been urging Murat to evacuate them, and hoped to arrange this shortly.[91]

This conversation confirmed Consalvi in the belief that Metternich was "sincerely well disposed towards us," and that "we have little to fear from Austria," though she might take the transpadane area of Ferrara.[92] The following months saw a series of cordial meetings, in which Metternich never tired of expanding on his good will towards the Papacy and the need for trust and cooperation between the two courts.[93] It was during this period that Metternich and Consalvi, coming gradually to know and appreciate each other's abilities and outlook, developed the mutual understanding and respect that was to endure as long as Consalvi lived, making him the only political figure at Rome for whom Metternich had genuine respect,[94] while, for the Cardinal, Metternich became the one Austrian minister whom he could trust. "I trust first in God, and then in the efforts of the Prince," he admitted to Pacca.[95]

Little progress was made towards the restoration of the Papal State during the Fall of 1814.[96] The Prince continued to promise the return of the Legations, except for transpadane Ferrara. Though Consalvi warned that the Pope would have to protest this annexation as a matter of principle, he was in fact "delighted" that it marked the limit of Austrian ambitions.[97] The true threat to the Legations came from the other Powers, each of which seemed to have some candidate for whom it wished to create a principality there. France and Spain pushed vigorously for Maria Louisa of Bourbon-Parma, the ex-Queen of Etruria, who everyone agreed deserved compensation for her former state now to be returned to Ferdinand III of Hapsburg. Parma was the location she preferred; but the Treaty of Fontainebleau had assigned Parma to Marie Louise, Francis I's daughter and Napoleon's wife, and everyone agreed that she too had a legitimate claim to sovereignty—somewhere. It seemed at times inevitable that one or the other of these princesses would be given the Legations.[98] The Tsar urged the claims of his protege, Eugene Beauharnais, while the Prussians argued that the King of Saxony, whom they hoped to dispossess, might conveniently find a new realm at Bologna, and the English asserted that Ferdinand IV of Sicily, if he did not regain Naples, would deserve suitable compensation, such as the Legations.[99] These last suggestions were never seriously considered, but when in November the Powers began to discuss Parma, it became clear that the Legations were also at stake. "I fear that whichever princess does not receive Parma, will get at least Bologna," wrote Consalvi.[100] In the sporadic discussions that followed, Metternich argued that Parma should go to Marie Louise and the Legations to the Pope, while Maria Louisa should rest content with a pension. The Bourbons, however, insisted that Parma should go to Maria Louisa and the Legations to Marie Louise, with no compensation for the Pope.[101] No settlement could be reached. As the year ended amid rumours of war over Poland and Saxony, Consalvi feared that Austria would be driven to buy French support in that question, vital for her interests, by agreeing to install Maria Louisa in the Legations.[102]

Under these circumstance, Consalvi could do little during the closing months of 1814 to influence the fate of the Legations. He concentrated on remaining in close touch with Metternich, retaining his good will, and maintaining a steady but tactful pressure upon him by stressing that if Austria deprived Rome of its lands, the harmonious cooperation which they both desired would become impossible.[103] Beyond this, Consalvi made known to the assembled diplomats that the Pope would not suffer the loss of his territories in silence, but would publicly condemn whoever usurped them.[104] Metternich encouraged Consalvi to publicize this stand, hoping it would intimidate Maria Louisa and her supporters.[105] The ex-Queen was in fact so impressed that she assured the Pope she would in no case accept the Legations.[106] Talleyrand, intent on reviving Bourbon influence in Italy, was less scrupulous: "you may be sure your Legations will compensate whoever does not get Parma," he warned Consalvi in November. He proceeded to draw up several plans on this basis—ignoring his King's instructions to support the Papal claims.[107] Metternich rejected all his proposals, partly to please the Pope, partly to ward off a revival of French influence in Italy.[108] Consalvi was much impressed by the contrast between the Austrian and French attitudes: "our only hope lies in Austria," he concluded,[109] while "on France we cannot count at all."[110]

The French attitude showed no improvement with the new year, for Talleyrand continued to draw up plans that involved depriving the Pope of the Legations.[111] But Metternich assured Consalvi that the Legations were no longer in danger—and he spoke truly, for he had just concluded certain secret negotiations with Louis XVIII, and was about to resolve the questions of Parma and the Legations with a master stroke that would not only settle the future of those territories, but would seal the fate of Murat and pave the way for the establishment of Austrian predominance in Italy.

Before describing that stroke, we must first survey the negotiations over the Marches during the second half of 1814. Metternich had greater freedom of action in dealing with the Marches than with the Legations: since the Pope had never formally ceded them, their fate could be decided between Austria, Naples, and Rome, rather than by the Congress.[112] As we have seen, Metternich had been urging Murat to evacuate the Marches since the end of the Italian campaign in March, 1814.[113] Murat resented the loss of his anticipated gains; but in the face of Bourbon hostility, he could not afford to antagonize his only ally and his nearest neighbor by an intransigent stand. In July, 1814, his Foreign Minister, Campochiaro, met Consalvi and offered to hand over not only the Marches, but also Benevento and Pontecorvo, two small Papal enclaves in Neapolitan territory which Napoleon had seized and Murat now occupied. In return, he insisted that the Pope grant Murat formal recognition as King of Naples. Unfortunately, Papal recognition would inevitably lead to tension with Murat's Bourbon enemies, whom Consalvi did not wish to provoke. Moreover, it was a fundamental principle of the Papacy not to recognize any new government until the majority of the Powers had done so. Consequently, Consalvi felt obliged to reject Murat's offer, and his negotiations with Campochiaro broke down. In retaliation, Murat announced that without Papal recognition, he would not evacuate the Marches.[114]

At his first meeting with Metternich in Vienna, Consalvi complained of Murat's stand. The Prince replied that he had already told Murat that he would not be allowed to annex the Marches, that he should evacuate them immediately, and that the Pope was not obliged to recognize him until the Powers had done so. Since Austria was not yet in a position to apply stronger pressure at Naples, he hoped that the Papacy and Murat could reach a friendly settlement. However, Consalvi might rest assured that the provinces would in time be restored.[115]

But Murat had by no means abandoned all hope of retaining the Marches or, at the least, of using them to force Papal recognition. Moreover, as long as he continued to occupy them, he could draw upon their revenues and spread propaganda for his dream of uniting Italy under his rule. He was thus in no hurry to evacuate. At Metternich's urging, he reopened negotiations with Rome, but continued to insist on the recognition that he knew the Pope would not grant.[116] At last Metternich reluctantly decided to intervene. He was anxious to bring about a prompt evacuation for several reasons: to please Rome, to weaken Murat by depriving him of revenue, to end the nationalist propaganda that Murat's agents were spreading in the Marches, and to prevent a Papal break with Naples that might compel him to turn against Murat before he was prepared to do so. In October the Prince suggested an arrangement that Campochiaro considered acceptable. Murat would evacuate the Marches immediately, without insisting on Papal recognition, on two conditions: first, that the Pope adopt a neutral attitude as between the rival claims of Murat and Ferdinand IV; second, that if a foreign army—presumably Franco-Spanish—entered the Papal State in order to attack Naples, the Pope would resist its passage. Consalvi accepted the first condition. As for the second, the Pope was in no position, morally or militarily, to offer armed resistance to a foreign invasion, but he would publicly condemn it. Campochiaro was prepared to recommend this compromise to his King.[117] Unfortunately, Consalvi now received orders from Rome to insist that Murat must evacuate Benevento and Pontecorvo as well as the Marches. Pacca had learned that Murat, hoping to win the assistance of Talleyrand—whom Napoleon had named Prince of Benevento—had offered to turn that principality over to him in full sovereignty at the end of the Congress. Hence, Pacca had convinced Pius, Rome must regain possession of Benevento as soon as possible.[118] Metternich was taken aback, for he foresaw that Murat would never accept this new condition unless the Pope granted him formal recognition, and the negotiation would fail.[119] He therefore urged Consalvi to accept his original proposal, pointing out that in this way the Pope would secure immediate possession of the Marches, while Murat would surely have to evacuate Benevento and Pontecorvo—to which he had no shadow of a legal claim—when the Congress ended.[120] Consalvi approved his reasoning, but Pacca was overcome with moral indignation: "a robber who has stolen a hundred and then offers to return fifty if given immunity for the rest—that is Murat." The "robber" must return everything at once, or the Pope would denounce him.[121] Consalvi patiently explained that "in affairs of state, one cannot always follow the same rules, however just, as in private life,"[122] but not until December did Pacca reluctantly agree to accept Metternich's proposal.[123]

Meanwhile, weary of Papal intransigence and alarmed by signs that Murat was moving towards a less accommodating position, Metternich decided that Austria would have to play a more active role. On November 29, he instructed Lebzeltern to persuade Pius to accept a compromise and, if the Pope wished, to act as mediator in arranging it.[124] Since tension was growing over the Poland-Saxony question, Metternich explained, Austria could not afford an Italian crisis as well. It was imperative that the Papal-Neapolitan dispute not be allowed to come to a boil, nor must Murat be allowed "at present" to feel that Austria had deserted him—for then, in despair, he would try to start an Italian national revolution.[125]

Lebzeltern had great difficulty in persuading Pius and Pacca to seek a compromise with Murat, for both were skeptical of the King's intentions.[126] Their pessimism was soon justified. On November 29, Metternich had also directed Count Mier, his representative at Naples, to urge Murat to negotiate with the Pope.[127] But Murat's confidence had revived. He felt that Austria would not dare antagonize him now that war seemed likely over Poland and Saxony, and he took a firm stand on the Marches: not only did he insist on Papal recognition as the *sine qua non* for an evacuation, but he implied that he still expected at least part of the promised territorial compensation. As for the agreement that Metternich and Campochiaro had worked out, he rejected it.[128]

Murat's intransigence forced Metternich to admit that at present a settlement on the Marches was unattainable.[129] He allowed the question to rest through January, 1815, but continued to assure the anxious Consalvi that Austria would compel Murat to return the Marches as soon as the Polish question was settled: "If we must go to war to return the Marches to you, we will do so."[130] He hinted that such a war, ostensibly on behalf of the Papacy, would not be unwelcome at the right moment; but in the meantime, the Pope must refrain from any step likely to precipitate a crisis prematurely.[131]

By late January, the Poland-Saxony question was at last on the way to settlement, and Metternich felt free to come to terms with France for the destruction of Murat.[132] In essence, he offered to cooperate with France in overthrowing Murat once the Congress had ended, in return for a satisfactory settlement of central Italy: the Legations were to go to the Pope, Parma to Marie Louise, and a tiny principality at Lucca to Maria Louisa. Louis XVIII readily agreed, and by the end of February, the fate of Murat had been settled, along with that of the Legations and Marches.

Consalvi was the first foreign diplomat to whom Metternich revealed his plans—a striking demonstration of the confidence that had grown up between them. The Prince explained that Austria would send Murat an ultimatum demanding the immediate evacuation of the Marches. Murat would presumably refuse, giving Austria the pretext to declare war. Austrian and Bourbon armies would then invade Naples, depose Murat, restore the Bourbons, and return the Marches to the Pope.[133]

But Napoleon's return from Elba temporarily upset these plans.[134] Distrusting the Allies, Murat threw in his lot with Napoleon. In March he invaded the Papal State, calling upon all Italians to join him in a war of liberation against Austria.[135]

Austria declared war on Naples on April 11. On the following day, Metternich requested the cooperation of all the Italian rulers in the common struggle. While the secular princes were asked to provide troops, the Pope was called upon to provide moral support.[136] "The conduct of the Holy Father, in words and deeds, must be a perfect union with Austria," Metternich announced.[137] Consalvi was alarmed, fearing that the Allies might expect Rome to excommunicate Murat. That idea was certainly discussed at Vienna, and Talleyrand in particular demanded it.[138] Consalvi felt able to ignore Talleyrand's demands, in view of his generally unfriendly attitude towards Rome, but if Metternich were to second his request, the Pope would be placed in a difficult position. Consalvi was anxious to keep Austria's good will; but Murat had given the Pope no grounds sufficient to justify his excommunication, and Consalvi was not prepared to misuse the Church's sanctions for purely temporal ends.[139]

To his relief, Metternich soon explained that he had no intention of requesting Murat's excommunication. All that he meant by Papal moral support in this instance was that when Naples invaded the Papal State, Pius should flee from Rome and denounce the invasion, thereby demonstrating to the world that Murat was an aggressor against whom Austria was fighting a just war.[140] In fact, Pius had already fulfilled this request. When Murat had invaded his state in March, Pius had issued a formal protest, ordered the small Papal army to join forces with Austria's, and fled to Genoa.[141] Metternich was delighted with the Pope's conduct, and asked no more from Consalvi. In any case, it soon became apparent that the Austrian army needed little help from any quarter to deal with Murat, whom it decisively defeated before the end of April.[142]

The way seemed open for the restoration of the Papal State, when Consalvi suddenly encountered a new problem. He had expected Benevento and Pontecorvo to be restored as a matter of course, since they did not fall within the class of territories at the disposal of the Allies. Unfortunately, Naples had long wished to incorporate these enclaves, and the newly-restored Ferdinand IV now offered Talleyrand 6,000,000 francs to secure Benevento for Naples. Moreover, the Tsar had formed the plan of establishing Eugene Beauharnais at Pontecorvo. Beauharnais indicated that he would prefer a pension, which left the way open for Talleyrand to seek to acquire Pontecorvo too for Naples. Taking his stand on the principle that enclaves were a menace to peace and stability, Talleyrand set about winning the assent of the Congress to the incorporation.[143]

Meanwhile, Ferdinand had also won Metternich's support. Having agreed to the Bourbon's restoration, Metternich wished to win his good will so as to prevent French influence from becoming completely dominant at Naples. Moreover, the principalities would serve to compensate Naples for renouncing her claims to the Tuscan Presidios, Piombino, and Elba, all of which Metternich wanted transferred to Tuscany. He felt that the Pope could hardly resent this minor loss, since he had been given "lands so large and important as the Legations and Marches."[144]

Consequently, when in April Consalvi invoked Metternich's support against Talleyrand, he was startled to hear the Prince insist that the Pope must cede the principalities. The Cardinal "opposed an insuperable resistance" to this demand,[145] and Metternich, taken aback, gradually reversed his stand.[146] He did not wish to alienate Rome over so minor an issue. Moreover, by May he no longer needed to conciliate Naples, having won its agreement to a secret treaty that would bind it closely to Austria.[147] There remained Talleyrand, who was determined to get his pound of flesh, and also Prince Eugene; but Metternich knew that both were more interested in cash than in territorial jurisdiction. Consequently, he was able to negotiate a new settlement, which he revealed to Consalvi on June 11.[148] Both principalities would be returned to the Pope, on two conditions: first, that if Naples should wish to exchange equivalent territory for Benevento, he would agree; second, that he would contribute 500,000 francs to the King of Naples. Metternich expressed regret at these conditions, but they were necessary: only by promising that Ferdinand would pay Talleyrand 2,000,000 francs for his interest in Benevento, and a similar sum to Prince Eugene in lieu of Pontecorvo, had Metternich been able to persuade them to accept the restoration of the principalities to the Pope. Since these payments would be a heavy burden for Naples, it seemed only fair that the Pope should shoulder a small part of it. Consalvi gratefully accepted the arrangement.

The essentials of the Papal restoration had now been worked out; but several loose ends remained to be tied during the final days of the Congress. One problem concerned the Po frontier. As we have seen, Metternich had agreed to annex transpadane Ferrara so that Austria would have a stronger defensive line. Consalvi made no serious objection, and though he warned that he would have to make a formal protest as a matter of principle, he promised to make it "with that moderation and those sentiments of respect and attachment to the Emperor that are truly in our hearts."[149] He was less complacent over Metternich's second concession to the Austrian military: asserting the right of Austria to garrison the citadels of Ferrara and Comacchio. Consalvi disliked this as a violation of Papal sovereignty, and feared it might lead to the infringement of Papal neutrality should Austria go to war. But Metternich was insistent, and in the end Consalvi yielded, though here too he would have to make a mild public protest for the sake of principle. Metternich awaited such protests with equanimity, as well he might since he had gained both his points without antagonizing Rome.[150]

Their discussions were less cordial on two other points: first, the Austrian demand that, in keeping with an Allied decision, the Pope, like all other Italian rulers, should contribute either troops or money to the new struggle against Napoleon; second, the date when Austria would evacuate the Marches and Legations. Metternich defended the first as a matter of simple justice. Since Napoleon threatened the peace and security of all Europe, Austria and her allies were fighting for the common interest, and all states must contribute to their struggle. Consalvi was reluctant to accept new burdens for the empty Papal treasury, but he finally yielded when Metternich agreed to a two-thirds reduction of the sum demanded, to 1,700,000 scudi.[151] Consalvi was also able to obtain a satisfactory settlement on the Austrian evacuation. Metternich had originally planned to evacuate the Papal territories as soon as the Congress ended.[152] After Napoleon's return, when it seemed that war might drag on for months, he came under pressure from the Austrian military and from the finance ministry to postpone the evacuation until the final peace with France: the military argued the strategic value of the Papal State should the war spread to Italy, the finance ministry pointed out the advantage of drawing revenue from the occupied lands to compensate for the expense of the renewed fighting. Though initially reluctant, Metternich was finally compelled to accept their arguments, and in mid-May he informed Consalvi of the intended delay.[153] Since Rome too desperately needed revenue, a "stormy interview" followed. To the Cardinal's protests, the embarrassed Metternich could answer only that Consalvi was "preaching to the converted, since he too felt that the Pope should take prompt possession," but that he was not the sole architect of Imperial policy.[154] Weeks of discussion followed, until in June Metternich persuaded the Emperor to intervene with the military and finance officials. The result was a treaty of June 12, 1815, stipulating that the Papal territories would be turned over to Rome within four weeks, that being the minimum time in which the necessary arrangements could be made.[155]

On the day the treaty was signed, Consalvi wrote jubilantly to Pacca that his mission had "at last been crowned with happy success": the Papal State had been recovered virtually intact, the financial settlement reduced to tolerable proportions, and the evacuation set for the earliest possible date.[156] It was indeed a triumph, and the Cardinal deserved the praise that he received from all sides. As Metternich recognized, he had carried out his mission with great skill, and if favorable circumstances had contributed much to his victory, his own ability to exploit them and his determination in the face of temporary reverses had justly entitled him to success.[157] This was the climax of his career. Never before had he known such general acclaim; nor would he ever again, for his efforts to adapt the Papacy to the modern world would soon turn many who now applauded him into bitter enemies. It is well that the Cardinal had this moment of triumph; it would not last long.

II

The Union of Throne and Altar, 1815–1820

1. The Foundations of Austro-Papal Cooperation

For Metternich too the Congress had been a "happy success," and perhaps the climax of his career. When he had come to office in 1809, the very survival of the Habsburg Empire had been in doubt. Now in 1815 a revived Austria again ranked among the Powers. A vast area from the Alps to Transylvania acknowledged the rule of Francis I, while the influence of the Empire indirectly dominated Italy and Germany. Metternich had come close to realizing the concept of *Mitteleuropa* in the Habsburg realm, a great power bloc sufficient to balance off the restless and expansionist extremes of the continent—the old enemy France, the new rival Russia—and prevent their intrusion into Central Europe. As long as this favorable central position could be preserved, Austria would survive as a great Power; should it be lost, the days of the Empire's greatness, and perhaps of its very existence, would be numbered.

But it was by no means only the preservation of Austria's international position against her rivals that Metternich had to consider as he formulated policies to ensure the Empire's survival. There was another threat, less immediate perhaps, but in the long run no less dangerous: the liberal-nationalist movement, now at low ebb, but far from dead. The threat which this movement posed to the existing order or society, plus the memory of the disasters which a generation of revolution and war had brought to Europe, were sufficient to arouse the hostility of most Restoration statesmen. But Metternich's aversion had a deeper cause: liberalism threatened the dynastic authority and the traditional aristocratic-clerical society which served as cement for the Empire, while the centrifugal force of nationalism, once given its head, would surely whirl the multinational Empire apart. The movement must therefore be held in check, its popular appeal undercut by timely moderate reform, the spread of its ideas halted, its every violent outbreak repressed—and this throughout all Central Europe, for revolution anywhere within that region would upset Austrian predominance and might spread to the Habsburg realm itself.

It was thus with mingled satisfaction and apprehension that Metternich could survey Europe as the Congress of Vienna ended: satisfaction at the extent of his achievement in reviving the Empire and creating a European order

21

that would buttress it; apprehension at the fundamental weakness of the Empire and the many challenges that it must face. His latest career would be devoted largely to preserving the achievements of 1815 and meeting the challenges to them. To succeed in this task, he would have to mobilize all those forces that might strengthen the 1815 settlement and neutralize all those that might weaken it. Prominent among such forces was the Papacy, which could be a major source of either strength or weakness.

Some degree of concern for good relations with the Papacy had always been inevitable for any Catholic Power, for the sake both of prestige in the Catholic world and of smooth church-state relations within the Power's own frontiers. Austria, like France or Spain, had traditionally striven to secure a position of influence at Rome and cordial relations with the Pope. But during the Restoration Metternich's interest in the Papacy went beyond traditional concerns, for Rome intersected at three vital points with the policy which he had devised for the defense of the 1815 settlement.

First and most fundamental, Metternich planned to use the Papacy as a bulwark of the conservative order.[1] "Essentially conservative in its very nature," the Papacy was the "best collaborator" the monarchs of Europe could hope to find in their struggle against revolution: "among the Powers of whatever nature, there is none that is in its essence further removed from, or more directly opposed to, all that smacks of revolution."[2] Therefore, rulers must alter their attitude towards the Papacy: instead of regarding it as a rival for the loyalty of their subjects, as they had done in the eighteenth century, they must see in it their "potent ally" in a "Union of Throne and Altar" against revolution.[3] Since the true strength of the revolutionary movement lay in the appeal of its ideals, material means alone could never eradicate it. A rival moral authority was needed, and this Metternich hoped to find in the reviving spiritual prestige of the Papacy.

The concept of a Union of Throne and Altar was not, of course, original with Metternich, but was an old idea that had revived to become a political axiom of the Restoration. Such conservative theorists as De Maistre and Bonald had argued forcefully that only a revival of the old unity between church and state could save society from revolutionary anarchy, and their arguments were widely accepted. Few rulers of the time would have dissented from the judgment of Francis I that they must act in harmonious cooperation with the Church, which "renders subjects faithful to their sovereigns because it renders them faithful to God and clothes sovereigns with the authority of God Himself."[4] Hence, it was not surprising that Metternich should have set as the primary goal of his Papal policy the creation of such a union, a "perfect accord *sacerdotem inter et imperium,*" in which the Pope would join his moral authority and spiritual weapons to the material might of the conservative Powers for a combined assault on the forces of revolution.[5] To obtain this unity, monarchs must be prepared to make major concessions to Rome, particularly by relaxing their claims to authority over the church in their territories; however, such concessions should never be carried so far as to make the state subservient to the church, for Metternich never doubted that, in the last analysis, the secular power should be in the senion partner in the Union of Throne and Altar. Nor should the Papcy be allowed to carry its conservatism too far: its assault on the forces of revolution must never be allowed to develop into a reactionary attack on modern society as a whole. Metternich was inflexibly hostile to any attempt by Rome to revive the old ecclesiastical claims to authority over the state, or the old religious controls over society associated with the Middle Ages. Such a course was not merely repugnant to Metternich personally—man of the Englightenment that he was—but would discredit the conservative cause, furnish liberals with propaganda material, and risk splitting the conservative front by reviving the old clerical-regalist antagonism within its ranks. The Papacy could thus become a source of weakness rather than strength to the conservative order, and it was the duty of the Powers, above all Austria, to prevent such a transformation.[6]

On a second level, the Pope as a temporal sovereign was an important factor in Metternich's Italian policy, which aimed at preserving the hegemony in the peninsula which Austria had won at the Congress, and which was a major element in her international position.[7] Outside the Habsburg provinces of Lombardy-Venetia, Austria exercised this hegemony indirectly. With many of the Italian states, such as Tuscany or Parma, Austria had dynastic links which provided a means of influence; alliances gave her a measure of control with others, such as Naples; with all, she held the influence that naturally derived from geographical proximity, from possession of a large army, and from her role as defender of the *status quo* in the peninsula and hence as the protector of the Italian princes against revolution. These were potent advantages, which Metternich used effectively to protect Austrian predominance against three threats: first, the distrust of Austria widespread even among conservative Italians, who regarded her hegemony as a menace to their independence; second, the efforts of rival Powers, France in particular, to replace Austria as the dominant force in Italy; and third, the Sects or revolutionary secret societies, which aimed at creating a liberal Italy free from foreign control. As ruler of the second-largest Italian state, controlling the strategic center of the peninsula, the Pope's cooperation was "not merely desirable, but even absolutely necessary" for the maintenance of Austrian hegemony.[8] But, with the possible exception of Piedmont, the Papacy was the least susceptible of the Italian states to the means of indirect control which Austria had at its disposal. The two courts were linked by neither military alliance nor dynastic tie; moreover, the Papacy's peculiar spiritual status allowed it to count upon the intervention of the other Catholic courts against overt Austrian pressure. Papal cooperation could be gained only by skillful persuasion and offers of reciprocal advantages, not compulsion. Metternich must persuade Rome to renounce any distrust of Austrian predominance in Italy; to cooperate with Austria and follow her lead in Italy, resisting contrary pressures from rival Powers; and to cooperate in the counterrevolutionary struggle, both by taking suitable measures of repression against the Sects and by reforming the antiquated Papal regime so as to eliminate the popular discontent upon which the Sects thrived.

The third aspect of Metternich's Papal policy was religious, if only because the Pope's dual status as spiritual leader and temporal prince meant that religious questions tended to have political effects. Thus the Papacy's bitter hostility towards the Josephist state church in Austria tended to poison Austro-Papal relations in general. Metternich therefore felt obliged to intervene in Austrian religious affairs, which were not strictly within his jurisdiction, but whose effects on political relations with Rome he could not ignore. He soon came to the conclusion that he would have to support the Papal struggle against Josephism, up to a point. He had no sympathy for any lingering ecclesiastical pretentions to the predominance of church over state; but he could see that the power of the state relative to the church was so great that it was in no danger of subordination.[9] He was thus quite prepared to abandon the state church system and to support an extensive revival of Rome's authority over the Austrian church as an indispensable means of winning Papal good will. The real danger lay in the means by which the Papacy might attempt to attain its goal. A steady, tactful pressure, avoiding any display of fanaticism or intransigence, was in Metternich's opinion the only safe way to secure the dismantling of the Josephist system. But he knew that many in the Curia favored a frontal assault, which would have disastrous results: a bitter church-state quarrel just when their unity against revolution was vital, a split in the conservative front as regalists fought ultramontanes, and a great opportunity for liberals to cast discredit upon the conservative order. The last major aim of Metternich's Papal policy was to avert this danger by convincing the Papacy that religious moderation and cooperation with Austria offered the best hope of reviving its authority over the state church.

By 1815, Metternich had laid the foundations for cooperation between Austria and the Papacy. During 1809-1814, he had revived cordial relations for the first time in decades; then, at the Congress, he had exerted himself to win Papal trust and good will by securing the restoration of the Temporal Power; and he had succeeded. Consalvi was well aware that only the support of Austria had enabled him to regain the Papal State, while the other Powers —notably France, Austria's traditional rival for influence at Rome—had sought to advance their own interests at Papal expense. Consalvi left Vienna well disposed towards Metternich, and convinced that Austria was the best, perhaps the only reliable, friend the Pope had among the Powers—a conviction that long remained with him.[10] He left also with the understanding that he and Metternich would keep in touch via a confidential correspondence, in which they could discuss and settle on a friendly basis whatever problems might arise in the future, as they had done so successfully at the Congress.[11]

As the Congress came to an end, then, Metternich's new policy of Austro-Papal cooperation was well launched. In the years that followed, he worked steadily to consolidate it. He was careful to impress upon Lebzeltern and his successors at the embassy in Rome the great importance which he attached to Austro-Papal cooperation, whose maintenance and consolidation he regarded as their chief task.[12] Anxious to ensure Consalvi's continued support for cooperation, he frequently took advantage of their confidential correspondence to remind the Cardinal of their common interests and the need for them to stand united in defense of the Restoration order,[13] or urged similar views upon the Vienna Nuncio for transmission to Consalvi.[14] On the practical level, he attempted to settle the various political and religious questions that arose between the two courts in a way satisfactory to Rome.

Metternich's overtures for reorienting Austro-Papal relations from their old pattern of distrust to a new pattern of cooperation—a Union of Throne and Altar on the international level—had great appeal for Consalvi, who was acutely aware of the value of Austrian friendship in a world filled with dangers for the spiritual and temporal interests of the Papacy.

As Secretary of State, Consalvi was responsible for conducting Papal policy in all its aspects, religious and temporal, domestic and foreign; and in every field he found major problems. In domestic affairs, having regained the Papal State, he now faced an even more onerous task: to reform and modernize the regime so as to make it acceptable to its regained subjects, whom French rule had accustomed to efficient modern government. Without reform the Papal regime could never withstand the revolutionary challenge; yet reform was certain to meet with fanatical opposition from the powerful reactionary party at Rome. In foreign policy, Consalvi's task was complicated by the mingling of temporal and spiritual that arose from the Pope's dual status. He saw the ever-present danger that spiritual duties, the *raison d'etre* of the Papacy, might be sacrificed for political advantages; yet political questions might have consequences for religion that could not be ignored. In particular, he fully shared the prevalent belief—not so anachronistic in 1815 as it was to be by 1870—that the political independence of the Papacy was essential for its spiritual freedom, and hence must be defended. Political independence might be threatened overtly, by aggression or revolution; but it could also be endangered more subtly, by the encroaching influence of the predominant Power in Italy.

Yet even the most important political questions must be less significant for the Secretary of State than the religious problems which he had to face. The Revolution had had drastic consequences for the Church over much of Europe, sweeping away its privileges and weakening its hold on society, but also sparking a religious revival which, though often superficial, held the seeds of a genuine spiritual renewal. Moreover, the Revolution had upset the eighteenth century pattern of church-state relations, creating a new situation full of peril and promise: the peril foreshadowed by Napoleon of total control over the church by an essentially non-Christian state, but also the promise, arising from the weakening of monarchial authority and the revival of religious zeal, of a reassertion of Papal authority over the semiautonomous state churches which the rulers of Old Regime had established. The prospects of such reassertion were improved by the evident desire of many sovereigns for a common front with Rome against revolution. The situation was encouraging, but also challenging, for it would have to be handled with skill if the potential gains for the Papacy were not to be lost.[15]

And finally, lurking always in the background was the ominous specter of the Revolution, which the statesmen at Vienna had tried to exorcise, but whose reappearance at any moment Consalvi considered all too possible. How to defend the Papacy in the face of this threat?—such was the final problem that confronted Consalvi upon his triumphal homecoming.

The Cardinal could see that all these problems were linked to some degree with the question of Papal relations with Austria, which was not only of obvious importance for his diplomacy, both religious and temporal, but was also related to his major domestic problems. The formulation of a sound

Austrian policy was thus of primary importance, yet was no easy task. Metternich's proposal for Austro-Papal cooperation was certainly appealing, and, if workable, would go far towards solving many of the Cardinal's problems. But he could not avoid a degree of skepticism, less of Metternich's sincerity than of the likelihood that the underlying realities of Austro-Papal relations would permit his intentions to be realized. He could well remember the religious and political quarrels of the last four decades, the Austrian efforts to manipulate Rome for its own ends, its openly displayed appetite for Papal territory, the relentless encroachement of Josephism upon Papal authority. Even at the Congress—apparent triumph for Austro-Papal cooperation though it had been—there had been hints that the interests of Vienna and Rome might not be so "identical" as Metternich claimed[16]—that problems lay hidden below the surface of their relationship that might prove intractable.

At the very outset of the Congress, rival Papal and Imperial claims to religious jurisdiction in the lands newly regained by Austria led to mutual recrimination and controversy.[17] Consalvi had a bitter interview with Francis I, who had been convinced by the Josephists that the Papal claims represented a plot to overthrow his authority. Fortunately, Metternich saw the danger which religious controversy posed to his plans. He exerted himself to dispel his sovereign's suspicions of Rome and to show him the Papal side of the points at issue. In the end the Emperor's anger was dissipated and the controversies were settled peacefully. But the crisis had served to remind both Consalvi and Metternich that the present religious policies of Rome and Vienna were incompatible, and that if they were not brought into harmony, the inevitable collision would sooner or later make cooperation impossible. Metternich consequently set out upon a campaign to modify the Austrian religious system so as to make it acceptable to Rome; on his success depended Consalvi's ability to cooperate with Austria.

In the political field, the problem centered on the nature of Austria's Italian policy and its implications for Papal independence. Here Consalvi's fear was not of Austrian territorial ambitions, even though it was still widely believed that Vienna was only awaiting some favorable moment—an attempted revolution, perhaps, or the death of Pius VII—to annex the Legations, or even the entire State.[18] These suspicions were unfounded. As Consalvi realized, Austria could have taken the Legations at the Congress if she had wanted them.[19] Having decided against doing so, she did not afterwards reverse this decision, and ignored the opportunities which the death of Pius VII or the revolution of 1831 might have given her.[20] Beyond the harm it would have done to Austro-Papal relations, any attempt after 1815 to annex the Legations would have met with the opposition of the other Powers, and would have been contrary to the basic principle of Metternich's Restoration diplomacy—the maintenance of the 1815 settlement intact.

Consalvi's distrust of Austrian policy in Italy arose from a different but better-founded apprehension. For centuries it had been an axiom of Papal policy to fear and oppose the predominance of any Power in Italy, since this might restrict Papal independence; and now Austria was predominant.[21] For Consalvi, the true danger from Austria was not annexation, but the gradual extension of her influence over the Papal State to the point where the latter would become a mere satellite or protectorate. Aware that "Austria seems to believe that she has the right...to a position of dominance in Italy,"[22] he perceived that the logical aim of her Italian policy must be "the acquisition of a direct influence on the governments of all the Italian states, indeed, political control over them."[23]

Consalvi's suspicions were not groundless. As we have seen, Metternich considered Austria's predominance in Italy as essential for her international position, and had prepared the way for it at the Congress. If "Austria must exercise in Italy an influence preponderant and exclusive," the logical position of the lesser states could only be that of Austrian satellites.[24]

Metternich's preferred instrument for consolidating this hegemony was an Italian Confederation, similar to that in Germany, and serving the same purpose of maintaining Austrian control over the lesser states while providing a sop to the growing demand for national unity.[25] He had to move cautiously, partly to avoid alarming the Italian rulers, partly because a Confederation might be in violation of Article VI of the First Peace of Paris.[26] Hence he did not formally propose a Confederation at the Congress, but only suggested privately the advantages of a defensive league or Italian league, which Italian diplomats were given to understand would be merely a military alliance to defend the peninsula against invastion.[27] After the many invasions of recent decades, this suggestion had considerable appeal for Italian leaders such as Consalvi, who regarded it favorably when Metternich first presented it in the Fall of 1814. His only concern then was how to reconcile membership even in a defensive league with the principle of Papal neutrality.[28] But gradually he realized that the league might be the thin end of the wedge for expanding Austrian hegemony, particularly when Metternich began to speak of it as designed to ensure the "internal tranquility" of the Italian states as well as their external security; such an interpretation might justify Austrian interference in the internal affairs of the Papal State.[29] Consalvi was therefore relieved that Metternich, though often expressing his intention of having a long discussion with him on the Papal role in the league, never reached the point of doing so.[30]

In fact, by 1815 Metternich had decided on a still more cautious approach, to head off opposition from the Italian states or the rival Powers: instead of proposing the immediate formation of a league or confederation, he would work indirectly by arranging defensive alliances with the individual states, which would link them to Austria and commit them to join the Confederation when the time was ripe to erect it.[31] Such alliances were signed in 1815 with Naples and Tuscany, bringing those states firmly under Austrian hegemony.[32] The tiny states of Modena and Parma were already Austrian satellites by location, dynastic ties, and dependence for protection. Only two states remained to be enticed within the Austrian orbit: Piedmont and the Papal State. Metternich approached them simultaneously, though in different ways, during 1815–1816.

In June, 1815, he opened negotiations with Piedmont for a defensive alliance, but the Piedmontese, traditionally suspicious of Austria, had no intention of tying themselves to her by an alliance; with Russian backing they were eventually able to resist Austrian pressure and reject the treaty.[33]

Metternich's inability to persuade Piedmont to sign a treaty brought his plans to a halt, since a Confederation without so major a state as Piedmont would be worse than useless—it would only weaken Austrian predominance by formalizing and publicizing Austro-Piedmontese hostility. He therefore decided to postpone the implementation of his plans indefinitely, and to concentrate for the present upon consolidating informal Austrian influence over the peninsula.

Whether Metternich had ever seriously planned to offer the Papacy a formal treaty of alliance, as Consalvi had feared, is uncertain. Considering the absence of any firm reference to such a project in his correspondence, and considering the general nature of his Papal policy, it seems likely that he had from the beginning seen informal Austro-Papal cooperation as the best way to bring Rome into the Austrian sphere. Hence, his persistent effort, at the Congress and afterwards, to convince Rome that Austria was its best friend, that their interests were the same, and that in consequence cooperation with Austria was Rome's natural policy.[34]

Consalvi was aware of what lay behind Metternich's proposals, and was convinced that the Confederation which was his ultimate goal was incompatible with Papal independence.[35] However, Metternich had never formally proposed a Confederation to the Papacy, and since his failure with Piedmont he had ceased even to speak of it. Consalvi deduced correctly that Metternich had decided to abandon the Confederation, at least temporarily, and to rest content with the status quo in Italy. While this situation lasted, Austrian and Papal interests were not in conflict, and Consalvi could pursue a policy of cooperation with Metternich, provided it offered genuine advantages; and such advantages were not hard to find.

One lay in the inescapable fact that, with France in eclipse, Austria was both the greatest Catholic state and the predominant power in Italy. Its enmity would be dangerous, while its good will could be extremely useful. The Napoleonic era had demonstrated the truth of Metternich's claim that the Papal State was too weak to defend itself, and that neither Rome's principle of neutrality nor its spiritual weapons could be relied upon to deter a ruthless aggressor. Only the military power of Austria had liberated the Papal State, first from the French, then from Murat; only that military power could be relied upon to defend the State against any future invader. Moreover, even if no external danger threatened, Consalvi realized that "the Revolution is far from over, and in Italy as elsewhere there is still fire under the ashes." Who could say when revolution might break out in the Papal State?[36] The Papal government lacked the military strength to repress a major uprising; as in the past, the spiritual sword needed the temporal sword to protect it; and for this role Austria was clearly indicated.

Austrian diplomatic support could be useful to the Papacy, as had just been convincingly demonstrated at the Congress. Her support continued to be valuable in the years after 1815, especially when Rome had to deal with non-Catholic courts. For example, Russia, despite her sizable Catholic minority, refused as a matter of principle to open reciprocal diplomatic relations with the Pope; thus, when friction arose between the two courts, Austria's good offices were often of value.[37] Austria was equally useful to Rome in its interminable controversies with the Protestant German princes over the administration of the Catholic Church in their territories, and on several occasions Austrian intercession at Constantinople halted persecutions of Catholics in the Ottoman Empire.[38] Such diplomatic support was by no means automatic; it was given at Austria's good pleasure, and might be withdrawn should Rome antagonize her.[39]

Taking all this into account, it is not surprising that Consalvi remained convinced during 1815-1820 that Austria was "the best protector" of Papal interests.[40] It was certainly desirable to retain the good will of a Power whose aid was so useful, provided that its policy remained as innocuous as at present.

But Consalvi could see a greater advantage in cooperating with Metternich: the downfall of Josephism. Metternich often advised that a friendly and cooperative Papal attitude, blending with the Emperor's growing conviction that the Church should be strengthened as a bulwark against revolution, might induce Francis I to abandon the state church system. The Prince also made clear his own willingness to work against Josephism for the sake of good relations with Rome. Since the overthrow of Josephism was among the most cherished aims of the Papacy, the opportunity to bring it about was sufficient in itself to justify experimenting with a policy of cooperation.

Consalvi's most immediately pressing motive for cooperating with Austria, however, was his need for support against the two extremes of the Restoration political spectrum: the revolutionary Sects on the left, and the reactionary faction at Rome known as the *Zelanti.*[41] Each was in its own way a threat to the Temporal Power: the Sects because they planned to overthrow it as an obstacle to their dream of a united liberal Italy, the *Zelanti* because their reactionary policy, if adopted by the Roman government, would arouse such discontent as to make revolution inevitable.

To preserve the Temporal Power, then, Consalvi had to fight on two fronts at once, repressing the Sects while overcoming reactionary opposition to reform. This battle, if difficult, was not unique, for it was one which he shared with Metternich, and, indeed, with all those moderate statesmen typical of the Restoration who set as their goal not "to wipe out the Revolution and all its works," but rather "to reestablish a stable order while keeping under control the Revolution and all its works."[42] All were engaged to some degree in the same two-front battle, against revolutionaries for whom this goal was inadequate and reactionaries for whom it was excessive. There was thus a natural sympathy and understanding between Consalvi and Metternich, since they were fighting the same battle against the same enemies. Moreover, Metternich realized that Austria's own interests were involved in the Cardinal's struggle: unless Consalvi overcame his enemies, revolution was sooner or later inevitable in the Papal State, to the detriment of the tranquillity of all Italy, perhaps of all Europe. Metternich was therefore eager to aid the Cardinal. The Austrian police would supplement the inefficient Papal police in keeping the Sects under control, while the assurance of Austrian military support in the event of revolution would relieve one of Consalvi's major anxieties—indeed, it might well deter the Sects from attempting revolution at all. Equally important, Austrian diplomatic support for Consalvi's reforms would help counterbalance *Zelanti* influence at Rome. Here was a point on which the interests of Consalvi and Metternich were truly as identical as the Prince claimed.

Consalvi's response to Metternich's overtures was, then, favorable. During the five years following the Congress, the Cardinal made a sincere effort to cooperate with Austria in every way that did not threaten the temporal independence or spiritual authority of the Papacy.[43]

The reservation was crucial. Consalvi never forgot those aspects of Austrian policy that were potentially dangerous to the political and religious interests of Rome, and his willingness to cooperate with Austria was based on the assumption that Metternich would prevent such aspects from coming to the fore in Austrian policy. Here his personal confidence in Metternich was vital, for he had little trust in the rest of the Imperial government.[44] As he warned Metternich at the outset:

> I earnestly desire a close union with Austria..., and I will do everything possible to achieve it. But there are certain things which are impossible for us to do, and certain things which His Holiness cannot tolerate. I beg Your Highness for the love of God to oppose with all your influence things of this nature.

If Metternich did not oppose such things, or if his influence was insufficient to prevent them, then the experiment in Austro-Papal cooperation would fail.[45]

In 1815, however, success seemed possible. At the dawn of the Restoration, with the dangerous aspects of Austrian policy submerged, and Metternich and Consalvi agreed on the importance of cooperation, the prospects for Austro-Papal relations seemed bright. "I anticipate the closest unity and friendship with the Court of Rome," Metternich predicted.[46]

Clairvoyance or mirage? Only events would tell.

2. *Cooperation against Revolution*

Nothing strengthens friendship like a common enemy. Metternich and Consalvi shared two: the *Zelanti,* to be described in the next section, and the *Settarj,* the members of the Sects.[47]

The Italian Sects, like those of Europe in general, formed the left wing of the liberal-nationalist movement. In contrast to the numerically superior moderates, who hoped to attain their goals by peaceful means, the *Settarj* held that their aims could only be attained by revolution; hence their history consists of an endless series of plots and uprisings against the established order. Their origins are still obscure. Arising in the midst of the masonic orders, apparently linked to the Bavarian *Illuminati,* and certainly inspired by the ideals of the Enlightenment and the Revolution, the Sects first clearly appeared in Italy as resistance movements against Napoleonic rule. After the expulsion of the French, they turned against the Restoration order which was as incompatible with their ideas as Napoleon's despotism had been.

These ideals differed among the various groups making up the movement, but certain aims were generally held: the expulsion of foreign rule, some form of national unity, the reduction of the influence of the Church—which in the Papal State meant abolishing the Temporal Power—and such customary aims of nineteenth century liberalism as constitutional parliamentary government, while among the more advanced leaders primitive socialist ideas were widespread. The Sects drew their main support from ex-officials of the French regime, intellectuals, and limited sectors of the bourgeoisie and aristocracy. They normally drew little support from the lower classes, which tended to be either politically apathetic or loyal to the established order, although they might occasionally be aroused to action in time of economic crisis.[48]

Since the aims of the Sects involved overthrowing the existing order, while their means included conspiracy, assassination, and revolution, the Italian governments naturally regarded them as a threat to be repressed. Austria took the lead in repression, not merely because of her European role as champion of the conservative order, but also because her rule in Lombardy-Venetia and her Italian predominance were threatened.[49]

Reports of *Settarj* activity began to reach Metternich even before the Congress of Vienna opened. His first move was to learn more about the Sects, "to become acquainted with the full extent of the evil," so as to be able to estimate the degree of danger which they posed and to devise effective countermeasures. Accordingly, a Central Observation Agency (Central Beobachtungs Anstalt) was secretly established at Milan as center for "a system of surveillance which would eventually include all the Italian states."[50]

As the above implies, Metternich was less concerned with the Sects in Lombardy-Venetia, where he felt good government and efficient police would easily keep the situation under control, than in the rest of Italy. In the independent states, he feared, misgovernment and the discontent which it bred, plus the lack of an effective police, were creating conditions favorable to the growth of the Sects. The Austrian intelligence network must therefore be extended to cover the lesser states. The *Settarj,* a peninsula-wide organization, could be fought effectively only on a peninsula-wide basis.

Some information about the Sects in other Italian states could be gathered by Austrian secret agents, but the amount of ground they could cover was limited, and their reports were often unreliable.[51] The accurate and comprehensive information Metternich needed could only be obtained through the cooperation of at least some of the independent states. With this in mind, he had planned in 1814 to create a General Police Commission at Milan which would coordinate and direct the anti-*Settarj* activities of all the Italian police. All information gathered by the police would be sent to the Commission for evaluation and correlation, then used as a basis for coordinating the police activity of all the states. Such a system would no doubt have been the most effective way to organize a general attack on the Sects. However, when Metternich sugggested this plan to Consalvi and other Italian leaders at the Congress, their reaction was unfavorable, for the plan would give Austria effective control over all Italian police activity and thus strengthen her hold over the lesser states.[52]

Faced with this opposition, Metternich abandoned the General Police Commission in favor of the Central Observation Agency at Milan. In the new system of surveillance, Milan was the northern point of a triangle. The other points were Florence, "an intermediate point," and, more important, Rome, which "offers the greatest advantages for the observation of the south of Italy," and would therefore play the same role in the south as Milan played in the north. Then "all that was necessary was to establish a regular exchange of information between these three points, and we could be confident that no event of the slightest importance for public tranquillity would escape our knowledge."[53]

To ensure this "regular exchange" the Austrian ambassador in Rome was made responsible for the systematic collection of information on the Sects in central and southern Italy; this he sent to the Central Observation Agency, which in turn sent him all the information which it had gathered pertaining to his area. The whole system, operating in the greatest secrecy, was ultimately under the authority of Metternich as Foreign Minister. If the system worked as planned, Metternich could expect to be so well informed of the nature and plans of the *Settarj* that, should they ever be in a position to stage a revolution, he would be forewarned and able to take prompt and effective countermeasures.

The Agency, in contrast to the abandoned General Police Commission, was fully Austrian in its composition and direction. Nonetheless, Metternich still needed the cooperation of the other states, and Rome's in particular was essential if the Agency was to operate effectively in the south. He approached Consalvi early in 1816 to request his cooperation, not only in the passive sense of allowing the system of surveillance to operate in the Papal State, but in the active sense of turning over to it all information on the Sects uncovered by the Papal police.[54] This cooperation, he stressed, would be mutually beneficial: "in watching over police suspects we are working as much for you as for ourselves,"[55] since "the Sects are our common enemy . . . , and must be fought in common." The more information Austria had, the better she could wage this fight for the common good.[56] Moreover, if the Papal government cooperated in the system of surveillance, Austria would provide it with all the information which she gathered on the Sects in the Papal State: "we have more ways than you to learn such things, and so in many cases can be of great help to you.[57]

To his great satisfaction, Metternich found in Consalvi a "willingness to support us fully," for "this worthy minister is as convinced as we of the need to unite all our forces to keep the ill-intentioned under control."[58] Although Consalvi was alert for any sign that Metternich's plan encroached on Papal independence, he was fundamentally very favorable to it. Even during the Congress he had been acutely aware that the revolutionary spirit was far from dead in the Papal State,[59] and since his return to Rome he had received constant reports of *Settarj* activities in the provinces. At Rome itself the Sects were weak. Here the mass of the people were attached to the Papal regime by religious sentiment and economic interest—the Papacy was directly or indirectly the chief source of income for most Romans—and the city remained a stronghold of Papal loyalty down to 1870. The provinces, however, were a different story. Loyalist sentiment seemed strong in Umbria, but once the Apennines were crossed, discontent was widespread. Anti-Papal sentiment was strongest in the Marches and especially in the Legations, forming in such cities as Bologna and Ravenna the main current of public opinion. These were lands with a long tradition of local autonomy, whose people still resented the consolidation of Papal authority; moreover, they had lived under French rule since 1797, and the ideas and institutions of the Revolution had taken deeper root there than anywhere else in the State. The return of the inefficient ecclesiastical regime aroused bitter hostility among the educated classes, particularly since they now lost the opportunity of participating in the administration, which the French had opened to them. Consequently, it was in the Legations that the Sects were strongest, and Papal authority weakest: here was the Achilles' heel of the Temporal Power.[60]

Consalvi read the reports from the provinces with growing alarm. Though the Sects were only a small minority, their aims and zeal made them a danger he did not underestimate: "where revolutions are concerned, you must never confuse that part of the population which is most numerous, with that which is most active; it is the latter that is decisive, not the former."[61] Against this threat Consalvi could muster only an inefficient and unpopular administration, a tiny army, and an inadequate police.[62] Given time, Consalvi believed, he would be able to strengthen the military and police forces to the point where they could be relied upon to keep the Sects under control, while his planned reforms would undercut the Sects by eliminating the many abuses which won them popular support. For the present, however, the regime was dangerously weak, and he therefore welcomed Austrian cooperation, which would enable him to hold the Sects in check until Rome could stand alone. He willingly agreed to participate in the system of surveillance, which went into full operation in the Fall of 1816.[63]

Hereafter, as long as he remained in office, Consalvi maintained a regular exchange of information with Metternich, who considered it "of immense value."[64] But the Prince wanted not only Rome's participation in the intelligence system, but the full alignment of Papal policy towards the Sects with that of Austria. This too he obtained, for his views and Consalvi's coincided on this subject.

Prior to the 1820 revolutions, Metternich's attitude towards the Sects could be summed up as one of watchful waiting. At first, he held back from action against them until the system of surveillance could provide him with adequate information on their strength; then, when the information began to come in, he was somewhat reassured, for the *Settarj* were more a future threat than an immediate danger. Down to 1820, his information led him to believe that, provided they were kept under careful supervision, they could become a serious danger only if they secured the support of some rival Power—perhaps Russia, which was mounting an anti-Austrian campaign in Italy during these years—or if a general war broke out.[65] Consequently, he could see no immediate need for a campaign to extirpate the Sects; indeed, such a campaign would only do harm, by arousing them to more violent action in retaliation, and by creating popular sympathy for them as martyrs. He opposed any systematic repression or "inquisition" against the Sects, favoring the arrest and prosecution only of those who actually plotted revolution or who committed crimes in the course of their political activities. Those who confined themselves to talk—and they were the majority—were not to be sought out and persecuted.[66]

There is no foundation for the charge that Metternich tried to compel a reluctant Consalvi to adopt harsh measures against the Sects.[67] In reality, he was more concerned that Rome might adopt overly-severe measures. For example, when in 1817 the Governor of Rome, Monsignor Tiberio Pacca, proposed a mass arrest and prosecution of all suspected *Settarj* in the State, Metternich hastened to warn him that "his plans are too contrary to the principles of the Emperor for us to be able to tolerate them."[68] A year earlier, when incorrectly informed that Consalvi planned to exile all suspected *Settarj*, he strongly advised against the move as being too harsh and unjust. The Papal government's best course would be to keep close watch over the Sects and transmit all discoveries to Austria, which was in the best position to decide when the peril had grown to the point where action was needed. Until then, he advised Consalvi, "your role must be that of a vigilant observer."[69]

Metternich's advice was superfluous, for Consalvi had never contemplated the drastic step attributed to him.[70] In reality, his views on the Sects closely resembled Metternich's. Like the Prince, he was fully aware of the potential danger from the Sects, and was ready to act severely against those who actually plotted revolt or committed crimes, for "their way of thinking will not be changed by leniency; only fear of punishment will deter them."[71] It was not Austrian pressure that led him to act against such *Settarj*, but his own realization that he must do so to maintain public order and the authority of the state.[72] But he also agreed with Metternich that there should be no persecution, no white terror or witch hunt. Action was to be taken only against those who actually conspired, not against those who merely held liberal ideas. Nor was anyone to be punished on mere suspicion, but only after undeniable evidence of his guilt had been obtained.[73] Consalvi did his best, though with only limited success, to repress the common tendency of Papal officials to proceed arbitrarily and ignore legal forms in dealing with political suspects; those subordinates whose zeal led them beyond the boundaries of strict legality received crushing rebukes.[74]

Given this similarity of views, the coordination of Papal and Austrian policy towards the Sects was not difficult, at least in theory. It was less easy in practice, because of the innumerable difficulties which Consalvi experienced in securing the implementation of his policy by his subordinates. Here as in every other aspect of the administration he was severely handicapped by the chronic disease of the Papal regime, the lack of loyal and competent officials.[75] His plans for action against the Sects therefore often suffered the same fate as did many other projects: either they were not carried out, or they were carried out in such a way as to do more harm than good. Many of his subordinates were too incompetent, too lethargic, or—especially in the Legations—too frightened to act against the Sects, while those who did act all too often displayed an arbitrary severity and contempt for legality that aroused general resentment and attracted sympathy for those convicted.[76] The shortcomings of the Papal officials were a continual source of exasperation to Met-

ternich; but, realizing the Cardinal's difficult position, he consistently paid
tribute to the soundness of Consalvi's policies, only lamenting that they were
so poorly executed by his subordinates.[77]

Cooperation against the Sects was intensified after the 1820 revolutions,
which came as a rude shock to Metternich. Only a few months earlier he had
felt so confident of the weakness of the Sects that he had virtually dismantled
the system of surveillance.[78] Now he decided that he had seriously under-
estimated them, and that more rigorous measures would be necessary.
Therefore, while tightening up Austrian security, he urged Consalvi to do the
same in Rome and to intensify their cooperation. Consalvi, with *Settarj* activity stimulated by the apparent success of the Neapolitan revolt, needed no
urging to redouble his vigilance, and readily agreed to greater cooperation.[79]
In particular, he agreed to carry out special investigations of those individ-
uals or groups in the Papal State whose activities had aroused Austrian
suspicions.[80]

This intensified cooperation against the Sects continued for the rest of
Consalvi's ministry, reaching its high point when the Pope condemned the
Carbonari at Metternich's request in 1821. Cooperation against the *Settarj,*
successful and mutually beneficial as it proved to be, constituted one of the
foundations on which Metternich and Consalvi based their experiment in
cooperation, and, despite later political and religious disputes, it long remained a major link between them.

3. The Problem of Reform in the Papal State

In his last dispatch to Pacca before leaving Vienna in June, 1815, Consalvi,
after describing the difficulties he had met in recovering the Papal State,
turned to a subject that had increasingly preoccupied him of late:

> If it has been, God knows, so very difficult to recover what we have
> recovered, I will tell you frankly that it will be still more difficult to
> *keep* it. Your Eminence, believe what I am going to tell you: if we do
> not take the right path, then *we will not keep the recovered lands six
> months*. God grant that events do not justify my prediction!—but *it
> will be so* if we take the wrong path.[81]

The "wrong path" was that of reaction—a path advocated by many at
Rome, Pacca included, but which Consalvi saw must lead to disaster. Even
before the revolution, the Papal system of government had been outdated
and in serious need of reform.[82] Now, after the long French domination had
accustomed the people to efficient government and modern ideas, any attempt to return to the old system would arouse vigorous opposition and discredit the Papal regime. "You must realize that in these lands the way of
thinking has utterly changed," Consalvi warned Pacca; "most of those with
whom we must deal do not think as we do . . . , yet it is with them that we must
deal, and there is no help for it."[83]

Consalvi returned to Rome convinced that the Papal regime could survive only if adapted to the new ideas and needs created by the Revolution. This conviction did not reflect any particular sympathy with the aims and ideals of liberalism: he had "never paid court to the *philosophes.* "[84] Constitutional parliamentary government, whatever advantages it might have elsewhere, was incompatible with the nature of the Papal State, whose *raison d'etre* was to guarantee the Papacy's freedom from secular control. If the Pope were to grant a constitution or other reform which limited his freedom of action, he would lessen his necessary political independence.[85] When it came to reform, the Cardinal's outlook was essentially that of the Enlightened Despots or their recent incarnation, Napoleon. He was not a creative political theorist, but a highly gifted pragmatist, adept at grasping the realities of his world and skilled in adapting to the special circumstances of the Papacy the ideas and institutions of whatever provenance—even those derived from the hated Revolution—which seemed best suited to its needs.[86] "We must come to terms with the spirit of the age," he warned the unheeding reactionaries at Rome;[87] "when the current is of such force that it cannot be resisted, better to seek to control and direct it than to let oneself be swept away by it."[88] Here was the fundamental insight which united Consalvi with Metternich and the other moderate statesmen of the Restoration, the touchstone dividing conservative from reactionary—Consalvi from the *Zelanti,* Metternich from Francis I. Only if absolutist regimes adapted themselves to the new climate of opinion in so far as their nature permitted could they hope to survive.

This adaptation was the ultimate objective of Consalvi's reforms. His immediate plans, intended to meet the most pressing needs of the State, called for a general modernization of the administration, financial reform to provide adequate revenue, the creation of a coherent and humane legal system, and the abolition of feudal survivals. He particularly wished to satisfy the educated classes by admitting layment into the administration in large numbers.

The Cardinal had felt the need for reforms of this type during his first ministry, but reactionary opposition and his own preoccupation with diplomatic problems had kept him from carrying them out. The French occupation, however, had disrupted the old system of government, and Consalvi saw in this a heaven-sent opportunity for a thorough reorganization: "if a whirlwind knocks down a dangerous wilderness, we may, without approving of the whirlwind, benefit from its effects."[89] He returned from Vienna determined to carry reform through.[90]

The reforms which he proposed were moderate enough, even by the standards of 1815; nonetheless, they aroused fanatical opposition at Rome, forcing Consalvi for the rest of his life to carry on a bitter struggle against forces that in the end proved too strong for him.

Consalvi's opponents were the *Zelanti,* the powerful faction of "Zealots" in the Papal government.[91] Their hostility represented in part a struggle for power within the government, for they resented Consalvi's influence over Pius VII and his predominant role in the government and they hoped by causing his downfall to revive their own power. But beyond these personal rivalries lay two more fundamental sources of conflict. The first—to be treated in Chapter III—involved religious policy. The second, which concerns us here, centered on the Secretary of State's plans for reform, for the *Zelanti* felt that "the old pontifical system of government is best in every way..., and must be revived in its entirety."[92] This strange blindness to the glaring defects of the old system had several causes. The Revolution had been a traumatic shock for the *Zelanti*, who, like reactionaries elsewhere, became hostile to all innovations: they could see no good in reform, and their most heartfelt wish was to return to the prerevolutionary situation as quickly and as completely as possible.[93] In the case of the Zelanti, these general reactionary tendencies were strengthened by religious preconceptions: on the one hand, they considered the Revolution, which had attacked the Church and raised blasphemous hands against the Pope, as quite literally Satanic in nature, and any compromise with it or its works was therefore damnable; on the other, they saw recent events as virtually guided by the hand of God, Who after long tribulations had assured the triumph of the Pope over the demonic pride of Napoleon.[94] With such striking proof of divine support, what need had Rome to compromise with the new ideas as Consalvi advised? Then too, on a less exalted level, they were concerned to preserve the monopoly of political office which the clergy had traditionally held, and the opportunities for personal gain and family advancement which the corruption and inefficiency of the old system made possible. Such material considerations explain the opposition which Consalvi met from many ecclesiastics who were anything but "zealots."[95]

Given such widely divergent views on religious and political questions, conflict between Consalvi and the *Zelanti* was inevitable, and, indeed, began even before his return to Rome. His absence during the first year of the Papal Restoration left the *Zelanti* a free field to gain control of the government and begin their policy of reaction in the territory around Rome. Led by Pacca as Prosecretary of State, they lost no time in overturning the innovations of the French and returning to the Old Regime.[96] The efficient French administration was swept away, to be replaced by the old Papal system, antiquated even in 1796 and now hopelessly inadequate. The equally unsatisfactory financial system of the past was restored. The Napoleonic Code gave way to the Roman code, "compiled thirteen centuries ago, containing over fourteen thousand laws, often mutually contradictory, and entirely incompatible with the customs and outlook of modern times."[97] Vaccination and street lighting were abolished, simply because they had been introduced by the French. The Jews were returned to the Ghetto, the Inquisition reestablished, and the feudal rights and jurisdictions of the nobility restored. French sales of church property were annulled—a step that threatened financial loss to many of the well-to-do. Particularly annoying to the educated classes was the wholesale removal of laymen from the administration, ending a French innovation which had given them a first taste of the rewards of government service.[98] At the same time, punitive measures were taken against those of the clergy who had collaborated with the French; though hardly constituting a "white terror," these did provide a basis on which enemies of Rome could spread exaggerated accounts of persecution to alienate European opinion.[99]

This reactionary course aroused great hostility in the Papal State, especially among the politically conscious upper and middle classes.[100] The reaction was equally unfavorable abroad, and at Vienna Consalvi found his task of regaining the Papal State becoming even more difficult as enemies of Rome acquired new arguments against its Temporal Power, and even friendly statesmen like Metternich began to have doubts about the wisdom of returning additional territory to such a government.[101]

Metternich, indeed, was deeply disturbed by *Zelanti* policy, of which Lebzeltern kept him well informed.[102] As historians from Srbik onwards have made clear, Metternich was not the reactionary obscurantist depicted in nineteenth-century liberal histories, but an intelligent conservative, keenly aware that the Restoration order could survive only if it won the support of public opinion by a program of moderate non-political reform.[103] He was convinced that under normal circumstances the revolutionaries would constitute only a small minority of fanatics, too few to threaten the existing order; only if they somehow acquired mass backing would they become a serious threat. Such support they would hardly win with their abstact ideals, since "the masses are and always will be conservative."[104] But should legitimate rulers fail to provide for the needs of their subjects, the Sects would be able to exploit the resulting discontent to swell their ranks to the point where successful revolution would be possible.[105] Reform from above was essential to forestall revolution from below.

Since Metternich's ideal of government differed greatly from that of contemporary liberalism, his concept of reform was also different. For liberal ideas of popular sovereignty he had only contempt mixed with fear. He never doubted that an enlightened absolutism would best provide for the common good. Any innovation that would weaken the foundations of absolutism was out of the question—his reforms were intended to strengthen absolutism. He hoped that the adoption of the administrative, financial, judicial, and humanitarian innovations of the revolutionary era would be sufficient to satisfy public opinion so that revolutionary political innovations would no longer be demanded. A modern, efficient administration responsive to popular needs; humane and equitable laws; a sound financial system; a paternalistic welfare policy for the poor; government encouragement of economic development—these and similar measures which would promote popular contentment without weakening royal authority were the core of his reform program. He recognized the growing desire of the educated classes to participate in government, but hoped to satisfy them by measures short of genuine representative government: by opening the ranks of the administration to all men of talent; by giving local notables a share in the handling of local affairs; by granting municipal self-government; and by creating consultative councils to offer advice to the ruler. For regions where traditions of autonomy or primitive nationalism were strong—such as Lombardy-Venetia in the Habsburg Empire, or the Legations in the Papal State—he advocated a separate regional administration adapted to their traditions.[106]

Metternich worked for reform along these lines not only in the Habsburg Empire, but also throughout the Austrian sphere of influence, particularly in Italy.[107] Nowhere, however, did he demonstrate a more serious or long-lasting interest in promoting reform than in the Papal State. There his efforts stretched from the dawn of the Restoration to its very end, and constituted a major theme in his relations with the Papacy which will recur frequently in the course of this study.[108] His reasons for particular concern with the Papal State were threefold: first, because of its proximity to Lombardy-Venetia, revolution there was more likely to spread to the Empire; second, the moral authority of the Papacy, which he intended to use in the defense of the Restoration order, would be weakened should misgovernment produce revolution in the Papal State; third, the Papal State was probably the most poorly governed in Italy, so that the need for reform was especially urgent there.[109]

Metternich's attention was first drawn to this problem in the summer of 1814 by Lebzeltern's reports on the reaction and incompetence that prevailed in the Roman government.[110] The envoy's warnings and arguments seemed to make no impression upon Pacca or the other *Zelanti* who dominated the aging Pope, and he could only hope that Consalvi's return would bring a change for the better. Otherwise, the survival of the regime was in doubt.

Metternich was not minded to await the end of the Congress in the hope of improvement. He at once took up the question of reform with Consalvi, and was delighted to find him in complete agreement as to its necessity and the general form it should take. Only on one point was Metternich disappointed: isolated at the Congress, Consalvi was unable to influence the course of events at Rome. He wrote repeatedly to Pacca advising a more reasonable policy and warning of the consequences which reaction might have for the Temporal Power; but to no avail.[111] The Prosecretary, firm in his convictions, continued his reactionary course.[112]

This disappointment aside, Metternich was fully satisfied by his discussions with Consalvi.[113] Since he soon perceived that the Cardinal's ideas on reform paralleled his own, he was able to refrain from urging on him a specific program of reform—which might have aroused suspicion that Austria wished to dictate Papal policy—and to confine himself to listening and commenting upon Consalvi's plans, suggesting specific measures only when they seemed of particular importance. They readily agreed on the general lines that reform should follow: a centralized, efficiently organized administration run by a professional bureaucracy recruited from all men of talent—especially the hitherto excluded laity—but which would leave a certain scope for participation by the educated classes in the form of municipal self-government and consultative councils; a legal system purged of the confusion, inequity, and inhumanity of the Old Regime, incorporating the principle of equality before the law and some guarantee of individual rights against arbitrary procedures; a financial system that would produce adequate revenue without overburdening taxpayers; an efficient police and military capable of maintaining public order—in short, the non-political institutions which revolutionary France, following in the tracks of the enlightened despots, had developed and which her enemies had found themselves compelled to imitate. As a convenient example of such modern institutions, Metternich pointed to those which he planned to introduce into Lombardy-Venetia; with some modifications, they would do equally well for the Papal State.[114] On a more immediate level, the Papal government would have to grant a general amnesty for actions under the French regime and to confirm the possession of confiscated ecclesiastical properties, in keeping with the general policy of the Congress.

Consalvi welcomed Metternich's interest in his plans. He realized how strong the opposition to reform was at Rome, and how valuable Austrian support would be in combatting it. As the predominant Catholic Power, Austria inevitably exercised great influence at Rome, despite widespread Austrophobe sentiment in the Curia. Cast on the side of Consalvi and reform, this influence might mean the difference between success and failure. Before the Cardinal left Vienna, he and Metternich had come to an understanding: Consalvi would do his best to reform the Papal regime, and Metternich would provide him with all possible support.[115]

The Prince was as good as his word. Soon after Consalvi's departure, he instructed Lebzeltern to neglect no means of supporting the Cardinal against *Zelanti* opposition or Papal reluctance: "I authorize you to use the strongest language on this point, and to declare that the Emperor will never tolerate the adoption of measures whose effect would be to disturb the tranquility of those lands, and consequently of our own; and that you have the most definite orders to watch for his and oppose it."[116]

Austrian support was soon needed. Upon his return to Rome, Consalvi at once set about undoing the reaction of the past year by edicts granting a general amnesty, guaranteeing possession of the *biens nationaux*, setting up a provisional administration which preserved much of the French system, and promising a modern administration and other reforms.[117]

With these edicts, battle was joined between Consalvi and the *Zelanti*. Accusing him of "having imbibed Jacobin ideas" from Metternich (!), they began a vigorous campaign to persuade the Pope to dismiss him and reject his reform plan.[118] Less than two weeks after his return to Rome, Consalvi was fighting for his political life.[119]

The struggle that now began was to last without intermission until the end of Consalvi's career. It was an unequal contest from the start. The *Zelanti* formed the majority of influential cardinals and prelates, dominated the Curia and the congregations, and filled most posts in the civil government.[120] "Against this multitude of enemies the Cardinal stands almost alone," reported Lebzeltern.[121] Consalvi had perhaps a half-dozen effective supporters among the cardinals, and somewhat greater, but still minority, support among the lesser prelates. This meant that he had to carry on the government almost singlehanded, using his few loyal supporters for the most important posts, but perforce filling the remaining offices with the less loyal or less competent. The problems inherent in trying to carry out a reform program through subordinates the greater part of whom were hostile to reform can be readily imagined. "He is charged with trying to do everything himself; this is true, but if he leaves the smallest affair to his subordinates it will inevitably be frustrated and brought to a conclusion contrary to what he intended." Now, and for the rest of his career, "the greatest difficulty which the Cardinal meets in seeking to alter the course of the government is that most of those with whom he must work do not think as he does and seek constantly to undermine his policies."[122]

Immediately upon returning to Rome, Consalvi set to work on a plan of reform, which was completed by the end of Summer. He had next to submit it to a congregation for its comments. He had hoped to implement the plan at the new year, but the *Zelanti*-dominated congregation held up its passage with endless procrastination. Not until March, 1816, was Consalvi able to pry it loose from the congregation, and then only at the cost of abandoning several projected reforms.[123]

Now began the most critical stage of the struggle as the plan went to the Pope for final decision. Without the confidence of Pius VII, Consalvi's position would long since have become untenable. But since his imprisonment, the aged Pope retained little interest in worldy affairs; and the *Zelanti,* who had acquired much influence over him during Consalvi's absence, skillfully played upon his growing religious scruples by asserting that the Cardinal's reforms would be harmful to the spiritual interests of the Church.[124]

At this critical moment, Austria provided one of Consalvi's few reliable sources of support. Lebzeltern threw himself into the struggle for reform with such concentration that he neglected the other business of his office.[125] He had been a valuable friend to Consalvi during the long struggle, listening sympathetically to his problems, encouraging him in moments of depression, and reassuring him of continued Austrian support: at times it seemed that in all of hostile and uncomprehending Rome it was only at Palazzo Venezia that the Cardinal could find a sympathetic hearing.[126] But of far greater value was the influence that Lebzeltern, in the name of Austria, brought to bear upon Pius VII for the passage of the reform plan. Subjected to constant pressure from almost all those about him to reject the plan, Pius, despite his old trust in Consalvi, began to waver in his support.[127] But Metternich had foreseen this danger, and at his orders Lebzeltern devoted himself to counteracting it: "whenever I see the Pope, I speak to him with a frankness and vigor which no minister would dare to use..., I support Consalvi and his policies with every means at my disposal...."[128] These forceful arguments—delivered by a man for whom Pius had great liking, the envoy of the greatest Catholic Power, to which Pius felt sincere gratitude for the help which Austria had given him during his captivity and at the Congress—made a great impression upon the pontiff, balancing to some extent the pervasive influence of the *Zelanti.*[129]

For two months the fate of the reform plan hung in the balance while Consalvi and Lebzeltern fought to win the Pope's approval. At the end of May, 1816, the outlook was so discouraging that Consalvi spoke of resigning if the plan were not approved. Convinced that this would be disastrous, Lebzeltern made a supreme effort to convince the Pope, warning in the bluntest terms of the marh reaction would do the Papacy and the displeasure it would give Austria.[130] Pius seemed impressed by his arguments, and, since the long-delayed formal approval was given a few days later, they were evidently not without effect, though the native good sense of the Pope and his trust in Consalvi were probably more important. In any case, Consalvi expressed the greatest gratitude for Austrian support, while the *Zelanti* bitterly criticized Austria for the same reason.[131]

Papal approval finally secured, the plan appeared as the *Motu proprio* of July 6, 1816,[132] which provided for the creation of an efficient centralized administration. Most offices were opened to laymen, though the highest were

still reserved for the clergy. Papal absolutism continued to be the foundation
of the regime, but each province (a Delegation or Legation according to its
governor's title) would have a consultative council of local notables to advise
the governor. The rationalization and simplification of the judicial system
was begun: new codes are to be drawn up, and new tribunals instituted. The
old ecclesiastical tribunals survived, but their much-criticized jurisdiction in
civil cases was eliminated. Torture and arbitrary arrest or punishment were
prohibited. The principle of equality before the law was introduced, and the
intricate network of aristocratic and municipal privileges of the Old Regime
largely suppressed. The financial system was modernized, with more
equitable taxes and uniform customs duties and government monopolies in
all provinces.

The *Motu proprio,* as its preamble indicated, constituted only a first step
towards reform. Consalvi "willingly admits the imperfection of his work, but
defends himself by pointing out the insurmountable opposition which
rendered his original benevolent goals unattainable, and feels he has done
everything possible under the circumstances."[133] Metternich agreed: the
reform, "if still far from being in perfect agreement with the needs of the
situation, nonetheless approaches them sufficiently to defeat those who have
not moved with the times.[134] He praised the plan and its originator lavishly,
and promised the Cardinal his full support for the further reforms that they
agreed were necessary.[135]

With all its limitations, the reform of 1816 gave the Papal State the most
efficient and modern government it every enjoyed under pontifical rule, thus
meeting in part the chief demand of public opinion. Doctrinaire liberals were
not appeased, of course; but they were as yet a small minority. At this time,
the educated classes were in general less concerned with liberal ideals than
with satisfactory government, which Consalvi seemed in the process of introducing. The influence of Consalvi's reforms can be seen in the tranquillity
which prevailed in the State during the 1820–1821 revolutions in contrast to
the upheavals in Naples and Piedmont, and in even more significant contrast
to the revolution that broke out in the Papal State in 1831 after Consalvi's
plan had been revoked and all hope of reform from above had vanished.[136]

Still, much remained to be done, and Consalvi devoted his remaining
ministry to further efforts at reform.[137] But little was accomplished. The budget was balanced by 1821. The army and police were reorganized and became
somewhat more effective in dealing with the Sects and the perennial scourge
of brigandage. But in more fundamental areas Consalvi could make little
progress, because of constant *Zelanti* opposition.[138] He was unable to complete the reorganization of the administration, while of the judicial reforms
promised in 1816 only the code of civil procedure ever appeared. Even when
he managed to secure the promulgation of a reform, its effect was usually
blunted, for the *Zelanti* who filled most offices either ignored his directives or
interpreted them in a sense contrary to his intent. Indeed, because of this
ceaseless opposition, many provisions even of the *Motu proprio* of 1816 remained a dead letter.[139]

The central tragedy of the Papal Restoration was that the one man who
had both the vision to perceive the necessity of reform, and the position of

authority from which to carry it out, was prevented from doing so by the blind opposition of the *Zelanti*.[140] It is, of course, unlikely that a reform program of the type envisaged by Consalvi could have won the permanent backing of public opinion, given the spread of liberal-nationalist ideals after 1830, and the Sects would never have been satisfied by anything less than the overthrow of the Temporal Power. But his program would, at the least, have given the people of the State infinitely better government, strengthened the regime by reconciling moderate opinion to it, and to some extent saved the Papacy from the unenviable reputation for obscurantism and reaction it acquired in the nineteenth century. The opportunity was lost, and with it the last hope of saving or at least prolonging the Temporal Power. Even the limited reforms introduced by Consalvi were abolished by his successor. Thereafter, the State was ruled by men without vision, increasingly out of touch with the modern world. By 1846, when another man open to reform came to power, it was too late: public opinion had moved beyond the point where it could be satisfied by any concession which even the most conciliatory pope could make, as the disastrous end of Pius IX's attempt at reform was to show.

Fortunately for his peace of mind, Consalvi could not foresee what was to come; his success in securing the *Motu proprio* encouraged him to push on with his plans for reform.[141] It also encouraged him to persevere in his policy of cooperation with Austria, as did the steady support which he received from that quarter after 1816.[142] Metternich too found in the Cardinal's reforms justification for his policy of cooperation, for thanks to it the most glaring defects of the regime were being corrected, and to that extent not only the Papal State, but the Restoration order in Italy of which it was the weakest link, were being strengthened.[143] He therefore continued to provide the Cardinal with all possible support. Lebzeltern, who had been Consalvi's friend as well as ally, was transferred to Russia in 1816, and the Cardinal never again found so effective an ally at Palazzo Venezia.[144] However, Metternich took care to instruct subsequent ambassadors to support Consalvi and reform: first Count Apponyi as Minister *pro tem* during 1816–1817, then Prince Kaunitz in 1817–1820, finally Apponyi again as ambassador after 1820.[145] His support did not waver even when Austro-Papal relations began to cool in the wake of religious controversy, for Metternich never forgot that only Consalvi could save the Papal State from the dangers that reaction would surely produce.[146] This common front against reaction persisted throughout Consalvi's ministry, and even beyond: at the conclave of 1823, the Cardinal and Metternich united in one more effort to thwart the *Zelanti* by electing a moderate pope. Appropriately, the final act of Consalvi's public career saw a last rally of the policy of Austro-Papal cooperation, based, like that policy itself, upon the natural alliance of two great Restoration statesmen against the forces of obscurantism and reaction.

4. The Aftermath of the Austrian Occupation

The course of Austro-Papal cooperation did not run entirely smooth during 1815–1816. An "endless series of difficulties" grew out of the Austrian occupation of most of the Papal State after Murat's defeat. The Austrian troops were often guilty of brutal mistreatment of Papal citizens, while their commanders caused widespread hardship by levying heavy contributions in money and kind. In response to Papal complaints, Francis I offered profuse apologies, and explained that he had ordered that his troops should not be supported by the Papal State, but the occasional breakdown of their supply system had made forced requisitions necessary; however, the Papal government would be fully reimbursed for these exactions.[147]

In any case, such abuses would end with the evacuation—but here arouse a more serious problem: the apparent determination of the Austrian army to prolong its occupation indefinitely. As we have seen, Metternich and Consalvi had agreed that the evacuation would be completed by July 10. On his return to Rome, however, Consalvi learned that Count Saurau, in charge of the occupying forces, had refused to evacuate until several demands had been met—in particular, that Rome agree to pay certain debts of the Napoleonic Kingdom of Italy. Even if the Papacy met these demands, the transfer of the provinces to it would still be only *pro forma:* they would be evacuated only over several months, and in the interim would be administered by Austria.[148]

Saurau's demands had aroused great indignation at Rome. Pacca had protested forcefully, while the *Zelanti,* always distrustful of Austria, called for a public denunciation. Fortunately, Consalvi returned before action could be taken; he preferred to put Metternich's good will to the test, and sent a secret request for his intervention. The Prince responded promptly: the attempt to prolong the occupation was the work, not of Vienna, but of Saurau, who wanted the forces under his command to be supported by the Papal provinces, not the Imperial treasury. Metternich brought the situation to the Emperor's attention, and the last troops were evacuated by the end of July.[149]

Meanwhile, another problem had arisen. Ancona, the State's only good port on the Adriatic and a town of considerable strategic importance, had been strongly fortified by the French. Consalvi stipulated in the convention of June 12, 1815, that these fortifications should be turned over to the Papacy intact, but in mid-July he learned that they were being systematically destroyed by the Austrian garrison prior to evacuating the town. He at once turned to Metternich, but both the Prince and Francis I were absent from Vienna when his appeal arrived. Not until August did Metternich receive the letter. He at once secured Imperial orders suspending the demolition, but by that time the fortifications had been largely destroyed. Though the incident led to rumors of a sinister Austrian plot to weaken the defenses of the State,[150] its true cause was confusion within the Austrian government. During the war with Murat, Francis I had ordered that the fortifications should be destroyed so the Neapolitans could not use them if they retook the city.

Preoccupied with other problems, the Emperor forgot to revoke the order after Murat's defeat, and the army carried them out. However, Rome was promised full compensation.[151]

Annoying though these incidents were, they did not turn Consalvi against Austria; rather, his trust in Metternich was strengthened by the Prince's effective intervention. The Cardinal was increasingly confident that he and Metternich, working together, could solve any Austro-Papal problem on a mutually satisfactory basis.[152]

With one problem, unfortunately, Metternich had to be less accommodating. As was mentioned earlier, during the Hundred Days Austria had demanded that the Italian states furnish men or money for the struggle; Consalvi had reluctantly agreed to pay 1,700,000 scudi in installments to be completed by June 12, 1816. But the Papal finances were in critical condition: the French had left the treasury empty, the foreign occupations of the last year had deprived Rome of the revenue from its richest provinces, and a postwar depression was weakening the State's economy. In the midst of this, Consalvi had somehow to find money to finance his reforms, relieve popular economic misery lest it turn into revolutionary discontent, revive the many religious orders and activities whose properties the French had confiscated, make a dozen other unusual expenditures—and find 1,700,000 scudi for Austria. He consequently asked Metternich either to reduce the sum or to allow him to postpone payment until 1817. Lebzeltern advised granting his request. Metternich too was sympathetic, but the matter was not primarily within his jurisdiction, but that of the Finance Minister, who insisted that prompt payment in full was essential for Austria's own shaky finances. The Prince could only direct Lebzeltern to insist upon payment of the entire sum in keeping with the terms of the convention.[153]

Consalvi managed to meet the first installment, but by December he had to announce that additional payments were literally impossible for the time being. Once again he requested reduction or postponement of the debt; but the most Metternich could obtain from the Finance Ministry was the suspension of further payments until June, 1816, when the entire balance would have to be paid in full.[154]

By heroic efforts Consalvi managed to raise the necessary sum before the deadline. The Austrian attitude made an unfavorable impression at Rome, where, Lebzeltern reported, public opinion was "most critical of Austria for demanding so much when the Holy Father was in such dire straits." Consalvi's reaction was more complex: he did not criticize Metternich, who would have made concessions had the Finance Ministry not stood in the way.[155] However, the incident had again brought home to him an inherent weakness in Austro-Papal cooperation: Metternich, who had devised that policy, had only limited authority at Vienna, and could not always prevent the adoption of measures damaging to Rome. Still, if Metternich had failed to modify Austrian policy on the debt, he had dealt successfully with the problems of the evacuation and Ancona; the Cardinal therefore felt, as of 1816, that he had good cause to hope that the Prince's influence would usually be adequate to modify Austrian policy in a sense beneficial to the Papacy. With this in mind, Consalvi refused to allow the problems growing out of the occupation, annoying though they had been, to prevent him from cooperating with Vienna.[156]

5. *The Projected Imperial Visit to Rome*

In the Fall of 1816, Francis I announced that, after a tour of his Italian states, he would visit Rome in the Spring as the guest of Pius VII.[157] It was an announcement that caused Metternich and Consalvi great satisfaction, for they had long been working to bring about a visit from which they expected great benefits.[158] Both realized that, although at the moment all was well between their courts, the fundamental incompatibility of Austrian and Papal religious policy would lead to conflict sooner or later. Metternich hoped to avert this danger by dismantling the state church system, but Francis I remained attached to the Josephist principles in which he had been brought up, and most of his advisers at Vienna encouraged him to persist in that policy. Metternich and Consalvi hoped that if the Emperor were removed from the Josephist atmosphere of his court and brought into personal contact with Pius VII, he could be persuaded that the claims of the Papacy were not so unfounded as his advisers asserted. A meeting at Rome would give Pius—whose obvious honesty and genuine saintliness rarely failed to impress those whom he met—a unique opportunity to break through the Emperor's Josephist convictions and explain the Papal side of the religious situation. Francis might then be persuaded to abandon or at least modify his Josephist principles, thus eliminating the greatest single threat to good Austro-Papal relations. Moreover, the visit would enhance Austria's prestige at Rome, and would strengthen Consalvi against the *Zelanti,* since Francis and Metternich would seek to "confirm the Pope in his support of the liberal principles held by Consalvi."[159] Finally, the visit would have a salutary effect on public opinion by demonstrating to the world the good will and solidarity of Throne and Altar, thus discouraging the *Settarj.* With these advantages in view, Metternich and Consalvi had begun to discuss the visit during the Congress, and after its conclusion Consalvi dispatched an invitation to the Emperor on the Pope's behalf, which Metternich persuaded him to accept.[160]

But the possible effects of the visit were also apparent to the Josephists at the Imperial court, who made "a supreme effort to persuade the Monarch not to follow his original plans."[161] In December, 1815, Severoli reported that all the ministers except Metternich had appealed to Francis I not to visit Rome: "the reason given is the needs of the state; that which is not given, is fear of the discussions between the Holy Father and His Imperial Majesty."[162] Metternich fought back, but to little effect:

> The visit is strongly opposed by those immediately around His Majesty. . . . They believe, despite all that I can tell them, that our good Master will be forced to pass at least one or two nights bareheaded, barefoot, and without his shirt in the courtyard of the Quirinal, as

was the Emperor Henry IV of unhappy memory. When I point out that times have changed, they reply in professorial tones that one cannot be certain. . . .[163]

Moreover, it gradually became apparent that the current administrative reorganization of Lombardy-Venetia would require the Imperial presence for so long that no time could be left for him to visit Rome before affairs at Vienna called him back. The Josephists now had a solid argument to bolster their stand, the wavering Emperor was convinced, and in February, 1816, Metternich regretfully informed Consalvi that the visit could not take place.[164]

The cancellation of the visit caused Consalvi "the greatest distress," for it meant not only the loss of the advantages which he had anticipated, but a humiliation for the Papacy and a blow to his own prestige. Moreover, the *Zelanti* seized upon it to illustrate the alleged illwill and unreliability of Austria, while the apparent rift between Rome and Vienna encouraged the Sects.[165] Hoping to counterbalance these negative effects, Metternich decided to visit Rome himself in the summer of 1816.[166] Consalvi welcomed the plan, only to be disappointed once more: negotiations with Bavaria held Metternich in Vienna longer than expected, and the Prince soon began to suffer from a painful eye disease which made travelling out of the question. He had to cancel his visit in June, and his promise that he and Francis I would come to Rome at the first opportunity only partially consoled Consalvi, who warned that Austro-Papal relations might suffer from these repeated disappointments.[167]

In fact, after the cancellation of the visits a certain ebbing of the high tide of Austro-Papal good will became perceptible. The failure of the Emperor and Metternich to appear, after so many expensive preparations had been made to receive them, inevitably annoyed even those so well disposed towards Austria as Consalvi, while the *Zelanti* regarded it as evidence of Austria's disregard for the welfare of the Papacy, perhaps even a deliberate insult.[168] The most serious result of the cancellations was that Pius and Francis I did not have the opportunity for a personal discussion of religious affairs. Had they met, it is probable that they would have reached an understanding on religious questions, as they did when the Emperor finally visited Rome in 1819; the various religious problems that had been developing during 1815–1816 could then have been settled peacefully. But as matters stood, the Emperor's Josephist convictions remained unshaken and no understanding had been reached with the Pope; consequently, when religious questions came to the fore in 1816–1818, they led to prolonged controversy that gave a serious check to Austro-Papal cooperation.

Changes in the Roman diplomatic corps during 1816 also contributed to the erosion of Austro-Papal unity. As long as Lebzeltern represented Austria, her influence at Rome was undeniably predominant. His diplomatic skill and personal charm, his well-known sympathy for the Papacy, and the advantages he derived from his long friendship with Pius—all these combined to give him an influence over Pius which no other diplomat could match, while with Consalvi he was on close and friendly terms.[169] Unfortunately, in the

Spring of 1816 Alexander I, who had come to know and respect Lebzeltern during the negotiations of 1813–1814, imperiously demanded his transfer to St. Petersburg. Given the importance and delicate state of Austro-Russian relations, Metternich was in no position to reject the Tsar's request. In June, 1816, the Ambassador left Rome, to Consalvi's lasting regret.[170] Had Lebzeltern remained, he might have been able to smooth over the disputes that were to put so great a strain on Austro-Papal relations after 1816, just as he had calmed the Pope during the tense days of the Congress and prevented any open quarrel until Metternich's plans for restoring the Papal State could reach maturity. His successors were of lesser caliber, and lacked his advantage of long friendship with Pius and Consalvi. His immediate successor, on a provisional basis, was Count Apponyi. Although he was an experienced diplomat, well-liked by Pius and Consalvi, his "caractere doux et timide"[171] prevented him from exerting Austrian influence as boldly as Lebzeltern had done. He proved unable to calm Papal irritation at the religious disputes which arose during his stay, and could not check the slow decline of good relations which now set in.[172] The next ambassador, Prince Kaunitz-Rietberg, grandson of the great Chancellor of Maria Theresa, was even less satisfactory.[173] Ignoring his duties, he embarked upon a course of dissipation that scandalized even the blasé Roman society. His reputation was ruined, Austrian prestige declined, and the religious negotiations with which he was charged went badly; these failures produced a state of acute depression, climaxed by a nervous breakdown and his recall in 1819.[174]

Benefiting from this decline of Austrian prestige, and further contributing to it, was the revival of French influence.[175] In contrast to the inadequate Austrian diplomats, France was represented at Rome after 1816 by the Duke of Blacas, a diplomat of considerable ability, whose influence was enhanced by his reputation for devotion to the Church and his prestige as the favorite of Louis XVIII. Blacas set about replacing Austrian predominance with that of France. In 1817 he seemed to carry the day when he negotiated a new concordat favorable to Rome, in striking contrast to the religious controversy then straining Austro-Papal relations.[176] French prestige soared—to fall abruptly when the Chamber refused to ratify the concordat. The Curia was indignant, and Consalvi disgusted to see the results of his long negotiations lost.[177]

Moreover, though France had temporarily pulled ahead of Austria in the religious sphere, in the political field her rival remained well in the lead during 1815–1820. France did not offer Consalvi the same valuable support for his reforms as did Austria, nor was Paris in a position to be of equal assistance against the Sects; hence the Cardinal regarded France as a less useful ally,[178] while the *Zelanti* looked askance at her constitutional government. Nor could France now win Papal gratitude by playing her traditional role as counterbalance to an overbearing Austria, since Metternich's policy during these years did not seem to threaten Papal independence.

Nonetheless, the French revival was not totally reversed, and Blacas remained influential. France had once again emerged, as in the eighteenth century, as the Habsburgs' chief rival at Rome.[179]

The other Powers could offer only a feeble challenge to Austria's position. Spain had lost most of her once-great influence, partly because of the general decline of her power, partly because Consalvi was aware that her reactionary government was hostile to his policy of religious moderation and political reform.[180] Though Metternich was at times concerned at the cordial relations between Spain and the more intransigent *Zelanti,* Spanish influence was in general too slight to worry him.[181] Far more alarming, at least briefly, was the major effort made by Russia during 1815–1819 to gain influence at Rome, as part of a broad campaign aimed at undermining Austrian predominance in Italy. Consalvi, however, was unimpressed by the anti-Austrian arguments of the Russian Ambassador, Prince Italinski. Moreover, the growing persecution of Catholicism in Russia was not likely to endear its government to anyone at Rome. Even before the Tsar ended his campaign in 1819, it was clear that it had failed at Rome.[182]

Despite, then, the rivalry of other Powers, religious disputes, and the deficiencies of her ambassadors, Austria managed to retain a generally predominant influence at Rome during the five years following the Congress. Balancing in his mind the merits and drawbacks of cooperation with Austria, and the relative potential of the Empire and its rivals for the defense of Papal interests, Consalvi did not hesitate to conclude that Austria was "still the best protector" of the Papacy.[183] He accordingly persisted in his policy of cooperation, with such sincerity that Apponyi, at the end of his first year in Rome, was fully convinced of the Cardinal's "profound devotion to the Court of Vienna,"[184] and Metternich in 1819 professed himself "perfectly satisfied with the Court of Rome" and with the "most happy relations of confidence that exist, despite the efforts that have been made to weaken them," between Austria and the Papacy.[185] The meeting between Francis I and Pius VII, long postponed, was now definitely scheduled for 1819, and was expected to resolve whatever problems remained.

But storm clouds were building up on the horizon: as early as 1816, signs of a renewal of religious controversy were impossible to ignore. In the next three years, the unresolved contradictions between Austrian and Papal religious policy were to strain their alliance to the utmost, and when the long-awaited Imperial visit to Rome at last took place, it came less as the symbol of a triumphant Union of Throne and Altar than as a determined effort to halt the deterioration of Austro-Papal relations and to present to the world an appearance of unity and good will that increasingly failed to correspond to reality.

III

The Revival of Religious Controversy

1. The Legacy of Joseph II

The five years after the Congress of Vienna saw Austro-Papal cooperation flourish in the political sphere. Yet the dual nature of the Papacy meant that Consalvi could not judge his Austrian policy solely upon the basis of political effectiveness. If cooperation with Austria proved incompatible with Papal spiritual interests, then political benefits, however considerable, could not justify him in persisting in it. This was a point which the Cardinal had considered carefully, and his decision in favor of cooperation stemmed in large part from his belief that cooperation offered the best means of attaining one of Rome's chief religious objectives: the overthrow of Josephism.

The origins and nature of Josephism have long been disputed. Some historians have seen it as an attempt to reform and modernize Catholicism; others consider it only a move to establish state control over the church. Neither interpretation has won universal acceptance, perhaps because each contains an element of truth: it seems equally undeniable that a sincere wish for reform motivated many Josephists, and that the chief practical effect of Josephism was to implement the theory of absolute, if enlightened, despotism by extending the authority of the state over religion.[1]

The second objective was largely attained by Joseph II with the creation of a state church under Imperial control. Papal authority was rendered little more than nominal as virtually all direct links with Rome were severed; henceforth, the Austrian church was under the control of an Ecclesiastical Court Commission appointed by the Emperor, which regulated its administration, religious practices, and all else, in the most minute detail. Particular attention was given to clerical education, where great pains were taken to instill Josephist principles, with considerable success. Religious orders were suppressed, except for those involved in teaching or medicine, which survived only under tight government control and cut off from their superiors in Rome.

Whatever reforming ideals its intellectual leaders may have held, Josephism was always seen by the Papacy as simply another and unusually thorough attempt by the secular power to dominate the spiritual realm. The Papacy did its best to resist Joseph II, but the political and intellectual climate of the

age was unfavorable. In the end, Rome had to acquiesce in *de facto* Imperial
control over the Austrian church, though it remained always unreconciled to
the loss of its authority. When Consalvi first came to power in 1800, he found
Josephism more deeply entrenched than ever. Francis I, though pious, had
been raised in Josephist principles and was determined to defend what he
considered his sovereign rights over the church.[2] Most of his ministers,
bureaucrats, and high churchmen were firm Josephists, whose convictions
reinforced his. Far from reviving Papal authority, Consalvi had to resist efforts to extend Imperial authority yet further, as when Francis I sought to
deprive the Nuncio in Vienna of the last remnants of his ecclesiastical
jurisdiction or to reorganize various dioceses on his sovereign authority
alone. The Cardinal's diplomacy smoothed over the resulting disputes and
saved the principle of Papal authority, but could not prevent the Emperor
from winning the substance of his demands.[3]

As the Restoration opened, the Vienna Nuncio could find no sign of
change in Austrian policy: "we here are still as much as ever in the old
system, and very far from expecting change; instead, we shall see consolidated
in our midst the old abuses."[4] His reports painted a gloomy picture of the
religious conditions he felt Josephism had produced in the Empire. "The
clergy present a truly horrible aspect": uncontrolled by Papal authority and
with the disciplinary power of their own bishops hampered by the state,
educated in seminaries where the chief stress was upon political reliability
rather than spiritual qualities, the clergy had declined noticeably in morality,
learning, and religious zeal. Consequently, popular respect for the clergy, the
church, and religion had diminished, while immorality, irreligion, and
revolutionary principales were spreading.[5] And if the continued predominance of Josephism within the old frontiers of the Empire were not sufficient
cause for alarm, the Nuncio warned Rome that "there is no doubt that they
are planning to revive or introduce the laws of Joseph II into Lombardy and
the newly acquired territories."[6]

This last was a policy that would make conflict with the Papacy inevitable.
That Josephism flourished in the traditional Habsburg lands was bad enough
from the Papal standpoint; that it should be extended into new ground was
not to be endured—above all, not in Italy. There the Pope had a special interest and exercised a special authority, for there he ruled not only as Head of
the Church, but also and in a more immediate sense as Primate of Italy. "All
religious innovations made in Italy touch the Pope in his most sensitive
spot," Lebzeltern warned. "It is, so to speak, his exclusive domain, and he
draws perhaps greater advantage from his title of Primate of Italy than from
that of Head of the Universal Church," Therefore, many things which the
Pope might tolerate beyond the Alps he would never accept in Italy.[7] But this
warning, though backed by Metternich, could not prevail against the
Josephist counsel which the Emperor received from most of his advisers, and
the decision was made to extend the state church system into the territories
gained in 1815.

Conflict was thus unavoidable, especially since aggressive impulses and
dissatisfaction with the *status quo* were not lacking at Rome. There the circumstances of the Restoration were seen as unusually favorable to the revival

of Papal authority and the overthrow of Josephism. The *Zelanti* had been exhilarated by the spectacular and unexpected triumph of Pius VII over Napoleon, seeing in it manifest proof of divine support that would ensure Rome's ultimate victory over any secular foe if it only held fast to its God-given rights.[8] Even on a more worldly level, the *Zelanti* found cause for optimism. Josephism had been born during the Enlightenment, whose prevailing intellectual currents had been hostile to the Papacy and to Catholicism. The consequent weakness of the Pope's moral and intellectual position had had much to do with his inability to resist Joseph II. But in 1815 a new spirit was stirring Europe: the Age of Reason was submerged beneath the flood tide of Romanticism. The writings of Chateaubriand and his imitators, the stream of conversions of prominent intellectuals, the new intellectual respectability of religion, all bore abundant witness that this new spirit was favorable to Catholicism. A new Age of Faith seemed to be dawning as everywhere the rationalism of the eighteenth century retreated—to the joy of the *Zelanti*, who felt, not without cause, that the new emphasis on sentiment and faith would work to the advantage of the Church.[9]

Equally encouraging to Rome was the trend among European rulers towards reviving the Union of Throne and Altar. Frightened by the wave of revolution that had sprung from the rationalism of the Enlightenment, "rulers have realized that the best defense of their thrones...lies in the true religion, which makes subjects faithful to their sovereigns."[10] Even Francis I, that stout Josephist, admitted to Pius VII that "the temporal authority alone cannot carry out this salutary work," the extirpation of revolutionary ideas, for "the source of the evil is in the field of religion and morality, the field Your Holiness rules, and it is from you that I ask assistance."[11] If, the *Zelanti* argued, the secular power so greatly needed Papal moral backing, why could not Rome exact in return the restoration of its authority over the state churches? Not in centuries had the European situation seemed so favorable to the assertion of Papal authority, and the *Zelanti* were determined to make the fullest use of this opportunity. There must be no more compromise with regalist states such as Austria, no more backing down in the face of Josephist encroachments. No expansion of Imperial religious authority should be tolerated, nor should its extension into the newly acquired lands be allowed. In fact, it was imperative that the Emperor should first prove his good will by the "prompt and sincere revocation...of all laws contrary to the principles, maxims, and laws of the Catholic Church" before Rome would agree to enter upon the Union of Throne and Altar with him.[12] A merely defensive policy was not enough, the *Zelanti* felt. If the Emperor persisted in upholding Josephism, the Papacy must take the offensive, preferably by a bull condemning the entire state church system and all its adherents. The *Zelanti* were confident that such a bull, backed by the revived prestige of the Papacy, would shake the power of the Emperor and quickly bring him to submission.[13]

Consalvi was appalled by the policy advocated by the *Zelanti*, though not because his views on the aims of Papal religious policy differed from theirs. No *Zelante* was more convinced than he of the justice of the Pope's claim to supreme religious authority throughout the Catholic Church, and his basic objective was to make that claim effective in practice. This objective necessarily implied the destruction of the state churches of regalist Europe, and no one of his time did more than Consalvi to prepare the way for their destruction and the triumph of Papal authority.[14] Hostile to Josephism on principle, he also agreed with the *Zelanti* about its disastrous effects on the Austrian church, whose state he considered "a hundred thousand times worse than in France at the worst of times." [15] As early as 1805, the Austrian ambassador in Rome had warned his government that Consalvi intended to revive Papal authority to the fullest extent possible, but would proceed with caution, for he perceived the dangers of an aggressive policy.[16]

This last comment offers the key to Consalvi's attitude. He shared the *Zelanti's* aims, but not their exalted view of the power of the Papacy in the affairs of this world. His innate realism and long diplomatic experience had given him a just appreciation of Rome's true weakness *vis-à-vis* the Powers. The Papacy might persuade; it could not compel. Consalvi considered the tendency of the *Zelanti* to rely upon divine assistance in worldly affairs presumptuous: "God is not required to save us from the consequences of our own folly."[17] Nor was he so impressed as they by the altered intellectual and political climate of the Restoration. The currents of Romanticism might stir poets, but statesmen would continue to guide their policy by the dictates of reason of state, as before. The desire of rulers for a Union of Throne and Altar did work to the advantage of the Papacy, and Consalvi intended to exploit this desire to the utmost; but it was a weapon that must be used with care, for it was not so all-powerful as the *Zelanti* imagined. Monarchs could if necessary do without the Union, and might well choose to do so if the Pope demanded excessive concessions as its price.[18] Moreover, the Union was a weapon that cut both ways: revolution could threaten Rome as well as the Powers, and if the state needed the moral support of the Papacy, Rome needed the material power of the state.

Consalvi's policy started from the premise that the Papacy was too weak to force Austria to abandon the Josephist system. Far from intimidating Francis I, a direct assault would probably provoke him into a yet more intransigent stand than before, perhaps even to the schism at which Austria occasionally hinted.[19] "Great moderation seems to me to be necessary in dealing with this ruler," the Cardinal cautioned. "We must avoid any action of a startling or aggressive nature; only thus can we hope to reach a satisfactory conclusion."[20] Consalvi planned to undermine Josephism gradually, by tactful diplomacy. In dealing with Austria, as with other Powers, he followed a policy of studied moderation and conciliation. When a principle or a fundamental Papal interest was at stake, he was courteously unyielding; but on all else he was flexible, prepared to make concessions if it seemed necessary for the good of the Church, or if desirable concessions could be obtained in return.

Consalvi's motives were incomprehensible to the *Zelanti*, who accused him of betraying the Papacy, or, at least, of sacrificing its spiritual interests for petty political gains.[21] The same uncomprehending opposition which Consalvi's political reforms aroused was directed against his religious policy. Because of their control over the Curia, their influence over the Pope, and their domination of the congregations, the *Zelanti* were able to interfere constantly with his conduct of religious affairs. Of special importance was their control of the Congregation for Extraordinary Ecclesiastical Affairs, through whose hands concordats and all other major religious negotiations had to pass.[22] A long struggle with this potent opposition was usually necessary before Consalvi could proceed with the conciliatory approach he knew was most likely to prove successful, and all too often he had to give in and adopt a more rigid stance than he would have liked.

Despite these obstacles, Consalvi was able to negotiate a series of important concordats and less formal agreements with various states by which church-state relations were adapted to the changed circumstances of the post-revolutionary era.[23] These arrangements in general marked a significant advance for Papal authority at the expense of the state churches.

In dealing with Austria, Consalvi intended to pursue his customary policy and secure a concordat if possible, or at least an agreement regulating Austrian religious affairs that would begin the decline of the state church.[24] He was well aware of the difficulties in his path, but hoped they might be overcome if he proceeded with tact and moderation, taking advantage of the Emperor's genuine piety, the religious revival now under way, and in particular the desire for Papal cooperation against revolution. Above all, his hopes of success were encouraged by the appearance of a ray of light amid the Josephist gloom of Vienna: the obvious willingness of Metternich to abandon the state church system.

2. Metternich's Campaign against Josephism

By 1815, Metternich had come to believe that Josephism was no longer in the best interests of the Empire.[25] The claim that it was necessary to prevent domination of the state by the church seemed to him too anachronistic to be taken seriously. Instead of regarding the Pope as a rival, the Emperor should look upon him as a valuable ally.[26] Nor was Metternich impressed by the argument that Josephism had strengthened Austrian religious life—on the contrary, it seemed to him to have weakened religious sentiment, which he valued as a barrier against revolutionary ideas. Moreover, especially in Lombardy-Venetia, many devout Catholics who would otherwise have been firm supporters of the Imperial government had been alienated by its Josephism.[27] Yet, for the sake of this unnecessary and detrimental system, important interests in foreign policy were being sacrificed.[28] As Metternich saw it:

> This is the moral situation of Austria: she is engaged in a secret war against the church and its central see, while she is in a state of open war against the Revolution. The secret of our weakness lies in this struggle that we carry on against two diametrically opposed powers....This situation, absurd in itself, will sooner or later render our political system untenable.[29]

To extricate Austria from this position and enable her to concentrate all her energies, in union with the papacy, against the real enemy, revolution, Metternich in 1815 launched a campaign against Josephism. Although his ultimate goal was to abolish the state church system, he prudently refrained at first from suggesting so drastic a step to Francis I. During the decade after 1815, he was ostensibly working only to prevent the extension of Josephism and to modify those aspects of it most offensive to Rome; later, when Josephism had been undermined and the Emperor's mind prepared, the time would come for a more sweeping assault.

But even Metternich's immediate objectives were not easily reached. Everywhere in the Imperial government, the principles of Joseph II were still accepted—perhaps because to those of liberal inclination, they represented anticlericalism and the secular society, while to conservatives they by now seemed part of the traditional fabric of absolutism. Metternich's later claim to have been "alone on the side of the right" was no great exaggeration.[30] Above all, the Emperor was still firmly attached to Josephism. Metternich's primary goal, therefore, was to win over Francis I. To do this, he moved forward along two lines.

His first approach was to give Francis a more favorable picture of the Papacy, which the Josephists customarily depicted as aggressively plotting to extend its power at the expense of the Emperor's rights. Metternich explained the Papal side, pointing out that actions which the Josephists denounced as aggression were usually the result of misunderstandings, or of the exercise of what Rome might reasonably consider its traditional rights. His second approach was to stress the need for Papal cooperation against their common enemies, for Francis I too was increasingly inclined to regard the Union of Throne and Altar as essential for the counterrevolutionary struggle.[31]

Impressed by Metternich's arguments, Francis I began very gradually to reconsider his unquestioning adherence to Josephism. However, his fundamentally cautious nature made him reluctant to abandon any traditional policy. Accordingly, his retreat from Josephism was a long-drawn-out process, in which a step forward was usually followed by a half-step back—a process far from complete at the time of his death in 1835. During Consalvi's second ministry, this process had barely begun, and its ultimate outcome remained in doubt, though there were frequent hints that the Emperor's religious ideas were being transformed.

The first evidence that Metternich could modify Imperial religious policy in a sense favorable to Rome was provided by his successful intervention during the Congress in several incidents that seemed likely to provoke serious disputes. The first of these involved the Patriarchate of Venice. This post had been vacant since 1804 because of Pius's captivity, and the long vacancy had brought about much disorder in Venetian religious affairs. Upon his liberation in 1814, Pius appointed an Apostolic Administrator, Bishop Peruzzi of Chioggia, to deal with the situation. Count Lazansky, president of the commission charged with incorporating the newly acquired territories into the Empire and a staunch Josephist, chose to regard Peruzzi's appointment as a deliberate encroachment upon Imperial authority. Traditionally, the Patriarch had been nominated by the Venetian government; now that Venice was ruled by Austria, Lazansky claimed, the Pope should have consulted the Emperor before making this appointment. Lazansky's report led Francis I to believe that this was the opening move in a Papal campaign to deprive him of his sovereign rights over the church; he reacted with a strong protest to Consalvi. The Cardinal, however, found a more sympathetic audience in Metternich, to whom he explained that the Pope had not intended to encroach upon the Emperor's rights: since Venice had not yet been legally incorporated into the Empire, Pius had not felt compelled to delay the appointment until he received Imperial approval. Moreover, Pius, anxious to avoid any cause for controversy, had first consulted Lebzeltern, and had made the appointment only after the envoy had mistakenly declared that there would be no Imperial objection. Metternich, as anxious as Consalvi to avoid a quarrel, used these facts to appease the Emperor, and good relations were restored.[32] He was also successful in smoothing over two incidents minor in themselves, but which the Josephists sought to make into major controversies. The first arose from a Papal attempt to conduct a survey of the regular clergy of Venetia without prior Imperial approval, the second from a Papal brief that had placed under the jurisdiction of the Swiss Bishop of Coire a part of the Tyrol which, unknown to Rome, had been restored to Austria—an affront to the Josephist principle that no foreign bishop might hold jurisdiction over Austrian territory.[33]

Meanwhile, Lazansky had seized an opportunity to reaffirm Josephist principles by persuading the Emperor to decree the reorganization of the recently regained dioceses in the Tyrol on his sovereign authority alone, though by canon law Papal approval was necessary. This *de facto* extension of Imperial authority aroused resentment at Rome, but once again Metternich intervened at Consalvi's request. By explaining the legal basis of the Papal position and warning of the dangers of an unnecessary quarrel, he persuaded Francis I to request the Pope's approval before carrying out the reorganization.[34]

Early in 1815, Lazansky returned to the attack by suggesting to the Emperor that he should forbid the Lombard bishops to ask Papal authorization before granting dispensations for marriage within the third and fourth degrees of kindred. This prohibition was more significant than it seemed, for it would have cut one of the few remaining direct ties between the Lombard church and Rome. However, Metternich was able to persuade the Emperor to reject the proposal.[35]

Metternich's success in these disputes convinced Consalvi that the Prince had both the will and the ability to influence Austrian religious policy. It was now clear that Rome could have a powerful ally within the Imperial government in the fight against Josephism, provided that it was prepared to cooperate as Metternich wished. Consalvi left Vienna convinced that "the conciliatory spirit of Prince Metternich" offered the best hope of overthrowing Josephism.[36]

Despite this encouraging beginning, Metternich was to have no easy victory. Along with his successes during the Congress, he had to accept several minor failures, and in 1816 he suffered a major defeat when he could not prevent the Emperor from adopting three measures aimed at consolidating Josephism in Lombardy-Venetia.

The first of these measures was the prohibition of the *Romreise,* the obligation of those nominated to bishoprics in northern and central Italy to visit Rome, there to be personally examined (preconised), instructed in their duties, and consecrated by the Pope. This obligation, traditional since the Middle Ages, reflected the special authority of the Pope over the clergy of Italy in his capacity as Primate. Given the decline of Papal authority over the clergy since the rise of regalism, this obligation had acquired particular importance in that it both symbolized the continued authority of the Pope as Primate of Italy, and enabled him to preserve some degree of influence over the Italian bishops who otherwise tended to direct their loyalty towards the prince who had nominated them. As Consalvi admitted, "the Italian bishops are not in the least called to Rome to be examined and instructed, but solely to remind them, and the people as well, that the Holy Father is Primate of Italy." The popes were most tenacious of this obligation. The Cardinal was only expressing the general sentiment of the Curia when he declared that "since there only remains to the Holy See, of all its former power, little more than the canonical institution of bishops throughout Christendom, and this direct primatial influential on the Italian bishops, it is essential to preserve these two rights, of which the first has in most countries been reduced to little more than a formality."[37] So fervently had the Papacy clung to the *Romreise* that even Joseph II had ended by formally recognizing this obligation in the *Conventio Amicabilis* of 1784, which had regulated religious affairs in Lombardy.[38]

In February, 1816, Francis I forbade the bishops of Lombardy-Venetia to make the *Romreise.* [39] The official reasons given were the expense and inconvenience which the trip caused the bishops, and the need for administrative uniformity with the rest of the Empire, where the *Romreise* was not required. The real motive was the Josephists' fear that the bishops would come under Papal influence at Rome and "return to their dioceses as Roman converts..., doing more harm than good to church and state."[40]

In his second innovation of 1816, the Emperor claimed the power to nominate bishops in the newly acquired or regained lands without obtaining a specific Papal grant of this privilege. Arguing that he had inherited all the powers of the former rulers of those lands, including that of nominating bishops, Francis I proceeded to nominate a Patriarch of Venice in May, 1816, followed by a Bishop of Vicenza in July and an Archbishop of Salzburg in August.[41]

The Pope refused to confirm these nominations. Although the Papacy had long since been compelled to grant the power to nominate bishops to secular rulers almost everywhere, it clung to the principle that this power belonged by right only to the Pope; others might exercise it only as a special privilege he had granted. This was no mere legal quibble: as long as the Papacy maintained the principle, hope remained that one day favorable circumstances would enable it to reassert its right in practice—as it was in fact to do in the coming century. Therefore, the Papacy insisted that since Francis I had never been granted the privilege of nominating bishops for the new lands, he had no right to exercise it there.[42]

The third policy to arouse Papal opposition was the introduction of the Austrian marriage laws into Lombardy-Venetia. The Papacy had strongly opposed these laws on the principle that, by bringing marriage under state control, they degraded a devinely instituted sacrament to the level of a mere civil contract. Moreover, many specific provisions were contrary to canon law. With uncharacteristic prudence, Joseph II had refrained from introducing his laws into Italy, and their extension there by Francis I outraged the Curia.[43]

These innovations, as Metternich had predicted, aroused fierce resentment at Rome. The *Zelanti*, with their usual violence, demanded a public condemnation of Austria, and even the mild Pius VII was alarmed and indignant, particularly over the marriage laws, which he felt "went beyond anything Napoleon had done."[44] Though Consalvi agreed that the innovations would have to be fought, he rejected the *Zelanti* clamor for vigorous retaliation. Cooperation with Metternich would be the best way to defeat these manifestations of Josephism. After the usual debate with the *Zelanti,* he persuaded Pius to agree.

Consalvi's first step was to impress upon Metternich the gravity with which the Papacy regarded these innovations. Both directly by letter, and indirectly through Lebzletern, he hit repeatedly at the same theme.[45] The Papacy was eager to cooperate with Austria, and would willingly grant her anything that did not harm the essential nature of the Papacy. To the recent innovations, however, Rome, with the best will in the world, could never consent, for they were "destructive of its authority..., and opposed to the principles of Catholicism."[46] Continued Austrian insistence upon these innovations would only antagonize the Pope, strengthen the *Zelanti,* and perhaps compel Consalvi himself reluctantly to abandon his policy of cooperation.

To reinforce these warnings, the Papacy refused to accept any nomination made by Francis I in the newly acquired lands, or to confirm his nominees to Italian bishoprics who did not make the *Romreise.* To demonstrate the strength of his opposition to the marriage laws, the Pope refused to confirm the nomination of Monsignor Augustin Gruber to the Bishopric of Laybach. This prelate was of unimpeachable character, but, while acting as religious adviser to the Milan Gubernium in 1815, had signed the decree introducing the marriage laws into Italy. Pius declared that to accept his nomination would seem to confer Papal sanction upon those laws in the eyes of the world.[47]

But Consalvi accompanied this show of firmness with conciliatory gestures. Traditionally, each Catholic Power had the privilege of nominating one "crown cardinal" to act as its unofficial representative in the Sacred College. In July, 1816, Francis I—already represented as Emperor of Austria by one crown cardinal—requested the Pope to grant him a second in his capacity as successor to the Venetian Republic. However, he did not demand this as his right, but only as a special favor for which he would be forever grateful. Since the request gave Consalvi an opportunity to display good will towards Austria without weakening Papal authority in any way, he agreed. In order to avoid arousing the resentment or emulation of other Powers, the Emperor's request was kept secret, and the appointment was made ostensibly as the Pope's own selection—a precaution that reinforced the desired impression that the Pope was prepared to go to great lengths to grant any reasonable Austrian wish.[48] In the same month, Consalvi arranged a settlement on the nomination of Monsignor Gruber. Having demonstrated Papal repugnance to the marriage laws, Consalvi agreed that Gruber would be confirmed as Bishop of Laybach, on the secret condition that after assuming his see he would declare his support for official Catholic teaching on marriage in a pastoral letter.[49]

Having thus demonstrated both the determination of the Papacy to defend its rights and its willingness to conciliate Austria whenever possible, Consalvi in August, 1816, proposed that negotiations be opened for a concordat regulating religious affairs in Lombardy-Venetia.[50] As a basis for the talks, he declared that the Pope was willing to grant the Emperor the right to nominate to every see in Lombardy-Venetia, even those to which the Pope held the right of nomination, on two conditions: that the Emperor make a formal request to the Pope for this privilege, and that his nominees make the *Romreise.*

Consalvi's proposal reached Vienna at an opportune moment. For some time Metternich had been endeavoring to persuade the Emperor to adopt a more conciliatory religious policy. He had made his first effort when Rome refused to accept the nomination of Monsignor Gruber. Citing this refusal as proof of the Pope's determination to defend his authority, he advised Francis I that Rome was eager for cooperation with Austria and would grant whatever she asked, provided its essential rights and the welfare of the Church were respected; but where these last were concerned, the Pope could never yield. Such was the case with the recent innovations. To insist upon them would result, not in Papal acquiescence, but only in antagonizing Rome to the point where she would refuse to cooperate with Austria.[51]

Francis found these arguments sufficiently impressive to seek an opinion upon them from his spiritual advisers. They, however, being staunch Josephists, defended the innovations as just and necessary, and convinced the Emperor that the Papacy would yield if he held firm. He accordingly rejected Metternich's advice.[52] But after several months passed with no sign of Papal weakening, Metternich returned to the battle. In July, 1816, repeating his previous arguments, he urged the Emperor to establish a commission to study the desirability of a concordat to regulate religious affairs in Lombardy-Venetia. At this point Consalvi's proposal arrived—at so opportune a moment that we may suspect that he had received some hint from Metternich of which no trace has survived in the archives. Metternich promptly seized upon his proposal, as well as upon Papal moderation in regard to Monsignor Gruber and the second crown cardinal, as proof of Papal good will and readiness to reach a settlement.[53]

Under the impact of Metternich's arguments, Francis I now wavered in his support of Josephism for the first time. In October, 1816, he accepted Metternich's suggestion to set up a commission. However, in his usual style, he balanced this departure from Josephist tradition by appointing a commission composed entirely of Josephists, with predictable results. The commission's report, presented in January, 1817, firmly rejected the very idea of a concordat. It declared that all the recent innovations were necessary and came within the legitimate authority of the sovereign. Even to negotiate on them would encourage Rome to advance new pretensions subversive of Imperial authority. Rome would have to yield if the Emperor stood firm.[54]

This report reconverted the Emperor to the Josephist fold, and he decided against a concordat. But Metternich continued to insist that some sort of arrgeement with the Papacy was necessary to place religious affairs in the new territories on a stable basis. The Emperor could not deny that some sort of settlement was imperative. Because of the long Papal captivity, followed by the dispute over the nomination power, many sees in Italy had been vacant for years, leading to a breakdown in clerical discipline and growing immorality and irreligion. These conditions offended both the Emperor's piety and his hope that strong religious faith among the people would halt the spread of liberalism. Since only an agreement with Rome would permit the sees to be filled, Metternich was at last able to persuade his August Master to agree that Prince Kaunitz might open informal negotiations with the Pope when he arrived in Rome as ambassador in June, 1817.[55]

Victory—but a very limited one, as Metternich soon realized. The Emperor agreed to the negotiations, but only on terms that left them little chance of success. The conduct of the negotiations was virtually removed from Metternich's hands and put in those of the Josephists. Kaunitz, who represented Metternich's conciliatory policy, was to be joined by Councillor Jüstel, a firm Josephist, whose guidance he was to accept in religious questions. Although Metternich drew up Kaunitz's instructions, he had to submit them to Lazansky for final revision.[56]

The instructions as they emerged from Lazansky's hands retained little trace of the conciliatory policy favored by Metternich. They were founded on the assumption that the state church system was both just and necessary, and must be extended in full to the newly acquired territories. The purpose of the negotiations was not to work out a mutually satisfactory settlement of religious affairs, as Metternich had intended, but only to secure Papal approval for the extension by obtaining five major concessions: 1) that the Emperor be given the right of nomination to all Venetian sees; 2) that the *Romreise* be abolished; 3) that the Emperor be given the right to nominate the Archbishop of Salzburg, who should retain all the special privileges which his predecessors had held as sovereign prince-bishops of the Holy Roman Empire; 4) that the Lombard-Venetian bishops be given full power to grant marriage dispensations in the third and fourth degrees of kindred; and 5) that the Papacy formally approve the new diocesan organization which the Imperial government had drawn up for Lombardy-Venetia, the Tyrol, and Vorarlberg.

The Pope was to be persuaded to grant these concessions, not by the offer of reciprocal concessions, but by playing upon his gratitude for past Austrian assistance and his fear of a break with Austria. The sole concession that he might be offered was the withdrawal of Austrian garrisons from Ferrara and Comacchio. No religious concessions of any sort could be considered, and indeed, Kaunitz was if possible to avoid even discussing Austrian religious policy.

The talks would be secret and informal. Negotiations conducted on the lines which the Josephists had laid down were a far cry from those Metternich had envisaged, and he knew well how little chance they had of success. Better that negotiations never formally open than that they do so only to end in failure, thus revealing to the world the break between Rome and Vienna. In fact, his chief concern now was not with making the negotiations succeed, but with preventing their inevitable failure from doing lasting harm to Austro-Papal relations. He realized the extent to which Consalvi's cooperation rested upon his hope of inducing Austria to modify her religious system. The intransigent Josephism imposed upon Kaunitz by his instructions was certain to make the worst of impressions upon the Cardinal, and might well shake his faith in the value of cooperation with Austria. Metternich therefore ended the instructions by alerting Kaunitz to this danger. Above all, Kaunitz must prevent religious controversy from upsetting political cooperation between the two courts: upon this "delicate nuance" depended the success or failure of the talks.[57]

Consalvi too feared the possible adverse effects of the negotiations. He knew that for the Pope and the Curia these talks constituted a test case for Austro-Papal cooperation. If they led to a significant modification of the Josephist system, then the policy of cooperation would seem justified, not only to Consalvi, but to his ruler and the *Zelanti;* but if they failed, he would have great difficulty in persisting in that policy in the face of reinforced *Zelanti* criticism and Papal doubts. His initial satisfaction at learning of the negotiations gradually evaporated as disquieting reports came in from Leardi, whom he had sent to Vienna in 1817 to replace Severoli, whose criticism of the Austrian government had made him *persona non grata*.[58] In early June, Metternich explained the situation frankly to the new Nuncio, carefully disassociating himself from the Josephist demands which Kaunitz would present. He admitted that those demands were excessive, but advised against flatly rejecting them. The very fact that the Emperor had agreed to negotiate with the Pope indicated that he had begun to depart from strict Josephist views. A blunt rejection would only anger him and push him back towards rigid Josephism. All the efforts of Metternich and Consalvi would thus be wasted.[59]

Consalvi realized the force of his argument, but his ability to act upon it was limited. Though willing to make reasonable concessions, he would not sacrifice any major Papal interest even to prevent an Imperial relapse into Josephism. Moreover, he had always to reckon with the *Zelanti* who dominated the Congregation for Extraordinary Ecclesiastical Affairs: they would not only reject any attempt by Consalvi to make unreciprocated concessions, but would seize upon it as evidence for their old charge that he was willing to sacrifice religious interests for political advantages. The Pope was particularly susceptible to their influence now, for he had been seriously ill for weeks. His nearness to death intensified the religious scrupulosity upon which the Zelanti could play with great skill; under their influence, he refused to sanction any arrangement with Austria that did not receive the approval of the Congregation.[60] Consalvi directed Leardi to explain his difficult position to Metternich, and to warn him that if Austria insisted on conducting the negotiations along Josephist lines, he could prevent neither their failure nor the decline in Austro-Papal cooperation that would surely follow. Only if Metternich could alter Kaunitz's instructions could these consequences be averted.[61]

But Metternich could do nothing, for he was no more able than Consalvi to overcome the influence over his sovereign of those whose ideas were the opposite of his own. Kaunitz arrived in Rome with his original instructions. At his first meeting with Consalvi, on June 16, 1817, he presented the Cardinal with the list of concessions demanded by the Emperor.[62] The Secretary of State pointed out that since these concessions would mark a major advance for at the expense of Papal authority, Austria could hardly expect to receive them without making concessions in return. Kaunitz tried to play upon Papal gratitude for the recovery of the Papal State and upon fear of a rupture with Austria, but without effect. The meeting ended with both diplomats pessimistic.

After much argument, Consalvi—heeding Metternich's advice not to reject the requests outright—managed to win the approval of the Congregation to offer Kaunitz a compromise. The Pope would grant all the Austrian requests—except that for the power of dispensation, which Pius was resolved to keep—provided "His Majesty does something for the Church by eliminating the most serious of the abuses in his Empire." In particular, the Emperor must agree to: 1) modify the Austrian marriage laws in Lombardy-Venetia to eliminate those provisions contrary to canon law; 2) grant the Papacy a voice in the education of Austrian clergy; 3) allow the Pope free communication with the Lombard-Venetian bishops, without government interference; and 4) allow Papal bulls relating purely to dogma to enter the Empire without the *placet regio*. Consalvi suggested that Metternich come to Rome to work out a final settlement on the basis of this compromise.[63]

Kaunitz, alarmed by the strength and intransigence of the *Zelanti,* advised acceptance of this proposal, which he felt was the most Austria could hope to obtain. Consalvi had extracted the utmost concessions possible from his colleagues. If this settlement were rejected, the *Zelanti* would only make greater demands in the future, when Consalvi, weakened by his failure to obtain concessions from Austria, would no longer be able to restrain them. In any case, concessions were desirable to reassure Consalvi as to the value of cooperation with Austria. "As in any negotiation," Kaunitz concluded, "we will not obtain what we want except by agreeing to some things we dislike."[64]

Metternich agreed, but he could not persuade Francis I to accept any modification of the Austrian demands or make any religious concession. There was no point in Metternich's coming to Rome: no doubt he and Consalvi could easily work out a mutually satisfactory settlement of religious affairs, but the Emperor would not endorse it. In religious questions, Metternich was "only a negotiator, merely a go-between," bound by the Emperor's decisions which he could not alter. In the future, he hoped to be able to accomplish more, but at present he could only instruct Kaunitz to reject the Papal proposal, and to express to Consalvi his hope that religious controversy would not be allowed to disturb "the great political interests which link our states"—a hope which he knew was unlikely to be realized.[65]

The rejection of Consalvi's compromise killed the last real hope for a settlement, though negotiations continued into July. Consalvi and Kaunitz held several more conferences, in which each merely reiterated the customary arguments and claims of his court. Since Consalvi could offer no greater concessions than earlier, and Kaunitz none at all, these meetings were an exercise in futility. Jüstel also tried his hand at dealing with the Cardinal, but with no greater success: Consalvi shrugged off the Councillor's stereotyped Josephist arguments for the state church system and merely repeated that the Papacy would never yield its undoubted rights without reciprocal concessions[66]

"I no longer expect any favorable outcome from this negotiation," Kaunitz reported after a final meeting on July 13. The Pope would agree to the diocesan reorganization in Venetia, the Tyrol, and Vorarlberg, if some minor changes were made; he was also willing, as he had been since 1816, to grant the right of nomination for Venetia if the Emperor would request it as a special privilege. But on all other points, especially the *Romreise*, he would not yield.[67]

The reasons for the failure of the 1817 negotiations are obvious. The Papacy, understandably, would not accept the considerable advance of the state church system which the Imperial demands represented, unless the Emperor agreed to balance that advance by a retreat on other aspects of the Josephist system. Since Francis was still too tightly wedded to Josephist principles to consider making religious concessions, the negotiations had been doomed from the start.

As Metternich had feared, the failure of the negotiations led to a deterioration in Austro-Papal relations. The rigid Austrian attitude had made a highly unfavorable impression at Rome. The Pope was bitter at the Emperor's intransigence and inclined to listen to the *Zelanti*, who redoubled their pressure for an open attack on the state church system. Consalvi continued to oppose their pressure, but his arguments for moderation had been weakened by his failure to bring about any significant improvement in the Austrian attitude. Nor was the Secretary of State himself entirely unaffected by the failure of the negotiations. His personal regard for Metternich remained undiminished, since he realized that the Prince had sincerely tried to change Austrian policy. But if his trust in Metternich's good intentions remained strong, not so his faith in the Foreign Minister's ability to translate those intentions into practice. The Cardinal did not abandon his policy of seeking to weaken Josephism through cooperation with Metternich, if only because no plausible alternative existed; but his willingness to make cooperation the basis of his foreign policy inevitably suffered, as did his ability to defend it against *Zelanti* criticism.

The unfavorable impression which the Austrian stand made upon Consalvi was heightened by the contrast with the success which he was then attaining in religious negotiations with France, Naples, and Bavaria. Writing to Metternich to express his regret at the failure of the negotiations, he significantly chose to conclude with the remark: "I cannot refrain from telling Your Highness that...the ratification of the concordat by the King of France has just arrived."[68] The implication was unmistakable: the Papacy was not dependent upon Austrian good will, but could find other friends better disposed towards Papal religious interests.

The point was not lost on Metternich, who found in it another argument against Josephism. The Emperor's immediate reaction to the failure of the negotiations, however, had been irritation that his services to the Papacy in the past had not induced it to grant him the concessions he desired.[69] Consequently, Metternich's first problem was to restrain Francis I from acting on his impulse to retaliate against Rome. In his report on the negotiations, he outlined a moderate course of action for the future. The most pressing necessity was "to provide for the vacant bishoprics of Lombardy-Venetia and... for the new diocesan organizations." Therefore, even though it meant accepting the Papal position to some extent, the Emperor should request the power of nomination as a special privilege, and should ask Papal approval for the diocesan reorganization. As for the other points in dispute, the Papacy had shown its determination not to yield; further Austrian pressure would thus be useless, and it would be best to await a more favorable moment before raising them again. This was especially true of the *Romreise,* whose formal abolition the Emperor should cease to demand. Instead, he should instruct his nominees to approach the Pope individually, each requesting a dispensation on some ground such as health or age. The Pope would no doubt grant most of these requests, so that the Emperor would gain the substance of his wish. Finally, Metternich advised that it was imperative to "avoid new subjects for misunderstanding with the pontifical court; this means, above all, halting the promulgation of any new ecclesiastical ordinances for the Lombard-Venetian Kingdom." This was the "only means of mitigating the somewhat unfavorable impression that might be produced" by the contrast between the concessions made to Rome by France and other courts and the rigid Austrian attitude, "which could do serious harm to our political interests."[70] Francis I grudgingly accepted his minister's advice, and the danger that he might provoke an open break with Rome by adopting a more aggressive policy was averted.[71]

Nonetheless, Austro-Papal relations cooled as the unsettled religious disputes continued to fester. After Francis I had made a formal request, Pius granted him both the nomination power and its approval for the diocesan reorganizations; but even these concessions led to recrimination. The *Zelanti,* unable to prevent the Pope from granting the nomination power, persuaded him to include in the bull conferring it a strong reaffirmation of Papal authority over the Lombard-Venetian Church and an implicit criticism of Imperial claims to religious authority. Consalvi had tried to prevent this gratuitous provocation, but this influence in religious affairs had declined since the failure of the negotiations, and the most he could do was to moderate the criticism of Austria. As usual, the intransigence of the *Zelanti* stimulated that of the Josephists, who tried to persuade Francis I to reject the bull and nominate bishops on his own sovereign authority. Metternich defeated this move, which would have further embittered relations with Rome, but the Emperor could not be dissuaded from expressing his displeasure to Leardi in the strongest terms.[72] Metternich apologized to the unfortunate Nuncio and assured him that he would continue to work for good relations with Rome, but added that the Emperor now rarely consulted him on religious policy. For the time being, he could do more than prevent the adoption

of new Josephist measures likely to lead to controversy; he would have to
await a more favorable moment before making another attempt to induce
Francis I to abandon Josephism. "God knows where all this will end," Leardi
concluded gloomily. Of only one thing was he certain: there was more trouble
to come, and its center would be the Archbishopric of Salzburg.[73]

3. The Salzburg Question, 1818-1819

Prior to the Revolution, the Archbishop of Salzburg had been prominent
among the autonomous ecclesiastical princes of the Empire. As such, he had
enjoyed many unusual privileges, such as that of not merely nominating his
suffragan bishops, but of confirming them without awaiting Papal approval.
When Napoleon suppressed the ecclesiastical principalities, Salzburg was incorporated into the Austrian Empire. Francis I then requested the right of
nominating the Archbishop, but agreed that the latter should lose his special
privileges. Various minor disputes prevented a settlement, and in 1809 the
imprisonment of Pius VII and the loss of Salzburg to Bavaria ended the
discussion.[74]

Austria's recovery of Salzburg in 1815 led Francis I to request the nomination power once again, but now his claims had increased: under Josephist
influence, he demanded not only that he have the power to nominate the
Archbishop, but also that the Archbishop should retain all the special privileges which had once made him "virtually independent of the Holy See.[75] The
Pope had tolerated this virtual independence, though reluctantly, while the
Archbishop was a sovereign prince elected by his cathedral chapter. But it
was a very different matter to allow the same powers to an Archbishop chosen
by the Josephist Emperor, who would thus acquire even greater religious
authority in Salzburg than in the rest of his Empire. The Archbishop's power
of confirming his own suffragans seemed especially dangerous under those
circumstances. Consalvi also realized that if the Papacy were to agree to the
concentration of such power in the hands of an Imperial nominee, a precedent would be set which the Josephists would surely try to expand to the rest
of the Empire—indeed, Leardi reported that the Josephists were already urging that the Archbishop of Salzburg be made Patriarch of Germany, with full
power to confirm all bishops there.[76] Consalvi therefore resolved not to grant
the Emperor the power to nominate the Archbishop unless the latter sur-
rendered his extraordinary privileges.[77]

Francis I made his first move in August, 1816, by nominating Count Fir-
mian, Prince-Bishop of Lavant, to the Archbishopric of Salzburg. No mention of the Archbishop's privileges was made, implying that they were to be
retained as a matter of course. Pius refused to confirm the nomination, arguing that the Emperor had never been given the nomination power for
Salzburg.[78] Consequently, during the 1817 negotiations Kaunitz was directed
to secure for the Emperor the power to name the Archbishop, his suffragans,
and their chapters, with the Archbishop to retain all his privileges.[79] Little

was said of Salzburg during those negotiations, since both sides were preoccupied with Italian questions. However, Consalvi made clear to Kaunitz that
the Emperor could have the nomination power only if the Archbishop lost his
privileges.[80]

Discussions on Salzburg continued in desultory fashion through the Fall
and Winter of 1817. Since neither side would abandon its previous stand,
no progress was made.[81] In the Spring of 1818, Francis directed Kaunitz to
make a new attempt. Consalvi replied by offering the Emperor a choice:
either to acquire the power to nominate the Archbishop, with the latter losing
his privileges, or to preserve the *status quo,* with the Archbishop, retaining
his privileges but being named by the metropolitan chapter of Salzburg.[82]

Francis I rejected both alternatives as unsatisfactory, and continued to
press for his original demands. Negotiations continued into the Fall of 1818,
with growing bitterness on each side. The Emperor complained angrily of the
Papal reluctance to grant "his most reasonable requests," to which he felt his
"innumerable services to the Holy See" fully entitled him.[83] His displeasure
was shown in more tangible form when he withdrew Austrian support from
the Papacy in its dispute with the Protestant states of the upper Rhine. The
prevailing attitude at Vienna was well illustrated by Councillor Hudelist, who
told Leardi bluntly that "Austria could easily sweep aside" the problems
which the German states were creating for Rome, but could see no reason to
aid the Papacy in this or any other matter in view of its stand on Salzburg and
the *Romreise.* Hudelist did not conceal the satisfaction of his court at the difficulties which Rome was now meeting in securing the ratification of its concordat with France. Austria, Leardi concluded, "would be delighted to see
Rome humiliated and on its very knees begging support."[84]

The Imperial attitude aroused anger and resentment at Rome. The *Zelanti*
seized this opportunity to revive their long-cherished project for a bull condemning the entire Josephist system. Pius VII was persuaded to approve a
provisional draft of the bull, and it took all Consalvi's skill to convince him
not to sign a formal version.[85] Even Consalvi, though still convinced of the
political value of cooperation and determined to prevent an open break, was
no longer so firm in his support for cooperation as before.[86] The events of the
past year had weakened his confidence that this policy could transform the
Austrian religious situation. Despite several years of cooperation, Josephism
seemed as well entrenched as ever, and Francis I as unwilling to make any
significant concession. The Secretary of State consequently began to harden
his policy: he resolved to make no further concessions until Imperial policy
had shown a substantial change, which he increasingly considered unlikely.[87]

The coolness which had entered Austro-Papal relations after the failure of
the 1817 negotiations now threatened to become actual hostility. Negotiations over Salzburg and the *Romreise* dragged on interminably but fruit-
lessly. At Rome, Consalvi was hard pressed by the *Zelanti,* who asserted that
his policy of conciliation had failed and demanded the condemnation of the
state church system. Ironically, he was at the same time the subject of bitter
criticism from Vienna, where he was generally blamed for the deterioration
in relations.[88] This unfair criticism of the one man at Rome who sincerely
wanted to cooperate with Austria was too much for Consalvi, and in the Fall

of 1818 the usually self-controlled Cardinal allowed his feelings to burst forth in a bitter, eloquent protest to Metternich:

> I am certain that for a long time everything possible has been done to satisfy the wishes of the Court of Vienna, except for those few things which His Holiness *could not do*. . . . Austria's policy towards the Roman government and these unjust and slanderous accusations have wounded me to the heart. . . . To have to carry virtually the whole burden of the world upon my shoulders here; to be slandered as a man without principles; to be accused of laxity, because within reasonable limits I try to adapt myself to modern ideas; to arouse hatred as a supposed partisan of Austria—and then to find those attached to Austria, not defenders and supporters, but slanderers and unjust critics—I confess to Your Highness that I cannot endure it. . . . Were it not for the unlimited attachment that links me to His Holiness, I would certainly retire from a post which yields me nothing but slanderous accusations.[89]

The outspoken bitterness which marks this letter, in contrast to the Cardinal's usual restrained style, seems too great to have been produced merely by the petty backbiting of the Viennese court; rather, it represents the bursting forth of the intense disappointment and frustration he felt at the whole course of Austrian religious policy since 1816. He had cooperated with Austria in political matters, followed a moderate religious policy, checked the anti-Austrian intrigues of the *Zelanti*—and his reward from Austria had been, not friendship and reciprocity, but Josephist intransigence and unjust criticism. Clearly, the Cardinal was close to jettisoning the whole idea of Austro-Papal cooperation.

But at that very moment, unknown to Consalvi, the situation at Vienna had taken a turn for the better. Rome's stubborn resistance had at length forced the Emperor to admit that it could not be beaten down by Austrian pressure. Metternich was always at his elbow to warn that the Josephist system must be moderated if Papal cooperation was to be retained. For three years now, the Emperor had been hesitating, torn between his fundamental aversion to change and the advice of the Josephists on the one hand, and Metternich's arguments on the other. In the Fall of 1818, he at last began to move gingerly in the direction urged by his Foreign Minister. Metternich, hoping to give his August Master a definite impulse towards a policy more sympathetic to the Papacy, now revived the plan for an Imperial visit to Rome. All the arguments that had favored such a visit in 1815 were doubly valid now, though in order to pacify the Josephists Metternich took care to present the visit as political rather than religious in nature—part of a general tour of Italy aimed at consolidating Austrian influence there. After some hesitation, Francis I agreed to go—and thereby took his first halting step away from Josephism.[90]

Metternich could thus send a soothing and encouraging reply to Consalvi's protest. Denying that he himself had ever criticized the Cardinal, he expressed the highest appreciation for the "enlightened changes" which Consalvi had made in Papal policy. In answer to the Cardinal's implicit reproach at his failure to secure a major modification of Austrian religious policy, he reminded him that they were in essentially the same situation: "like all ministers, you have a limited authority; the same is true of me. I can do much, and I try to do it; but I cannot do everything." It was a defense whose justice Consalvi could not fail to admit, nor could he help but be touched by the appeal to his sympathies as one who suffered from the same handicaps and frustrations as his colleague in Vienna. After thus explaining and apologizing for the failures of the past, Metternich concluded by offering hope for the future: he and Francis I would spend the Easter season of 1819 at Rome.[91]

This letter impressed and reassured Consalvi, and the news of the projected visit aroused the same hope in him as in Metternich for a change in the Emperor's religious views and a revival of Austro-Papal cooperation. He sent a cordial, even enthusiastic, reply.[92] Yet the impression made upon him by Austrian conduct in the past two years was not entirely effaced, and the pessimism about Imperial religious policy which had taken root in his mind was too deep to be entirely removed by one letter, however impressive. When, early in 1819, Austria proposed that negotiations be resumed on Salzburg and the *Romreise,* his continued skepticism was evident in his comments to Leardi:

> I fear that this will be a new source of sorrow for the Holy See..., for I cannot help but foresee that new demands and new claims will be raised. Since, given the principles known to prevail in Austria, the spirit in which they will want to discuss religious questions will certainly differ from ours, the Holy Father has every reason to fear that this will be a new source of affliction for the Holy See.[93]

But for once the Cardinal's pessimism was unjustified, for the Emperor had finally begun to accept Metternich's arguments. The Prince had pointed out that if the questions of Salzburg and the *Romreise* were left unsettled, the Pope would no doubt raise them at his meeting with the Emperor. Francis I would then be in the difficult position of having either to yield on both points, or to reject the requests to the Pope's very face. Won over by this reasoning, Francis agreed to accept a compromise. With regard to the *Romreise,* he would recognize the obligation in principle, by agreeing that "the first bishop nominated in Lombardy-Venetia after each succession to the Imperial throne or the pontifical sovereignty would make the trip." In return, the Pope was to "dispense the other bishops from this obligation." In regard to Salzburg, of the alternatives presented by Rome, Francis I decided in favor of preserving the *status quo,* though with certain modifications: he wanted the power to nominate to all the canonicates, prebends, and other dignities of the metropolitan chapter. In February, 1819, Metternich informed Kaunitz that the Emperor, "desiring that his stay in the capital of the Christian world be marked only by the expression of a mutual confidence and understanding so well established that the criminal hopes of the enemies of public order will be discouraged thereby," had authorized him to propose the above compromise to the Papacy.[94] Although the offer was to be presented as an "ultimatum," Metternich advised Kaunitz confidentially that if the

Papacy rejected parts of it, modifications could be made to secure its acceptance.[95] The striking difference between the tone of these instructions and
those sent for the 1817 negotiations is the measure of the success which Metternich was beginning to achieve in his campaign to convert the Emperor
from Josephism, and of the distance which Francis I had already traveled
from his original principles.

Since Kaunitz had now begun to sink into the mental decline which would
soon cause his recall, the proposal was made to Consalvi by the Secretary of
the Embassy, Chevalier Gennotte. The Imperial proposal was considerably
more favorable than the Cardinal had feared, and he rejoiced at this evidence
that the Emperor was at last moving towards a more moderate position.
Nonetheless, he was unable to accept it in full. The proposal on the *Romreise,* in particular, though accepting the principle of the trip, would in practice have eroded its substance. Since Consalvi was as determined as ever to
preserve this link with the Lombard-Venetian bishops, he rejected this part
of the compromise. A more satisfactory settlement was reached on Salzburg.
The Emperor's decision to accept the status quo rather than insist on the
power to nominate the Archbishop made a favorable impression on Pius VII,
who agreed to grant him the power to name the metropolitan chapter.[96]

With this agreement ended the long controversy which had arisen from the
Imperial attempt to impose the full Josephist system upon the newly acquired
territories. Francis I professed himself satisfied with the settlement of the
Salzburg question. As for the *Romreise,* though disappointed that his proposal had been rejected, he decided to pursue the point no further, to acquiesce in the obligation of the trip, and "not to hold its refusal as a grievance
against the Holy See," with which, he stressed, he desired better relations.[97]

Consalvi too had cause for satisfaction. His careful mixture of firmness
and conciliation had secured a settlement more satisfactory than could have
been anticipated a few years earlier. Given the political and religious conditions of the Restoration, some degree of Imperial control over the Austrian
church was inescapable. The task of Papal diplomacy was to reduce that control to the smallest degree the Emperor could be induced to accept. Consalvi
had performed this task successfully, fighting to a standstill the Imperial attempt to impose the full Josephist system on the newly-acquired lands and
thereby preserving at least a modicum of Papal influence there, a basis on
which Papal authority could be rebuilt in more favorable times. Moreover, he
had secured this result without an open break with Austria, though relations
had been severely strained. Of course, Consalvi's ability was only half the
story—he could never have won without the support of Metternich, whose
persistent efforts to modify Imperial religious policy were at last showing
results. In the religious as in the political field, Consalvi and Metternich were
fighting the battle typical of the moderate statesmen of the Restoration: the
struggle against the extremists in their own camp—and at last the battle
seemed to be turning in their favor.

4. The Imperial Visit to Rome and Its Aftermath

And now the long-awaited Imperial visit to Rome was at hand. As planned by Metternich and Consalvi, its fundamental purpose was to repair the damage done to Austro-Papal relations by the religious controversy, reestablishing mutual trust and good will so that they might once again cooperate effectively.[98] This purpose required a discussion of religious affairs. Although the disputes arising from the attempt to extend the state church system into new territory had been settled, there remained the fundamental question of Josephism's continued prevalence in the Empire as a whole, a perennial stumbling block to truly cordial relations. Both statesmen saw in the trip to Rome an opportunity for the Pope to explain the case against Josephism directly to Francis I, at a time when the Emperor would not be surrounded by his Josephist advisers. This personal discussion, they hoped, would accelerate the retreat from the state church system which certain signs indicated the Emperor was now contemplating. The modification of Austrian demands during the 1819 negotiations, the acceptance of the *Romreise,* the Emperor's announcement of plans to reform Austrian religious orders as the Papacy had long wished, and above all, his decision to visit Rome despite the almost unanimous opposition of his advisers—all seemed to demonstrate that he was wavering in his allegiance to Josephism.[99]

The Imperial party arrived in Rome on April 3, 1819, and remained until April 26; then, after visiting Naples, the Emperor returned to spend June 2-11 as the guest of the Pope. Between ceremonies and tours of the Eternal City, the visitors found time to discuss religious affairs with Pius.[100] Since these discussions marked an important stage in the development of Austrian religious policy, it is unfortunate that no record of them seems to have survived.[101] Fortunately, a reasonably accurate idea of the topics discussed can be formed by studying the various reports and *memoires* on Austrian religious conditions which Pius ordered drawn up to guide him in his discussions with the Emperor.[102] Particularly useful is a summary of the most objectionable features of the state church system, "whose revocation the Holy Father cannot avoid asking."[103] The seven points discussed in this summary—which are also the points most frequently mentioned in the other materials in this file—had long been the subject of Papal complaints, for they went to the heart of the Josephist system: 1) the marriage laws, the point on which Pius himself felt most strongly, and which he had decided to bring up first of all;[104] 2) the "instruction in the universities and schools" of the Empire, which "includes many perverse or condemned ideas," and was generally antipapal in tone; 3) the requirement that all bulls or other papal documents receive the *placet regio* before being admitted into the Empire; 4) the prohibition on the admission into the Empire of various bulls, particularly those condemning regalist or Jansenist ideas; 5) the prohibition of appeals in religious cases by Austrian subjects to Papal courts; (6) a new ceremonial for the installation of bishops stressing their duties to the state rather than to the church; and 7) the rules for the instruction and ordination of novices, which were objectionable because they prescribed the inculcation of Josephist ideas.

In all probability, these—especially the first five—were the points which Pius raised in his talks with the Emperor, and whose revocation he requested. Beyond this, they seem to have discussed the general religious situation, giving the Pope an opportunity to explain the Papal case against Josephism—a case to which Francis I seems to have given a favorable hearing.[105] Now for the first time,—and this is the chief importance of the talks— Francis I was presented with the Papal position on Josephism, not through the mouths of hostile intermediaries, but by the Pope himself, whose sincerity and piety he could not doubt. As one historian has commented:

> The Pope said virtually nothing that was new to the Sovereign; but it was of decisive importance that *he* said it, that he had broken through the magic circle of the rationalist court, branding as un-Catholic what they had described as primitive Christian doctrines, and thereby planting the first doubts as to the validity of the Josephist state-church system in the mind of the Emperor.[106]

The talks made a profound impression on Francis. Years later, Metternich declared that Pius and Francis had come to a complete agreement on religious questions, so that the Emperor left Rome with the intention of abandoning Josephism.[107] The claim seems plausible. Certainly, Metternich himself returned to Vienna highly pleased with the visit, which he felt had undone the damage inflicted by the recent controversies, restored "most happy relations of trust" between Rome and Vienna, and paved the way for a new flourishing of Austro-Papal cooperation.[108]

It remained to be seen, however, whether the effect of his talks with the Pope would persist after Francis I had returned to the Josephist atmosphere of Vienna; and even if it did persist, how long would it take for so innately cautious a mentality as his to bring itself to make so drastic a break with the past as the abandonment of Josephism. His first moves were promising. Shortly after his return from Rome, he broke with long Josephist precedent by agreeing to a Papal request to admit the Redemptorist order to his realm.[109] A more startling break with the past came in 1820, when he decided to allow the return of the Jesuits, whose defense of Papal authority had always made them anathema to Josephists.[110] The immediate impact of this move was limited: the Jesuits admitted into the Empire were a handful of refugees expelled from Russia, who were admitted at least partly from motives of charity, and whose activities at first were restricted to one town in Galicia. Even here their situation long remained precarious, as the Josephists made endless and at times nearly successful efforts to expel them. Only in the late 1820s, as we shall see, were they able to win Imperial approval for a gradual expansion. The ultimate significance of their return thus remained unclear; nonetheless, the decision to allow it was unmistakably a radical departure from Josephist tradition, and Francis carried it out over the fervent opposition of virtually all his advisers. Significant too was the Emperor's newly sympathetic response to Papal complaints. For example, in March, 1820, Leardi protested against the "scandal of the theses defended at the Catholic University of Vienna," which he asserted were contrary to Catholic doctrine.[111] Such protests had often been made before, with no discernible result. Now, however, Francis I, brushing aside Lazansky's claim that the theses contained nothing incompatible with Catholic doctrine, ordered that in the future all theological theses must be submitted to the local bishop for prior approval.[112] Later that year, the Nuncio learned that the government planned to introduce into the Lombard-Venetial seminaries the same system of instruction, antipapal in tone, that was in force in the rest of the Empire. He protested to the Emperor, and the plan was quietly dropped.[113]

Even in the face of *Zelanti* provocation, the Emperor did not abandon his new attitude towards Rome. In January, 1820, a *Zelanti*-dominated congregation placed on the Index of Forbidden Books the standard texts on canon law and church history that were used in Austrian religious instruction. Since these works contained the epitome of Josephist principles, their condemnation implied that of Josephism itself. This represented a step towards the *Zelanti's* pet project of a formal condemnation of the state church system, and for that reason Consalvi had unsuccessfully opposed it.[114] A few years earlier, such a condemnation would have provoked at least a strong Imperial protest. In 1820, Francis I—ignoring the belligerent advice of the Josephists—took no action except to order the preparation of new texts to replace those condemned.[115]

These signs of a new Imperial attitude on religious questions caused much satisfaction at Rome. Consalvi's attitude towards Austria, distinctly chilly in 1818, thawed rapidly, to the point where in 1820 Metternich felt justified in assuring Apponyi that the religious conflict might be regarded as settled, so that nothing stood in the way of Austro-Papal cooperation.[116] But the Prince had overestimated the extent of Consalvi's satisfaction. Though pleased by the Emperor's latest moves, the Cardinal did not consider them sufficient proof that his policy of cooperation was producing a major revision of Austrian religious policy. For Consalvi—rendered skeptical by the disappointments of 1817-1818—such proof would be furnished only if the Emperor definitely broke with Josephism by satisfying the major complaints against the Austrian religious system which Pius had explained to him during their meeting.

At the conclusion of their talks, Pius had given Francis I a memoir listing the chief abuses in the Austrian religious system, presumably the same abuses of which he had complained during their meeting.[117] The Imperial response to this memoir constituted for Consalvi the touchstone for appraising the reality of the Emperor's conversion from Josephism, and hence the validity of a policy of cooperation with Austria.[118] A favorable response would both restore Consalvi's faith in the religious advantages of cooperation, and provide him with an irresistible argument with which to convince the doubtful Pope and the critical *Zelanti;* a negative response, demonstrating that the Emperor was unwilling to change his religious principles, would undermine the foundations of Austro-Papal cooperation.[119]

The Emperor's first reaction to the memoir was favorable. Even before leaving Italy, he sent it to his ecclesiastical adviser, Councillor Jüstel, instructing him to comment upon it according to its intrinsic merit, regardless of whether it happened to be in agreement with the existing state church system. Jüstel's report, delivered in August, 1819, was what the Emperor

might have expected from this ardent Josephist: he bluntly declared that all
the Papal complaints were without foundation, and advised that the memoir
should be ignored.[120]

But the Emperor was still under the influence of his personal meeting with
the Pope, and this negative report failed to satisfy him. He at once directed a
prelate of more moderate views, Bishop Jacob Frint, to comment upon the
memoir. Frint's report, delivered in September, 1820, was generally favorable to the Papal complaints, though ambiguous on certain points. He
agreed that the Pope must have free communication with the Austrian
bishops if he was to perform his duties as Head of the Church, admitted that
Pius was justified in criticizing the teaching at Austrian universities and
seminaries, and in guarded terms opposed the exclusion of papal bulls and
briefs dealing with doctrine. However, he prudently refrained from attempting to delimit the respective spheres of authority of church and state in
regard to marriage, and contented himself with advising both parties to work
together in harmony. Nor was his position very clear on the question of appeals to Rome, though he did advise against unnecessary state interposition
between the Austrian clergy and the Pope.[121]

Favorably impressed, Francis seemed ready to act upon Frint's report.
Leardi announced jubilantly that the Emperor, "filled with good will towards
the Holy Father," had drawn up a reply to the memoir which would "correct
everything contrary to the sound doctrine of the Church," even if this involved "abandoning principles established for no less than half a century."[122]
Consalvi, though pleased, remained skeptical, for he had learned by sad experience how strong was the aversion of Francis I to a clean break with past
practice in any field, and how great was Josephist influence at the Imperial
court.[123]

The Cardinal's pessimism was justified by events, for the Emperor's determination to act on the memoir did not survive long. The Josephists fought a
delaying action to prevent him from sending his reply until they could win
him over. By the spring of 1822 the reply still had not been sent, and Leardi
began to fear that the Josephists had won again.[124] The final blow came in
July, 1823, when the Emperor's official spiritual adviser, Councillor Martin
von Lorenz, submitted his formal report on the opinions given by Jüstel and
Frint. Lorenz agreed completely with Jüstel that the Papal complaints were
unfounded. The Pope had only been persuaded to present this memoir by the
Zelanti, whose real aim was to place the Emperor and his predecessors under
suspicion of heresy.[125]

In the face of the strong Josephist opposition which culminated in Lorenz's
report, the Emperor shelved his original plan to return a favorable reply to
the memoir. Not until five more years had passed would he begin to consider
the memoir again; by that time Pius VII and Consalvi were dead, and
Austro-Papal relations had entered a new phase.

When Consalvi left office in August, 1823, Josephism seemed hardly less
entrenched in the Empire than when he had gone to Vienna in 1814. And yet,
all was not as it had been. With the advantage of hindsight, we can perceive
what was still obscure to contemporaries: Josephism had reached its high-
water mark around 1814, and by 1823 had begun, very slowly, to recede.[126]

As yet, its recession had not attained major proportions, and Consalvi himself ended his life uncertain whether real progress was being made. Nonetheless, the moderation of Imperial demands in 1819 and the acceptance of the *Romreise;* the readmission of the Jesuits into the Empire; the increased compliance with Papal protests; the trip to Rome; and the serious, if so far fruitless, attention given by Francis I to the memoir of 1819—all were indications, small but in sum significant, that the long slow trend away from Josephism had begun.

Consalvi and Metternich cannot be denied the chief credit for this development. The Prince's desire for Austro-Papal cooperation, and the Cardinal's willingness to consider that cooperation as the best means of attacking Josephism, were crucial. Metternich contributed by his cautious but persistent urging of reconciliation with Rome, by his counterbalancing of Josephist influence, and by his diplomatic skill in smoothing over potential quarrels. Equally important was Consalvi's skillful handling of the religious controversy: by exercising firmness when firmness was needed, he had demonstrated that the Papacy could not be bullied into surrender as the Josephists had claimed, but would have to be treated with respect and won over with concessions, while his generally moderate and conciliatory policy had averted quarrels and softened controversies which would otherwise have reversed the Emperor's retreat from Josephism.

But though Consalvi had done much during his second ministry to plant the seeds whose fruition would be the downfall of Josephism, he did not live to see the outcome; the harvest was gathered by his successors. To the Cardinal, in the last years of his life, it seemed that little progress had been made.[127] As 1820 became 1821 and no reply to the memoir came, he began to lose hope that his policy of cooperation could be the means of bringing about the downfall of the state church system; and just as this unduly pessimistic but natural judgment was eroding the religious incentive for cooperation with Austria, a sequence of events began that would undermine its political incentive as well. In July, 1820, revolution broke out in Naples, and the first great crisis of the Restoration began.

IV

The Revolutions
of 1820

1. Revolt in Naples

The revolt which broke out in Spain on New Year's Day, 1820 ushered in a year of revolutions. The repercussions were soon felt in Italy: in July, liberal officers of the Neapolitan army joined the *Carbonari* in a revolt that succeeded with amazing ease. The Spanish constitution of 1812 was adopted, a liberal ministry installed, and a parliament elected.[1] Elsewhere in the peninsula, revolutionary ferment redoubled. To Italian patriots and liberals, a new day of freedom seemed to be dawning, while conservatives looked on in horror.

Nowhere was dismay greater than at Vienna. Any successful revolution was distasteful to Metternich on principle, but that at Naples gave him particular cause for alarm. Not only did it end the Austrian influence which had prevailed at Naples since 1815, but if not suppressed it would surely encourage similar outbreaks that would threaten Austria's hegemony throughout the peninsula. This catastrophe would in turn encourage those Germans who resented Austrian predominance to imitate the Italian example, and the Empire's international position would totter.[2]

Consequently, Metternich had no sooner learned of the revolt than he decided that it must be suppressed, by military intervention if necessary. The execution of this decision was delayed until February, 1821, by his need to win the prior sanction of the other Powers, especially Russia, before the Austrian army could safely march south; but Metternich never wavered in his determination to crush the revolutionary regime.[3]

At Rome too, the Neapolitan revolution caused consternation.[4] The dangers were obvious, nor was it long before they began to materialize. *Settarj* activity increased almost at once. Still more alarming, on July 6 the local *Carbonari,* aided by Neapolitan volunteers, overthrew Papal rule in Benevento and Pontecorvo. Consalvi acted quickly to keep the Sects under control and prevent the events in the enclaves from being duplicated elsewhere, but unlike many of his colleagues he did not give way to panic. He believed that the majority of the people were loyal to the Papacy, especially since his reforms had given them hope that their lot would improve without revolution. Provided the government took reasonable precautions, the Sects did not yet have the strength or public support to carry out a successful revolution; only if Naples came to their aid would they pose a serious threat. Here lay the true danger, for the tiny Papal army, outnumbered ten to one by the Neapolitans, could not defend the State against a serious invasion. Consequently, one of Consalvi's primary aims throughout the crisis was to avert a Neapolitan attack: he accepted the new regime as the *de facto* government of Naples and carefully avoided furnishing it with any pretext for hostile action. In accordance with Papal tradition, however, he refused to grant the regime formal recognition until the Powers should have done so.[5]

The Papal position was rendered far more difficult by the Austrian decision to suppress the Neapolitan revolution, of which Leardi warned Consalvi in July.[6] The warning was soon confirmed by Metternich himself, in a confidential letter of August 2 requesting the Cardinal's cooperation in his plans, in particular by passing on to Vienna all the information which he could gather on Neapolitan events.[7] Needless to say, the elimination of a revolutionary regime on the Papacy's doorstep would not in itself have caused Consalvi the least regret. His concern arose from the geographical position of the Papal State, which, stretching across central Italy, lay directly between the Habsburg Empire and Naples. If Austria wished to suppress the revolution, her troops would have to march through the State to do so.

Consalvi's position was thus very delicate. On the one hand, the revolutionary regime threatened the security of the Papal State; its overthrow was obviously desirable. Moreover, his general policy of cooperating with Austria implied giving her aid against Naples; failure to do so would arouse resentment at Vienna. Yet there were serious obstacles to cooperation. The most fundamental lay in the spiritual character of the Pope: as befitted the leader of Christendom, he had long made it a basic principle to remain neutral in wars between Christian states. Only a decade earlier, Pius VII had adhered to this principle to the extent of breaking with the all-powerful Napoleon rather than siding with him against Protestant England; he could hardly do less in a war between Catholic Austria and Catholic Naples. Moral principle was reinforced by expediency: should Rome abandon its neutrality, the Neapolitans would have a legitimate excuse for the attack on the Papal State which Consalvi dreaded.[8]

Though this dilemma occupied most of Consalvi's attention during the Neapolitan crisis, he was also concerned by the crisis's long-range implications. Successful intervention by Austria would do more than suppress a revolution; it would also strengthen Austrian hegemony in Italy. The Kingdom of the Two Sicilies, occupied by Austrian troops and with its ruler indebted to Vienna for his restoration to absolute power, would remain under tight Austrian control for years to come—a serious matter for the Papal State, which, bordered on the north by Lombardy-Venetia and on the south by Austrian-occupied Naples, would be more susceptible to Austria's influence than ever. Moreover, since it was obviously in Austria's strategic interest to control the area through which ran her lines of communication with Naples, Vienna would have a stronger motive than in the past to seek control over the Papal State. Austria would thus have both motive and means for encroaching upon Papal independence. Perhaps she would resist the temptation to do so, but the contrary possibility was enough to alarm Consalvi, and goes far to explain the ambiguous attitude he took towards Austria's anti-revolutionary crusade.[9]

Austria at first gave Consalvi no overt cause for distrust. Indeed, Metternich, was anxious to placate him, being well aware of the value of Papal cooperation in an action against Naples. Here was an opportunity to put the Union of Throne and Altar into effect. Rome obviously could not be expected to provide military help, nor did Austria stand in need of it. Rome's moral backing, however, would be valuable indeed in shaping the Catholic attitude towards the revolution and the Austrian intervention. Metternich saw that the Pope could not issue a formal condemnation of Naples, which would provoke armed retaliation; but he did hope that, whatever lip service it might pay to the principle of neutrality, Rome would make clear to the Catholic world a general attitude of disapproval of Naples and sympathy with the counter revolution.[10] Furthermore, when conditions should make it practical, he wanted the Pope to issue a formal condemnation of the *Carbonari,* which, though unlikely to disturb hardcore *Settarj,* would encourage lukewarm supporters to drop off and would inoculate the devout Italian masses against *Carbonari* attempts to stir them up. Metternich had occasionally contemplated requesting such a condemnation in the past, but the need had never seemed pressing; now he had no doubt of its urgency. Moreover, Papal cooperation would be necessary for the passage of the Austrian army to Naples: if, as Metternich realized, the Pope could not give formal approval to an Austrian march through his State, he should at least refrain from criticizing it, encourage his subjects to offer the Austrians a friendly reception, and arrange for local pontifical authorities to provide the troops with the supplies they would need.[11]

Metternich approached these subjects cautiously, determined not to arouse alarm by any premature request for extensive Papal assistance. In his letter of August 2 to Consalvi, as we have seen, he merely urged a general attitude of cooperation on the part of Rome. His one specific request—that Consalvi send information on Neapolitan events—was technically unneutral, but could easily and secretly be granted, and grew naturally out of the existing exchange of information on *Settarj* activities.[12] The Prince emphatically denied any intention either of involving Rome directly in the coming conflict, or of using the crisis to expand Austrian control over the independent Italian states; the sole purpose of the intervention at Naples, he stressed, was to preserve the legitimate order in Italy against a revolutionary menace, for the common good of all the rulers of the peninsula.[13]

Consalvi was not entirely convinced, but tactfully denied any suspicion of Austrian motives.[14] In his reply to the letter of August 2, he stressed his eagerness to cooperate with Austria to the fullest extent possible. Unfortunately, "two compelling reasons"—the Pope's status as the common Father of Christendom, and the danger of retaliation from Naples—forced the Pope against his will to remain officially neutral. However, where assistance of an unofficial and secret nature was concerned, Consalvi pledged the fullest cooperation. As proof of his good will, he promised to transmit to Vienna all the information gathered by Papal agents on the situation in Naples.[15]

Metternich seems to have accepted this explanation—which was true enough, as far as it went—at face value during the early stages of the crisis. Admitting that Rome could not be expected to depart openly from her neutrality, he devoted himself to securing the utmost cooperation possible within this limitation.[16] During the first months of the crisis, the degree of cooperation which he needed was not very great. His most frequent request, which Consalvi unhesitatingly fulfilled, was for the continued collection and transmission of information.[17] In September came a request for a more serious, though still secret, departure from neutrality. Two Neapolitan diplomats, Prince Cimitile and the Duke di Gallo, who were returning from missions abroad, had halted in Bologna, arousing Metternich's suspicion that they were spying on Austrian military preparations across the border. Metternich asked Consalvi to expel them, and, in the meantime, to intercept their correspondence. Consalvi felt no qualms about agreeing: copies of the Neapolitans' intercepted letters were turned over to Austria, and the diplomats were soon persuaded to leave for Naples on the grounds that their presence was compromising Papal neutrality.[18] Thus far, Consalvi's attitude had been all that Metternich could wish, and relations between the courts seemed better than ever. "The eagerness with which the Cardinal has complied with these requests," Apponyi felt, "demonstrates in the most convincing way his good will and his determination to act in harmony with our August Court."[19]

But in general, Metternich had few demands to make upon Rome in the Fall of 1820, and, indeed, little attention to spare for it. During these critical months, he was obliged to concentrate upon the difficult negotiations involved in securing the agreement of the other Powers for the planned intervention at Naples.[20] Only after that agreement was secured at the Congress of Troppau did he once again turn back to Rome and Consalvi, for he now required a greater degree of Papal cooperation.

On November 22, after explaining his plans for the intervention, Metternich asked Consalvi for three forms of cooperation: first, that the Pope agree to the passage of the Austrian army through his State; second, that he arrange for the army to be provisioned during its passage; and third, that he take adequate military measures to guarantee Ancona against a Neapolitan *coup*, with the implication that if the Pope could not do this, he should allow Austria to garrison the city.[21]

Having long anticipated these requests,[22] Consalvi had his response ready.[23] First, the Pope agreed to the passage of the Austrian troops, but he could not give his formal approval without openly violating his neutrality and inviting Neapolitan retaliation. Instead, Consalvi suggested, he and Apponyi could work out a "suitable expedient" whereby Austria would not officially request permission for the passage, but simply announce its intentions when the troops marched; the Pope could then accept the apparent *fait accompli* without harm to his public neutrality. Second, Rome definitely could not provision the Austrian army, because doing so would violate its neutrality, because its treasury could not bear the expense, and because Austria had not yet repaid the Papacy for similar expenditures in the 1815 campaign.[24] As for Ancona, it was already too well defended to be in danger—an assertion that reflected more Consalvi's wariness of any move that might increase Austrian influence in the Papal State, than any confidence that the weak Papal garrison could beat off a Neapolitan assault.[25]

Although Consalvi's reply was more guarded than Metternich would have liked, he accepted it as probably the best that could be expected under the circumstances.[26] During the next month, he suggested several other forms of Papal cooperation against Naples. He was increasingly interested in implementing the theory of the Union of Throne and Altar by securing a Papal condemnation of the *Carbonari,* which, he felt, would be of "immense value" in demoralizing the *Carbonari* and discrediting them among the devout.[27] The Austrian army soon to march on Naples would crush the material strength of the Sects. But since the power of the Sects was moral as well as material, military defeat would not suffice for their destruction: the Pope, wielder of the spiritual authority of society, must employ his weapons to destroy their moral position forever.[28]

Consalvi was distinctly wary of the proposal for a condemnation, involving as it did the obvious and public use of a spiritual power for a political end. Moreover, it might provoke Neapolitan retaliation. He therefore "obstinately refused to reinforce the secular arm with spiritual weapons,"[29] despite the repeated arguments of Apponyi, several eloquent letters from Metternich, and—the heavy artillery—a personal appeal from Francis I to Pius VII.[30]

Another Austrian request received a more favorable reception. The conservative Powers had invited the King of Naples to attend the Congress of Laybach in January, 1821, partly so that he might give his approval to the intervention, partly to protect him from retaliation by the *Carbonari* afterwards. It seemed unlikely that the Neapolitan parliament would allow the King to depart. In the hope of influencing Neapolitan opinion, Metternich asked the Pope to throw his moral authority into the balance by a letter to the King advising him to attend the Congress in the interest of preserving peace. Consalvi had no objection to this step, which was in keeping with the Pope's traditional role as peacemaker, and the letter was sent.[31]

But Metternich was not alone in realizing the value of the Pope's moral prestige. The Russian minister, Capodistrias, had long been in sympathy with the Italian liberals and hostile to Austrian hegemony in the peninsula. Late in November, in a last bid to avert the Austrian intervention, he proposed that Pius VII be requested to act as mediator between the Allies and Naples. Metternich was hostile to the proposal, since he was determined to carry out the intervention come what might. To humor the Tsar, he agreed to the proposal, but only with the intention of sabotaging it. He directed Lebzeltern—who was charged with this mission to Rome—to seek, not a genuine mediation, but only the use of the Pope's moral authority to weaken Neapolitan resistance by "enlightening the nation on its fatal aberration," attesting the determination of Austria to crush the revolution, and urging the Neapolitans to allow their King to attend the Congress.[32]

Lebzeltern set out, but while passing through Florence he met the King of Naples, who, contrary to expectation, had been allowed to depart for Laybach. Here was a welcome pretext for abandoning the mediation, for now the King himself could discuss a settlement of the crisis with the Powers at

Laybach. Arriving in Rome, Lebzeltern had no difficulty in persuading the Allied ministers there to agree that no formal proposal should be made unless further instructions were received from Laybach. For Metternich's information, however, he confidentially sounded out Consalvi. To his satisfaction, the Cardinal, without flatly rejecting the mediation, pointed out that so many difficulties were involved that it would have no hope of success and thus was not worth undertaking. As for Metternich's desire for the Pope to use his moral authority to weaken Neapolitan resistance, Consalvi expressed sympathy for the idea, but explained that the Pope could not risk an act that would provoke Neapolitan attack. Metternich made no attempt to overcome his reluctance; he was satisfied that the plan for Papal mediation had in effect been killed.[33]

The Prince was more concerned over the response to his renewed request, conveyed by Lebzeltern, that Austria be allowed to garrison Ancona. He had been reluctant to raise this point again, but the Austrian high command insisted that control of Ancona was necessary for the success of the intervention. In Austrian hands, Ancona would be a natural base of supply and reinforcement for the army as well as an invaluable strong point to fall back upon in the event of a vigorous Neapolitan counterattack. Should Austria not occupy the city, the generals believed, the Papal garrison was too weak to resist either an attack by Naples or an uprising by the local *Settarj*. With Ancona in hostile hands, the whole plan of campaign would be disrupted, since the city would have to be recaptured before the Austrians could safely move south. Metternich considered that danger remote, but since the Austrian military had convinced the Emperor, he reluctantly instructed Lebzeltern to approach Consalvi again on this delicate subject.[34]

As Metternich had feared, the request revived Consalvi's distrust of Austrian policy in Italy. The effect was heightened when Lebzeltern incautiously revealed that the Austria high command was considering the occupation, not merely of Ancona, but also of Bologna, Perugia, and several other strong points. Coupled with earlier Imperial offers to station a garrison in Rome to protect the Pope, this conjured up for Consalvi the menacing vision of a general Austrian occupation of the State, whose destructive impact on Papal independence was obvious. Since he found the military arguments for the occupation unconvincing, the Secretary of State naturally suspected that they were merely a cover for deeper political designs and his attitude towards Austria became increasingly distrustful.[35] He therefore opposed to the arguments of Lebzeltern and Apponyi "an opposition so pronounced, indeed, so obstinate," as Apponyi reported, "that I can see little hope of success."[36] Lebzeltern, that old champion of Austro-Papal cooperation, was so alarmed by Consalvi's growing distrust that he spent most of January trying to argue him into a more confiding frame of mind.[37] But neither arguments nor appeals to their old friendship could lull Consalvi's suspicions or induce him to agree to the occupation.

On January 6, Consalvi sent a personal appeal to Metternich to use his influence to have the request withdrawn, on the grounds that it was not militarily necessary and would violate Papal neutrality.[38] Evidently the Cardinal had not yet lost all confidence in Metternich's good will. But on the same day he wrote another letter—to Count Blacas, who was with the French delegation at Laybach, requesting French intervention to prevent the occupation.[39] Clearly, Consalvi's confidence in Austria had now declined to the point where he was prepared to consider renouncing cooperation with her and returning to the old Italian game of balancing Habsburg power with that of France.[40] His move towards this policy was to continue for the rest of his ministry, checked less by a revival of trust in Austria than by the weakness of the French government, which often prevented it from giving him effective support.

For the moment, reliance on France seemed unnecessary: on January 18, Metternich replied to Consalvi that the Emperor, placing Papal good will above military advantage, had withdrawn his request for the occupation.[41] But appearance—and Austrian assurances—were deceptive: Austria had not abandoned the occupation, but only the intention of securing prior Papal approval for it. Instead, as the Austrian army passed through various Papal cities, it would leave troops behind to act as garrisons, thus presenting Rome with a *fait accompli*. Responsibility for the occupation was to be attributed to the initiatives of the local Austrian commanders.[42]

But Consalvi was soon alerted to this plan by the indiscreet remarks of Austrian officers. Nothing that Austria had done in his years as minister had so shocked him as this intended treachery. "I would never before have believed it possible that the Austrian court could even consider such a step," he wrote in indignation; now, disillusioned, he would resist this treacherous encroachment by every means at his disposal.[43] Metternich denied the existence of the plan,[44] but Consalvi no longer trusted him.[45] His confidence in Austria had received a blow from which it never recovered. Genuine cooperation with Austria could no longer form the basis of his policy; and should Austria persist in disregarding Papal rights, he would have to adopt a new policy, based not on cooperation but on distrust, and aimed above all at the stubborn defense of Papal independence against Austrian encroachment.

2. *The Congress of Laybach*

At the Congress of Troppau, Metternich had secured the approval of the Powers for the intervention at Naples. At the Congress of Laybach, he planned to secure the approval of the Italian states, so that the intervention would have greater moral authority as representing the will of all the legitimate rulers of the peninsula. The Congress was also to discuss the government to be given Naples once the revolution had been suppressed. Both purposes required the presence of representatives of the Italian states, and invitations were sent.[46] Since the new government for Naples was a matter of legitimate concern to the neighboring Papal State, Consalvi decided that participation in the Congress would not violate Papal neutrality. He appointed his most trusted diplomat, Cardinal Spina, to represent Rome.[47]

Consalvi's instructions to Spina revealed his continued preoccupation with the Papacy's neutrality and independence. Officially, Spina was to attend the Congress only to ensure that the new government planned for Naples contained nothing detrimental to the welfare of the Papal State. On any other question, Spina might give his personal opinion, but could not speak for the Papacy. In particular, he must not associate Rome in any way with the hostile measures to be taken against Naples, but must observe "the most perfect neutrality." Should the Allies again request Papal mediation, he was to refer the request to Rome. If Metternich pressed for a condemnation of the *Carbonari,* Spina should reply that Rome did not as yet have sufficient information on their religious principles to justify taking action against them. Finally, the Allies were reportedly planning to ask the Italian states to carry out various reforms to allay discontent. This plan Consalvi opposed, partly because he felt his own reforms were best adapted to the Papal State, partly because he feared it might be used to increase Austrian influence over the internal affairs of the Italian states. He warned Spina not to discuss any request for reform, but to refer it to himself.[48]

The Italian delegates were scheduled to participate in the Congress for the first time on January 26. Spina, having learned that they would then be expected to give their approval to the intervention, warned Metternich in advance that his comments would have to be made "in full accord with the principle of the most correct neutrality." The Prince replied that nothing more would be expected.[49]

The meeting on January 26 opened with an explanation by Metternich of the Allied plans. Naples was to be called upon to abolish the constitutional regime. An Austrian army would be sent to Naples, to maintain order during the change of regime if the Allied demands were accepted, or to impose the demands by force if they were rejected. Metternich then called upon the Italians to express their approval of this plan. Spina spoke first. Although praising the intentions of the Allies, he declared that the neutrality imposed by his spiritual office made it impossible for the Pope to approve any plan that involved the use of force against Naples. Though this was no more than Spina had warned Metternich to expect, the Allied ministers tried to persuade him to modify his stand. Metternich argued at length that Papal neutrality need not prevent the Pope from approving the plan, for it was essentially peaceful: only in the hypothetical case that Naples refused to accept the reasonable Allied requests would force be used. Spina replied briefly that the threat of force was still an essential part of the plan, which he therefore could not approve. He was then challenged by Capodistrias, who claimed that the Pope, by the very act of sending a representative to discuss a new government for Naples, had agreed that the present government should be replaced. Since he who wills the end, wills the means, the Pope had implicitly approved the plan which was to accomplish this aim. Spina retorted that the mere presence of a Papal delegate did not commit Rome to approving any changes in the Neapolitan government or the means by which they were to be put into effect. The Pope would gladly approve all peaceful means for settling the Neapolitan crisis, but his neutrality forbade him to approve a plan containing the threat of force.

The final attack on Spina came, rather surprisingly, from the English "observer," Lord Stewart, who remarked that although England, like the Papacy, was officially neutral, she nonetheless recognized that the revolution had been a disaster and approved of the Allied measures against it. Blacas now came to Spina's aid by pointing out that the Papal State, which had the revolution at its doorstep, could hardly adopt the same attitude towards it as England, half a continent away.

Since Spina obviously was not to be moved from his stand, it was agreed that he should prepare a statement for the journal of the Congress which would explain the Papal position. Composed with the help of Blacas, this statement put on record the Papal refusal to approve the intervention, but stressed that it stemmed only from the need to preserve Papal neutrality, and not from sympathy with the revolution or hostility to the intervention as such.[50] Metternich declared the statement fully satisfactory, as well he might since Blacas had consulted him before drawing it up.[51] Contrary to what certain historians have claimed, Metternich was neither surprised nor displeased by Spina's position: aware of Rome's difficult situation, he had anticipated the stand it would take and judged it "quite understandable."[52]

The new government for Naples was discussed at the session of February 20. It contained only two innovations: separate administrations for Naples and Sicily, and advisory councils appointed by the King. Asked for his comments, Spina replied that he lacked authority to endorse the plan, but that in his personal opinion it contained nothing harmful to Rome, and the Pope would no doubt approve it.[53] The other states approved the plan, which was formally adopted. On February 21, 1821, the Congress was dissolved, with the resolution that another Congress would be held in Florence in September, 1822, to discuss the development of the Italian situation. The representatives of the Powers remained at Laybach to observe the outcome of the intervention, but Spina returned home to receive the congratulations of Consalvi on the effective way he had carried out his instructions.[54]

3. Suppression

Now at last the Austrian intervention could go forward. On February 6, Austrian troops crossed the Po and marched south through the Papal State. As Consalvi and Apponyi had arranged, Austria did not formally request permission for the passage of its army. To all appearances, Rome was being presented with a *fait accompli* against which it was pointless to protest.[55] Consalvi had previously given instructions to the provincial governors in preparation for this event—instructions in which his willingness to satisfy Metternich's wishes was overshadowed by his growing concern at the danger of Austrian encroachment upon Papal independence. Since the Papacy was at peace with all nations—an official proclamation of neutrality was issued on February 8[56]—Papal officials were to treat all regular foreign troops as friends, offering no opposition to their passage. However, they should never furnish these forces with supplies nor admit them to any fortified place. Even in unfortified places, foreign troops should be allowed to remain only as long as obvious military necessity required, and during their sojourn no interference with the Papal administration or the lives of the people was to be tolerated.[57]

The restrictions laid down by Consalvi proved difficult to enforce. In particular, the rule against supplying foreign troops broke down under pressure of events. At Consalvi's suggestion, Austria had arranged with local agents in the Papal State to provision the army. Unfortunately, these agents often lacked adequate capital to buy the necessary supplies. Last-minute changes in the Austrian route of march further dislocated the supply system, which began to fail almost at once.[58]

Problems appeared as soon as the Austrians reached Bologna, the first Papal city on their route. Since the local Austrian agent had been unable to raise the money to buy what the army needed, its commander asked the Vice-Legate, Monsignor Amat, to help him find provisions and baggage animals. Amat agreed to help indirectly, by secretly persuading wealthy citizens to provide the Austrians with horses, against promise of repayment, and a local banker to honor an Austrian draft for 12,000 francs with which the commander could then buy food. Amat defended this step to Consalvi as the lesser of two evils, the greater being forced requisitions by the Austrians, which would have caused hardship to the local people. Consalvi accepted his explanation, and advised officials faced with similar problems to imitate Amat's example.[59]

The events at Bologna were repeated as the Austrians continued their march. Consalvi was forced to authorize a steadily increasing degree of aid: local officials might establish hospitals for the Austrian sick, they might persuade farmers to bring in supplies for the army, they might fix prices to ensure that the Austrians could buy what they needed at reasonable cost. Finally, in early March, when the Austrian supply system collapsed completely, Consalvi authorized his subordinates to take over the full burden of supplying the army.[60] Given the circumstances, the Cardinal had no real alternative; now his only concern was to arrange with Metternich for full repayment to the government and its subjects for the supplies furnished.[61]

The breakdown of the supply system caused Consalvi far less concern than Austria's simultaneous attempt to occupy cities in the Papal State. In his instructions to his subordinates, he had done what he could to guard against this attempt, but it had not been enough. When the Austrian army began to pass through Bologna, its commander demanded that Amat provide quarters for two thousand troops for an indefinite period. Despite the Vice-Legate's protests, a force of that size was left behind when the army moved south on February 14.[62]

Consalvi at once protested vehemently to Metternich who, after several denials, finally admitted that the army was supposed to leave troops behind to guard its communications, but insisted that they would not constitute a garrison, only a rear guard to be withdrawn as soon as the army reached Naples. He promised that the Austrians would not interfere with the Papal administration of the city and that Austria would bear the full expense of the occupation.[63]

Dissatisfied, Consalvi turned to France, asking Blacas to secure the withdrawal of the Austrian forces. Blacas agreed; however, though genuinely sympathetic to the Papacy and inclined to champion the Italian states against Austria, he was also bitterly hostile to revolution. When Metternich managed to convince him that the occupation of Bologna was necessary for the success of the operations against Naples, Blacas dropped the subject. Here, as so often during the Restoration, France was too weak and her diplomats too attached to the conservative cause to play effectively the old role of counterweight to Austria.[64]

Meanwhile, the Cardinal had resolved not to be caught off guard by Austria in other cities. On February 10, he learned that the Austrian supply agent had been ordered to arrange provisions for two thousand men in Ancona for an indefinite period. The implication was obvious. Consalvi at once instructed the Delegate of Ancona that when the Austrians approached his city, he was to inform them that he was aware of their plans and would not allow them to enter. The city gates were to be barred, so that the Austrians could enter only by assault, which they would hardly attempt for fear of the effect on public opinion.[65] The Delegate carried out these orders when the Austrians appeared on February 15. After a futile attempt to persuade him that Rome had granted permission for the occupation, the Austrian commander declared that he would refrain from occupying the city out of respect for His Holiness, and moved on.[66] Similar unsuccessful attempts were made to garrison Perugia and Spoleto, while Consalvi denied repeated Austrian requests to station troops in Rome.[67]

By early March, 1821, most of the army had passed through the Papal State and was marching victoriously on Naples. But just when the strain on Austro-Papal relations was being eased, revolution broke out in Piedmont on March 9. The new revolution being no less a threat to Austrian interests and the conservative cause than the one in Naples, Metternich resolved to deal with it in the same way. He easily secured approval from Russia and Prussia and soon Austrian forces were on the march towards Piedmont.[68]

Among the by-products of the Piedmontese revolt was a new and more imperious demand for the occupation of Ancona. The Austrian military, forced to campaign at both ends of the peninsula simultaneously, considered the secure possession of Ancona essential to safeguarding their overextended lines of communication. They won the Emperor's support, and on March 15 Metternich again requested permission to garrison the city. He pointed out that the suppression of the Neapolitan revolt had freed Rome from fear of retaliation, while the return of peace made the principle of neutrality irrelevant. Moreover, Vienna would cover all the expenses of the occupation and would undertake not to interfere with the normal course of Papal administration. The Papacy thus had no longer any plausible reason for refusal. Not only had Russia and Prussia supported this request, but Blacas promised his unofficial support.[69]

Consalvi was more reluctant than ever to agree, but, as Metternich pointed out, the defeat of the Neapolitan revolution nullified his official reasons for rejecting the occupation. Since he could hardly admit that it was distrust of Austria alone that motivated his opposition, he had to fall back on the feeble argument that the occupation would inconvenience the citizens of Ancona and might be misinterpreted abroad. Metternich easily demolished these flimsy pretexts, and at length the Cardinal gave in.[70] Consalvi and Apponyi set about planning for the occupation, when word suddenly arrived that Austria had decided to suspend it. The Piedmontese revolution had been suppressed with unexpected ease, and the Austrian military were no longer concerned for the security of their communications. Alarmed by the resentment which the proposed occupation had aroused at Rome, Metternich had promptly persuaded Francis I to suspend it.[71]

Consalvi greeted the news with relief, though he disliked an Austrian stipulation reserving the right to garrison Ancona in the future if a new revolutionary peril should arise. Consalvi accepted this stipulation, but on condition that the future peril must arise directly from the 1820–1821 revolutions.[72] When Metternich accepted this condition, the Ancona question was settled.

4. Aftermath

Austro-Papal relations emerged much changed from the crucible of the 1820 revolutions. The initial effect of the crisis had been to stimulate a revival of cooperation as Rome and Vienna drew together against the common enemy. The confidential correspondence between Metternich and Consalvi—that accurate barometer of Austro-Papal friendship, which had been falling since 1817—now attained its greatest bulk, and once again abounded in those imposing phrases "Austro-Papal cooperation," "Union of Throne and Altar", "identity of interest," which had disappeared during the disputes of 1817–1819.[73] Words were matched by actions, as Consalvi did everything possible in his position to aid Austria, which responded with assurances of protection against revolution or invasion. Down to the end of 1820, Consalvi's attitude towards Austria remained cooperative, while Metternich was satisfied that Rome had given all the help possible under the circumstances.[74]

Yet, even before 1821 was well under way, the initial impulse towards cooperation had spent itself, a victim of conflicting interests. Consalvi and Metternich were alike hostile to the Neapolitan revolution. But whereas for Metternich, with the Restoration Order and Austrian predominance in jeopardy, the suppression of that revolution was the overriding necessity of the time, to which all lesser interests must give way, for the Cardinal it was a goal for which he could work only so long as he could reconcile it with Papal neutrality and independence. From December, 1820, onwards, this reconciliation became increasingly difficult, and Consalvi found himself obliged to oppose Austria on several occasions. His "strange obstinacy towards the true friends of religion and the Good Cause" aroused surprise and anger at Vienna, and by the Spring of 1821 the Austrian attitude towards him had become extremely critical.[75]

For his part, Consalvi was "amazed that...Prince Metternich could even conceive the idea that he had cause for discontent with our policy;" in his view, Rome rather than Austria had legitimate cause for complaint.[76] Since he had cooperated with Austria whenever possible, he felt that he deserved gratitude from Vienna rather than criticism. Austria, in his opinion, had all too often ignored the rights and interests of its presumed partner in the Union of Throne and Altar. If, as now seemed clear, Vienna was prepared to violate Papal rights when it suited her convenience, he could no longer base his policy upon cooperation with her, but would have to devote himself to defending Papal independence against the Austrian encroachment which now seemed the greatest threat to it.

Metternich quickly perceived the change in Consalvi's attitude, and sought in alarm to regain his confidence. The suspension of the occupation of Ancona in May, 1821, was a step in this direction, as was the comparatively rapid repayment of the debts contracted by the Austrian army in its passage through the Papal State.[77] He also sought a rapid evacuation of Bologna, but the Austrian military continued to insist for over a year that the occupation was necessary for the security of their forces in Naples. Not until February, 1822, could Metternich persuade the Emperor to order the evacuation.[78]

As usual, Metternich supplemented actions with words in profusion. Although his confidential correspondence with Consalvi lapsed in 1821 as tension grew between them, he sought via Apponyi and Leardi to justify his policy to Consalvi: Austria had no ambition to extend its power in Italy, but only wished to maintain the status quo and prevent revolution; she was scrupulously respectful of the rights of the Italian states and would never consider infringing upon their independence; surely so enlightened a statesman as Consalvi must realize that Austria did not in any way constitute a threat to Rome, and that the best way for him to defend Papal interests was to return to his former trustful cooperation.[79]

Metternich's eloquence was foredoomed to failure, for it could not hide the fact that Consalvi's suspicions of Austria were well founded. Metternich's defense of Austrian policy was justified, as far as it went. He did not lie when he assured Consalvi that Austria's fundamental aim was to maintain peace and the established order in Italy. But by 1821 Metternich had become convinced that this aim could be securely attained only if Austrian control over the Italian states were increased. A renewal of revolution could be prevented only if the lesser states implemented the program of moderate reform and effective repression of the Sects which Metternich had been urging upon them for years. By 1821, he despaired of the Italian states' performing this essential task of their own accord; hence Austria would have to ensure that they did so. In the closing stages of the Congress of Laybach, Metternich accordingly began to claim for Austria a right to supervise and guide the Italian rulers, because, left to their own devices, they would follow policies which would in due course make another wave of revolutions and another Austrian intervention inevitable.[80]

How accurate this analysis was, the events of the next thirty years would abundantly demonstrate; but Consalvi could never accept a policy which would reduce the Papal State to the level of an Austrian satellite. Once the new direction of Austrian policy became clear, no words from Metternich could convince the Cardinal that Austria did not pose a threat to the vital political interests of the Papacy.

Contrary to what might have been expected, then, the end result of the 1820–1821 revolutions was not to draw Austria and the Papacy together again, but to drive them further apart. With Metternich determined to extend Austrian control over the Italian states, and Consalvi determined to oppose him, the death agony of their experiment in cooperation was at hand.

V

From Cooperation To Conflict 1821–1823

1. The Condemnation of the Carbonari

As if to deny that the life had gone out of Austro-Papal cooperation, the summer of 1821 witnessed a striking public manifestation of the Union of Throne and Altar: the Papal condemnation of the Carbonari.

As we have seen, Metternich had sought this condemnation since the early days of the Neapolitan Revolution, for "the Carbonari must be attacked by all weapons at once, spiritual as well as temporal."[1] This belief grew naturally from his confidence in the Union of Throne and Altar. Military power such as Austria possessed could break the material strength of the Sects; it could not destroy their moral foundation. If the moral authority of the Carbonari was allowed to survive, they would in time recover from even the severest military defeat, to flourish anew. They could be permanently crushed only if the moral power of Rome was joined to the military power of Austria.[2]

Metternich's first approach to Consalvi on this subject, in November, 1820, was framed with caution.[3] No doubt he foresaw that his request, involving as it did the diversion of spiritual powers to political ends, would encounter difficulties at Rome. As Consalvi explained, "the Holy Father, as a spiritual ruler, can pronounce spiritual penalties only against those societies whose institution is evidently contrary to the Catholic religion and which openly attack its principles." There was as yet no evidence that the Carbonari could be considered such a society—indeed, their constitution prescribed Catholicism as their official religion.[4] Moreover, a condemnation might provoke Neapolitan retaliation.[5]

In the months that followed, Metternich continued to press for a condemnation, but without success.[6] The suppression of the Neapolitan revolution only led him to step up his efforts, for the condemnation seemed to him more essential than ever. The revolution had been suppressed, but its instigators, the Carbonari, "still encourage the people to revolt from one end of Italy to the other." Unless the Papacy used its spiritual authority to destroy the moral position of the Carbonari while they were still weak from their military defeat, they would soon recover and stir up new revolutions. Rome must act, and act quickly.[7] So Metternich argued in a renewed appeal to Consalvi on April 21, 1821,[8] while Francis I lent greater weight to the request by addressing on the same day a personal letter to Pius VII urging the condemnation, "which involves the welfare of religion equally with that of society."[9] At Rome, Apponyi maintained a constant pressure on Consalvi,[10] while Metternich invoked the aid of the other conservative Powers: soon the Prussian and Russian ministers at Rome were instructed to second Apponyi, while Blacas lent his support on his own initiative.[11]

Faced with this conservative front, Consalvi was in a difficult position. Austria and the other Powers clearly attached the greatest importance to the condemnation, and would be seriously offended should Rome persist in refusing. No matter how distrustful the Cardinal had become of Austria, he had no wish to antagonize her unnecessarily; nor, of course, did he have the least sympathy for the *Carbonari*. Nonetheless, as he told Apponyi:

> Without a justifiable charge of irreligion or impiety the spiritual power finds itself involuntarily paralyzed....Furnish us with some irrefutable proof of an outrage to religion by the *Carbonari*, based on the rules of their organization, and we will eagerly use this excuse to second the temporal power's coercive measures with all the influence of the spiritual power.[12]

Since Consalvi would not budge from this stand, Apponyi decided to "devote all my efforts to searching for some official document to serve as the basis for an accusation against the *Carbonari* from the strictly religious viewpoint." His patient search was eventually rewarded with the discovery of:

> ...a book containing the ceremonies of initiation into the second grade of the *Carbonari*, ceremonies which enact the mysteries of the passion of our Lord in the most impious way: the initiate plays the role of our Lord, the members play those of Pilate, Caiphas, and Herod; the crown of thorns is put upon him, he is scourged, made to carry the cross to Calvary, the sacred words of the Gospels are put in his mouth and in those of his assistants; in sum, the whole ceremony is no more than a tissue of blasphemies and insults against all that is most sacred in our religion.[13]

Apponyi at once brought his discovery to Consalvi, upon whom it produced "the desired effect of most profound indignation and a marked willingness to agree that the spiritual power can now cooperate in this important work."[14]

Consalvi and Apponyi set to work collecting further evidence. Aided by the police of Rome, Milan, and Naples, they succeeded within a few weeks in gathering a sizable body of information about the ways in which the *Carbonari* had adapted the rituals and beliefs of Catholicism to their own purposes.[15] This adaptation was obviously intended to win for the sect the support of the devout: if the *Carbonari* used the language of Christianity, "the aim was not to make good Christians, but to turn good Christians into *Carbonari*."[16] To Consalvi, such practices represented "the most detestable blasphemy," which rendered the condemnation of the *Carbonari*, so desirable politically, morally desirable as well.[17]

By the end of May, sufficient evidence had been accumulated to justify Consalvi in drawing up a rough draft for a brief of condemnation. Before the brief could be issued, however, "all the formalities required by canon law must be scrupulously performed;" otherwise "the moral effect of the measure will be destroyed and the spiritual authority exposed to ridicule and distrust."[18] Metternich approved the Cardinal's caution, as well as his suggestion that "since the thunders of the Church alone may be insufficient to destroy this evil," Austria and the Italian states should enact new and stringent laws against the *Carbonari* to coincide with the condemnation. In order that these supplementary measures should harmonize with the brief, he asked Consalvi to provide him with a copy before its publication.[19] The Cardinal agreed, on condition that "the most inviolable secrecy be preserved" to avoid arousing suspicion of the role which Austria had played in instigating the condemnation.[20]

In fact, the formalities of which Consalvi warned did not long delay the brief, which, by the standards of the Curia, made rapid progress.[21] Metternich had feared that the *Zelanti* might hinder its passage. However, the events of 1820–1821 had so alarmed the *Zelanti* that their usual prejudices against Consalvi and Austria were submerged by fear of revolution. They willingly supported the condemnation, and the brief was formally approved by the end of July.[22] As the Cardinal had promised, he sent a copy to Metternich. The Prince was enthusiastic: "I consider it perfectly adapted to the intended purpose..., and have no doubt that it will make a profound impression everywhere."[23]

With Metternich's blessing thus secured, the brief *Ecclesiam a Jesu Christo* was promulgated on September 13, 1821. It declared anathema "that society, of recent origin but widespread in Italy and elsewhere, which, though divided into many sects and called by many names, is still substantially one by virtue of a common doctrine and common crimes, and is generally called the *Carbonari*." In effect, then, the condemnation was intended to apply to all the Sects. The brief went on to explain the reasons for the condemnation, notably the blasphemous misuse of Catholic ceremonies by the *Carbonari* and their "special hatred" for the Papacy. All present members of the sect who did not quit it immediately, as well as any who might join in the future, were excommunicated; they could only be absolved upon application to the Pope himself.[24]

Convinced that the brief would have a great effect, Metternich spared no effort to publicize it and to secure the adoption of complimentary measures by the Italian governments. In November, the Imperial government issued a decree imposing heavier penalties on the *Carbonari*.[25] Consalvi had already arranged for the brief to be distributed to every commune in the Papal State.[26] As for the other Italian states, Metternich and Consalvi had agreed that on September 13, the Papal representative at each Italian court would inform the sovereign of the condemnation; the resident Austrian minister would then join his Papal colleague in urging the ruler to adopt the desired measures. Most Italian rulers obligingly issued more stringent laws against the *Carbonari*.[27]

Metternich had thus obtained the "object to which I attach the highest importance": the condemnation that would "serve as the most potent weapon for the destruction of this pernicious sect."[28] He rejoiced that he had been responsible for the condemnation, for thus the glory of destroying the *Carbonari* would be his: coming after the suppression of the 1820 revolutions, the condemnation would surely give them the *coup de grâce*.[29]

The historian must wonder whether Metternich's expectations were justified—whether the condemnation did prove so potent a weapon as he hoped. It appears that in certain areas at least, the condemnation had considerable effect: a recent student of the *Carbonari* in Istria and Dalmatia, for example, believes that the edict undercut the popular appeal of the sect there and played a major role in its decline.[29] On the other hand, certain contemporaries and historians have denied that the brief had any significant effect, and at Naples the police reported that it had "irritated" the educated classes, who considered it "inappropriate for modern times."[30] A definite conclusion cannot be reached until we have more local studies similar to that on Istria; at present, it seems probable that the condemnation had considerable impact, especially in less developed areas and among the devout peasantry, but that the educated classes who provided the leadership of the society, and who were often anticlerical, paid it little heed. The brief doubtless played a role in the decline of the *Carbonari*, but the failure of their revolutionary efforts and the appearance of new and more appealing revolutionary organizations probably had greater significance. Certainly the revolutionary movement as a whole was only temporarily weakened.

From Metternich's viewpoint, the results of the condemnation, though not perhaps as thorough as he would have liked, were sufficient to reinforce his belief in the political efficacy of the Union of Throne and Altar. Nonetheless, the condemnation did not portend a revival of Austro-Papal cooperation, which was now in a state of dissolution.

2. From Laybach to Verona, 1821–1822

The development of Austro-Papal relations in 1821–1822 can be properly understood only in the context of Metternich's Italian policy.[31] His aim had not changed since 1815: to preserve Austrian predominance and the established order in Italy. But the 1820 revolutions imparted a new sense of urgency to his pursuit of this aim. Prior to 1820, he had been inclined to underrate the strength of the Italian Sects, considering them less dangerous than their counterparts in Germany and France. The Neapolitan revolution had come as a rude awakening; in reaction, he now tended, if anything, to exaggerate the danger from the Italian sects and the need for vigorous action against them. At present, true, Italy was tranquil, for the triumph of Austrian arms at Naples and Piedmont had broken *Settarj* strength and left them confused and disheartened. But this effect would be only temporary: given time, they would revive their courage, rebuild their power, and threaten the stability of the peninsula once again. Austria would then be faced once more with the unpleasant choice between allowing revolution to triumph—

which meant abandoning her predominance in Italy—and undertaking a new military intervention, with all the attendant risks and expense.

If this dismal future was to be averted, the time to act was now, while the Sects were still weak. Not only Austria, but all the Italian states, must take effective action of the sort Metternich had long advocated. First, of course, should come repression: the subversive activities of the Sects must be checked, their leaders and those actively engaged in sedition arrested, their organization broken up, and their circulation of inflammatory writings halted. All this must be done vigorously, but according to strict legality, without injustice or persecution; overenthusiastic repression, such as several states had undertaken in 1821, was as dangerous as undue laxity. But even now, Metternich did not expect repression alone to overcome the revolutionary movement: he was more than ever convinced that the Italian states must adopt nonpolitical reforms which would eliminate the misgovernment to which he ascribed popular support for the Sects.

But Metternich was now profoundly doubtful that the Italian rulers were willing or able to carry out this dual task successfully. By their failure to follow sound policies after 1815, he felt, they had brought the 1820 revolutions upon their own heads. Nor did they give any sign that they would do better in the future. Some, like the senile King of Naples, were incompetent; others, such as the Grand Duke of Tuscany, were too easygoing in their administrations and too indulgent of the Sects; even the few—like Consalvi—who possessed ability and sound principles, seemed unable to achieve adequate results. Metternich foresaw that the Italian rulers, left to themselves, would let slip the present opportunity to avert future revolution. Austria must therefore step into the breach: backed by the other conservative Powers, she would have to assert a greater measure of control over the Italian states than hitherto, in order to ensure that they successfully performed the necessary task of reform and repression.

Of course, Metternich had long aimed at greater control over the Italian states, in particular through an Italian Confederation; but after his reverses in 1815, he had abandoned his plans and accepted the status quo. Now the need to ensure more effective counterrevolutionary action served to revive his earlier ideas. When considering his Italian policy during 1821-1822, a point that must be stressed is its essentially *defensive* nature: the expansion of Austrian control was not sought for its own sake—though it was obviously not unwelcome—but rather as the only means of preserving the Restoration Order in Italy. Metternich's conviction that only effective reform and repression could prevent revolution was too genuine, and his distrust of the ability of the Italian princes too well founded, not to have been the true motive for his plans, rather than the mere pretext which Italian diplomats tended to consider it.[32]

The extension of Austrian control would take several forms. The time was not yet ripe for Metternich to seek his ultimate goal, the Confederation; this would arouse too much opposition, not only in Italy, but from France and Russia as well. Instead, he sought several intermediate objects, necessary both in themselves and as steppingstones towards a Confederation. The most important was a Central Investigating Commission—a revival of his 1815 plan for a General Police Commission—similar to that established at Mainz for the German Confederation, which would coordinate the fight against the Sects under Austrian direction.[33] The Commission would be located in Milan or—if this aroused opposition—in Parma, which was technically independent but in practice an Austrian province. Each state would send a commissioner, and would transmit all information on the Sects gathered by its police. By studying and coordinating this information, the Commission would discern the overall pattern of revolutionary activity; it would than either transmit its conclusions to the states for their police to act upon, or, in some cases, proceed itself to the questioning of suspects. The Commission would thus be in a position to draw up a common plan for counterrevolutionary activity to which the states would be expected to conform. In this way the common front of the Sects would be met in the only effective way: by a common front of legitimate governments.

The opportunity to propose the Commission would come at the congress of 1822, which, as had been decided at Laybach, would discuss the proper means to safeguard the tranquility of Italy.[34] This meeting would also furnish Metternich with the opportunity to implement the second part of his program, that dealing with reform. Before the Allied sovereigns departed from Laybach in May, 1821, they would, at Metternich's prompting, exhort the Italian rulers to promulgate reform, warning that they would have to justify their internal policies to the Powers at the congress in 1822. Should their reforms then prove to have been inadequate, as Metternich expected, then Austria, acting on behalf of the Allies, would assert a right to supervise and to some extent direct the internal administration of the Italian states to ensure that reforms were carried out.

These plans took shape in Metternich's mind during the Spring of 1821; in May, during the closing stages of the Congress of Laybach, he set about preparing the way for their implementation at the Congress of Verona. The first prerequisite was to secure the support or acquiescence of the other Powers. Since Castlereagh favored Austrian hegemony in Italy, English acquiescence was to be expected. Prussia had no vital interests in Italy; by appealing to her solidarity with the conservative cause, Metternich easily secured her moral support.[35] France, Austria's traditional rival in Italy, seemed the most likely opponent. However, during the Neapolitan crisis, the weakness and division of the French government and the conservative sympathies of its diplomats had allowed Metternich to ward off France's intended interference with his plans, and he hoped that the same factors would work in his favor now. The Tsar's attitude was crucial. Metternich's success during the crisis of 1820–1821 had been possible only because he won Alexander's backing. Russian support might be equally necessary now, to overawe the Italian states should they show signs of resistance, or France should she attempt to intervene. Therefore, Metternich's best efforts were directed towards winning the Tsar's active support for his plans.[36]

After describing the continued existence of the revolutionary threat, he explained to Alexander I that the inability of the Italian princes to deal with it by themselves required Austria, on behalf of the conservative Powers, to exercise a right of supervision over them. Such supervision and the control which it implied were fully justified: first, since the Italian rulers owed their survival in the recent crisis solely to Austrian intervention, that Power had gained the right to watch over them; second, since the weak and incompetent rule of the Italian princes endangered not only themselves, but neighboring Lombardy-Venetia as well, Austria had the right in self-defense to ensure that they governed well; and third, if a new revolution broke out because of Italian misgovernment, Austria would have to bear the burden of suppressing it. To satisfy the Tsar's most likely objection, Metternich argued ingeniously that this right of supervision was not contrary to the principle of noninterference in the affairs of sovereign states. The Italian states were certainly entitled to their sovereign independence; but so were the Powers. Any revolution that misgovernment might provoke in an Italian state would surely disturb the tranquility of its neighbors, notably Austria, and such disturbance constituted interference in those neighbors' internal affairs. Accordingly, Austria and her Allies had the right—in the name of their own sovereign independence!—to supervise the smaller states so as to prevent misgovernment and its consequences.

This supervision should take several forms. In occupied Naples and Piedmont, the Allied ministers, supported by the Austrian military authorities, would watch over the restored absolutist regimes to prevent any false steps. The remaining states would be warned of their obligation to demonstrate at the congress of 1822 that they had taken satisfactory steps towards reform. As a suitable example of reform, Metternich pointed to the plan for Naples drawn up at Laybach under his auspices: it provided for nominated advisory councils, some degree of communal self-government, and a general modernization of the administrative system.[37] The Powers should also provide for effective repression by establishing a "center for information, understanding, and joint decision"—in other words, the Central Investigating Commission.[38]

Had his plans won the Tsar's support, Metternich would have been in a strong position to secure their acceptance at the congress, even in the face of Italian or French opposition. But active Russian support proved unobtainable. Despite his conversion to the conservative cause, despite Metternich's growing influence over him, Alexander I was not yet willing to abandon completely his former role as champion of the small states of Central Europe or to support the expansion of Austrian power which was implicit in Metternich's plans. He agreed to support Metternich's plan for the reform of the Neapolitan administration; he agreed further to dispatch a circular to the Russian ministers in Italy, to be communicated to the princes, expressing support for the Austrian call for reform and repression; but beyond this he would not go.[39]

Metternich would have made further, and perhaps successful, efforts to win the Tsar's active support had not the Greek revolution of May, 1821 led to a major crisis. It now became far more important to prevent the Tsar from aligning himself with the cause of revolution by aiding the Greeks than to secure his backing for the expansion of Austrian control in Italy. Metternich soon found that the attainment of the first objective was so difficult as to require the use of all his influence with the Tsar, leaving none to spare for the second.[40]

The failure to win active Russian support was a serious blow, since without it Metternich would have difficulty if Italian and French opposition should materialize. He realized that his best hope of success lay in persuading the Italian states to accept his plans, or at least not to oppose them openly and invoke French intervention.[41] The means for such persuasion he could find not only in the reality of the revolutionary peril and the soundness of his plans, but also in the advantageous position of Austria vis-à-vis the Italian states—in particular, her dynastic connections, their dependence upon her for protection, and her military occupation of Naples and Piedmont. With these advantages on his side, his powers of persuasion might well suffice to convince the Italians that his plans were no real threat to their interests, but rather an essential move to protect them against revolt.

Metternich's work of persuasion with the circular of May 14, 1821, to the Austrian missions in Italy, which were to communicate it verbally to the Italian courts.[42] It began with a warning that the revolutionary danger still existed, despite the defeats of 1821, because rulers had failed to remove its causes. Austria, as a partly Italian state, the savior of the Italian princes in 1821, and their only hope of protection against future revolutions, was "in a certain sense authorized to insist that states adopt measures so that this inconvenient and expensive aid will not be continually necessary." The measures to be taken were not spelled out in detail, but it was clear that both reform and repression were involved. At Verona, the Italian rulers would have to explain their internal policies; if these were judged unsatisfactory, further action by the Powers might be necessary to ensure the tranquility of Italy. To reinforce the impact of this warning, Russia and Prussia dispatched similar circulars to their Italian missions.[43]

Metternich's circular, backed by all of his persuasive skill, met with a favorable response, officially at least, from most of the Italian princes. The Duke of Modena, who was a Habsburg and an ardent reactionary, and Marie Louise of Parma were eager to cooperate.[44] Naples, occupied by Austrian troops and dependent upon Vienna for protection against revolution, was also agreeable.[45] Piedmont too was under Austrian occupation; moreover, its King, frightened by the recent revolution and convinced by Metternich's eloquence that Austria "has, at least for the present, renounced its former ambitions," considered his proposals a sound basis for cooperation against the common revolutionary foe.[46] Lucca, whose dynastic link with the Bourbons made it a center of French influence, was willing to resist Austria, but its diminutive size made it of little importance. The Grand Duke of Tuscany, too, was unimpressed by Metternich's arguments, but his family connection with the Habsburgs limited his ability to offer open resistance.[47]

By elimination, this left the Papal State as the best placed in Italy to oppose Austria. It was restricted neither by dynastic ties nor—thanks to Consalvi's resistance in the past year, whose wisdom was now evident—by Austrian occupation. Moreover, as we have seen, Consalvi had a more compelling motive than other Italian leaders for dreading the extension of Austrian power: at the heart of his policy was the conviction that genuine political independence was essential for the Papacy's freedom to carry out its spiritual mission. This conviction, which in 1802–1806 had led him to oppose the all-powerful Napoleon's attempt to extend a protectorate over the Papal State, now made him the leader in the opposition to Metternich's plans.

Consalvi's attitude became apparent when Apponyi read him the circular. The Cardinal tactfully declared his confidence that Austria was inspired only by sincere concern for the welfare of the peninsula. Yet, he added, though Austria no doubt had no deliberate intention of encroaching upon Papal independence, "when between two independent sovereigns, one speaks of a right to compel the other to carry out duties which are imposed upon it, the latter's independence has necessarily ceased to exist." Apponyi pointed out that in the past Consalvi had willingly accepted Austrian aid in his struggle for reform and his efforts against the Sects; why could he not do so now? Consalvi replied that circumstances had changed. In the past, Austrian support had been given for his own policies, and could therefore be gratefully accepted. Now Austria was claiming the right to compel the adoption of policies which she, not Rome, considered desirable; announcing that the Papacy would have to justify its own internal policies before a general Congress; and threatening that if Rome failed to adopt satisfactory measures, she would be compelled to do so. No matter how well intentioned such dictation might be, no state could accept it without renouncing its independence.[48]

These comments alarmed Metternich, who realized the difficulties which Papal opposition could create at Verona. He at once set about persuading Consalvi that his plans were both essential for the security of Italy and not menacing to Papal independence.[49] The Secretary of State seemed favorably impressed by his arguments, and Apponyi at least felt that he had been won over.[50] Metternich apparently agreed, for in March 1822—at last finding time to spare from the Eastern crisis which had preoccupied him since the previous May—he revealed to Consalvi and certain other Italian leaders a further aspect of his plans: the Central Investigating Commission in Milan.[51]

Naples and Piedmont, still in the throes of reaction against the revolutions of 1820–1821, favored the Commission.[52] Tuscany, though hostile, seemed willing to acquiesce rather than offer open resistance to Vienna.[53] As for Consalvi, the Commission was first explained to him by Prince Alvaro Ruffo, long the Neapolitan ambassador at Vienna and a confidant of Metternich. Asked his opinion, the Cardinal replied evasively that the Papacy was in full agreement as to the need for a united effort against the Sects and would work wholeheartedly with Austria to that end whenever possible.[54]

Metternich apparently accepted this equivocal reply as indicating approval for the Commission;[55] but in fact Consalvi was implacably hostile to it, and to his plans as a whole, which, Consalvi realized, would give Austria "a direct influence upon the government of the Italian states, and, indeed, political control over them."[56] The Cardinal was resolved to do everything in his power to defeat Austria, even if it meant coming out in open and singlehanded opposition.[57]

Preferring to avoid single combat with Vienna if possible, Consalvi turned to France. His earlier attempt to enlist French support over the occupation of Bologna had failed, owing to the weakness of the French government and the conservative sympathies of Blacas. Now that the 1820 revolutions had been suppressed, however, Blacas could no longer see a legitimate need for Metternich's plans, which he consequently regarded as a mere cover for the expansion of Austrian power. Applauding Consalvi's determination to resist Austria, Blacas promised to use all his influence to secure French support for him.[58]

Blacas had no difficulty in fulfilling his promise. At Paris too, the old distrust of Austria had revived. The new President of the Council of Ministers, Villèle, regretted the weakness of his predecessors, which had in effect given Metternich a free hand to suppress the Neapolitan revolution and increase Austrian predominance.[59] He was therefore receptive to Consalvi's appeal: the French plenipotentiary at the Congress of Verona, Viscount de Montmorency, was instructed to oppose any Austrian move to increase her power in Italy or to encroach upon the independence of the small states, particularly by means of a Confederation or Central Investigating Commission.[60] Moreover, Blacas, while passing through Turin, had secured a promise of Piedmontese support.[61] If France kept her word, and if Rome was joined by Piedmont and other Italian states, the chances of defeating Austria at the Congress seemed good.

3. The Congress of Verona

The chief purpose of the Congress of Verona, as originally planned by the Powers at Laybach, had been to discuss the Italian situation with a view to determining further measures to ensure the tranquility of the peninsula. By the Fall of 1822, however, the Greek crisis and the Spanish question had come to be the dominant problems in international affairs, so that the Congress was in fact mainly concerned with them.[62] Nonetheless, Italian affairs would still be discussed, and decisions important for the future of the peninsula would be made: for here the Italian states would have to justify their policies of reform and repression, and if these were found inadequate, the Powers might impose some type of supervision or control over them.

This was the occasion for which Metternich had been waiting to launch his drive for greater Austrian hegemony in Italy—but in fact, he had had little time to prepare for it. For over a year, his preoccupation with the Greek crisis had prevented him from giving more than a fraction of his attention to his Italian plans. By the Summer of 1822, he had managed to persuade the Tsar not to go to the aid of the Greek rebels, and the Near Eastern situation had become less critical. He now felt free to turn to Italy; but almost at once he was again distracted by a new crisis, arising from the growing determination of France and Russia to suppress the Spanish revolutionary regime.[63] Since this crisis threatened to upset the delicately balanced diplomatic equilibrium, to the detriment of Austria, Metternich had to devote most of his attention to it throughout the Summer and Fall of 1822; once again he was too preoccupied to give his Italian plans the careful guidance necessary to ensure their success. He took no action to counter Consalvi's opposition—indeed, he seems to have been unaware of it.

Consalvi was now carefully concealing his hostility. His original criticism of Metternich's plans in 1821 had probably been made in the hope of influencing the Prince to abandon them; once it was clear that this hope was vain, further criticism would have served no purpose but to alert Austria to the opposition he was organizing. On the very eve of the Congress, Apponyi assured Metternich that Consalvi's "political principles are perfectly identical" with those of Austria, that he sympathized with her Italian policy, and that in particular "the plan for establishing a Commission...is entirely approved."[64]

Lulled by such misinformation, Metternich believed that he could count upon Papal support. In this delusion, he even made a major effort to persuade Consalvi to represent the Papacy at the Congress, confident that his personal support would facilitate acceptance of the Austrian plans. Consalvi too would have preferred to attend—though not to support Metternich's plans, but rather to manage personally the delicate task of ensuring their defeat. Unfortunately, since the Pope's health was now so poor that a crisis might arise at any moment, the Secretary of State could not absent himself from Rome. He therefore appointed as plenipotentiary Cardinal Spina, with whose skillful conduct at Laybach he had been well pleased.[65]

The instructions which Consalvi drew up for Spina's guidance at the Congress[66] opened with an analysis of Austrian policy in Italy, whose aim was seen as the attainment of a "supreme direction over all those interests common to the states of the peninsula," with "the right to compel all the other Italian governments to adopt those measures which she considers appropriate." In view of Austria's strong position *vis-à-vis* most of the Italian states, circumstances seemed favorable for her to attain this aim, especially since Russia and Prussia seemed to favor it. Fortunately, France was disposed to aid the Papacy; indeed, the likelihood of French opposition had apparently led Metternich to postpone his plan for a Confederation, and instead "to seek to prepare the way for it by securing the adoption of principles and institutions of such a nature as to lead little by little to a Confederation under Austrian protection." Hence, Spina would have to oppose, not only a Confederation, but also anything likely to serve as a step towards it, especially the Central Investigating Commission. When possible, he should offer other grounds for his opposition than the true motive, which was distrust of Austria. For example, the Commission should be opposed as unnecessary, because a voluntary exchange of information among the Italian states and cooperation among their police would serve the same purpose. The attempt to supervise the internal affairs of the Italian states in the name of reform and to impose upon them some common form of administration was equally dangerous to Papal independence; it too was to be opposed on the pretext that it was unnecessary, since Consalvi's reforms would satisfy all the requirements of good government. With unyielding opposition to every aspect of Metternich's plans as the theme of his mission, Spina set out for Verona.

By the Fall of 1822, the growing importance of the Spanish question had led the Powers to decide that the Congress should begin with a discussion of it, to be followed three weeks later by a discussion of Italian affairs. Castlereagh's suicide caused the opening of the Congress to be delayed until mid-October, and the discussion of Spain then dragged on longer than anticipated. When the Italian delegates began to arrive in Verona at the end of October, they found the Congress still deeply involved with Spain.

Aside from Spina, few of the Italian representatives who now gathered at Verona were likely to cause Metternich anxiety. Naples was represented by King Ferdinand and his minister, Prince Ruffo, Metternich's confidant. Terrified by the 1820 revolution, both were favorable to the Commission; and if they looked with less favor on Metternich's plans for the reform of their unhappy country, they were in no position to oppose the will of their protector.[67] Equally friendly to Metternich's plans were the representatives from Parma and Modena, both Habsburg-ruled.[68]

From Tuscany came the Grand Duke and his able minister, Prince Corsini. Despite Ferdinand III's dynastic link with Vienna, he was tenacious of Tuscan independence; moreover, he considered Metternich's fear of the Sects exaggerated—which it was, in so far as Ferdinand's own tranquil state was concerned—while Tuscany, long one of the best-governed European states, seemed in no need of reform. He was therefore inclined to oppose Metternich, but only if he did not have to take the lead in so doing, and could cloak his opposition under a pretext that would not betray distrust of his cousin in Vienna.[69] Also unfriendly to Metternich's plans but reluctant to lead the opposition was the Foreign Minister of Lucca, Count Mansi, though the diminutive size of his state meant that his hostility could have little more than nuisance value.[70]

Piedmont, represented by King Charles Felix and his minister, Count della Torre, played an ambiguous role at the Congress. Hostile to Austria by tradition and ambition, she had relied upon Austrian aid to repress the 1821 revolution, and might need that aid again. Moreover, the King, alarmed by the revolutionary ferment in Italy, was inclined to favor the Commission. He disliked the extension of Austrian influence which Metternich's plans would bring about, but was not prepared to offer open opposition. Della Torre was therefore instructed to encourage Rome, Tuscany, and France to oppose Metternich, but not to join with them; if these states could not defeat Austria, Piedmont would acquiesce in her plans.[71]

During the weeks of waiting before the discussion of Italian affairs began, Spina carefully sounded the views of the Italian delegates. He also sought audience with Francis I and Metternich. Both expressed alarm at the persistence of revolutionary agitation in Italy, and were very critical of the Italian governments in general and of Rome in particular, whose misgovernment they blamed for the general discontent. Spina explained Consalvi's plans for reform and repression, but the Austrians were not impressed.[72]

Spina found greater comfort in the French representatives, who repeated Blacas' promise of support. In fact, Montmorency had already made the French attitude clear to Metternich, who disclaimed any intention of extending Austrian hegemony with such vehemence as to give the impression that he had already abandoned his plans.[73]

But Metternich had by no means done so, though compelled thus far to neglect his plans by the need to concentrate on the Spanish question. His assurances to the French were intended only to lull their suspicions until he was ready to move. When, in late November, the Spanish question finally approached settlement, Metternich could at last turn to Italy. He found an unpromising situation: Papal hostility and Tuscan distrust were now unmistakable, while France was clearly disinclined to allow him a free hand in Italy as she had done in 1820–1821. Hopeful nonetheless of securing part—if not all—of his aim, he set about lulling the opposition Consalvi had stirred up. He concentrated his best efforts on the French, seeking to convince them that Austria had no desire to extend her hegemony, but that the incompetence of the Italian rulers made some degree of Allied supervision and control necessary.[74] Simultaneously, he sought to persuade Piedmont to give more active support, and to abate Tuscan and Papal opposition by stressing the desirability of his plans and the absence of any selfish Austrian ambitions.[75]

As a further move to weaken Italian opposition, he announced—first to Della Torre on November 19, then to Spina and Corsini shortly afterwards—that he had modified his original plan for the Commission. Instead of the Central Investigating Commission, he now proposed a Political Commission made up of commissioners from all the Italian states, whose duty it would be to "follow the movements of suspects in order to uncover all their activities and connections." Each commissioner would transmit all information uncovered by his state to the Commission, which would then investigate and return its findings to all the states for them to act upon. This modification, he felt, should eliminate all reasonable cause for opposition to his "salutary plan." Della Torre, faithful to his instructions, praised the plan, but secretly encouraged Spina to oppose it. Spina needed no urging: unable to detect any substantive change, he commented that "at first sight it seems only the old Commission under another name."[76]

Consalvi agreed. The new Commission was no more than a renamed and slightly modified version of the old, and must be opposed for the same reasons. Even if all the other states should accept it, the Papacy would refuse to take part.[77] Spina, foreseeing his chief's attitude, had meanwhile set about organizing resistance. Corsini agreed that the new Commission too must be opposed. Explaining the reluctance of his master, the Grand Duke, to display public distrust of Austria, he agreed with Spina upon several pretexts to cover their opposition.[78]

Spina and Corsini then sought the support of the other Italian states. The response was disappointing. Della Torre, though pleased to observe their opposition, was now cultivating Austrian good will by publicly favoring the Commission. Naples, Parma, and Modena were so obviously in the Austrian camp that no approach was made to them. Only tiny Lucca was inclined to join the opposition.[79]

With the Italian states disunited, Metternich pressed forward with his plans, redoubling his efforts to intimidate the Tuscans and persuade the French to abandon their opposition. "The affair of the Commission, far from being abandoned, is making progress," Spina reported in alarm.[80] Consalvi, unintimidated, instructed him to continue his resistance: even if the Papacy was abandoned by its allies, it would still refuse to accept or participate in the Commission. He realized the enmity that not only the Papacy but he himself would attract for this stand, but, having once abandoned hope of cooperation with Austria, he was resolved to hold firm: "knowing that I would betray my duty if I acted differently, I am prepared to accept any consequences that may befall."[81]

But matters did not come to a single combat between Austria and the Papacy. Despite Austrian pressure, Tuscany remained loyal; when Metternich appealed over Corsini's head to the Grand Duke, the ruler gave his minister full support.[82] The French also rebuffed Metternich, and Montmorency continued to make known his court's hostility to the Commission and support for Rome and Tuscany. His colleague, Count de la Ferronays, the French Ambassador to Russia, was able to convince the Tsar that the Commission was both unnecessary and an unwarranted infringement on Italian sovereignty. This was the final stroke. Faced with the resolute opposition of the Papacy and Tuscany, the hostility of France, and the disapproval of his most essential ally, the Tsar, Metternich saw that he had little chance of success. He therefore decided against proposing the Commission at Verona.[83]

His defeat was formalized at the session of December 8, which was primarily concerned with the Austrian occupation of Naples and Piedmont. That subject settled, Metternich announced that "it remains for us to warn the governments of the peninsula that, although they may view their internal situation in rosy colors, [Austria] has very different reports, and cannot doubt that ferment and discontent are everywhere, especially in the Papal States." At this point La Ferronays interrupted to ask "if he really planned to limit himself to warnings," as he had heard differently. When Metternich affirmed that this was his sole aim, the French delegate bluntly charged that "it is by now notorious among the plenipotentiaries that Your Highness has expressed other ideas, and in particular, that you have spoken...of a certain Commission." Metternich at first denied the charge, but, pressed by La Ferronays, finally admitted having mentioned the idea. However, he declared, he had never seriously intended to establish the Commission, but had only proposed it to frighten the Italian rulers, "convinced that without this they would have paid little heed to his warnings." Now, filled with apprehension, they would hasten to introduce the measures which the Powers urged. It is unlikely that this ingenious explanation convinced anyone, but as Metternich had now publicly disavowed the Commission, La Ferronays allowed the subject to drop.[84]

"I believe that the affair of the Commission will end here," was Spina's accurate prediction.[85] Metternich still considered the Commission "indispensable," but realized that the strength of the opposition made its implementation impossible; he therefore decided to postpone further efforts until a more favorable moment—which never came.[86]

The Commission had been defeated, and a Confederation not so much as mentioned. Metternich still hoped, however, to achieve at least one of his aims: the right to supervise the Italian states in the interest of reform. Since mid-November, he had been working to prepare the ground by demonstrating to the delegates of the Powers that the general misgovernment of the Italian rulers and their failure to adopt reforms made Austrian supervision necessary. As Papal opposition to his plans became evident, his criticism increasingly centered on the Papal State.[87] Spina worked energetically to counter his charges, explaining to the other representatives the reforms which Consalvi had introduced or was about to introduce. Corsini was similarly active on behalf of Tuscany. In the end, though Metternich easily convinced the Prussians of the truth of his claims, the Tsar remained noncommittal, and the French were actively hostile. Montmorency made clear to Metternich and the Congress at large that in his opinion, the Italian states were making satisfactory progress toward reform.[88]

The question was to be taken up at the session of December 11. Aware that Metternich planned to use this occasion to demand that reforms be imposed on the Italian states, Spina spoke with him on the previous evening, presenting a vigorous defense of Papal policy and stressing Consalvi's determination to tolerate no external interference.[89]

Spina's defense did not alter Metternich's unfavorable—and all too well justified—opinion of the Papal administration, but it did at least convince him that Rome would resist to the last. Since Tuscany, at least, would take the same stand, while Russia was unsympathetic and France evidently planning to support the Italians, Metternich once again decided that he had no hope of success at present. His plan to claim a right of supervision over the Italian states in the interest of reform therefore met the same fate as the Commission: it was deferred until a more favorable moment, which never arrived.[90] At the session of December 11, he merely read a declaration reminding the Italian rulers that the Powers expected them to consolidate their position by timely reform.[91]

The Italian states were to reply to this declaration on December 13. Metternich had originally intended this session as the climax of the Congress, so far as Italian affairs were concerned. Here the states would have to describe to the Powers the measures which they had taken in response to the Congress of Laybach. Since it was improbable that their measures would be considered adequate, Metternich would have the opportunity to advance his proposal that Austria supervise them in a program of administrative reform. Since, however, Metternich had already realized that his plans would have to be postponed, the course of events on December 13 was quite different.

The session opened with a defense by Spina of his government's policy. Agreeing with the claim of the Powers that reform was essential, he declared that fortunately the Papacy had long since realized this, and had adopted the necessary measures. After describing Consalvi's reforms, past and to come, he concluded that since they had established "perfect tranquility" in the Papal State, no alteration of Papal policy was necessary.[92]

Although the accuracy of this assertion was distinctly open to question, the Prince allowed it to pass without comment. The other Italian representatives then read their declarations, which tended to consist of general statements that all was well in their states, thanks to the enlightened administration which they all enjoyed. These declarations were accepted without complaint, and the meeting came to an end.[93] Metternich's great drive to organize the Italian states into an antirevolutionary front under Austrian hegemony thus expired in platitudes and anticlimax.

The reasons for Metternich's failure are not difficult to find. Fundamental, as he himself recognized, was the Papal opposition, conducted with skill and tenacity by Consalvi. It was the Secretary of State who led the resistance from start to finish, whose willingness to oppose Austria encouraged Tuscany to join the fight, and whose appeal to France gained the invaluable assistance of a great Power.

Certainly, fortuitous circumstances also played an important role in Metternich's defeat. First, the Greek crisis demanded Metternich's attention for over a year, just when we should have been devoting himself to preparing the way for the fruition of his Italian plan. No sooner did that cirisis subside in 1822 than the Spanish question became critical; once again, he was distracted from Italy, and Consalvi had the opportunity to organize resistance undetected and unhindered. By the time Metternich was free to turn his full attention to Italy, it was too late: the opposition to his plans was too strong to overcome.

But the intervention of chance, in the form of the Greek and Spanish questions, would not in itself have brought about Metternich's defeat had it not been for Consalvi, who alone was willing to lead the opposition and, skillfully taking advantage of the opportunities presented by fate, organized a resistance strong enough to defeat Austria. Spina was well justified in his claim that "if a minister may be congratulated because a certain Power has failed to accomplish anything that it had planned at the Congress," this "negative merit" belonged to Consalvi.[94]

Metternich was of the same opinion. The opposition Consalvi had stirred up was so strong that it was necessary to postpone the implementation of Austria's plans. However, Metternich remained convinced that his plans were essential if the Restoration order in Italy was to be safeguarded against revolution, and he regarded his defeat as only temporary. All that Metternich felt he needed was a means of overcoming Papal opposition: with Rome compliant, no other Italian state would dare to resist Austria, and France, given no excuse to intervene by Italian appeals, would be unable to thwart him. Soon after the Congress ended, he confidently assured Apponyi that "I will soon give you the means" to eliminate Papal opposition, and then the way would be clear for the realization of his plans.[95] What means he had in mind must remain uncertain, for in fact his promise remained without sequel. He apparently made no subsequent effort to compel Consalvi to cease his opposition, nor, as we shall see, did he attempt to win the support of the Cardinal's less competent successors. Most probably, he was awaiting a favorable turn in the international situation that would give him a free hand to deal with Italy as he wished. If so, he was doomed to disappointment. In retrospect, it is clear that 1821-1822 saw both the apogee of Austrian power in Italy, and the most propitious moment for its strengthening. In the years that followed, England became increasingly unsympathetic to Austria and the conservative cause; French hostility towards Austrian hegemony in Italy grew steadily stronger, especially after the July Revolution; and even Russia, though remaining conservative, increasingly asserted its independence from Austrian guidance after the death of Alexander I in 1825. Never again would the international situation be so favorable for the realization of Metternich's Italian plans as it had been in 1821-1822; defeated then, they were lost forever.

Metternich's failure obviously had unfavorable consequences for Austria, whose best chance of strengthening and formalizing her hegemony in Italy was lost thereby. The direction of Italian police activity which the Commission would have conferred, the opportunity to guide the internal policies of the states which the right of supervision would have provided—these would not merely have greatly extended Austrian predominance in themselves, but would have served as major steps towards the Confederation which would have provided it with a formal basis. Because of Metternich's defeat, none of this came to pass. Austrian hegemony, though it survived another three decades and more, remained vulnerable to the assaults both of the Italian liberal-nationalist movement and of Austria's rival, France, whose alliance in 1859 would spell the end of Austrian predominance in the peninsula and the beginning of her decline as a great Power.

The outcome was apparently more satisfactory for the Italian states. The danger that their tenuous independence might be replaced by complete subordination to Austria had been lifted. Yet, in the long run, they had little cause for jubilation. Though Metternich's plans had involved the extension of Austrian control, they had never been intended to achieve that aim for its own sake, but rather because Metternich saw them as the only means of strengthening the Restoration Order in Italy against the revolutionary threat. Only if compelled by Austria—Metternich feared—would the Italian states adopt the reforms necessary to preserve their subjects' loyalty and thus undercut the growing appeal of the Sects; only if their sporadic and inefficient efforts against the Sects were coordinated and directed by a Central Investigating Commission could a truly effective campaign of repression be mounted; only if a Confederation was established would Austria have a solid basis, legal and practical, not only to defend its own hegemony, but also to direct the united forces of the Italian states against both external intervention and internal revolution. His fears were fully realized. After 1822, the Italian rulers in general did fail to provide satisfactory government, thus driving their more enlightened subjects into the revolutionary camp—a process we shall observe in the Papal State; they failed equally to root out the revolutionary movement, which soon entered upon a period of rapid growth; and Austria, without the Confederation, experienced increasing difficulty and final failure in controlling the liberal-nationalist movement, restraining Piedmontese ambitions, and preventing French intervention. That Metternich's plans, if realized in 1822, could have reversed the course of history by preventing forever the overthrow of Austrian hegemony and the unification of the peninsula can hardly be asserted; yet it would be equally unconvincing to deny that his success then would greatly have strengthened both Austrian predominance and the Restoration Order in Italy, and appreciably delayed their downfall. By their unwillingness either to adopt adequate measures of reform and repression of their own volition or to allow Austria to compel them to do so, the Italian states doomed themselves to the final reckoning of 1859–1870, when all save one—ironically, Piedmont, which had played no role in defeating Austria at Verona, yet was now the sole beneficiary of that defeat—ceased to exist. However gratifying this outcome may have been for Italian patriots, it was hardly one which their former rulers could welcome; yet it was the predictable sequel of their victory at Verona.[96]

Metternich's failure in 1821–1822 is of particular interest in that it offers perhaps the first example of a recurrent problem confronting modern counter-revolutionary Powers. Such a Power will, of course, want to prevent revolution in the smaller, and usually less advanced, states within its sphere of influence. Unfortunately, the rulers of those states all too often tend to be reactionary and incompetent, so that they both drive their subjects into the revolutionary camp as the only alternative to misgovernment, and fail to adopt effective repressive measures against the revolutionary movement, which grows by leaps and bounds. The obvious move for the Power is to seek to persuade or compel its small allies to reform; yet this move tends to be self-defeating, in that the ruling class of the small state, fearful both of reform and of encroachment upon its independence, will tenaciously resist the Power's well-intentioned efforts and usually defeat them either by open opposition or by covert obstructionism. Thus the farsighted plans of the Power are thwarted, and—like the Austria of Metternich—it is eventually confronted, as the revolutionary movement makes headway, with the dismal choice between tolerating the victory of revolution, and a risky military intervention to save an incompetent regime. Recent examples of this dilemma come easily to mind; Metternich may have been the first to face it, but he was not the last to fail to find a satisfactory solution.

4. The Postal Controversy

Whatever the long-term consequences of Consalvi's victory at Verona, he had won his immediate objective: the preservation of Papal independence against the most serious threat it had to face during the Restoration. The price was the collapse of Austro-Papal cooperation for the rest of his ministry. Hereafter, he could expect Vienna's hostility; and he was soon to be reminded—if he had ever forgotten—that the power of Austria was still great. One more battle—the last of his career as Secretary of State—lay before him: the struggle to prevent Metternich from bringing the postal correspondence of the Italian peninsula under Austrian control. This attempt was of more than administrative significance: control of the Italian postal system, though desirable for financial reasons, was pursued mainly for political purposes—it was, in fact, another aspect of Metternich's search for greater Austrian control over Italy in the aftermath of the 1820 revolutions.[97]

Like most European states, Austria had long recognized the value of its postal system for purposes of espionage. All mail that passed through the Austrian post offices—particularly that of foreign diplomats and other prominent figures—was liable to be opened. The Restoration brought another motive for postal espionage—the counterrevolutionary struggle. Control over Italian correspondence would be of obvious value to the Austrian police, who, by intercepting the mail of suspected *Settarj*, could learn much about their activities.

Consequently, after 1815 Metternich made a vigorous effort to extend Austrian control over the entire Italian postal system. Much Italian correspondence normally passed through the post offices of Lombardy-Venetia, and so came into Austrian hands as a matter of course; but much also went via Piedmont. The complete control of correspondence which Metternich sought could only be won if the lesser states were persuaded to send via Lombardy-Venetia all the mail which passed through their hands.

Metternich's first target in Italy was the Papal State, whose correspondence would be particularly valuable: because of its location, virtually all mail between northern and southern Italy, as well as much of that between Northern Europe and Mediterranean lands, passed through its offices. In July, 1815, Metternich sent his most trusted expert in postal affairs, Baron von Lilien, to Rome to negotiate a postal convention which would give Austria control of all Papal correspondence.[98] Lilien's first dealings were with the Superintendent of Posts, Cavaliere Altieri, an unimaginative bureaucrat whom he easily persuaded to accept a draft convention binding Rome to send via Lombardy-Venetia virtually all the correspondence originating in or passing through the State.[99] At this point, however, Consalvi turned his attention to the negotiations and at once saw the dangerous implications of the draft convention.[100] Though foreign control over its correspondence must be distasteful to any state, Rome found it particularly undesirable. Unlike most states, the impoverished Papal government could not afford to send its diplomatic correspondence by special couriers, but had to use the regular mails. Papal correspondence with the Vienna Nuncio was already subject to Austrian scrutiny; should Rome agree to turn over all its mail to Austria, then all its diplomatic correspondence would become as restricted and hampered as that with Vienna already was.[101] Moreover, much Roman correspondence was concerned with spiritual matters, often involving personal moral problems or cases of conscience; it was clearly improper to allow such mail to be seen by anyone save the spiritual authorities whom it concerned. Consalvi therefore rejected Lilien's proposed convention, substituting a draft which eliminated the objectionable provisions.[102] After failing to win over Consalvi with the offer of financial concessions, Lilien accepted the Cardinal's draft as the basis for a convention which dealt only with the administrative and financial side of the postal system, leaving the political side in abeyance.[103]

Though disappointed by this outcome, Metternich did not wish to antagonize Consalvi by exerting pressure for a more favorable convention. Instead, he turned to another plan: seeking postal conventions with the central Italian states—Parma, Modena, and Tuscany—by which they would give Austria all the mail that passed through their offices. Added to Lombardy-Venetia, these states formed an unbroken line of territory across Italy from the Adriatic to the Ligurian Sea, through which Papal correspondence would have to pass to reach the North. Once this postal barrier was formed, Metternich believed, he would have little difficulty in bringing Rome to agree to his plans.[104] "We cut Italy in two and become its masters," he predicted.[105] In 1817 Parma and Modena signed agreements to turn over their correspondence.[106] Tuscany, however, jealous of her independence, proved uncooperative; she was encouraged to resist by Piedmont, whose location had long made it the natural route for most Italian correspondence with Western Europe. The Piedmontese were joined in secret by Consalvi, and openly by the French, who did not

want their Italian correspondence in Austrian hands. Thus supported, the
Tuscans were able to evade Metternich's pressure. By 1820, Austria still had
not managed to close the gap in its postal barrier, and the correspondence of
Italy remained largely free from its control.[107]

The 1820 revolution stirred Metternich to a new effort, for the knowledge
of *Settarj* activities that could be derived from the Italian mails now seemed
vital for preventing new revolts.[108] Moreover, such control was a logical part
of Metternich's revised Italian policy aimed at strengthening Austrian hegemony. Late in 1821, he renewed his pressure on Tuscany. With Austria's
power at its height, this pressure was too great to be resisted, and on September 4, 1822, a postal convention was signed by which Tuscany agreed to turn
over all correspondence to Austria.[109] The postal barrier was a reality at last.

Consalvi learned of the secret convention in October, and at once began
working against it. His appeals to France and Piedmont received encouraging responses. Villèle promised French support at Verona,[110] while della Torre
promised to "display the greatest firmness in the postal question."[111]

In reality, Piedmont was already wavering. Its plenipotentiary was indeed
directed to oppose the Austro-Tuscan convention; however, he was not to
carry this opposition to the point of seriously irritating Austria, whose protection was needed against revolution, nor was he to jeopardize the financial
interests of the Piedmontese postal service by clinging too firmly to the principle of freedom of correspondence.[112]

Soon after arriving at Verona, Spina met with Della Torre and Mansi, the
delegate from Lucca, to discuss ways of defeating the postal barrier. They
agreed that their only means of bringing pressure would be to deny Austria
and Tuscany the use of certain routes which they controlled, such as the Al-
pine passes through Piedmont and the Bologna road from Venice to Florence.
Unfortunately, Austria and Tuscany had alternate, if less convenient, routes
at their disposal. "Our situation is certainly most unpleasant," Spina concluded.[113] He would have been yet more pessimistic had he known that Piedmont was negotiating with Metternich in secret for a convention that would
bring her financial advantages, even at the cost of yielding control of her
correspondence.[114]

Spina had a brief flurry of hope in early December, when France and Brit-
ain intervened. Montmorency joined Spina in a determined effort to persuade Tuscany to abandon its convention with Austria; Della Torre came to
their aid, as did Lord Burgherish, the English minister in Florence. But even
this general effort, which continued for the rest of the Congress, had no effect.
Tuscany merely replied that its Austrian convention was far more advantageous than its former agreement with Piedmont; that in signing the convention
it had been moved only by financial and administrative considerations and
was unaware of any broader political implications; and that, in consequence,
it could see no reason to abandon the convention.[115]

The struggle against the postal barrier was weakened in late December
when Chateaubriand replaced Montmorency as Foreign Minister. Montmorency had been strongly opposed to Austrian policy in Italy; his successor
was primarily concerned with plans for French intervention in Spain, and
was indisposed to quarrel with Austria over Italy.[116] Although Chateaubriand

assured Consalvi of his support, he consistently evaded on one pretext or another every concrete proposal made to him.[117]

French unreliability was paralleled by Piedmontese duplicity. Once it was apparent that Tuscany would not yield, the Piedmontese decided that Austrian victory was inevitable. While encouraging Consalvi to resist, they pushed on with their secret negotiations with Austria for a settlement safeguarding their financial interests. Consalvi was dismayed to learn of these negotiations: Austria would "divide and conquer by dealing with Sardinia alone."[118] But Piedmont ignored his complaints; as the Papal chargé in Turin warned, the primary concern of this government is its financial interest; it will sign any agreement that safeguards it."[119]

"If Sardinia yields, all is lost," Consalvi foresaw.[120] Nonetheless, he was resolved to fight on alone. When in December Tuscany suggested negotiations for a new postal agreement in harmony with its Austrian convention, Consalvi refused, arguing that Rome could never accept that convention because it violated the right of the sender to choose which route his mail should take, because Austria and Tuscany had no right to sign an agreement disposing of Papal correspondence without consulting the Pope, and because the new Austrian route was longer and would delay the transit of Papal mail. Since Austria and Tuscany refused to allow Papal mail to pass freely, the Pope would exercise his sovereign right to refuse to allow them to use the Bologna road.[121] The Cardinal was so critical of the convention to Apponyi that the Ambassador, alarmed, suggested to Metternich that some concession be offered Rome to prevent a breakdown in relations.[122]

Metternich ignored his advice. Still smarting from the defeat which Consalvi had inflicted on his plans at Verona, he was little inclined to conciliate him; moreover, he saw the long-desired postal domination of Italy within his grasp. He replied with a rebuttal of Consalvi's arguments, in particular demonstrating that the new Austrian route, though longer in miles than the one through Piedmont, was in better condition and better organized, so that mail would actually move more swiftly along it. He thus undermined Consalvi's best argument, but did not weaken the Cardinal's determination to resist.[123]

Consalvi passed the Winter and Spring of 1823 in ceaseless efforts to prevent Austrian victory: protests to Austria and Tuscany, exhortations to Piedmont to hold firm and to France to enter upon active opposition, plans for new postal routes to circumvent Austria's, plans for a packet boat service to France, plans for a congress of all Italian states on postal affairs—all in vain. Austria could not be forced to abandon her strong position by any pressure Consalvi alone could bring to bear, and of his presumed allies, Piedmont now sought only a good financial settlement, while France refused to take any action that might anger Austria.

The final blow fell in March, 1823, when Piedmont signed a convention with Austria. In theory, this avoided the concentration of correspondence in Austrian hands: Piedmont would turn over all correspondence of the states on the left bank of the Po to Austria, but that of states on the right bank—including the Papacy—would be consigned to Parma. In practice, however, since Parma was under effective Austrian control, Metternich's victory was complete.[124]

Consalvi's last hope was to secure French intervention; but Chateaubriand at last admitted frankly that "in these times of conflict with Spain, he could not afford to quarrel with Austria." For the present, at least, he would have to "limit himself to language that will not displease Austria, and to give advice, not protests."[125]

Papal isolation was now complete. Since some sort of agreement was necessary to end the confusion into which Italian postal affairs had fallen, Consalvi and Metternich—after much preliminary skirmishing and maneuvering for position—at length agreed to open negotiations. In July, 1823, Lilien arrived in Rome to begin talks.[126]

While the negotiations were taking place, power was slipping from Consalvi's hands. On July 6, Pius VII suffered a serious accident, and by early August there was little hope for his life. During these weeks, Consalvi's greatest concern was with the life of his sovereign and friend; he could spare only a fraction of his time for the postal negotiations. Moreover, the Pope's illness imposed a time limit on the talks, for his death would mean the end of Consalvi's ministry. If the Cardinal hoped to complete the postal negotiations— and he knew that few others in the Curia could handle them effectively—he must fight not only Austria, but time as well.

Discussions between Consalvi and Lilien went on in halting fashion whenever the Cardinal could find time to spare from his vigil at the Pope's bedside.[127] Lilien's first proposal was that Rome accept a convention similar to that with Tuscany. When Consalvi rejected this, Lilien became more flexible, but insisted upon two key points: first, that Rome bind itself to consign to Austria all correspondence destined for north of the Alps; second, that this correspondence be consigned in open packages, not in sealed packets—the latter, of course, would hamper espionage. Lilien argued that the mail would travel more swiftly over the Austrian routes, which would be more economical for the Papacy; moreover, he pointed out, further resistance was useless, since both Tuscany and Piedmont were committed to consigning all Papal correspondence to Austria.

Consalvi was hard pressed to answer these arguments, and his position became still more difficult in the second week of August when Lilien began to offer various tempting financial concessions. He realized, of course, that in practice he could not prevent the consignment of Papal mail to Austria by Tuscany or Piedmont. What he was fighting for was a principle, the Papacy's right to consign its mail to whatever nation and by whatever route it wished. At present, that right could not be put into practice, but circumstances might well change. Perhaps when the Spanish war ended, France would feel free to intervene in the postal question; then, with French backing, the Papacy might once again be able to put its theoretical right into practice—provided it had not bound itself to give its correspondence to Austria.

Consalvi therefore rejected Lilien's proposals, despite promises of financial concessions and threats of Imperial displeasure. On August 14, Apponyi joined in the talks, and both Austrians soon agreed that no argument could make Consalvi budge; they also realized that if an agreement were not reached before the Pope's death, which was now clearly imminent, the whole question would have to be held over indefinitely, until the next pontificate was well under way. Such delay was unthinkable, in view of the urgent need to stabilize the Italian postal system. Consequently, Consalvi's tenacity was finally rewarded: the Austrians agreed to drop their demands, and to accept the principle of Papal freedom of action in postal matters. Late on August 19, a convention was signed, which stated that "the Papal Post Office will send, in closed and sealed packets, that correspondence which it may choose to consign to the General Post Office of His Majesty, the Emperor of Austria."[128] With this convention, the postal controversy came to an end—a final victory snatched by Consalvi from an apparently hopeless situation.

It was Consalvi's last service to the Papacy, and his last official contact with Austria. On the morning of August 20, 1823, Pius VII died, and Consalvi again left office, this time forever.

VI

Metternich And Leo XII,
1823-1829

1. The Conclave of 1823

Metternich had long been concerned with the succession to Pius VII, for it could have serious consequences for Austria, the Papacy, and the Restoration Order.[1] Should an intransigent *Zelante* mount the Papal throne, Metternich could reasonably anticipate that all hope for Austro-Papal cooperation would vanish, obscurantism and reaction would triumph over Consalvi's program of domestic reform, and a new assault on regalism would begin that would not only embroil the Holy See with Austria, but would lead throughout the Catholic world to church-state conflict that was sure to weaken the conservative front and open the way for liberal gains.

The Prince therefore considered the election of a pope who would "follow in the wise path of moderation and conciliation that distinguished Pius VII" vitally important, and he was determined to do everything in his power to ensure it. To attain this objective in the face of the great influence and numerical strength of the *Zelanti* in the Sacred College, he planned a coalition between the Italian moderates led by Consalvi, and the court cardinals of the various Catholic states, who would presumably be loyal to the sovereigns who had secured them the red hat.[2]

Metternich first elaborated this plan in 1817, when Pius VII was seriously ill and a conclave seemed imminent. Consalvi's cooperation was easily secured, sinced his views coincided with Metternich's.[3] To win the support of the court cardinals—of which Austria herself had few—Metternich approached the other Catholic states, especially France, Austria's traditional rival. The Bourbon-Habsburg rivalry which had marked previous conclaves would, if repeated at the next, open the way for a *Zelante* victory. Fortunately, Richelieu, then at the head of the French government, shared Metternich's aversion to extremism: he agreed that the common interest of all sovereigns demanded the election of a conciliatory pope, and he promised to work with Austria to that end.[4] Of the lesser states, Naples and Bavaria, ruled by ministers whose outlook resembled Metternich's, agreed to cooperate. Spain, ruled by the ultrareactionary Ferdinand VII, was determined to support the *Zelanti*. Portugal seemed likely to follow Spain, as did Piedmont, in whose case hostility to anything Austria suggested was more important than any religious motive.[5] However, a coalition between the Austrian, Bavarian, French, and Neapolitan court cardinals, and the Italian moderates led by Consalvi, would form a bloc which Metternich considered sufficient to defeat the *Zelanti*. His confidence was not put to the test on this occasion, since Pius VII recovered from his illness. Nonetheless, the Pope's health remained poor, and Metternich kept his plans in readiness for the conclave which must eventually take place.[6]

Late in 1822, Metternich's attention was recalled to the question when word came from Apponyi that Pius' health was deteriorating so rapidly that his death could not be far off. Apponyi requested instructions for the conclave, which he expected within a year.[7] Although Metternich was now preoccupied with the Spanish question, he agreed with Apponyi as to the importance of the conclave and promised to send him full instructions.[8] Unfortunately, the instructions were long delayed, less by Metternich's preoccupation than by the procrastination of Francis I, who characteristically insisted on making a minute personal examination of the question.

Though unable to hasten his August Master's decision, Metternich found ways to put the interval to use. In particular, it was necessary to choose the cardinal to be entrusted with the Austrian Secret—i.e., the authority to represent Austrian interests in the conclave as the Ambassador, a layman, could not do. The Secret was normally entrusted to a reliable Austrian-born subject. At the moment, however, the only living Austrian cardinal was the Habsburg Archduke Rudolf, who could not attend the conclave, partly because of ill health, partly because the presence in the conclave of a member of the Imperial family would stir up hostility to Austria among the other cardinals.[9] The other "Austrian" cardinals were natives of Lombardy-Venetia, and none was considered fully reliable. Since, then, the Secret would have to be entrusted to a Roman cardinal, the leading candidate was Albani. Of a noble Roman family with a long record of good will towards Austria, Albani had been useful in the past, and had made clear to Apponyi his willingness to be of service at the conclave—for a suitable recompense. "Albani is not only ambitious, but has difficulty in resisting the least financial advantage, so the moment is propitious to win him," for he wished to be named to the vacant post of Protector of the Churches of the Austrian Empire. This position carried few duties, but notable financial benefits. Apponyi advised conferring it upon Albani: despite—or rather, because of—his venality, that Cardinal was a desirable ally, being "highly intelligent, and familiar with the intrigues of his court, which he can conduct skillfully to our advantage."[10] Metternich accepted this advice, and Albani was entrusted with the Secret.[11]

In June, 1823, having at last received the Emperor's approval,[12] Metternich sent Apponyi the long-awaited instructions.[13] Austria's fundamental aim at the conclave was defined as:

> First, to secure the election as the next pope of the cardinal most worthy of this honor, with regard both to the welfare of religion, and to the great European interests, in particular those of Austria. Second, so to act that the new pope is convinced that Austria supported his election.

As we have seen, Metternich's conception of the interests of religion, Europe, and Austria, involved a pope who would follow in the footsteps of Pius VII by cooperating with Austria in the Union of Throne and Altar, by continuing Consalvi's policy of enlightened reform and prudent repression in the Papal State, and by following a conciliatory religious policy especially with regard to Josephism, that would not lead to renewed quarrels with the secular power.

Metternich next considered which of the fifty-three cardinals was "most worthy" in this sense. His conclusions were not encouraging. Most of the cardinals whose principles and ability he respected—Consalvi, for example— had little chance of being elected. Of the twenty cardinals he considered *papabili*, none was fully satisfactory, and most were *Zelanti*. The most dangerous candidate was Severoli, the most influential and intransigent *Zelanti* leader, whose hostility to Austria had led to his replacement as Vienna Nuncio in 1816; but a dozen others were only marginally less objectionable. In general, Metternich did not attempt to pass definitive judgments as to which cardinals should be supported or opposed; his comments were to be regarded as tentative, to be revised as necessary by Apponyi. The Ambassador was to be alert for information that might show the candidates in a new light, and to adapt his policy accordingly; he was in particular to consult the opinions of Consalvi and Albani.

The Chancellor then turned to the crucial question: "what strategy would be best suited to secure the election of a worthy pope?"[14] The basic obstacle to be overcome was the numerical advantage of the *Zelanti* in the Sacred College. In appearance, Austria was well equipped to do so by her possession of the exclusive—the right, held by Austria, as well as France and Spain, to exclude from election one cardinal of whom she disapproved. The exclusion had to be announced to the Sacred College before that cardinal won the necessary two-thirds majority, for, once he was elected, the exclusive could not be used against him.[15] A potent weapon; but "costly experience has proven that the use of the formal exclusive creates great difficulties," for this dramatic interference by a secular Power in the conclave inevitably aroused such resentment that the Power's influence at Rome was weakened for years thereafter. Moreover, the exclusive could be used only once. Hence, Metternich decided "not to allow its use except in the last resort, and only if an election which we must at all costs prevent seems certain." He hoped that matters would not reach that point, for an undesirable election could also be prevented by the indirect exclusive: since a two-thirds majority was necessary to elect, a coalition of one-third plus one of the cardinals would suffice to make a *Zelanti* victory impossible. Forty-nine cardinals were expected to attend the conclave; hence, seventeen would form the indirect exclusive. The various Catholic states had among their national cardinals at least fourteen, Metternich felt, upon whose loyalty they could rely. If these were joined by three or four of the Italian moderates led by Consalvi, a *Zelanti* election could be postponed indefinitely. Eventually the *Zelanti* would tire of the fruitless struggle, their less determined members would drop off, and then the courts could seize the advantage and obtain the election of a moderate who would follow in the footsteps of Pius VII.

Apponyi's first task would therefore be to form such a coalition. Metternich

would prepare the way by approaching the other courts to seek their cooperation. Of course, this policy would have to be executed with some care: "the
Sacred College always resents the intervention of the Courts in an election,"
and "therefore the best way for the Courts to exercise influence is to avoid
making their intervention too obvious." This rule applied especially to Austria, which the cardinals already tended to distrust because of her religious
policy and alleged designs on the Papal State. Realizing the harm such prejudices could do, Metternich directed Apponyi and Albani to neglect no opportunity to dispel them by demonstrating the "disinterested nature" of Austrian
policy. They were to point out to the cardinals that "Austrian power, far
from threatening the independence of the Italian states, is in fact the surest
defense of their legitimate authority..., and of the Catholic faith," as had
been proven during the 1820 revolutions. The cardinals should also be reminded of the valuable support given by Austria to Catholic interests in non-
Catholic areas.

Finally, Apponyi and Albani were directed to remain always in perfect
unity, and to strive to bring Consalvi into this harmony. If these instructions
were carried out, Metternich felt, there was good reason to anticipate a satisfactory election.

The instructions came none too soon, for on July 6 the Pope was seriously
injured, and his condition steadily deteriorated until his death on August 20.
The Pope's accident caused Metternich to accelerate his preparations. Leaving Apponyi and Albani to rally support at Rome, the Chancellor set about
persuading the Catholic courts to present a united front at the conclave. His
appeal was based on one of his favorite concepts: the unity of the Powers in
the Alliance, the bulwark of the Restoration order.[16] The courts must abandon
their selfish interests and stand together in defense of the Restoration order
"against all who think to overthrow it," whether reactionaries or revolutionaries. The united action of the Alliance would strengthen the hard-won stability of Europe by electing a pope whose principles would coincide with those
of the Alliance.[17]

This characteristically "European" approach stood in contrast to the
national rivalries that had marked most previous conclaves, but the initial
response of the other courts seemed to indicate that it would be generally
accepted. The French reaction was particularly encouraging: Chateaubriand
agreed that the courts must stand together and assured Metternich that the
French cardinals would cooperate with Albani.[18] A similar promise of support
was received from Naples, which depended upon Austria for protection
against revolution, and whose enlightened minister, De Medici, was sympathetic to Consalvi.[19] The Bavarian minister, Count Rechberg, likewise promised the support of his court's only cardinal, Haefflin.[20] Even Piedmont,
hostile to cooperation with Austria in 1817, responded favorably. Piedmont
too was acutely aware of its need for Austrian protection against revolution;
moreover, Turin realized the problems a *Zelante* pope could create. Della
Torre therefore promised the cooperation of Piedmont's cardinals.[21] As for
the other Catholic states, Portugal, which had neither cardinals nor an ambassador at Rome, could not influence the conclave, while Spain, just emerg-
ing from three years of revolution, was too distracted to play a significant

role.[22] Metternich seems in fact to have made no overtures to the Iberian courts, though he expected the support of the only Spanish cardinal, a known moderate. Encouraged by these promises of support, Metternich predicted that the conclave would be "the occasion for a new triumph of the European Alliance."[23] And indeed, his confidence seemed justified, for during July and August Apponyi was approached by the representatives of France, Naples, Piedmont, and Bavaria—the Duke of Montmorency-Laval, Marchese Fuscaldo, Count Barberoux, and Cardinal Haefflin, respectively—who assured him of their cooperation.[24]

Meanwhile, Apponyi and Albani set about arranging a coalition with the moderate Italian cardinals. They first approached Consalvi, the natural leader of the moderates. His support was easily won—indeed, he had long been urging Austria to take a prominent role in the conclave—since his "natural interest," his only hope for his career and his policies, lay in "joining with the Crowns to elect a wise and moderate cardinal."[25] Assuring Apponyi that "you will always find in me a good friend of Austria"—an assurance that, despite the quarrels of recent years, was not so improbable as it might sound— Consalvi eagerly joined him in devising plans to defeat the *Zelanti*.[26] Less optimistic than Metternich, Consalvi pointed out the strengths of the *Zelanti*, who were to be feared "because of their numbers, their fanaticism, and above all because they have long had time to plan their moves." For the moment, the moderates should limit their efforts to "preventing a bad election" by gathering enough votes for the indirect exclusive. Consalvi considered only twelve of the national cardinals reliable, though five others might be won over. Two Italian cardinals had already placed their votes at Consalvi's disposal, and he expected several others to do so once the conclave opened. Thus there seemed a good chance of forming a solid indirect exclusive of seventeen votes. The most dangerous *Zelanti*, whose election must be prevented at all costs, included Severoli, Della Genga, Cavalchini, and Pacca. The best of the moderate candidates were Arezzo and Turiozzi.[27] Should the courts be unable to elect a genuine moderate, they should turn to one of the less intransigent *Zelanti*, such as Castiglione or Opizzoni.[28]

Apponyi next contacted "several of the most distinguished cardinals"—a curious mixture of moderates and *Zelanti*—to dispel any prejudices they might have against Austria and to persuade them to elect a moderate pope. As might be expected, his listeners "paid full justice to our noble and generous policy" and gave vague assurances that a moderate should be elected. Apponyi "particularly addressed myself" to those cardinals native to Lombardy-Venetia, explaining the Emperor's policy at the conclave and his expectation that they would cooperate with it as loyal subjects. All "replied in a manner that gives me complete confidence in their cooperation."[29] The worth of these assurances Apponyi would learn in due course.

Other cardinals were less tactful, but more honest. When Apponyi sought to ascertain Della Somaglia's views on the conclave, he was "startled to hear him reply with a sort of sermon in truly fanatical language," denouncing Austrian religious policy and implying that "it was at the expense of sovereigns that religion must be revived."[30] Other *Zelanti* bitterly denounced Consalvi's reforms—down to such "useless innovations" as vaccination, street lighting, and the new firefighting company of Rome—and demanded their abolition. Many seemed to believe the old rumors that Austria was planning to take advantage of the interregnum to annex the Legations. "One may deduce from this the nature and aims of the *Zelanti*," Apponyi commented.[31]

Metternich needed no reminders as to the nature of the *Zelanti*, but he felt the situation at Rome was evolving in a manner likely to ensure their defeat. He was especially pleased that, despite their recent disputes, Consalvi had promised his support: he had never lost his high regard for the Cardinal, and was confident that he would "exercise a preponderant influence in the conclave." Apponyi was directed to cooperate with Consalvi in everything, and to seek and follow his advice on all major points. Indeed, if it were to happen that, a moderate pope having been elected, Apponyi should be in a position to influence his choice of Secretary of State, he was to support Consalvi in preference to Albani—a decision of which Albani was not to be informed just yet.[32]

On the international level too the situation was promising. There was only one small cloud on the horizon: a certain "ambiguity" in Chateaubriand's recent conduct. Although the French minister continued to assure Metternich of his cooperation, the efforts of the Austrian ambassador in Paris to pin him down to a definite plan of action were unsuccessful. This was disquieting, but Metternich was not unduly alarmed: probably Chateaubriand still feared that Austria's "European" approach to the conclave hid secret ambitions. Metternich therefore planned to present him with arguments that would "remove any doubt . . . as to the disinterest and altruism of our court." Surely, once Austria's policy had been properly explained, "the Court of the Tuileries cannot possibly fail to see our complete freedom from selfish ambition," and then French cooperation would become a reality.[33]

But Metternich's confidence rested upon an insecure foundation: neither of the two assumptions on which he based his policy was valid. His first assumption, that the other courts would cooperate with Austria, was already being undermined. The most serious defection was that of France. Despite his promises to Metternich, Chateaubriand wanted to revive French influence in Italy at Austria's expense. He was therefore resolved to oppose any pope who might be favorable to Vienna, even if this meant supporting a *Zelante* whose fanaticism he deplored. Indeed, as he explained to Laval, he regarded the *Zelanti* as France's natural allies, since they were hostile to Austria:

> Vienna has proposed to cooperate with us to form a crown party at the conclave. . . . You must take great care not to support an Austrian pope; and it is clear that France, not being able to secure the election of a French cardinal, must support the Italian party [i.e., the *Zelanti*] who are in the last analysis the French party.[34]

This spirit of hostility to Austria continued to mark his instructions to Laval: "No Austrian pope: that is the primary consideration. The second is to have an Italian [i.e., *Zelanti*] pope, the most friendly to France possible." Chateaubriand did not favor, certainly, a *Zelante* of extremist religious views, for such a pope could do great harm in the present disturbed state of the

French church, where ultramontanes and Gallicans were feuding. However, he was quite indifferent to the political views of the new pope, or to the harm which reaction might cause in the Papal State. One of the more moderate *Zelanti* would be France's best choice; Castiglione would be most suitable. However, even an extreme *Zelante* was preferable to an Austrophile. As for the exclusive, France would not use it, except against a few cardinals who had been too friendly to the Napoleonic regime—certainly not against the *Zelanti,* whose good will as to be cultivated as a means to rebuild French influence at Rome.[35]

Chateaubriand further sought to outmaneuver Austria by winning over the other Catholic states, especially Spain, Naples, and Bavaria.[36] His solicitations had some effect, but in truth, they were not needed to erode the support which Metternich expected from these states. Piedmont, her old hostility only partly counteracted by her need for Austrian protection, was unreliable. Although Della Torre had fulfilled his promise to direct the Piedmontese ambassador in Rome and the Piedmontese cardinals to cooperate with Albani, he added a secret reservation which largely nullified its worth: "if the views of Austria are in agreement with our own, well and good; but if the contrary is true, we are by no means committed to follow any guide but that of conscience. Insinuate this to our cardinals."[37]

In a sense, however, these instructions represented realism as much as disloyalty, for Piedmont was in fact not sure that it could control its cardinals.[38] Here was a factor which Metternich had failed to take into account, a weakness in his plans going beyond the calculated duplicity of statesmen: the new religious climate of the Restoration, which was making anachronistic his assumption—typical of the eighteenth century in which his own outlook had been formed—that a court could rely implicitly upon the obedience of its cardinals. The revolutionary era had begun this process. For decades most of Western Europe had been dominated by revolutionary regimes, to which the cardinals could not offer the same unquestioning loyalty as to legitimate monarchs by divine right; in consequence, they had lost the habit of obedience to their rulers, and had turned more and more to the Papacy for guidance. The religious revival of the Restoration carried this process further, creating among the cardinals a new sensibility in which the spiritual interests of the Church increasingly replaced royal wishes as their polestar. Hence, after 1815, even legitimate monarchs were to find that they could no longer control their cardinals as easily as in the past. The conclave of 1823 was to be the first great demonstration of this altered state of affairs. This was the fundamental flaw in Metternich's plan to organize the national cardinals: even had all the courts sincerely wished to cooperate with him, they could not with certainty have brought their cardinals to do so.[39] This was strikingly demonstrated by the behavior of the Neapolitan and Bavarian cardinals. Upon both these courts, the insinuations of Chateaubriand had been wasted: both were determined to fulfill their promise to Metternich, and so instructed their ministers and cardinals.[40] The Neapolitan minister in Rome, however, doubted that he could rely upon more than three of the six Neapolitan cardinals, and even this estimate was to prove overly optimistic.[41] Bavaria's Cardinal-Ambassador Haefflin pledged obedience to his King's orders, but before the conclave had ended he too would subordinate them to his sense of a higher duty towards the Church.[42]

Thus the religious currents of the age, combined with French and Piedmontese duplicity, undermined Metternich's assumption that a strong court party could be organized. His second assumption—that the Italian moderates would rally around Consalvi—was equally unsound. Not only the *Zelanti*, but most of the moderates had turned against Consalvi: though they might sympathize with his policies, they resented his long monopoly of power. As we have seen, Consalvi had found few coworkers among the cardinals, and had tended to concentrate the conduct of affairs in his own hands. This much-criticized tendency was the result less of an authoritarian personality than of a realization that most of the cardinals were too incompetent, too old, or in total disagreement with his policies.[43] Consalvi's "despotism" had aroused the envy and resentment of all shades of opinion in the Sacred College, where the feeling prevailed that the cardinals had the right to share in the Papacy's decision-making process and to hold the major offices regardless of ability or energy.[44] Hence, as Apponyi reported afterwards, "there was in this conclave a most unique tendency, shared by the great majority of cardinals—that of ruining Cardinal Consalvi forever, by electing a pope hostile to this worthy minister."[45] In the end, all but a handful of moderates deserted Consalvi during the conclave. Far from being a source of strength to the court party, Consalvi was a source of weakness, since many cardinals voted against its candidates simply from fear that their election would mean Consalvi's reappointment as Secretary of State.[46]

As both the premises upon which Metternich had based his policy were thus invalid, the conclave was unlikely to prove the "occasion for another triumph of the Alliance" that he had predicted. The cardinals entered conclave on September 2. The first votes revealed the weakness of the Austrian position. "I cannot hide from you that the affairs of the conclave go badly," Albani reported on the 7th. Severoli, the worst possible candidate from the Austrian point of view, had at once taken the lead. "Most of the other votes are given to men of a similar type." Arezzo and Turiozzi, the moderate candidates put forward by Albani, could secure only a handful of votes. "There is no court party": the Piedmontese and Neapolitan cardinals, as well as those native to Lombardy-Venetia, for the most part supported Severoli. Nor had Consalvi been able to win over more than two of the moderates. All that prevented an immediate *Zelanti* victory was the division of their vote among several candidates, plus their willingness to await the arrival of the French cardinals, whose support they seemed to expect. "All now depends on the French cardinals," Albani concluded. "If they support us, we can hope to resist the torrent; but if they desert us, all is lost."[47]

The same pattern marked the second week of the conclave.[48] Only the arrival of the French cardinals on September 15 provided a note of encouragement. Their leader, Cardinal de la Fare, expressed willingness to cooperate against the *Zelanti*, but insisted that the joint effort should be made on behalf of Castiglione. After some hesitation, Albani agreed. He had come to share the opinion that Consalvi had long since been urging upon him: since a genuine moderate could not be elected, the only hope was to support some less intransigent *Zelante* who could attract support from both parties—"he is the best we can do."[49]

With Castiglione as their candidate, the court-moderate party was able for the first time to win a significant share of the vote. On September 17, Severoli held steady at nineteen votes, while Castiglione received sixteen. Though encouraging, this was still far from adequate. Seventeen votes were needed for the indirect exclusive, and all the efforts of Albani, Consalvi, and de la Fare failed to win a stable seventeen votes for Castiglione. Meanwhile, the various factions among the *Zelanti* were gradually coalescing around Severoli, as one candidate after another abandoned his personal ambitions and advised his supporters to join the common cause: on September 19, Severoli received twenty-four votes. Albani was unable to stem his inexorable advance, and found discouragement and apathy growing among the moderates, who were beginning to drop away. "More and more of the undecided are going over to Severoli," he reported. "We have no real party, and in the end those few with us will desert and we will fall."[50]

The crisis came on the morning of September 21, as Albani warned in a hastily scrawled postscript: "I have no time to write—Severoli received twenty-seven votes this morning; he will certainly have thirty this evening, and to-morrow he will be pope."[51]

Only one means to defeat Severoli remained: the direct exclusive. Unwilling to take sole responsibility for so drastic a step—which invariably aroused bitter resentment against both the court that authorized it and the cardinal who delivered it—Albani summoned a meeting of the leading court cardinals. All agreed that the use of the exclusive was unavoidable. Consalvi—absent from the meeting, but consulted later—concurred.[52] That evening, as the cardinals were assembling for the vote, Albani, "trembling so that he could hardly speak," delivered the notice of the exclusion of Severoli in the name of the Austrian Emperor.[53]

The exclusive "fell like a thunderbolt" upon the *Zelanti*, who were thrown into "complete confusion."[54] Nonetheless, Albani was "full of fear for the future." Angered by the exclusive, the *Zelanti* were "now more determined than ever to defeat us, they have numbers on their side, so what hope have we?" The only course was to continue working for Castiglione, in the hope that the *Zelanti* might accept him as a compromise. It was a slim hope. Castiglione had refused to promise never to give office to Consalvi—the *Zelanti's sine qua non* for support. Moreover, the very fact that the courts supported him caused him to be regarded with suspicion. Only if the *Zelanti* lost all hope of victory on their own terms would they accept Castiglione, and this was far from being the case. Austria had exhausted its exclusive in vetoing Severoli, while the *Zelanti* had several candidates in reserve. Albani tried to persuade the French or Spanish cardinals to promise to use their courts' exclusives, but in vain: the French were not authorized to use the exclusive against the *Zelanti*, and the Spanish cardinal was not authorized to use it at all. Even had those exclusives been forthcoming, they could have eliminated only two of the three or four leading *Zelanti* candidates.[55]

The *Zelanti* thus had no reason to compromise. Instead, they began to unite behind a new candidate: Della Genga. Although less extreme on religious questions than most of his party, Della Genga was a political reactionary and a personal enemy of Consalvi; the dwindling court-moderate coalition thus had good reason to dread his election, but could do little to prevent it. The direct exclusive had been exhausted, the indirect exclusive could not be formed. In the days that followed, Della Genga grew steadily in strength, while Castiglione weakened as the *Zelanti* persuaded one cardinal after another to desert him—not only Italian moderates, but even the Bavarian Haefflin.[56] By September 27, Castiglione's strength had fallen to thirteen votes, while Della Genga "has twenty-seven certain votes..., and is rapidly gaining others."[57]

Both parties realized that the decisive moment of the conclave was at hand, and the evening of September 27 saw intense activity as the *Zelanti* worked energetically to win the few votes that stood between them and victory. Albani, seeing one cardinal after another defect, decided that only the French exclusive could defeat Della Genga. He persuaded de la Fare to request Laval's authorization to use it; but no answer came from the ambassador, who in fact considered Della Genga an acceptable choice.[58] Albani had to stand by helpless while the *Zelanti* consolidated the necessary majority. When the cardinals voted on the morning of September 28, thirty-four votes, one more than the necessary two-thirds, went to Della Genga, who shortly afterwards was proclaimed Pope Leo XII.[59]

2. *The Triumph of the* Zelanti, *1823–1825*

The conclave of 1823 ended an era in the history of the Papacy. For a generation, Consalvi had been the dominant figure at Rome, and Papal policy had in general been characterized by his realism, moderation, and diplomatic skill. Now his long ascendancy came to an end. The *Zelanti* had insisted upon his dismissal as a condition for their support at the conclave; nor was the new Pope well disposed towards him. Though Consalvi and Della Genga had once worked closely together, they had drifted into opposing camps after their quarrel in Paris in 1814: Della Genga was now critical of Consalvi's political reforms as a dangerous concession to the revolutionary spirit, and regarded his foreign policy as too worldly, too concentrated upon the institutional interests of the Papacy, with insufficient regard for spiritual concerns, particularly for the possibility of a Papal-led religious renewal of society. By 1823, these differences of opinion had long since hardened into enmity, so that Leo's election made Consalvi's exclusion from office inevitable. "We have seen the last of Consalvi," rejoiced his former friend.[60] To Consalvi, this rejection came as the final blow: sick, worn out by years of overwork and bitter conflict, within six months he followed to the grave the friend and sovereign he had served so well.[61]

Metternich sincerely mourned the passing of the Great Cardinal—as many in Rome also began to call him, once he was safely dead—for he had never lost his respect for his sometime friend and ally.[62] He knew that Consalvi's death was a blow to Austro-Papal relations, and to the Restoration Order in Italy as well; but only in years to come would he realize how serious that blow had been. Never again in Metternich's time would the Papacy be guided by a statesman of Consalvi's caliber, possessing not only great diplomatic expertise—as did some of his successors—but also insight into the realities of the modern world, able to perceive the need to adapt the Papacy to that world, and to attempt that adaptation with energy and skill. With Consalvi perished the last real hope of modernizing the Temporal Power[63]—and with that died Metternich's hope of establishing the conservative order in Italy on a solid basis. Hereafter, the unreformed Papal State would become a source of weakness and instability, the center of constant discontent, of unending plots and revolutions. With Consalvi too went the last man at Rome with whom Metternich had a genuine rapport: Metternich would find skilled diplomats at Rome again, but with none of them would he have the instinctive understanding that had marked his relationship with Consalvi.

Papal affairs now came under the personal direction of Leo XII. The new Pope was an experienced diplomat, having served as Nuncio at Cologne, Munich, and the Diet of Ratisbon in 1802.[64] He had had ample opportunity to observe the workings of the international system and the impact of the Revolution upon European society; and if his reaction to the new ideas was in general blindly negative, he had at least gained a lasting appreciation of the realities of the international order. At sixty-three, he was comparatively young, but weakened by long illness. His health remained poor; moreover, he was subject to fits of depression which at times robbed him of the ability to act decisively. But his realism in diplomatic affairs had not deserted him, and he had come to the throne acutely aware—unlike the more intransigent *Zelanti*—of the need to maintain good relations with the Powers.

At his first audience with Leo, Apponyi was pleasantly surprised at the Pope's apparent determination to "devote all his efforts to remain on good terms with the Courts," so that "if he manages to free himself from the evil influence of the party which elected him, he will act with wisdom and moderation" in his foreign policy. Leo's declaration that "we must do all we can to preserve friendly relations with the Austrian court" calmed Metternich's fears of overt Papal hostility.[65] Still, it was obvious that Austro-Papal relations in the new reign would be difficult, marked by greater distrust and a more fundamental lack of understanding than during the Consalvian era. Though Leo might be aware of the dangers of conflict with Austria, he and his advisers still shared the traditional *Zelanti* hostility towards her—a hostility reinforced by Austrian policy at the conclave, above all by the use of the exclusive, which symbolized for the *Zelanti* all they most hated and feared in Austrian policy: the threat of Austrian intervention in the affairs of the Papal State, the still more hated interference of the secular power in the affairs of the Church. Moreover, Leo himself would have been less than human not to remember and resent Austria's stubborn opposition to his candidacy. Not in years had Austria's influence at Rome been so weak.[66]

But the coolness in Austro-Papal relations sprang also from a more fundamental source: an incompatibility of outlook, a mutual incomprehension too great to be bridged. There was no one in the new regime analogous to Consalvi, with whom Metternich had had a basic rapport that made their actions always mutually comprehensible, even when they were at odds. Both were pragmatic realists, striving to understand the revolutionary experience and adapt traditional society and its institutions so that they might survive in the new age. By contrast, there was in the cast of mind of Leo and his advisers a strain essentially reactionary, even medievalistic, manifesting itself not merely in religious zeal, but in obscurantism, diehard hostility to change, and a fundamental denial of the realities of the modern world—a strain which was alien to Metternich, too greatly at odds with the mentality of that Restoration statesman *par excellence* for there to be any real understanding between them. Throughout the pontificate, even in its later years when relations between Rome and Vienna improved, this fundamental incompatibility of outlook and mutual incomprehension was to persist.

Adding to the strain on Austro-Papal relations was the revival of French influence at Rome, which had soared in the wake of the conclave: Laval's ambiguous maneuverings there and his covert support of the *Zelanti* had won him much good will among the victors. Stressing the contrast with Austria's open hostility, he now took credit for having contributed to Leo's election, and the *Zelanti* were properly grateful.[67] French prestige was further strengthened by the Bourbon monarchy's strong support for the revival of the French church, by its apparent success in controlling anticlerical liberalism, and by its intervention to overthrow the anticlerical regime in Spain and restore the absolute power of the reactionary and clerical Ferdinand VII.[68]

French influence was thus in the ascendant at Rome; and it was inevitably turned against Austria, whose predominance in Italy France had never ceased hoping to replace with her own. French diplomats were particularly given to discrediting Austria by reviving the old rumors of her ambitions in the Legations and keeping alive fear of her plans for a Central Police Commission and an Italian Confederation; these insinuations never lacked willing listeners in the Roman government.[69]

Thrown on the defensive, Metternich had to adapt his policy to the new situation, though without abandoning his essential objectives. Recognizing that for the time being Austria could not regain her former predominant influence at Rome, he adopted a policy of biding his time until more propitious circumstances should allow him to resume the pursuit of his aims. In the meantime, he was content to observe the course of events at Rome, cultivating Papal good will when possible, and carefully avoiding any move that might further antagonize Leo. Only thus, he realized, could he hope to overcome the prejudices of the *Zelanti* and erase the bad impression left by the conclave. In particular, he consciously avoided anything that resembled interference in the affairs of the Papal State, restraining himself from giving advice even when Papal domestic policy seemed potentially ruinous to Rome and threatening to the tranquility of the peninsula.[70]

Carefully watched by Metternich, Leo's policies began to unfold. Since Leo owed his election to the *Zelanti,* he was expected to be under their control, and to exemplify in his pontificate their ideal—framed in response to Consalvi's "despotism"—of a collegiate government of the Church, with the Pope formulating policy in close cooperation with the Sacred College.[71] But

Leo, despite his sympathy with the ideals of the *Zelanti*, had no intention of being a mere figurehead. His choice of Secretary of State revealed his determination to conduct an autonomous policy. Passing over several able *Zelanti* leaders, he selected the octogenarian Della Somaglia. The latter had long been prominent among the moderate wing of the *Zelanti*, who could not take exception to his principles; however, he was over eighty, and the skill and vigor which had made him a prominent figure at the court of Pius VI had drained away. His intellect had not failed, and his approach in diplomatic affairs was usually realistic, but he lacked the energy to control policy. This was the real reason for his selection: he would be only a spokesman for Leo, unable to pursue a personal policy or to thwart Papal policy of which he disapproved. "Leo XII will be his own Secretary of State," was Apponyi's accurate prediction.[72]

Leo's domestic policy, as Metternich had feared, was founded on his aversion to Consalvi's reforms and his determination to execute the *Zelanti* program of a return to the prerevolutionary order.[73] The chief expression of his policy was the *Motuproprio* of October 5, 1824, which reorganized the administrative and judicial systems in a retrograde sense.[74] The jurisdiction of the ecclesiastical tribunals, restricted by Consalvi to spiritual matters, was reextended over secular affairs, so that civil and canon law were once again confused. The civil code, promised by Consalvi and now near completion, was suppressed, while the procedure of the tribunals, which Consalvi had modernized on the French pattern, was restored to what it had been in 1796, even to the compulsory use of Latin in civil cases. In the administration, all major officials were once again to be ecclesiastics. The consultative councils set up in 1816 were retained, but brought under the control of the nobility, for among Leo's aims was "to restore to the nobility that distinction which it enjoys in all civilized countries." Indeed, Leo hoped to revive the old feudal institutions, and for this purpose invited the Roman princes to request the restoration of their former baronial jurisdictions, which the *Motuproprio* of 1816 had largely constrained them to renounce.[75] The administration of the communes was also reorganized to bring them under closer noble domination. This rearrangement reflected partly the medievalizing trend of Leo's thought, and partly his hope of creating in each town a closed patrician caste that would dominate the area and owe loyalty to the Papal regime; in practice, the ill will aroused among those excluded outweighed any benefits the loyalty of the nobles might have brought.

The *Motuproprio* was accompanied by further measures, not merely reactionary but truly medieval, such as the abolition of Consalvi's provisions for vaccination, the replacement of the study of science by that of theology at provincial lycées and the revival of humiliating restrictions on the Jews.[76] Particularly unpopular were Leo's efforts—inspired by the moral rigor typical of the *Zelanti*—to improve public morality by such measures as restrictions on the public sale of wine, the closing of theatres and taverns during Lent, and a notorious Edict on Women's Clothing dated December 14, 1824.[77] Such regulations were cheerfully ignored by the Romans, and served only to make the government seem both tyrannical and absurd to many who had no interest in political questions.

More sympathetic motives inspired Leo's reorganization of financial policy, particularly his reduction of taxes, which was prompted both by sincere concern over the tax burden on the lower classes and by the hope of offsetting the unpopularity of his other policies. Unfortunately, since the result was to deprive the government of much-needed revenue, the balanced budget which had been among Consalvi's achievements was soon a thing of the past, and the financial position of the government deteriorated steadily. Public services, from education to street lighting, had to be reduced, and the government's ability to carry out its essential functions was weakened—for example, the army and police were greatly reduced, at a time when brigandage and *Settarj* activity posed a growing challenge to the authority of the state.

"These measures have aroused general discontent," Apponyi reported. As one reactionary policy followed another, Leo's initial popularity vanished, and sullen hostility took its place.[78] So far as the educated classes were concerned, this negative reaction was the result, not merely of Leo's specific measures, but of their general implication—that Consalvi's program of reform and modernization had been permanently abandoned. As long as Consalvi's spirit had dominated the government, even those dissatisfied with his actual achievements could still hope for greater progress in the future within the framework of the Temporal Power; Leo's unmistakable repudiation of reform meant that this hope would have to be abandoned. Hereafter, the educated classes became increasingly convinced that reform and modernization could not be expected from the voluntary action of the Papal government, but would have to be extracted from it by force, and perhaps—a conviction that steadily gained ground—only by the overthrow of the Temporal Power. The stage was being set for the revolutions of 1831 and 1848; the crisis of the Temporal Power was soon to begin.

An unpopular regime can maintain itself in power in the face of strong popular hostility for a surprisingly long time, provided it is capable of dealing firmly with the challenges which its unpopular course provokes. But this was not the case with the Papal regime, which under Leo failed to deal with two such challenges: the growth of brigandage in the southern provinces, and the systematic terrorism of the *Settarj* in the Romagna.

The *Settarj* posed the more serious political problem: growing in numbers and support as Leo's reactionary policy unfolded, spurred to boldness by the government's obvious incompetence, yet realizing that any revolution would be crushed by Austria, the *Settarj* of the Romagna turned to systematic terrorism. The Spring of 1824 saw a series of assassinations of officials and prominent supporters of the government, with which the local authorities—themselves often either in sympathy with the Sects or frightened into inactivity—were completely unable to cope.[79]

Equally alarming, if less dangerous politically, was the epidemic of brigandage along the Neapolitan frontier. Brought under control by Consalvi, brigandage had revived during the disturbances of 1820–1821. In 1824, a deteriorating economic situation, combined with the obvious weakness and unpopularity of the government, led to a spectacular expansion against which the local officials—often in league with the brigands—accomplished little. Within a few months the situation was so far out of control that communications with Naples were jeopardized and the exactions of the brigands had paralyzed the economy of the frontier provinces.[80]

By the Summer of 1824, brigandage and *Settarj* terrorism had led to a virtual collapse of public security and of the authority of the state over a wide area. Leo, deciding that drastic measures were necessary, appointed as Legates *à latere*, with extraordinary powers, two prominent *Zelanti*: Cardinal Rivarola to deal with the Sects, and Cardinal Pallotta to extirpate the brigands.[81]

Neither was a happy choice for missions requiring a delicate combination of vigor and tact. Pallotta's failure was total: unable to track down the brigands, he attempted to undercut them by striking at their accomplices among the peasantry; but his harsh and arbitrary measures seemed to strike the innocent more often than the guilty. Moreover, his arrogance soon alienated the local authorities and gentry. A chorus of protest from local notables and officials soon forced Leo to admit his mistake, and in midsummer of 1824 Pallotta was recalled.

Rivarola's failure was more protracted, but equally complete, and in the long run more serious for the Papal regime. He set about his mission with great vigor; but he shared the tendency to ignore legal forms that was all too common among Papal officials, and proceeded with inquisitorial methods that both discredited his results and further weakened public confidence in the justice of the government. Moreover, he failed to disrupt the organization of the Sects in the only effective way—through the arrest of their leaders—for his numerous arrests struck only the underlings. The leaders went undetected, or escaped due to timely warnings from sympathizers in the local government: striking proof of the moral weakness of the Papal regime in the Romagna. In August, 1825, Rivarola announced the sentencing of over five hundred *Settarj;* but virtually all were minor figures, and the excessive number of sentences together with the arbitrary nature of his proceedings enabled the *Settarj* to win sympathy as victims of persecution and to use his excesses as antigovernment propaganda. Rivarola was no more successful in his attempt to fight fire with fire by encouraging the pro-Papal secret societies, the *Sanfedisti.* These were too weak to be an effective counter to the Sects, and only added to the disorder by giving it something of the character of a civil war. Despite Rivarola's mission, then, the organization of the Sects in the Romagna remained intact, their hold on public opinion was if anything strengthened, and their activities suffered no check.

Metternich was kept well informed of these developments by his agents in Rome, who painted the situation there in somber colors: "the whole trend of the regime is retrograde," Apponyi reported, "aimed at restoring the state of affairs of a century or more ago."[82] In consequence, "though the government wishes to suppress the Sects, its policies and procedures have aroused general discontent..., which is all too easily exploited by the enemies of tranquillity to win support."[83] As the government could neither conciliate nor repress this discontent, the danger of revolution was growing.[84]

Metternich did not doubt the accuracy of these reports, nor did he differ with Apponyi's gloomy prognosis; yet, in contrast to the past, he made no attempt to persuade the Papacy to modify its policy. As he explained to Apponyi, "however unfortunate this policy may be for the future, it is not for us to seek to give it another direction, for it is not to a government such as that of Leo XII that we can venture to offer advice." The *Zelanti's* fundamental hostility to modern institutions was probably invincible in any case; but, given their long-standing distrust of Austria, advice from Vienna would be particularly ineffective. To approach Leo on so sensitive a matter would be counterproductive, increasing his suspicion of Austria without altering his course. Under these circumstances, "we must avoid anything that gives the appearance of interference, and limit ourselves to observing carefully the policy of the government." And in view of the probable consequences of Leo's policy, "we must keep ourselves in readiness to repress any outbreak that could endanger the tranquility of the peninsula."[85]

Only when some legitimate Austrian interest was so clearly involved that he could not be suspected of ulterior motives did Metternich attempt to influence Papal policy. This was the case, for example, with the brigands, who by the Summer of 1824 had grown so bold as to attack Austrian couriers and supply trains en route to the garrison in Naples. This threat to Austrian communications obviously could not be tolerated, especially since some of the brigands were reputed to be in league with the Sects, and the Chancellor asked the Papal government to take effective measures to end it.[86] But his request was ignored, and the attacks continued. In January, 1825, he felt obliged to make a new and stronger protest, demanding that Rome "take energetic measures of repression" and offering the cooperation of the Austrian garrison at Naples.[87] By this time Leo was so well aware of the gravity of the situation that he agreed to replace Pallotta with Monsignor Benvenuti—a confession of *Zelanti* failure, since this energetic young prelate had been a protege of Consalvi—and directed him to cooperate fully with the Austrian and Neapolitan forces. In the Spring of 1825 a full-scale joint campaign was mounted against the brigands, which made their operations so hazardous and unprofitable that those who were not hunted down were glad to accept an amnesty. By the end of the year brigandage had again become merely a local nuisance rather than a major threat to public security.[88]

Metternich walked more warily in regard to the Sects, in order not to arouse resentment and suspicion. In his "representations" to the Pope, he confined himself to expressing in general terms his alarm at the progress of the Sects and his hope that the Pope would deal with them firmly, in cooperation with the other governments of Italy.[89] His pessimism was justified: Leo and Della Somaglia, ignoring his suggestions, replied only that they were aware of the danger and had sent Rivarola to deal with it.[90]

Rebuffed by Leo, the Chancellor, next sought to influence Papal policy through Monsignor Bernetti, the rising young prelate who as Governor of Rome was in charge of the Papal police. Metternich directed Gennotte—in charge at Palazzo Venezia while Apponyi was on a mission to Naples—to win Bernetti's confidence, so that through the Governor's efforts "the Papal government will abandon the reserve it has constantly maintained towards us since the death of Pius VII" and return to Consalvi's policy of cooperation against the Sects, particularly by resuming the exchange of information.[91] Bernetti's response was friendly, if alarming. He agreed that the danger from the Sects was growing, and that the measures taken against them so far were inadequate. He had frequently urged Leo to take more effective steps, and would continue to do so, but thus far his advice had been ignored. Leo seemed to underestimate the danger from the Sects. Bernetti promised to do what he could against the *Settarj*, but his means were limited, since Leo was diverting revenue from the civil government to his religious projects. However, he welcomed the idea of cooperation with Austria, provided it was kept secret; thereafter, he met weekly with Gennotte to exchange information on the Sects.[92] The information which Metternich thus gained was useful, but hardly reassuring. Leo continued to underestimate the danger, and to begrudge the money necessary to improve the police; in December, 1824, he went so far as to contemplate "suppressing the Department of Police as an economy measure." Only Bernetti's frantic protests dissuaded him.[93]

The year that followed saw no improvement: "never has there been less security than at the moment," Gennotte reported at the beginning of 1826. "Bernetti does his best . . . , but the ever-growing discontent combines with the weakness of the government to paralyze the action of the police."[94] Gennotte and Bernetti continued to exchange information, but no progress was made towards winning Leo's cooperation: the Pope was as distrustful of Austria as ever, fearing that cooperation against the Sects would lead to a Central Investigating Commission and thence to a Confederation.[95]

In this depressing situation Metternich, for lack of any better alternative, continued his policy of watchful waiting; but he had little hope of improvement in Leo's policies, and seems to have resigned himself to awaiting the next conclave to secure change for the better. In any case, relations with Rome had receded to the back of his mind, for his attention was now concentrated on events elsewhere—in France, the Iberian Peninsula, and the Near East.

But in the Summer of 1825, his attention was recalled to Rome by a series of alarming reports from Gennotte, describing a trend in Leo's policy that threatened not only to embitter Austro-Papal relations, but to undermine the conservative front on which the Restoration order rested. The Ultramontane Crisis, the turning point of Leo's reign, was at hand.

3. *The Ultramontane Crisis*

As we have seen, a principal reason for Metternich's hostility to the *Zelanti* was fear of their religious principles, which might lead them, once in power, into policies dangerous to the Restoration order, whether in the form of an effort to revive the Church's medieval authority over society—a move which would alienate enlightened opinion—or in the more immediately dangerous form of an assault on regalism in general and Josephism in particular.[96]

Metternich had found Leo's first year reassuring on this score. Experienced diplomat that he was, Leo knew too well the balance of strength between Rome and the Powers to believe that a frontal assault on the state churches could succeed. So far as Josephism was concerned, he apparently soon came to share Consalvi's belief that the best hope of overcoming it was a policy of religious moderation aimed at winning the Emperor's good will. To the disgust of those who had elected him, Leo avoided criticizing Josephism openly and sought a friendly settlement of the various minor religious questions—rearrangements of diocesan boundaries, appointments to bishoprics, etc.—that arose.[97]

Anxious to encourage this conciliatory attitude, Metternich resumed his cautious chipping away at the state church system, in whose weakening he saw the best means of regaining Austro-Papal cooperation. As usual, progress was made with glacial slowness: Francis I was averse as ever to drastic or sudden changes, and his Josephist advisers still contested every concession to Rome. Nonetheless, the trend of Imperial religious policy continued to be away from Josephism. The Jesuits had been on the verge of leaving the Empire because Josephist legislation forbade them to communicate with their General at Rome and interfered with their traditional teaching methods and discipline; now Francis I not only permitted them to follow their traditional methods and to communicate with Rome, but encouraged them to open new schools.[98] Other religious orders banned by Joseph II were allowed to reenter the Empire. Control of the seminaries was returned to the bishops, religious instruction in schools and universities was increased, the obligatory use of books on the Index was discontinued, and certain professors who had taught "perverse doctrines" critical of the Papacy or Catholic dogma were dismissed.[99] And Rome might expect greater things in the future: at the end of 1825, Metternich explained to the Nuncio that Francis I had definitely turned against Josephism and was resolved to abolish it; however, "he sees that this cannot be done at one stroke . . . , without causing a great uproar," so he planned to "weaken it gradually so that in time it will collapse by itself."[100]

As intended, the changes in Austrian religious policy impressed Leo and strengthened his belief that a moderate policy would produce better results than the intransigence urged by his *Zelanti* advisers.[101] But in 1825 Leo came under the influence of a new, and from Metternich's standpoint, very dangerous religious current which was now beginning to manifest itself at Rome: the ultramontane movement associated with Lamennais.

The career of Lamennais is too well known to require description here.[102] The Breton Abbé was at this time in a stage of transition from his original position as a conventional Catholic ultraconservative, defender of the Union of Throne and Altar along lines which De Maistre had made familiar, to his post-1830 role as prophet of liberal Catholicism. By 1823 he was becoming disenchanted with the Restoration monarchies, which he had at first hoped would crush the revolution and guide society back to a stable order based on Catholic principles. This hope was incompatible with the nature of the Restoration order, which was based not on an antirevolutionary crusade, but on an attempt at compromise between the revolution and the Old Regime. Lamennais disdained this compromise, regarding it as disastrous for both society and the Church. It was disastrous for European society because it allowed the germs of revolution to survive eventually to break forth in an outbreak of even greater dimensions. The Restoration order was equally harmful to the Church, from which Restoration monarchs demanded much—its full cooperation against revolution as well as its acquiescence in the loss of much of its property and its former role in society—but gave little in return. Not only did such monarchies as France and Austria grant civil equality to Protestants and Jews, making a truly Catholic society impossible, and refuse the Church the monopoly of education and censorship which he considered necessary to inculcate sound Catholic principles; worse yet, they would not give the Church real freedom of action so that it could spread its message to the people, but hampered it by a maze of regulations and restrictions.[103]

Therefore, Lamennais was coming to believe, it would be best for the Church to cut itself free from the domineering and doomed Restoration monarchies. National churches must abandon their reliance upon the state and turn to Rome for leadership, while the Pope in turn must rely for support not upon a Union of Throne and Altar, but upon popular religious devotion. Lamennais was not yet by any means an admirer of democracy; as of 1823–1826, his political ideal was a sort of theocratic authoritarianism. But he realized that, however irreligious the intellectuals and the bourgeoisie might be, the masses were still devout. Properly stimulated and guided, this popular devotion, would provide the Church with a far more solid support than the decaying monarchies, whose downfall the Church would survive to become the moral guide of postrevolutionary society. The Papacy could then proceed to reconstruct the social order on the basis of Christian principles, which alone could ensure stability. The first task of the Church, therefore, must be to cut its ties with the monarchical order—thereby dissolving the Union of Throne and Altar dear to earlier clerical-conservative publicists and to Metternich—and set out on a new autonomous course.

This curious mixture of reactionary and forward-looking elements, presented with all Lamennais's romantic enthusiasm and literary skill, won some converts in France; but it also made him many enemies. He was increasingly regarded with suspicion by the government, the French hierarchy, the still-numerous Gallicans, and by conservatives in general who sought to use the Church to strengthen the established order.[104] Faced with this hostility, Lamennais looked to Rome for support. In 1824, partly to assure himself of Papal approval, partly to spread his ideas, Lamennais visited Rome. He found that his ideas had preceded him and had already become the dominant influence on the Italian ultramontane movement.[105]

This movement emerged as a reaction to the 1820 revolutions. Previously, the Restoration order in Italy had seemed too secure to be in pressing need of intellectual defense. The transient revolutionary success of that year dispelled such comfortable optimism and an energetic counterrevolutionary movement emerged at Naples, Turin, and Modena, where it conducted an active propaganda inspired by French ultramontanism.[106]

By 1823, Lamennais's ideas were widely accepted in the movement, and were vigorously championed by its most gifted leader, Gioacchino Ventura. This Sicilian priest, a vigorous polemicist, had first become prominent at Naples in 1821 as editor of a counterrevolutionary journal noted for its bitter criticism not only of liberalism, but also of those conservatives, like Metternich, who did not seem sufficiently fanatical and uncompromising in their detestation of revolution and its works. This extremism aroused the distrust of the Neapolitan government and its Austrian protectors, as did Ventura's ultramontanism, and the journal was suppressed in late 1822.[107]

Leo's election brought new hope to Ventura, as it did to ultramontanes in general, who hoped to find in him the new Gregory VII who would revivify Papal authority. Ventura hastened to establish himself in Rome, which he dreamed of making the center of a far-reaching propaganda activity along Lamennesian lines, aimed at the missionary reconquest of society for Catholicism, which alone could save society from the revolutionary peril.[108]

The opening stages of the pontificate did nothing to dampen these hopes. Leo's reactionary policy in the Papal State was encouraging, as was his attack on the Sects through the Rivarola mission. Still greater enthusiasm was aroused by Leo's first encyclicals: *Ubi Primum* of May 5, 1824, which condemned religious indifference in terms gratifyingly reminiscent of Lamennais, and *Quod Divina Sapientia* of May 17, 1824, which reorganized the educational system of the Papal State to make its primary function the inculcation of sound moral and religious principles.[109] The most striking demonstration of Leo's affinity for the ultramontane program was his proclamation, in May, 1824, that 1825 would be a Holy Year, in which pilgrims from the whole Catholic world might come to Rome to participate in spiritual exercises under Papal auspices; here, it seemed, in a great spiritual initiative aimed at reviving Papal contact with the masses, was an unmistakable sign that Leo intended to implement Lamennais's program.[110]

Against this encouraging background Lammenais in 1824 journeyed through Italy, receiving an enthusiastic welcome from his disciples in the leading ultramontane centers. At Rome he was given a very cordial welcome by Leo XII, who had several discussions with him and seems to have expressed sympathy with his aims and principles; this occasioned much comment, and even the rumor that Leo planned to name Lamennais a cardinal.[111]

Under these favorable circumstances, Lamennais's ideas prospered at Rome, and Ventura began to make headway with his plans. In 1825, he found a new vehicle for his ultramontane message, this time under the direct patronage of the Pope, with the foundation of the *Giornale Ecclesiastico*, of which he was the guiding spirit. Here Ventura poured forth his Lamennesian ideas in a series of fervent articles that aroused great interest.[112] To remove any doubt that his ideas met with Papal approval, Ventura was appointed in October, 1825, to the chair of ecclesiastical civil law at the Sapienza—the Papal university in Rome—which provided him with both an important official position and a new means of propagating his theories.

But the Lamennesian variety of ultramontanism was not everywhere so enthusiastically received, even in conservative circles. Hostility was growing fast at the Catholic courts, notably at Vienna. The first manifestations of the ultramontane movement at Rome aroused little Austrian concern. After describing them in 1824, Apponyi added confidently that such "petty matters" deserved little attention, since they would "not harm the interests of the great Powers."[113] Metternich apparently agreed; at least, neither in his correspondence with Apponyi nor in his conversations with the Vienna Nuncio in 1824 did he so much as mention the subject. Even Lamennais's visit to Rome was mentioned only casually by Gennotte and elicited no comment from Metternich.[114] Apparently, as long as the Roman ultramontane movement seemed harmless to the Austrian religious system and the Restoration order, the Chancellor saw no reason to act against it, despite his habitual distrust of religious enthusiasm and mysticism.[115] The announcement of the Holy Year attracted Metternich's attention only from a political standpoint: the influx of pilgrims from all lands might allow the Sects to move freely into the Papal State and concealed among the multitudes of pilgrims, carry out their plots.[116] When Leo agreed to take appropriate precautions against this danger, Metternich lost interest in the subject.[117]

Not until May, 1825, was Metternich roused from his indifference by the arrival of the first of a series of alarming reports from Gennotte. Leo, the chargé reported, had come under the influence of the ultramontanes, whom Gennotte described as a "party of fanatics" whose ideas revived "the principles of Gregory VII." The ultramontanes were engaged in a vast work of propaganda whose ultimate goal was to realize the medieval claim to supreme authority for the Pope in temporal as well as spiritual matters. The Holy Year had been designed to bring enthusiastic Catholics from all over Europe to Rome so that, having been indoctrinated there, they might return to their homelands to spread ultramontane ideas. An accelerating work of recruitment by the religious orders had the same end: "the youth of all lands are being recruited to spread Papal principles." The success of these operations "surpasses all expectations," encouraging the ultramontanes to "claim that they will need only five more years to regain all the influence and all the alleged rights of the Holy See." Their aims were "no longer a mystery, for they have just been revealed" in a series of articles by Ventura in the *Giornale Ecclesiastico*. Encouraged by the Pope and inspired by Lamennais, Ventura's articles "revive outdated Papal claims..., and deny sovereigns any rights *circa sacra*." What made the *Giornale* particularly dangerous was that it was written with great skill so as to "influence the unenlightened multitude and inculcate it with the principles of the court of Rome," with the obvious intent of using popular religious fanaticism as the basis for a revived Papal authority.

Further evidence of this alarming plan was furnished by the works recently published at Rome, with the approval of the censors, by the renowned antiquary, Abbé Fea. The first of these attacked the French government for upholding the Four Articles of 1682, the cornerstone of the regalist claim to sovereign authority in religious affairs; it was so written as to "have little effect on the educated, but a great impact on the ignorant masses." This was truer of Fea's second work, which bore the alarming title *Ultimatum per il dominio indiretto della Santa Sede sul Temporale dei Sovrani*. Gennotte described it as "in a word, the apotheosis of Gregory VII and a defense of his principles." The other diplomats at Rome were equally dismayed, and the Russian minister had already joined Gennotte in complaining to Della Somaglia, who professed himself unaware of Fea's works and seemed critical of them.[118]

Gennotte's report was the work of an old Josephist who had long since taken to regarding Papal policy in the most sinister light, and his account was certainly exaggerated, as Metternich probably realized. The recruitment by the religious orders was no more than a continuation of their long-term effort to augment their numbers after the heavy losses of the revolutionary era. Fea's pamphlets were the works of an unwordly octogenarian scholar unaware of their potential political impact; they had been approved because the censor, a dying man, had not bothered to read them. Gennotte tended to confuse the aims of the ultramontanes with their accomplishments—as events were to show, their influence was by no means as strong at the Papal court as they hoped and Gennotte feared.

Nonetheless, a substratum of fact certainly underlay Gennotte's exaggerations: the ultramontane movement did exist, its influence at Rome was growing rapidly, and it did aim to overthrow sovereign authority in religious affairs, reject the Union of Throne and Altar, and revived Papal authority on a basis of popular religious enthusiasm. So much was obvious to Metternich from the copies of the *Giornale* which Gennotte sent him. Ultramontanism was a reality, and one which he could not ignore, for it posed a even more dangerous threat to his policies, to Austrian interests, and to the Restoration order than the older *Zelantismo* which it seemed to be supplanting.

The immediate reason for Metternich's hostility to the ultramontane movement was the threat it posed to Austro-Papal relations. Not only was the movement consciously hostile to the Union of Throne and Altar on which his policy was based, but its uncompromising assertion of Papal authority and its active opposition to regalism would inevitably lead the Papacy into a more critical attitude towards the Austrian religious system, probably into open war against it. The result would be a church-state quarrel of epic proportions, which would be fatal to Metternich's plans. All the motives that impelled Metternich to seek Austro-Papal cooperation necessarily impelled him to oppose ultramontanism.[119]

But the danger from the ultramontane movement was even greater than this, for it imperilled not only Austro-Papal relations, but the stability of the Restoration order. The movement implied an assault on regalism that would lead to a major church-state conflict not only in Austria, but throughout Catholic Europe. The Papacy, which in Metternich's opinion should be the firmest support of the established order, would instead become its foe; only the revolutionary movement would profit. Moreover, the anachronistic revival of old Papal claims to an authority of medieval dimensions would surely antagonize not only liberals, but also many conservatives whose latent anticlericalism—laid aside in the interests of the counterrevolutionary struggle—would revive. The outcome would be a fatal split in the conservative front as ultramontanes and anticlericals fought among themselves, while liberals used the conflict to win support and freedom of action. Conceivably, the downfall of the Restoration order might ensue.[120]

Metternich's fears may seem to have been exaggerated; but that the danger was not imaginary was soon to be demonstrated in France, where Lamennais's bitter attack on the Gallican church and its association with the monarchy was leading to just such consequences. As old Gallican fears and hostilities revived, many even of the conservative aristocracy joined in the assault on the position of the church, an assault in which the government—partly from fear of ultramontanism, partly to conciliate public opinion—felt obliged to participate. The result was a rupture of the conservative front as Gallicans and ultramontanes turned on each other, to the sole benefit of the liberals, placing the Bourbon monarchy in an impossible position and initiating that rapid weakening of its hold on public opinion which paved the way for the July Revolution.[121]

If the ultramontanes were able to consolidate their influence over Leo XII to the point where he would be ready to act openly in their favor, the tragedy enacted in France would be repeated throughout Catholic Europe. That this did not take place was due in large part to Metternich's skillful intervention at Rome.

The Chancellor certainly had compelling reasons to intervene, but he proceeded with caution, anxious not to arouse a counterproductive resentment. Avoiding his formal channels of communication with Rome, he took up the question informally with Albani—who could be relied upon to handle it skillfully and precisely as Metternich wished—when the Cardinal paid a courtesy visit to the Emperor at Milan in May, 1825. Giving no hint that Austria felt alarm for her own sake, Metternich spoke as one concerned only for the welfare of religion and the Papacy. He concentrated his fire on Fea's works, the most extreme and so the most vulnerable public manifestation of ultramontanism to date. Gravely warning of the harm which they had done to the religious situation in France and to the progress of Catholic emancipation in England, he advised Rome in its own interest to prevent the appearance of such works in the future.[122]

Much impressed by Albani's report of this conversation, Della Somaglia hastened to reassure Metternich that Fea's works had been published only by accident and did not represent the views of Rome, which was determined to follow a policy of religious moderation and cooperation with the courts.[123] This assertion was certainly true in so far as Della Somaglia himself was concerned, for the Secretary of State was an opponent of ultramontanism, fearing the quarrels which it would breed with the Powers: "the Papacy has already too many enemies with whom it cannot avoid conflict for it to seek imprudently to procure others by borrowing needless quarrels."[124]

Whatever calming effect Della Somaglia's reply may have had on Metternich was dissipated when a visit to France in the Summer of 1825 enabled him to observe for himself the effects of the ultramontane attack on Gallicanism. Passing through Genoa on his return, he took advantage of a meeting with the Archbishop, Lambruschini, to warn of the "immense damage" to religion, church-state relations, and the conservative cause in France that Lamennais and his followers had done by their "fanatical attacks" upon Gallicanism; if the Pope gave his approval to the ultramontane movement—or even if he merely appeared to do so by such *faux pas* as permitting the publication of Fea's works—similar attacks would soon be launched throughout Catholic Europe, with similar consequences but on a vastly wider scale.[125]

Metternich's alarm continued to grow during 1825. In France, Lamennais published the first volume of his *De la religion considerée dans ses rapports avec l'ordre politique*, his most bitter public denunciation of the Restoration Order thus far. Condemning Gallicanism, he urged the French clergy to break with the "atheistic" state and turn instead to the Papacy, to which he ascribed supreme authority in political as well as religious matters. The overthrow of the Restoration Order by a new and more violent revolution was at hand, he predicted, but the church, if led by the Pope and based on popular rather than royal support, would survive to become the architect of a new society. The infuriated Gallicans launched a fierce counterattack, in which the liberals enthusiastically joined. A gaping rent opened in conservative ranks in France, as what had begun as a Gallican attack on ultramontanism was guided by the liberals into a full-scale assault on the church and its relationship with the Bourbon monarchy, which served as the thin end of the wedge for an attack on the monarchy itself.[126]

With this example of the effects of ultramontanism before him, Metternich was inevitably dismayed at the reports which Gennotte continued to send him on the progress of the movement at Rome.[127] Ventura's articles in the *Giornale* were attracting wide attention, but scandalizing conservatives and the diplomatic corps by their critical attitude towards the monarchies. He had won over many of his students and colleagues at the Sapienza, and was now planning to publish his lectures to bring them to a wider audience. Many prominent figures in the Curia had expressed sympathy with the ultramontanes. A society to spread ultramontane principles had been organized with official approval, and a *Biblioteca Cattolica* founded with Papal support to publish translations of the works of Lamennais and his school. To the panicky Gennotte, the ultramontane tide seemed irresistible.[128]

Though Metternich discounted Gennotte's exaggerations, he stepped up his effort to turn Leo against ultramontanism by contrasting its dangers with the solid advantages of cooperation with the Powers. During the Fall of 1825, he dispatched a stream of subordinates to meet informally with the Internuncio, Monsignor Ostini, and warn him of the harm that ultramontanism was doing: at Vienna it was strengthening the hand of the Josephists and causing "distrust and bitterness" even to "those most attached to the Holy See," such as the Chancellor.[129] Having thus prepared the ground, Metternich himself visited the Internuncio to discuss the reform of the Austrian religious system. After reviewing all that had thus far been accomplished to weaken Josephism, he explained that Francis I, impressed by Leo's "wisdom and moderation," had decided to abolish the state church system completely, though gradually, over the next few years—if the Papacy continued in its present wise course. Ostini saw the point: Papal moderation would keep the Emperor in his present path, while ultramontane extremism would drive him back to Josephism.[130] Nor was the point lost on Della Somaglia, who assured Metternich that the ideas of the ultramontanes did not represent official policy: Leo, he asserted, only tolerated them "from a just regard for those who err only from an excess of zeal." In any case, opposition to the movement was growing at Rome.[131]

On this last point at least, Della Somaglia was correct. The surviving Consalvians, men like Spina, had long been hostile, and they were now joined by those *Zelanti* who, like Pacca, distrusted the popular side of Lamennais's doctrine, or who, like Della Somaglia and Bernetti, were concerned to preserve good relations with the courts.[132] That ultramontanism threatened those relations was increasingly obvious, for Austria was not the only Power to express concern and disapproval. France—or at least its Ambassador—had initially favored the ultramontanes, apparently regarding them, like the *Zelanti*, as natural allies against Austrian influence;[133] but the religious controversy stirred up by Lamennais in France had led to an abrupt reversal, and by 1826 France had prohibited the entry of the *Giornale* and was making clear its displeasure with ultramontane influence at Rome.[134] Russia and Prussia had long been critical; the Dutch government, alarmed and suspicious, contemplated breaking off its negotiations for a concordat, while in England the rise of the ultramontane movement was cited by opponents of Catholic emancipation as evidence of Papal intransigence and claims to political supremacy.[135] The general disapproval of the courts caused Leo to waver in his support for ultramontanism, the more so as other arguments against it were accumulating. He was disillusioned by the results of the Holy Year, whose impact had been largely limited to Italy instead of serving as the springboard for the missionary reconquest of Europe, as the ultramontanes had predicted.[136] Moreover, he was alarmed by the religious controversy that Lamennais's pronouncements had touched off in France, and the subsequent weakening of the church and the conservative cause there. However, his sympathies with the movement were still strong, his personal relationship with Ventura remained close, and he made no effort to restrict ultramontane activities at Rome.

Metternich, kept informed of Leo's waverings by Gennotte, maintained a steady pressure on Rome via frequent warnings to the Internuncio. For example, when Ostini came in April, 1826, to thank him for the recent Imperial suppression of antipapal textbooks, which he had secured, Metternich replied that this was only a minor step in the Emperor's plans, which were aimed at abolishing Josephism. Unfortunately, this policy was now being endangered by Ventura and his associates, whose works liberals and Josephists alike were already quoting as evidence that the Papacy wished to dominate state and society.[137]

Against this background of steady Austrian pressure, the ultramontane crisis was brought to its climax by the appearance of declarations by the Irish and French hierarchies. The Irish declaration, issued in January, 1826 by the Primate and twenty-two bishops, appeared in the context of the struggle for emancipation by Irish Catholics, then at its height but hampered by English prejudices. The declaration was intended to refute these prejudices, and consisted of a solemn denial that Catholics held that the Virgin Mary deserved divine honors, that all non-Catholics were damned, etc. However, it also contained a declaration of political loyalty to the government, firmly denying that the Pope could claim supremacy over sovereigns in temporal affairs. Though this too was essentially a response to English suspicions, coming as it did at the height of the ultramontane crisis it was seen as a deliberate rejection of Lamennais's claims for Papal authority. This implication was immediately grasped by the ultramontanes, who urged Leo to condemn the declaration.[138]

Meanwhile, in March of 1826, Lamennais brought out the second volume of his *De la religion considerée...*; still more uncompromising than the first in its denunciation of Gallicanism, state control over the church, and the Union of Throne and Altar, it provoked an even more violent reaction. French liberals seized upon it as proof of the dangerous extremism of the clergy and stepped up their offensive against the church and the monarchy which supported it. Partly from genuine anger, partly in the hope of disarming the liberal offensive, the government brought Lamennais to trial for criticizing the ecclesiastical laws of the state. Simultaneously, at government urging, the French episcopate issued in April, 1826, a declaration denouncing Lamennais's ideas, proclaiming their own loyalty to the Gallican principle of total state independence from the authority of the church, and calling upon the King to warn the Pope against ultramontane activity.[139]

The French declaration, following hard upon the Irish, precipitated a crisis at Rome. When the French Ambassador presented the declaration to Leo, the Pope received it in complete silence, though with obvious displeasure.[140] His reserve reflected the conflict then raging both in his mind and in his councils as to the proper way to react to the declarations, which involved the greater issue of the Papal attitude towards Lamennais and towards the relationship between church and state. For three years Leo had edged gradually closer to ultramontanism, without ever giving it his full support; at once attracted to its program and fearful of its consequences. Now Ventura and his allies sought to persuade Leo to commit the Papacy openly to their cause by formally condemning the declarations.[141]

Leo's sympathy for the ultramontanes was still great, and he was much offended by the declarations with—as he saw it—their gratuitous criticism of Papal authority. But he could not fail to see the dangers of a condemnation: it would represent a virtual declaration of war on the monarchies, and inaugurate a struggle of incalculable dimensions whose outcome might well prove disastrous. The results of recent church-state conflicts did not encourage optimism. The declarations had also brought home to him that he could not rely upon the support of the national hierarchies in a showdown with the state. As for the popular support which the ultramontanes anticipated, after the limited success of the Holy Year Leo could hardly be confident that it would be forthcoming in sufficient strength to safeguard the Papacy. In any case, a church-state conflict under existing circumstances would surely weaken the conservative cause throughout Europe, as it had already done in France.

Swayed by these conflicting arguments, torn between his hopes for a great spiritual renewal of European society under Papal leadership and his realistic appreciation of Papal weakness in a confrontation with the Powers, Leo hesitated; but by May the ultramontanes seemed to have gained the upper hand. In his most alarming dispatch to date, Gennotte explained that "the fanatics have succeeded in convincing the Holy Father that it is necessary...to condemn the declarations and the principles contained therein;" all that remained was to decide on the form which the condemnation should take. The condemnation would be a deliberate challenge to the rulers of Europe, intended to "propagate and establish the principle of the supremacy of the spiritual power over the temporal."[142]

Upon receiving this report, Metternich decided that he must act before the Pope could take a step that would have fatal consequences. He at once saw the Internuncio, and—more agitated than Ostini had ever seen him—delivered a stern warning against the disastrous mistake which Leo seemed resolved to make:

Here is the Pope throwing himself into battle with the governments on a point so delicate that they can never yield. Here is the Pope throwing himself into battle with his own bishops.... The liberals, who were reduced to silence by the declarations, will now arise again, exulting at the discrediting of ecclesiastical authority.... What can I say now to the diehard supporters of the Josephist laws, who are thus provided once more with plausible arguments, when, regaining the courage they had partly lost, they advise the Emperor to uphold those laws and beware of the Pope? I, who had set to work to have these laws abolished, and had by infinite labor won over His Majesty, must now reluctantly yield to the Josephists and break with the Pope. I am utterly appalled. Here end the affairs so well begun of the texts used in the schools, of religious instruction, and those which would have followed, such as the marriage laws: the opposition... will now become insurmountable. What can the Emperor reply to those who seek to dissuade him from agreeing to the requests of the Holy Father, when they tell him that the days of Pius VII are past..., and now fanaticism reigns at Rome?

The Chancellor continued in this vein, with growing agitation, for over an hour, and Ostini was unable to calm him; his feeble attempts to defend Leo were brushed aside by Metternich, who repeated his warning and departed.[143] On the same day, Metternich instructed Gennotte to warn Leo "in the strongest language" that his policy would "bring ruin to Throne and Altar alike."[144]

Metternich's outburst, which represented both genuine horror at Leo's policy and a calculated effort to persuade him to alter it, crystallized the Pope's doubts as to the wisdom of an ultramontane policy. Whether Leo would otherwise have committed himself to ultramontanism must remain unknown—though he had certainly seemed to be moving in that direction—but as it was, Metternich's skillfully timed and phrased intervention, coming as it did at the moment when the issue hung in the balance, proved decisive.[145] Within a week the fate of the ultramontane movement had been decided.

Reluctantly, without abandoning his sympathy for Lamennais and Ventura, but convinced that their policy involved risks that were too great, Leo retreated from his earlier support. In June, 1826, he abandoned the plan to condemn the declarations, placed restrictions on the *Giornale*, and began a campaign to convince the Powers of Papal moderation.[146]

Metternich, naturally, was the first target of this campaign. Ostini was instructed, "by express order of the Holy Father," to "tranquilize Prince Metternich." He was to declare that Leo had no intention of condemning the declarations or of aligning himself with the ultramontanes. Metternich need not fear that Leo would ever "stray from the path of moderation;" thus reassured, Leo hoped, the Prince would feel able to proceed with his plans "to consolidate the alliance between the Holy See and the Empire for the triumph of the common cause" in confidence that "his wise policy will never have anyone who will support it with a more sincere and energetic zeal than His Holiness."[147]

Ostini promptly read these instructions to Metternich, whom they "filled with joy."[148] To confirm the Pope in his decision, Metternich described his latest victory over the Josephists—persuading Francis I to remove certain Josephist texts and professors from the seminaries—and his plans for reforming the marriage laws, adding that "only the moderation of the Holy Father will make this success possible." Ostini advised Della Somaglia that "the time has come to heal the wounds inflicted by Joseph II; we have the best Emperor possible, and a minister who seconds him effectively." Surely cooperation with Austria and the abandonment of ultramontanism were a small price to pay for such an achievement.

Leo agreed: to the protest against ultamontanism which Gennotte delivered in early June, as Metternich had ordered, the Pope replied that he would remove all cause for suspicion by suppressing all ultramontane activity at Rome, and, moreover, would soon give the Powers a "striking demonstration" of his good will and wish for cooperation.[149]

This demonstration took the form of a special diplomatic mission to reassure the courts—Vienna, St. Petersburg, Berlin, and Paris—as to Leo's renunciation of ultramontanism. The mission was entrusted to Bernetti—the rising sun of the Curia, now growing steadily in influence—who had taken a leading role in opposing ultramontanism. His first stop was Vienna, where he arrived on June 19, 1826. After a long conversation with Metternich—of which, apparently, no record exists, but whose central topic was undoubtedly ultramontanism—Bernetti presented the Emperor with a personal letter from the Pope, which praised the Emperor's plans for dismantling Josephism, denied all sympathy for ultramontanism, and promised moderation in all religious affairs.[150]

This letter marked Leo's formal break with the ultramontane movement. With his abandonment of the dream of regaining for Rome the spiritual hegemony of European society through an appeal to popular religious sentiment, a turning point had been reached in his reign, and in the history of the Restoration Papacy. Hereafter, Leo made cooperation with the Powers in defense of the Restoration Order the cornerstone of his policy—a policy that would long be followed by his successors. The reverse side of the coin was that henceforth Rome became increasingly distrustful of any tendency towards a liberal or popular interpretation of Catholicism. In the ultramontanism of the 1820s, reactionary elements certainly predominated; nonetheless, it contained the potential for developing in a more progressive sense, as Lamennais's later career was to demonstrate so dramatically. His disillusionment with the restoration monarchies drove Lamennais inexorably towards reliance upon popular forces, and hence towards the democratic liberalism which he championed after 1830. Had his ultramontanism prevailed at Rome, this tendency towards a more liberal position would surely have affected the policy of the Papacy, bringing it into closer harmony with the dominant spirit of the nineteenth century, and thus preventing or at least attenuating that fatal split between Rome and the progressive forces of the age which was to have such detrimental effects on Catholicism.

By renouncing ultramontanism, Leo closed off this potentially fruitful line of development, and placed the Papacy instead on the path of rigid and suspicious ultraconservatism that, with brief interludes, it would follow for the better part of a century. His successors lacked even his genuine, if fruitless, sympathy for Lamennais. After 1826, disillusioned by Leo's repudiation, Lamennais evolved in a direction more liberal but less propapal; by 1834 his alienation had reached the point where he was prepared to break with Rome rather than abandon his liberalism. Simultanously, as the Papacy became increasingly committed to alliance with the Powers, it became increasingly suspicious of his liberalism, to the point where Gregory XVI was prepared to drive Lamennais from the Church if he would not abandon his ideas. So far as relations between Lamennais and the Papacy were concerned, then, Leo's decision of 1826 was final. The outcome of Lamennais's famous appeal to Gregory XVI in 1831 was predetermined by the evolution of the Papal attitude which followed logically from Leo's decision, just as Lamennais's willingness to defy Rome was the end-product of his own evolution provoked by that decision. Thus, the crisis of 1831-1834 and its resolution were merely the confirmation of Leo's decision of 1826.

Yet, if Leo did cut short a line of development that might have proven beneficial to the Church, his decision was a natural one, quite comprehensible in the context of the Restoration. Metternich had not exaggerated when he warned Leo of the dangerous consequences of an ultramontane policy: a prolonged conflict with the Powers, in which the Papacy would be the weaker party by far; a conflict with many of the upper clergy, whose defection would weaken Papal authority over the Church; the revival of regalism in all its forms, and the loss of the present opportunity to restore Papal authority over the state churches; finally, the splitting of the conservative front, the strengthening of liberalism—which, it must be remembered, was strongly anticlerical, so that its victory would surely lead to a new assault upon Catholicism[151]—and perhaps the downfall of the Restoration order in a new revolution. These were risks that no responsible pope could lightly undertake—especially since it was clear that the masses of Catholic Europe, devout though they might be, were not yet so well organized and articulate as to provide the Papacy with a source of strength sufficient to enable it to fight on two fronts simultaneously: against the Restoration monarchs on the one hand, and the anticlerical liberals on the other. In such a conflict—which the commitment to ultramontanism sought by Ventura would have made unavoidable—the prospects for Papal victory were dim.

Leo's decision, then, made sense; where he—or, more accurately, his successors—erred, was in the extent to which they carried it. Leo himself never lost his personal sympathy with the Lamennesian cause, and maintained private contacts with its leaders;[152] but Pius VIII, who followed him, was unreservedly hostile, and the attitude of Gregory XVI is too well known to need description here.[153] Yet, in the transformed circumstances produced by the revolution of 1830, the drawbacks of Papal support for Lamennais were less grave, and the potential benefits more plausible, than had been the case in 1826. His ideas then deserved more serious and sympathetic consideration at Rome than they received; but by that time, especially after the shock of the 1831 revolt in the Papal State, hostility to Lamennais and the policy of participation in the conservative alliance were too well entrenched for the Papacy to contemplate abandoning them for a more liberal attitude.

To return to 1826: after the crisis in June, Leo proceeded as he had promised to liquidate Roman ultramontanism. The *Giornale Ecclesiastico* was given into safely conservative hands; ultramontanes were eliminated from positions of influence at Rome; strict censorship was applied to ultramontane works; and finally, in October, 1826, Ventura was removed from his position at the Sapienza and banished from Rome—with a pension and an expression of Papal regret, but banished nevertheless.[154]

Metternich followed the liquidation of ultramontanism with triumphant satisfaction, for, whatever regret it may have caused Leo, it was for Metternich an unadulterated victory, which had removed a major threat to his policies and to the Restoration Order, and consolidated Papal participation in the conservative front. Not the least cause of his satisfaction was that the way was now clear for the revival of Austro-Papal cooperation. The defeat of ultramontanism was the foundation on which Metternich rebuilt Austrian influence at Rome.[155]

4. Twilight of a Pontificate, 1826–1829

The last years of Leo's pontificate saw Austro-Papal relations grow steadily closer. Having once decided to reject ultramontanism in favor of cooperation with the Powers, Leo was naturally inclined to make a particular effort to cooperate with the Power which had persuaded him to make that decision; having accepted Metternich's advice then, he was more inclined to accept it in other matters. This inclination was strengthened by the decline of his confidence in France in the wake of the snowballing liberal assault on the French church, which the Bourbon regime apparently could find no way to meet except by concessions.[156] Leo was also displeased by French intervention on behalf of the Greek rebels, fearing that it would lead, in the short run, to Turkish persecution of Greek Catholics, and in the long run to an independent Greece in which Catholics would suffer persecution from the Orthodox majority.[157] Leo could not but appreciate the contrast—frequently pointed out by Metternich—between Austria's stand for peace and nonintervention in the Greek crisis, and the attitude of France, which, disregarding Leo's appeal to preserve the peace so as to prevent a massacre of Greek Catholics, took a prominent role against the Turks.[158] Moreover, once France had gone to war against the Sultan, she could no longer perform her traditional role as protector of Catholicism in the Near East, and Leo inevitably turned to Austria as a substitute. It was Austria whose influence halted a persecution of Armenian Catholics at Constantinople; Austria which persuaded the Sultan not to persecute his Catholic subjects in his fury at the Christian Powers; Austria whose consuls gave protection to local Catholic communities throughout the Empire. Leo's disappointment in France was matched by his gratitude to Austria.[159]

The decline of French influence at Rome was not halted even by the appointment of Chateaubriand as Ambassador in 1828; on the contrary, since his recent writings seemed to display sympathy with the liberal attack on the

French church, he was met with suspicion. Moreover, Chateaubriand was bitterly disappointed at not having been named Foreign Minister again, and regarded his appointment to Rome as merely a polite exile, whose end he eagerly awaited. To Metternich's relief, he displayed little energy in seeking to revive French influence.[160] His inactivity was doubly welcome to Metternich in view of the great writer's undeniable superiority in talent and prestige to the new Austrian ambassador, Count Lützow, who was earnest and conscientious, but without a shred of his opposite number's genius; had there been a serious contest between the two, Metternich could have had little optimism as to the outcome.[161]

The French decline certainly worked to Austria's advantage, but two other factors were of more fundamental significance in the revival of her influence at Rome: the favorable trend of Austrian religious policy, and the growing revolutionary agitation in the Papal State.

Leo's renunciation of ultramontanism had the desired effect on Francis I, who under Metternich's discreet prodding resumed his slow retreat from Josephism. The Jesuits—those *bêtes noires* of the Josephists—were given increased support for their existing establishments and encouraged to found others.[162] The purging of seminaries of antipapal or uncanonical instruction was carried forward with the elimination of offending texts and professors.[163] A drive against such instruction at the universities was also launched, and Francis I sought to stem irreligious tendencies there by requiring students to participate in numerous religious exercises; whether this strengthened either the devotion of the students or their enthusiasm for their ruler is open to question, but it did at least convince Rome of the Emperor's "exemplary piety."[164] Decrees for the reform of discipline among the regular clergy were issued, and their execution entrusted, not to the bureaucracy as in the past, but to the bishops.[165]

Though these measures were still comparatively minor, they served to provide Leo with proof of the Emperor's good intentions, and encouraged him to believe that more sweeping changes were being planned. Late in 1827, the new Vienna Nuncio, Monsignor Spinola, reported that the Emperor had at last decided to act on the *memoire* which Pius VII had given him in 1819. He planned to appoint a commission of ecclesiastics and legal experts, which, on the pretext of unifying religious legislation in a single code, would in fact modify the legislation so as to bring it into conformity with canon law. In this way, Spinola explained, Francis hoped to avoid the controversy that was inevitable if he attacked Josephism overtly. But the Nuncio warned against impatience, for though the Emperor would certainly move in the right direction, he would move slowly, and any attempt to hurry him would only "alarm the spirit of His Majesty." Instead, the Pope should offer lavish praise to the Emperor at every step forward, and "though seeming to speak only of that step, end by explaining in passing that the Holy Father, trusting in His Majesty's exemplary piety, hopes to see other effects of his zeal, without entering into specific details that might alarm or displease His Majesty."[166]

Spinola's warning was justified, for, as usual with Francis I, progress was exasperatingly slow, and the winter passed without the commission's being appointed.[167] Fortunately, Leo had taken Spinola's advice to heart: instead of showing impatience, he wrote to the Emperor in December, 1827, expressing his "holy joy" at Francis's recent measures, and mentioning in passing his confidence that Francis would carry through the "great object" of reforming Austrian religious legislation.[168] The letter made a good impression on the Emperor, who in reply promised that he would bring religious legislation fully into line with canon law.[169]

Meanwhile, Metternich was "acting with all diligence to bring the matter to a good end." Having failed to persuade Francis I to proceed directly to the reform of the religious laws without wasting time on a commission, he sought to spur him to action by presenting his own plan for a commission in April, 1828. The Emperor seemed favorable, but insisted upon obtaining the opinion of an expert in ecclesiastical law, and at Metternich's suggestion selected the Bishop of Leitmeritz to evaluate the plan. As Metternich had anticipated, the Bishop's report echoed his own opinion: the reform of religious law was imperative, but the appointment of a commission was unnecessary and would only cause delay. The Emperor should proceed to carry out the reform himself, disregarding whatever criticism the Josephists might make. Francis finally accepted this opinion in August, 1828. Metternich was jubilant: "the end is in sight!" he exulted to Spinola, declaring with great satisfaction that he would "show the world that what had seemed difficult, he could make easy."[170]

Metternich's boast was premature. Even though Francis seemed resolved to act on the *memoire* of 1819, he continued with instinctive caution to request the opinion upon it of various prelates; since each prelate took several months to draw up an answer, the process was still incomplete when Leo died in January, 1829.[171]

In any case, it was not only at Vienna that obstacles to the downfall of Josephism appeared. At Rome the more intransigent *Zelanti* still pressed for vigorous action against Austrian regalism. Leo consistently rebuffed their pressure and sought to keep them under control, but they managed at times to escape his vigilance and express their hostility in an anti-Austrian move, usually petty but still likely to annoy Vienna. In 1828, for example, a *Zelanti*-dominated congregation, acting without Leo's knowledge, placed upon the Index certain works by Bishop Frint, an influential adviser of Francis I. The condemnation was particularly offensive in that neither the writer nor the Imperial government had been previously informed that it was even under discussion. Francis I was irritated, and the Josephists sought to use the incident to revive his distrust of Rome. Warned by Metternich, Leo produced an acceptable explanation and a quasi apology; the condemnation was revoked, and the case was closed.[172] Such incidents did not check the steady improvement of Austro-Papal relations. Shortly before Leo's death, Francis assured Spinola that he was well satisfied with Leo's handling of religious policy and with his attitude towards Austria. Now that he had full confidence in the Pope, he would proceed with his plans for dismantling the Josephist system. All the ecclesiastics whom he had thus far consulted had approved his plans for reforming the religious laws, and the ultimate outcome would surely be satisfactory to the Pope.[173]

"For a long time now the Holy Father has received no news so encouraging as this," was the reply from Rome;[174] and indeed, in the closing months of his reign, Leo regarded the downfall of Josephism as imminent. The reorientation of Austrian religious policy produced a growing cordiality towards Vienna, which by 1829 was regarded at Rome with an approval unmatched since the early days of the Restoration. As early as February, 1828, Lützow reported that the Emperor's religious measures were rapidly dissipating Papal distrust: "even the most fanatical and exaggerated defenders of the rights of the Holy See admit" the Emperor's good intentions, while Leo and his advisers looked to him with "hope and confidence."

In the same report, Lützow indicated the second reason for the growth of Papal good will: Rome's increasing alarm over the growth of revolutionary sentiment in the Papal State, and the consequent realization that Austrian military aid might soon be needed to save the Temporal Power. This was rapidly eroding the second fundamental obstacle to good Austro-Papal relations: the old distrust of Austrian predominance in Italy, which now seemed less a threat to Papal independence than an essential safeguard for it.[175]

Leo was keenly aware that opposition to the Papal regime had grown steadily throughout his reign. This was partly due to the stimulus of events elsewhere. The growing success of the Greek rebels, and particularly the aid given them by England, France, and Russia, which revealed the breakdown of the conservative Alliance, aroused new hope among the enemies of the *status quo* in Italy, as did the struggle in Portugal between absolutists and constitutionalists and the aid given the latter by England. Equally encouraging was the liberal revival in France, where liberals won control of the Chamber in the election of November, 1827.[176]

But as always the fundamental reason for the strength of the revolutionary movement in the Papal State was to be found, not in external influences, but in the deficiencies of the Papal regime itself, which Leo's reactionary policy had gravely aggravated. Instigated by Metternich—who was still reluctant to offer Leo direct advice lest he revive the old resentment of Austrian interference—Albani, now Legate of Bologna, sought to persuade Leo that only reform of the administration and especially of the arbitrary and ineffective judicial system could restore tranquility to the Papal State.[177] But neither advice such as this nor the obvious growth of popular discontent and revolutionary activity convinced Leo of the need for a more progressive policy. Reactionary measures continued to appear. At the end of 1827, the judiciary was reorganized to increase the arbitrary power of the judges still more and weaken what little protection suspects enjoyed. The aim was to strengthen the authorities in their struggle against the Sects; but the effect was to alienate public opinion yet further and create sympathy for arrested *Settarj*. "Such laws in modern times," Lützow observed, "are harmful rather than useful to authority, which is secure only when based on the most careful administration of justice." He had hinted this to Leo, but "unfortunately this government wishes to preserve an absolutism beyond just limits."[178]

Leo's efforts to stem the rising revolutionary tide with his own resources had failed dismally. His greatest effort against the Sects, the Rivarola mission, had ended by strengthening rather than weakening them. Whatever faint hope Leo might have cherished that Rivarola, if he did not extirpate the

Sects, might at least frighten them into quiescence, were dramatically dispelled in July, 1826, when their terrorism reached its climax in a daring and almost successful attempt to assassinate the Cardinal-Legate himself.[179] Nothing could have brought home more clearly, to Leo or to the world, the total failure of Rivarola's mission, the contempt of the *Settarj* for the Papal government, and the virtual collapse of state authority in the Romagna. Rivarola was recalled and a commission under Monsignor Invernizzi sent to investigate the attempted assassination. But Invernizzi was no more successful than his predecessor: the *Settarj* were now too deeply entrenched in public sympathy—the result partly of conviction, partly of fear of their vendetta—to be rooted out by an inefficient government fallen far into public contempt. After two years of investigation, the commission managed to convict a few of those involved in the attempt on Rivarola or in other assassinations, but the leaders as usual remained undiscovered or were able to flee the country, thanks to timely warnings from friends in the administration. The network of Sects remained intact and their power and audacity continued to grow, while the authority of the state steadily diminished.[180]

Leo was no more successful against the Sects in Rome itself. For religious and economic reasons, the capital had always been a stronghold of Papal loyalty where the Sects found little support. It was thus a matter of particular concern to Leo when the police there uncovered a lodge of the *Carbonari* in the Summer of 1825, whose members retaliated by murdering a suspected police spy. Horrified by this extension of the terrorism of the Romagna to the capital, Leo ordered a rigorous police investigation, which led to several arrests. But as usual the workings of Papal justice were robbed of much of their effect by the arbitrary manner in which they were conducted: for example, at Leo's orders, the judges in the case were informed that for a condemnation in a political crime such as this, "proof in the strictly legal sense will not be necessary,. . . but only a moral certainty of guilt."[181] Consequently the accused were widely regarded as victims of persecution, and when two of them were executed, Gennotte was appalled to observe "signs of sympathy and pity" among the onlookers, "especially the young."[182] The sentences thus had little effect, and the Sects continued to be active in the capital: "never has there been less security or more discontent in Rome than at present," Gennotte reported in 1826.[183]

Under these circumstances, Austrian power in Italy increasingly became a source of comfort to Leo XII as a potential instrument of defense against an uprising which the Papal government itself might be too weak to suppress. The first clear expression of this new attitude came in 1827, when in keeping with treaty commitments, Austria withdrew her garrison from Naples. The prospect of this withdrawal caused much apprehension at Rome, where the value of the garrison in overawing the Sects had come to be appreciated.[184] When, therefore, the withdrawal was accompanied by the announcement that troops evacuated from Naples would be stationed in Lombardy as a deterrent to revolution throughout the peninsula, the Papacy reacted, not with the suspicion it would have shown a few years earlier, but with satisfaction and gratitude. The inevitable attempt of the French Ambassador to ascribe this decision to sinister Austrian ambitions fell on deaf ears: Leo told him bluntly that, far from fearing the presence of Austrian troops on his frontier, he welcomed it, since—given the internal problems of France— "Austria is in reality the only Power that can protect and preserve the legitimate order in Italy, and we must rely upon her with complete trust."[185]

The new Papal attitude was also apparent in Leo's first audience with Lützow, in July, 1827. The audience was devoted mainly to the revolutionary movement in Italy; Leo considered it to be under control at present, but only because of the firm measures taken since 1821 by Austria, which he regarded as the "eldest son of the Church and its chief support." Nonetheless, the Sects were increasingly dangerous, and Austria and the Papacy would have to work together to watch and contain them.[186]

These were grateful words to Metternich, who had aimed at such cooperation since 1814. The exchange of information between the two governments was accordingly increased and formalized, while Austrian and Papal police again cooperated in tracking down suspects. The benefits to the Papacy were immediately apparent, since the more efficient Austrian police obligingly uncovered and turned over to their Papal counterparts numerous *Settarj* who had fled from the Invernizzi commission.[187]

The reconciliation between Rome and Vienna was unaffected by the retirement of Della Somaglia in 1828. The extremist *Zelanti* urged that his successor be Cardinal Giustiniani, the ideological heir of Severoli;[188] but since Giustiniani was distasteful to the courts, above all to Austria, Leo rejected him. Instead, he appointed Bernetti, known as a leading supporter of cooperation with the Powers. Though in the past he had been more sympathetic to France than to Austria, Bernetti, like Leo, had been convinced by recent developments that Austria alone could be relied upon to protect Papal interests. His belief tenure as Secretary of State was marked by a consistent effort to cooperate with Vienna.[189]

By 1829, then, Leo XII—whose pontificate had begun in reaction against what he considered Consalvi's overly close relationship with Austria—was approaching a relation with that Power closer to dependence than the late Cardinal would ever have accepted. This was the natural, if ironic, consequence of Leo's rejection of Consalvi's reforms in favor of a policy of sterile reaction, which was undermining popular support for the regime to the point where soon the Papacy could no longer hope to control the domestic situation without Austrian support. Once that point was reached—and in 1829 it was not far distant—genuine Papal independence would become impossible, as Consalvi had foreseen and tried to forestall with his reforms. It was Leo who set up the fatal situation which was henceforth to haunt the Papal regime: hereafter, the Papacy would in the last analysis depend for its survival upon foreign military support against its own discontented subjects. With that support, the Papal regime could survive—but only as the dependent of a protecting Power, and thus without the genuine political and spiritual freedom of action that was the only *raison d'etre* of the Temporal Power; and once that backing was withdrawn, the Papal regime would fall.[190]

Given the political conditions prevailing in France after 1827, the necessary support could come only from Austria. The situation which Leo had created in the Papal State would in the long run prove fatal to the Temporal Power;

but from Metternich's point of view, it had its short-term advantages. Summing up the state of Austro-Papal relations in 1828, he declared complacently that Leo XII, rejecting the "absurd charges" of Austrian ambitions in Italy, had come to a policy of close cooperation with Austria in the realization that since she had but "a sole aim: the preservation of all that exists legally," she was the natural ally and protector that Rome needed against revolution. He thus looked forward to a steady expansion of the present cooperation between the two courts, which in the end would achieve the fundamental aim of his Papal policy since 1814: the Union of Throne and Altar in practice.[191] This generally satisfactory situation, he admitted, had still one most unfortunate aspect: Leo persisted stubbornly in his reactionary policy, which would surely have serious consequences for Italy. But there was nothing to be done: even the most tactful hints which Metternich ventured to make as to the wisdom of a less reactionary course were rebuffed. Hence "I am convinced that no advice given by a foreign government, even with the best will in the world, can ever attain this aim" while Leo ruled, for "the pontifical government would see in it only an unjustified and threatening interference in its internal affairs." Rome could only be allowed to pursue its own course, no matter how deplorable the effects, until the present reign ended.[192]

This insistence on nonintervention was all the more necessary now in that Metternich was otherwise fully satisfied with Leo's policy, both religious and political, and with the cordial relationship—closer than it had been for ten years or more—existing between Rome and Vienna. But like most diplomatic achievements, this satisfactory situation proved transitory. On February 10, 1829, Leo XII died after a short illness. Summing up his reign, Lützow praised his religious moderation and his "political wisdom" in cooperating with Austria; his death was certainly a blow to Austria and the good cause.[193] On the debit side, however, Lützow could not overlook the harm which Leo's reactionary policy had done in alienating public opinion from the regime. In contrast with the general mourning that had greeted the passing of Pius VII, Leo's death was received with indifference or even with satisfaction, and the popular satirists were savage in their epitaphs.[194] It could not be denied that the Papal regime was weaker in 1829 than it had been at Leo's accession, and that the opposition to it was far stronger. At present, revolution was unlikely—but only because the Sects feared Austrian intervention. Should some international crisis occur to distract Austria's attention from Italy, revolution would not be long delayed.[195]

Metternich agreed with Lützow's evaluation; but for the moment, his chief concern was that, for the second time in less than six years, his progress towards Austro-Papal cooperation was to be subject to the vagaries of conclave and the election of a new pope.

VII

Metternich And Pius VIII, 1829-1830

1. The Conclave of 1829

Annoying though the interruption of the smooth course of Austro-Papal relations caused by Leo's death was, Metternich looked forward to the conclave with far less anxiety than in 1823, for no fundamental change for the worse in Papal policy seemed likely to result.[1]

The conclave of 1823 had been a battleground between two opposing conceptions of the Papacy and its role in the Restoration world—a matter of vital significance for Metternich's policy. In 1829, by contrast, the conclave would be largely a conflict between rival personal ambitions, in which questions of fundamental policy or principle would play relatively little part. "It will be self-interest above all else which directs the conclave," Lützow predicted.[2] The old split between moderates and *Zelanti* was no longer so crucial, for the latter had declined greatly in both confidence and intransigence since 1823. Then they had by a supreme effort carried their candidate to victory; but the outcome had been disillusioning. No great revival of Papal authority over state and society, no great offensive against the regalist state churches, had followed. Leo XII's attitude towards the Powers and their state churches had come to be virtually indistinguishable from Consalvi's—and it was now obvious to all but the most "exalted" among the *Zelanti* that such a mutation had been as unavoidable for him as it would be for his successor, given the realities of the international situation. The events of Leo's reign had revealed the true weakness of the Papal position and the unrealism of *Zelanti* hopes. During the ultramontane episode many *Zelanti* abruptly realized the need for caution in asserting Papal authority, lest the Papacy find itself isolated in a hostile Europe. The continuing religious controversy in France, where the Church was in steady retreat under the hammer blows of a revived and fiercely anticlerical liberalism, was a demonstration of the perils of an intransigent assertion of ecclesiastical claims, as well as a reminder that the Church could have more dangerous foes then regalist monarchs. This last point was further driven home by the upsurge of revolutionary agitation throughout Europe, most ominously in the Papal State itself—a warning that the Papacy must brace itself to face a new revolutionary assault. Clearly, Rome must rearrange its order of priorities: the defeat of regalism, however desirable, must take second place to the defeat of revolution by means of the Union of Throne and Altar. As the European situation became increasingly unfavorable to the Papacy, the exalted view of its practical power which the *Zelanti* had cherished earlier in the Restoration began to crumble, and the more realistic among them were rapidly modifying, if not their theory of Papal authority, at least their plans for implementing it. In practice, then, the gap between the moderates and the majority of the *Zelanti* had narrowed appreciably, and the minority of the *Zelanti* who preserved their old intransigence found themselves isolated and impotent.

Moreover, *Zelanti* prestige had suffered from the resounding failures of their champions, Rivarola and Pallotta, in their respective missions against the Sects and the brigands, which had demonstrated the incapacity of the extremists to deal with the problems of the temporal government; while the absurd extremes of puritanical legislation to which their moral rigorism had driven them under Leo XII had aroused both general mirth and popular resentment. The extremists were further weakened by the loss of their best leaders: Severoli had died in 1824, several others had soon followed him, and there was no one of equal stature among the survivors.

Finally, the factor that had done more than anything else to cement the coalition of 1823, holding *Zelanti* of all degrees together until victory, had been removed: "Cardinal Consalvi is no more, and there is no one of similar influence to be fought."[3] Without their great enemy to impose unity upon them, the *Zelanti* were free to quarrel among themselves—less over principle than over personal ambitions—and they had done so freely since 1824, with the result that their unity was now a thing of the past.

With no great question of principle at stake and no great minister to be overthrown, "the election will be marked by the clash of selfish ambitions, which will decide its outcome."[4] It was true, Lützow reported, that those *Zelanti* who held fast to their old intransigence were working for the election of Cardinal Giustiniani; but he lacked the prestige of his mentor, Severoli, and his followers were a minority with little hope of victory. All the other likely candidates were more or less acceptable to Austria, since none posed a serious threat to her interests or to the Restoration order. Among the more moderate *Zelanti,* the leading candidates were Pacca, whose religious moderation was balanced by his hostility to political reform, and De Gregorio, whose religious rigorism was reminiscent of Severoli's, but whose attitude towards the courts was more conciliatory, and who favored reform in the Papal State; on the other hand, he was known for sympathy with France and aversion to Austria. Castiglione, who in 1823 had been classed among the moderate *Zelanti*, had moved gradually into the camp of the true moderates, whose leading candidate he now was; but his health was poor, and those moderates who felt that the interests of the Church demanded a long pontificate under a vigorous pope were turning to Cardinal Cappellari, who would be particularly welcome to Vienna since he was an Austrian subject with great respect for the Emperor.[5]

Of these candidates, some were obviously more desirable than others; but none posed a threat to the Restoration order of the magnitude that Severoli had. Nor did any pose a serious threat to Austrian interests, for few cardinals even among the *Zelanti* were as hostile to Austria as they had been in 1823. The Emperor's obvious retreat from Josephism had appreciably diminished the once-strong antipathy of the Sacred College towards Austrian religious policy. Perhaps even more influential, the growth of revolutionary activity in the Papal State, coupled with the obvious weakness of the regime, had engendered a growing sense of insecurity among the ecclesiastical elite: it was obvious that revolution was quite possible, and that if it broke out Rome would have to seek Austrian aid to suppress it. Once elected pope, few cardinals would be likely to adopt an anti-Austrian policy; most would surely try to conciliate that Power whose protection might soon be necessary, whose predominance in Italy now seemed reassuring instead of disquieting, and whose religious policy was becoming satisfactory.[6]

Metternich's awareness of these changes explains the serene confidence that pervaded his instructions for the conclave: "We are convinced that any worthy pope, any enlightened pope, will always be an *Austrian* pope, since he cannot help but see in Austria a neighbor as reliable as powerful, and the most zealous protector of the interests of the Church and the social order."[7] Since Austria now had less to fear, she had less reason to intervene directly in the conclave. Moreover, Metternich had learned in 1823 that direct intervention, above all by the use of the formal exclusive, was counterproductive. A less obtrusive, more restrained strategy was indicated. Lützow was not to show partiality for any specific cardinal; he must confine himself to stressing to the Sacred College and the diplomatic corps that Austria did not favor any particular candidate, and had no intention of interfering with the free choice of the conclave, but only hoped for the election of a "wise and moderate" pope. He was to concentrate on winning their agreement that the election of such a pope was necessary for the welfare of the Church and the European order, pointing to such evidence as the religious crisis raging in France, the question of Catholic emancipation in England, and the rising tide of revolutionary agitation everywhere. Albani would again bear the Austrian Secret in the conclave, and in that capacity he could work more forcefully than Lützow; but he too was to avoid partisanship and private ambitions, and to work sincerely for the election of any cardinal whom the majority in the Sacred College supported, provided he seemed likely to make a reasonably satisfactory pope, even if he were a *Zelante* or a notorious Gallophile. "In a word, it is a *good* pope we want above all else; whatever may be the nation or party that supports him, if he satisfies this great primary condition, everything else will be of secondary importance in our eyes," since such a pope would inevitably see the need to cooperate with Austria. Above all, Albani was not to use the formal exclusive, except against a cardinal "notoriously unworthy or incompetent." Even though Chateaubriand reportedly planned to exclude any Austrophile cardinal, Austria would not retaliate: "neither the circumstance of having been put forward by a party hostile to Austria, nor even that party's intention of excluding any cardinal who is an Austrian subject or loyal to Austria, would form in our eyes motives sufficient to give the exclusive against a candidate of that party, provided he is also wise, moderate, and desirable for the general welfare of the Church and the Roman State."[8]

This much Metternich had learned from the experience of 1823: better to accept the election of a pope unfriendly to Austria, but who in due course would surely come to recognize the need for Austrian good will, as Leo XII had done, than to seek by blatant intervention to defeat him, thereby stirring up resentment that would last for years.

Another lesson he had learned was the futility of attempting to form a court party: his instructions did not even mention this possibility, which had loomed so large in his plans for 1823. The other courts had then proven themselves either unreliable, like France, or unable to control their cardinals, like Naples. Apponyi, now Ambassador in Paris, had on his own initiative sounded out the intentions of the French government, which "responded in...a way completely in agreement with our opinions." But Metternich observed skeptically that "even if we accept these as the real intentions of the French government, as I would like to do,...it would be difficult to place full confidence in them,...for who can believe that M. de Chateaubriand, with his independent spirit, will conform to the orders of his government?"[9] As for the other states, Metternich apparently made no move to secure their support or even to ascertain their intentions. When the Neapolitan government approached him about the conclave, Metternich declared his willingness to cooperate, but only for the general purpose of influencing the Sacred College to elect any moderate cardinal, not to secure the election or defeat of a specific candidate. This disappointed the Neapolitans, who wished to defeat De Gregorio; but Metternich, although agreeing that the latter's religious views were undesirably extreme and his Gallophilism notorious, refused to use Austrian influence against him, much less to employ the direct exclusive as the Neapolitans wished.[10] There would be no court party at the conclave of 1829: Austria would play a lone hand.

Metternich had correctly assessed French intentions. Charles X, like Metternich, instructed his cardinals to work for the election, not of a specific candidate, but of any cardinal of moderate religious principles. However, the King also insisted that the pope must not be Austrophile. Regarding French and Austrian interests at Rome as incompatible, he felt there could be no true cooperation between the two courts; instead, France should work to undermine Austrian influence and replace it with her own. As in 1823, France should seek the election of a moderate *Zelante*, for "it is among them that Austria will no doubt find its most determined opponents." This group included several satisfactory candidates: Castiglione was an obvious choice, but others, such as De Gregorio, were equally acceptable. In contrast to Austria, France was prepared to use the exclusive, either against an extremist *Zelante*, like Giustiniani, or against an Austrophile. The King was confident of success, but he failed to realize the extent to which hostility towards Austria in the Sacred College had declined since 1823.[11]

This misunderstanding of the situation contributed to the failure of French diplomacy at the conclave, but more important in that regard was the personal policy followed by Chateaubriand. Despite his quip that "three things no longer make popes: the intrigues of women, the efforts of ambassadors, and the power of courts,"[12] this Ambassador, in order to revive his political reputation at Paris, was determined to "make a pope" who would be obviously pro-French. Since De Gregorio's Gallophile sympathies were well known, Chateaubriand threw the full weight of French influence behind him.

He thereby irritated many other cardinals, especially Castiglione, and allowed them to be captured by Albani for the Austrian camp. By the end of the conclave, Castiglione—in 1823 the French candidate reluctantly accepted by Austria—had become so definitely the Austrian candidate that his election would be an undeniable defeat for France.[13]

On February 23, 1829, the cardinals entered conclave, heavily guarded by troops for fear of a *coup de main* by the *Settarj*—a striking commentary on the decline of public security in recent years.[14] On the following day, the first vote revealed Castiglione and De Gregorio in the lead and roughly equal in strength, with Pacca, Cappellari, and Giustiniani trailing behind.[15] The next two weeks were a period of great activity for Chateaubriand, who hoped to secure De Gregorio's election before the arrival either of Albani, whose influence he feared, or of the French cardinals, with whom he did not wish to share his triumph. All the influence he could muster was vigorously exerted on behalf of De Gregorio. He was supported by the Spanish ambassador, for De Gregorio was linked to Spain by family ties, and the Spanish court found his religious extremism to its taste. De Gregorio's candidacy was further assisted by the skillful guidance of Bernetti, whose support he had won with a promise to reappoint him as Secretary of State. Gradually De Gregorio began to pull ahead, winning votes from both Pacca and the moderates: by March 6, he had twenty-four of the twenty-eight votes necessary for victory. "De Gregorio has virtually been elected," the Piedmontese minister reported on March 7.[16]

But Chateaubriand and De Gregorio had missed their best opportunity, for on March 7 Albani entered the conclave. Illness had delayed his arrival in Rome until late on March 5. Lützow spoke with him the following day, reading Metternich's instructions and especially stressing the need to "avoid the spirit of partisanship" and work for any satisfactory candidate. Albani agreed— with private reservations, for the wily Cardinal was determined to seize this opportunity to realize his lifelong ambition to become Secretary of State, and he was determined to elect only a pope who would give him the coveted post. This ambition excluded not only De Gregorio and Pacca, who like the *Zelanti* in general despised Albani as a self-seeking opportunist, but also Cappellari: though the latter would have been highly acceptable to Austria, he too despised Albani and would never appoint him Secretary of State. Albani had in fact decided to work for the election of Castiglione, who was linked to him by family ties and by their alliance in 1823. Moreover, as Castiglione had little interest in political affairs, Albani could be confident that as his minister he would enjoy a wide freedom of action. Albani carefully hid these calculations from Lützow, and they quickly reached apparent agreement on aims and tactics, though Albani was disconcerted to find that he was not authorized to use the exclusive.[17]

Though Albani would hold the Austrian Secret, he would be assisted by Cardinal Gaystruck, Archbishop of Milan and a native of Austria, who had also arrived on March 5. His reputation for piety and his "unlimited devotion to the person of His Imperial Majesty" would make him a valuable ally for Albani—and also a check on any possible inclination his Italian colleague might harbor to subordinate Austrian interests to his own ambitions.[18]

Albani's entry into the conclave—whether he came "like a lion," as one observer put it,[19] or like a "treacherous fox," in another's opinion[20]—put an end to Chateaubriand's hopes of a quick victory for De Gregorio. Albani at once assumed the leadership of the moderates, and began to promote Castiglione's candidacy with a vigor and skill which had previously been lacking. A series of maneuvers of dazzling complexity followed, as Albani worked to undermine De Gregorio's position and gather votes for Castiglione—seeking support in every quarter by lavish promises; frightening the Gregorians by hints that he was authorized to give the Austrian exclusive against their candidate; forming momentary tactical alliances with the most diverse groups, from the supporters of Pacca to the *Zelanti* extremists, while holding the moderates united; seeming at times to withdraw Castiglione in favor of a variety of other candidates who might draw support from De Gregorio and split the ranks of his followers—so that in the end everyone was baffled as to his true intentions and the Gregorians were left divided and disoriented. Albani's tactics deserve closer study as a model of how to win a papal election, if one is sufficiently indifferent to all considerations except victory.[21]

Even his opponents were driven to grudging admiration of this virtuoso performance: "Albani is an able man.... Call him the Devil if you will; he is nonetheless by his skill, his ability at managing men, and his talents perfectly suited to succeed in any affair he undertakes."[22]

An error on Chateaubriand's part played into Albani's hands. It was customary for each ambassador to deliver a "harangue" to the conclave, usually a bland and unexceptionable expression of his sovereign's good will and views on the election. Thus, on March 9, Lützow addressed the cardinals, expressing the Emperor's benevolence towards the Holy See, his determination to protect it, and his hope for the speedy election of a moderate pope.[23] These platitudes made no particular impression on the cardinals. Not so Chateaubriand's speech, given the following day: departing from the conventional formulas, he used the occasion to set forth his own progressive interpretation of the role of the Papacy in the modern world.[24] The Papacy must make fundamental adaptions to the "Spirit of the Age;" its true function in the modern world must be to work for the spread of knowledge and liberty. "Impiety has vainly claimed that Christianity favored oppression and reaction," but "the Christian religion has faith in civilization and moves with the times." Therefore, the Sacred College must elect a pope who, "firm in doctrine and the authority of the past, is no less familiar with the new needs of the present and the future."

A noble vision, which liberal Catholics would echo—vainly, for the most part—for a century to come; but a vision hopelessly out of touch with the mentality of most of his hearers. To an audience composed largely of *Zelanti*, with all that implied in terms of aversion to change, Chateaubriand spoke of the need to move with the times; men for whom the Revolution had been a traumatic experience, and who feared its imminent recurrence, he urged to devote themselves to the cause of liberty! Little wonder that the reaction of the cardinals was frigid—the more so as they were not accustomed to being lectured on the proper role of the Church by a outsider of dubious orthodoxy. Even the moderate and conciliatory Castiglione—chosen by the College to give the customary reply to this harangue—did not entirely hide his dissatisfaction. Despite many polite expressions of good will, despite the echoed wish for a "wise and moderate pope," his reply was a discreet rebuke: the Church had no need to adapt to the modern world in essentials, for it was solidly founded on divine authority; its policy must be based on "Holy Scripture and venerable tradition, the only school of good government." If the Church would but remain true to its divine tradition, God would protect it against the "immoderate desire to overthrow all authority." In other words, in so far as essentials were concerned, it was not the Church that should adapt itself to the modern world, but the reverse.[25]

Castiglione concluded with lavish praise of Chateaubriand, which so delighted the Ambassador that he managed to ignore the previous criticism, and prided himself on having made a highly favorable impression on the cardinals.[26] Metternich was more perceptive: "The discourse of M. de Chateaubriand contains, undeniably, many great and beautiful thoughts; but I nevertheless found in it more wit than judgment, and I doubt that it was approved by the August Senate to which it was addressed," for he suspected that "the greater part of them found in the eulogy that M. de Chateaubriand wished to offer the Catholic religion...an innovating tendency aimed at placing the eternal truths of Christianity in a state of willing submission to the philosophical pretensions and ideas of the age."[27] His evaluation was justified, for the majority of the cardinals had indeed been unfavorably impressed by Chateaubriand's address, which they saw in precisely the light Metternich suspected.[28] Their reaction weakened French influence in the conclave, and the position of De Gregorio deteriorated.

Aided by Chateaubriand's *faux pas*, Albani's tactical skill soon reversed the balance of the conclave: by March 15, Castiglione had twenty-four of forty-eight votes, while De Gregorio had sunk to fifteen.[29] But though Albani had dealt De Gregorio a fatal blow, he seemed unable to carry Castiglione to final victory by winning the necessary two-thirds vote. During the weeks that followed, Castiglione remained in the lead, but could not win more than twenty-four votes. The stalemate seemed unbreakable, and the conclave entered a period of stagnation. But most of the cardinals were becoming weary of the struggle, which was entering its second month; if a decision was not reached by the beginning of Holy Week in early April, the conclave, in keeping with tradition, would have to suspend its operations until the third Sunday after Easter. This was a prospect that few cardinals enjoyed, particularly since the disturbed condition of the Papal State and the difficult international situation obviously required that a pope be elected quickly to cope with any upheaval that might take place.

In an attempt to break the stalemate, the Gregorians—guided by Bernetti, a politician as subtle as Albani himself—staged a counterattack. On March 22, as Albani reported:

> De Gregorio saw Castiglione and pointed out that, since the votes were evenly divided, a pope could never be elected; therefore, each of them should abandon the idea of becoming pope...and ask his followers to select some other candidate. Castiglione, who was not himself at all ambitious to become pope, agreed to this suggestion....

It was arranged that a compromise candidate should be put forward by both parties: Cappellari, who could surely be elected with their combined votes.[30]

The precise motive behind this suggestion is uncertain. It may well have represented a sincere willingness on De Gregorio's part to sacrifice his own ambitions for the good of the Church, provided Castiglione did the same. For Bernetti, it represented a means of remaining Secretary of State, since Cappellari too had agreed to give him that post.[31] Albani, however, denounced it as "merely a ruse" intended to "split the party of Cardinal Castiglione" and throw it into confusion, after which De Gregorio's candidacy would be revived.[32]

Whatever the motive, the plan seemed likely to succeed. For most of the moderates and moderate *Zelanti,* Cappellari was as acceptable as Castiglione; Gaystruck was particularly favorable, in view of Cappellari's links with Austria. By March 25, Bernetti felt that he had won over thirty-eight of the forty-eight cardinals, more than enough for victory.[33] But Albani remained hostile; for no matter which interpretation of the plan was correct—whether it was a sincere move to elect Cappellari, or a feint to pave the way for De Gregorio's victory—it would prevent him from becoming Secretary of State. He therefore resolved to defeat it by any means possible.[34]

Albani went to work on two fronts. On one, he encouraged the intransigent *Zelanti* to hold firm in opposition; on the other, he persuaded many of Castiglione's supporters to ignore their leader's expressed wish that they turn to Cappellari. Consequently, when on March 25 Bernetti put his plan to the test by proposing Cappellari as a compromise candidate, he could gather only twenty-two votes instead of the thirty-eight he had anticipated.[35] As Bernetti withdrew in confusion, Albani seized the initiative, determined to push Castiglione to a quick victory, not only because he, like his colleagues, was weary of the long contest, but also from fear that his maneuvers and ambitions might cost him Metternich's confidence. Shortly after Cappellari's defeat, Albani had a "heated quarrel" with Gaystruck, who had seen through his intrigues:

> [Gaystruck] warned him that it was a grave offense to delay the election...for his personal interests. The wise Archbishop added with great dignity that the authority given Albani did not include the right to misuse it for his own selfish interests and ambitions: for His Imperial Majesty, in giving him this honor, had never imagined that it would be used to make an election impossible, but only to prevent the choice of an extremist pontiff.[36]

This rebuke alerted Albani to his danger. Should Vienna learn that he had misused his authority by defeating so satisfactory a candidate as Cappellari, he would forfeit Metternich's confidence forever; this would mean the end of the close relationship with Vienna which was a major factor in his political position at Rome. His only hope lay in securing the election of Castiglione; if he could do so, Metternich would be satisfied and would not investigate Albani's conduct too closely. But quick action was essential, for only thus could he prevent Gaystruck from informing Vienna of his suspicions before the tranquilizing news of Castiglione's election could arrive.

Albani therefore went to work with redoubled energy. As the solid nucleus of the Gregorians, held firm by Bernetti, proved irreducible, Albani concentrated on winning over Pacca—who had kept a small party intact throughout the conclave—and the *Zelanti* extremists. The latter, driven to admit that they had no hope of victory, proved like many extremists to cherish a greater aversion to a moderate of their own party—in this case, De Gregorio—than to a declared opponent such as Castiglione. Having won the support of both these groups, Albani on March 31 brought the various threads of his intrigue together in a victorious drive to place Castiglione on the papal throne: in the voting of that day, Castiglione at last won the necessary two-thirds majority, the remaining votes going to De Gregorio. Soon afterwards the conclavists proclaimed to the crowd waiting outside the election of Pope Pius VIII.[37]

Victory—for the moderates, for Albani, and for Austria: there could be no doubt on any of these three points. The new Pope's religious and political moderation was well known, and was confirmed by his choice of regnal name, for he thereby affirmed his respect for his predecessor Pius VII and his determination to imitate that Pope's moderate policy. Apparently, after six years of *Zelanti* rule, the Papacy was once again to pursue Consalvi's policy of conciliatory diplomacy and moderate political reform.

It was equally a victory for Albani, for, in Lützow's words, "it was surely he who motivated, sustained, and brought about this election; he had to combat the whole Gregorian party, sustained by the French Ambassador."[38] To the victor, the spoils: "shortly after the election, the Holy Father summoned Albani...to name him Secretary of State; Albani replied that he could not decline a post where he could be so useful...."[39]

Finally, the election was undeniably a victory for Austria, and not merely in the sense that Castiglione, like any other moderate candidate, was compatible with her interests, for the new Pope made no attempt to hide his particular sympathy for Austria. Indeed, a major reason for his appointment of Albani had been his wish "to give a testimony of his respect for the House of Austria;"[40] and certainly he could hardly have given a more striking and public testimony than to choose as his Secretary of State the man whom Chateaubriand bitterly described as "the Austrian chargé d'affaires in Rome."[41] In his first audience with Lützow, Pius not only lavishly proclaimed his "affection and attachment" for Austria and "eulogized the views and principles of our government," but went so far as to declare that "he has always considered himself an Austrian subject, since his family was of Lombard origin."[42] Similar expressions of "devotion to our August Court" continued to mark Pius's audiences with Lützow, leaving the Ambassador in no doubt as to the "sincere attachment of His Holiness for Austria and the unlimited confidence which he places in our government."[43]

Metternich was jubilant: the victory that had escaped him in 1823 was now his. The news of the election was "so pleasing that I immediately hastened to inform our August Master," who received it "with the most marked satisfaction."

> And indeed [Metternich continued] nothing less than a choice as perfect as this would have met the needs of the Catholic Church and of public tranquility, threatened from all sides.... It is to be ap-

plauded equally from the political and the religious viewpoint. . . , and will not fail to have the most happy influence on the great interests of each.

The election of Pius VIII was welcome above all because it offered "a most certain guarantee" that the relationship of "close friendship and complete confidence" which he had so long desired between Austria and the Papacy would now become a reality.[44]

Victory for Austria, defeat for France—and in particular, for its Ambassador, since the King would willingly have accepted Castiglione, while Chateaubriand by his lavish support of De Gregorio had not merely backed the wrong horse, but had alienated and driven into the arms of Austria the winning candidate. Chateaubriand did his best to conceal his defeat. "Victory!" he wrote to a friend; "I have one of the popes on my list: Castiglione."[45] To the Foreign Minister he described Pius VIII as "an entirely French pope," elected by his own efforts.[46] But he was hard put to explain how so pro-French a Pope could have chosen Albani, that "Austrian chargé d'affaires," as his Secretary of State. The only possible explanation must be that "this is a small consolation to Austria for the election of an entirely French pope."[47]

His reasoning failed to satisfy the Foreign Minister, who demanded an explanation of this apparent debacle.[48] For the remainder of his stay at Rome, Chateaubriand labored frantically to convince his sceptical government that Pius was indeed firmly pro-French, while Albani was not so pro-Austrian as was believed.[49] In any case, if Paris found Albani unwelcome, it need only bring pressure to bear for Papal interests in the Near East, and Pius would soon see the need to dismiss him.[50]

All to no avail. In a severely critical dispatch of April 25, the Foreign Minister systematically refuted the Ambassador's arguments, always returning to the same conclusion: no pope could have appointed so Austrophile a minister as Albani without himself being partial to Vienna. The election had thus been a disastrous defeat for France, which Chateaubriand's blunders had made possible.[51]

Stung by this rebuke, Chateaubriand returned a bitter reply that signalled his break with the Ministry and led to his recall.[52] It was the end of his Roman mission, and also—because of the unforeseen outbreak of the 1830 revolution—the end of his diplomatic career.[53] For Metternich, this was by no means the least pleasing result of the conclave of 1829.

2. *Austro-Papal Cooperation Revisited*

As Pius VIII ascended the Papal throne, Metternich confidently "cast the most favorable horoscope" for his pontificate. With a "Pope so enlightened as Pius VIII, and a Secretary of State so endowed with insight, intelligence, and experience as Cardinal Albani," he looked forward to a bright future of renewed Austro-Papal cooperation; of religious moderation that would smooth the way for the downfall of Josephism; of reform that would remove the causes of unrest in the Papal State and make it a source of strength rather than weakness to the Restoration Order; of effective joint action against the Sects that would check their perilous growth.[54]

An optimistic horoscope, but one which Pius's reign largely justified— except on one crucial point, which nullified all the rest: its duration. Elected in March, 1829, Pius died in November, 1830, after a reign of just twenty months. This abrupt end upset Metternich's expectations and kept Pius from achievements that seemed otherwise within his grasp. In the fields that mattered most to Meternich, Pius undertook policies that were full of promise; but all were cut short by his death.

Until this denouement, however, Metternich felt that his horoscope was being realized, for he found much to praise and little to blame in Papal policy. Certainly the attitude of Pius and Albani towards Austria was everything he could have wished: respectful, trusting, eager to cooperate with the Power which they clearly regarded as the Papacy's best friend and natural protector:

> The Holy Father told me [reported Lützow] that "after God, it is only upon the Emperor of Austria and the help he is prepared to give the Church that I allow myself to count. The personal character of the sovereign, his high and sincere piety, the wise and unchanging principles of his government, which has the great merit of fighting with wisdom and perseverance the designs of the enemies of order and all authority whether civil or religious: all this", he continued, "inspires me with confidence and courage for the task Providence has imposed upon me."[55]

And this was no mere flattery: throughout his reign, Pius did in fact continually demonstrate his reliance upon Austria, turning to Vienna for advice and support whenever Rome was confronted by some intractable problem, particularly in international affairs. When Turkish persecution of the Armenian Catholics at Constantinople flared up again in 1829, it was Austria whose aid Pius at once invoked. Metternich, "tireless in the service of the right," intervened effectively, not only securing an end to the persecution, but arranging a permanent solution to this old problem: he persuaded the Sultan to grant the Armenian Catholics for the first time a distinct legal status, independent of the schismatic Armenian Patriarch whom they blamed for stirring up the persecution.[56] When Pius hesitated to recognize the newly independent Greek state, it was Metternich's advice he sought and followed; it was likewise Metternich whom he asked to safeguard the rights of Catholics in the new state, and once again the Chancellor was glad to oblige.[57] When Albani learned that the Russian government was planning to confiscate certain properties of the Catholic clergy in Poland and to reduce their pensions, his first thought was to ask the Nuncio to "consult Prince Metternich..., who knows but that his fertile mind may suggest some opportune means of averting this storm." The Prince's fertile mind was equal to the occasion: arguing that a contented clergy would be a source of stability, while clerical discontent would inevitably strengthen the revolutionary movement in Poland, he persuaded the Tsar to modify his plans.[58] Metternich's advice was eagerly sought,

given, and followed by the Papacy on a wide range of problems, whether religious—e.g., the disputes with the Protestant princes of the Rhineland—or
political—e.g., the recognition of Dom Miguel as King of Portugal.[59]

Metternich's willing and usually successful responses to these numerous
requests naturally strengthened Papal confidence in him still further. With
every "new proof of the truly edifying zeal of Prince Metternich for the welfare
of our holy religion,"[60] as in one affair after another Austria "ceaselessly
wins new titles to the gratitude of the Holy See,"[61] Pius and Albani were increasingly convinced that "truly, Austria is the only protector of the Church."[62]

This attitude of trust and good will marked the course of Austro-Papal
relations in every field. Religious affairs had never gone so smoothly. As Metternich had anticipated, Pius intended to follow the general policy of his
namesake and of Consalvi, combining firmness in matters of principle with a
conciliatory attitude towards the courts: "he is certainly determined to defend
that which belongs to the authority of the Church," Lützow reported, "but
moderation and wisdom form the basis of his principles." In consequence,
his religious policy "could never give any government legitimate cause for
alarm, and Austria has less cause to fear than any other."[63]

In fact, Pius's "moderation and wisdom" were not seriously tested by relations with Austria, since no controversy arose to disturb their smooth course;
but in the various minor questions that did come up, his reaction was always
fully satisfactory to Metternich. An example is his response to an Imperial
request in December, 1829, that the Congregation of the Index, before issuing a formal condemnation of any work by an Austrian subject, would first
inform Vienna of the reasons for it. This was intended by Metternich to eliminate a long-standing source of misunderstanding and controversy between
the two courts, which the Josephists had often exploited to arouse the Emperor against alleged Papal ill will and obscurantism, as in the case of Frint's
works in 1828. To prevent any repetition of that incident, Metternich originally advanced his request to Leo, who rejected it on the grounds that it would
constitute an infringement on the Congregation's freedom of action and a
special favor which other courts would resent. The confidence which Pius VIII
felt in Austria was too great for such qualms to restrain him, and, "appreciating the true motives for His Majesty's request," he agreed at once, on
condition that strict secrecy be observed lest other rulers "less worthy of the
unlimited trust which the Holy Father has in His Imperial Majesty" should
make the same request.[64] "What a striking demonstration...of the special
regard of the Holy Father for our August Sovereign this is!" exulted Lützow,
with good reason. Not even Pius VII, he felt, had ever shown such "notable
condescension;" surely Austrian influence at Rome had never been so great.[65]

A few months later, Albani gave another remarkable demonstration of this
"special regard": in May, 1830, he advised Vienna that it had too few cardinals, and hence less influence in the Sacred College than it deserved. He urged
the Emperor to send some "young men of good family" to Rome to enter the
prelature, so that in due course they would be eligible to receive the red hat,
which Pius would be glad to bestow upon them. Once again, all must be done
in secrecy lest offense be taken by courts less deserving of this special favor.[66]

For Metternich, the surest proof of Pius's religious moderation was probably his refusal to repeat Leo's flirtation with ultramontanism or to take up the cudgels for Lamennais despite the latter's appeals.[67] Lamennais had not ceased his violent polemic against Gallicanism and the Restoration monarchies, thereby providing further fuel for the controversy between Gallicans and ultramontanes, and more ammunition for the liberals' assault on the Church and the Bourbon monarchy. Lamennais eagerly sought Papal support for his position. Pius, however, carefully abstained from taking sides in the controversy, partly from reluctance to exacerbate the quarrel that was tearing the French church apart, partly from distrust of Lamennais. This prudent silence, though it did not commend itself to the disillusioned Lamennais, was probably wise under the circumstances, and it certainly met with Metternich's approval.

If Metternich was pleased by the Papacy's religious policy, Pius had cause for reasonable satisfaction with Austria's. Here the central question was still the reform, long meditated but still hanging fire, of Austrian religious legislation. Francis I was still engaged in considering the *memoire* given him by Pius VII, taking the advice of one religious or legal expert after another as he inched towards decisive action. There could be no doubt of his good will towards the Papacy, or of his determination to bring Austrian religious legislation into harmony with Catholic principles—so Metternich assured the Nuncio just after the conclave. The Emperor had turned all the papers relating to the question over to him for his opinion, and it was merely a matter of working out the exact reforms to be introduced and the procedures to be followed. He expected to "see the affair ended within a few months."[68]

But as so often in this question, Metternich's optimism was unjustified; after a year had passed without action, the Nuncio made a more realistic appraisal of the situation. Metternich had indeed been given the papers, but "his many preoccupations"—and, perhaps, a lack of enthusiasm for sorting out theological niceties?—"have thus far prevented him from dealing effectively with this difficult task, especially since the basic case has been swelled enormously by the opinions of the many experts whose advice has been sought." The ecclesiastics consulted had generally agreed that some sort of reform was necessary, while the legal experts had been largely opposed. In the hope of giving the Emperor a decisive impulse towards reform—while simultaneously freeing himself from the morass of theological subtleties for which he had little taste—Metternich persuaded Francis to turn the whole question over to his confessor and former Court Chaplain, Bishop Wagner. Since Francis I had great confidence in Wagner, Metternich hoped that he would accept his opinion as definitive and act upon it; and since Wagner was known to be in sympathy with the Papal position, the nature of his opinion was predictable. In May, 1830, in fact, Wagner confidentially advised the Nuncio that it would be well if the Pope were prepared to send a trusted person to Vienna in the near future to collaborate with the Emperor and himself in drawing up a draft project for the reform.[69] As the Summer of 1830 came on, Francis seemed about to act decisively at last; but the outbreak of the July Revolution distracted him, and not until the reign of Pius's successor did serious negotiations on the modification of the Austrian religious system finally get under way.[70]

Austro-Papal relations were equally cordial in political affairs. The particular confidence which Pius and Albani felt in Austria ensured that Metternich would have no difficulty in obtaining his basic aim: Papal acceptance of and cooperation with Austrian predominance in Italy. From the beginning of the pontificate, the Pope and his Secretary of State left no doubt that they regarded Austrian hegemony in the peninsula not as a threat, but as an essential bulwark for the Temporal Power and the established order. They not merely welcomed Austrian power, but encouraged its strengthening, for example, by increases in the size of the garrison in Lombardy. "The tranquility of the peninsula," Albani felt, "is essentially linked to the presence there of numerous Austrian troops, which from the banks of the Tincio and the Po exercise a salutary influence on the spirits of the Italians outside the Imperial domains, and reassure their governments by throwing the necessary terror into the souls of the discontented."[71] This attitude arose, as it had under Leo XII, from realization of the Papal government's inability to defend itself against a serious revolt; but it was reinforced by the confidence which Pius and Albani felt in Austria's benevolence: "the Pope knows that he need fear nothing as long as Austria watches benignly over Italy."[72]

Firm in this conviction, Pius was impervious to French hints of Austrian ambitions; in any case, French influence was now declining at Rome as Pius's basic preference for Austria over France was strengthened by the contrast between Austria's support for the Church's interests and the alarming growth of anticlericalism in France. French prestige was further weakened by the series of reports, bitterly critical of the new Papal regime, which Chateaubriand and his successors sent to Paris; these were intercepted by the Austrian police, and copies were turned over by Metternich to Pius and Albani, whom they greatly irritated.[73]

Metternich was delighted by the confidence and acceptance of Austrian predominance in Italy which the Pope displayed: on this score, the reign of Pius VIII was even more satisfactory than that of Pius VII at its best. He was equally satisfied with Papal policy on another point of great concern: the counterrevolutionary struggle, in its dual aspects of domestic reform and repression of the Sects.

Though Pius VIII had never been much concerned with political affairs, his long association with Consalvi had given him some appreciation of that minister's program, and he had disapproved of the reaction under Leo XII. Moreover, during his early career as bishop of a poor diocese, he had acquired an intimate knowledge of the misery and discontent widespread among his subjects: "he has seen human misery and at close range, and he knows the evils that oppress his people," Lützow reported; hence he was determined to introduce reforms, and "only seeks the means best suited to carrying out his excellent intentions." Even had he been less interested in reform, his attention would have been imperatively directed to it by the general chorus of protest against Leo's reactionary policies: "too many complaints have been made . . . against the measures and innovations of Leo's reign for his successor not to be aware of them and seek to remedy them."[74] Discontent had attained menacing proportions by the end of Leo's reign, as the Sects daily grew stronger while support for the Papal regime withered. Reform was clearly essential, and Pius intended to carry it out along Consalvian lines.[75]

However, Pius was determined to proceed without haste, avoiding any such drastic, sudden reversal of his predecessor's policy as Leo had carried out: "there is no question of immediately reversing everything that was done then, to set up a new structure without plan, which will soon collapse for lack of a solid foundation."[76] His initial moves were confined to suspending or re- voking the most unpopular or most obviously unwise of Leo's measures, such as his hated moral regulations. More fundamental and far-reaching reform would come only when Pius had had time to orient himself to his new role. His past experience having been confined to ecclesiastical posts, he felt keenly his lack of practical administrative and political experience: "I have lived the life of an ecclesiastic," he admitted to Lützow, "and I never thought to reign over the State and its people; I understand nothing about it."[77] He would move slowly, cautiously, until he became acquainted with this unfamiliar political world. Partly from this awareness of his own inexperience, but also partly because he had learned from the errors of his predecessors, he wished to involve the cardinals in the work of reform. Their participation would un- doubtedly retard the pace of innovation, but it might also enable Pius to avoid the position of isolated impotence, ringed about by enemies, into which Con- salvi had fallen towards the end.[78] His first move towards reform was there- fore the appointment in April, 1829, of a congregation of cardinals—carefully chosen to eliminate any who were fundamentally hostile to reform *per se*—to study the measures of Leo's reign and recommend their modification or aboli- tion as necessary.[79]

It was primarily upon Albani, however, that Pius relied to remedy his own lack of experience. Impressed by Albani's long administrative experience and great political skill, the Pope "gives him full confidence in all that con- cerns domestic administration."[80] But Albani's undeniable abilities were matched by undeniable drawbacks—above all, by that which Lützow foresaw at the time of his appointment: "it remains to be seen if an old man, almost eighty, will long be able to sustain the burden of affairs."[81] Lützow had soon to report that Albani, though "animated by the best principles," lacked energy and stamina, tended to sink into apathetic inaction in the face of ob- stacles, and seemed unable to carry major projects through to completion.[82] Yet at the same time he attempted to concentrate all power in his own hands, refusing to delegate to others the authority which he himself could not wield, and in particular jealously excluding the cardinals from participation in the government. It was not long before he sabotaged the congregation appointed to consider reform so that it accomplished nothing, thus undercutting Pius's attempt to associate the cardinals in the work of reform and arousing much unnecessary opposition. An additional problem was that "the personal ten- dencies of Albani tend to make themselves felt in the administration," above all his notorious parsimony: "all expense is avoided . . . , no great enterprises are undertaken, and parsimony reigns throughout the administration." This economizing was by no means entirely undesirable: the Papal financial situa- tion was desperate at the end of Leo's reign, to the point where many state employees had gone unpaid for months. Albani's mania for economy placed the government on the road to financial recovery; but it also made him reluc- tant to embark upon the fundamental reforms whose necessity he admitted, but whose expense he dreaded.[83]

For all Pius's good intentions, then, the pace of reform during his reign was slow. In normal circumstances this would not have been an unmitigated evil; hasty, ill-planned reform would only have produced greater confusion and discontent than already existed. But circumstances were not normal. A revolutionary situation was developing in the Papal State, and only rapid and sweeping reform could halt it. Pius knew something of the danger; but he did not foresee the July Revolution, which had a catalytic effect upon the Italian political situation, producing revolt in the Papal State much sooner than would otherwise have been the case. Nor, of course, could he foresee that his own premature death would cut short his reign before his slow-maturing reforms could be implemented.

Not that the pontificate, brief though it was, was entirely devoid of accomplishments. The most unpopular of Leo's measures were revoked. The financial situation of the government was greatly improved over its low ebb of 1829: the government once again found sufficient revenue to meet its obligations; public employees were again being paid regularly; the traditional system of poor relief—a major factor in Roman devotion to the Papacy, which Leo had unwisely cut back—was resumed; and the postal system and customs were modernized to provide better service and revenue.[84]

These achievements were not to be despised; and it was also to Pius's credit, as Lützow stressed, that if reform was slow in coming, reactionary policies and unpopular measures were conspicuous by their absence: "those who judge him most severely say only that thus far in his reign he has done neither good nor evil; and when critics are prepared to grant that a sovereign has done no ill at all, it is a notable admission, rarely made."[85] True enough; yet, compared with the needs of the State, it was insufficient. None of the fundamental reforms planned by Pius materialized; and as the revolutionary crisis of 1830 approached, it was fundamental reform that was required more than ever.

Metternich made no attempt to accelerate the progress towards reform, for—no more foreseeing the brevity of the pontificate than did Pius himself—he considered the Pope's attitude highly satisfactory: he agreed that hasty and ill-planned reform would do more harm than good, and praised the Pope's intention to weigh his plans carefully before implementing them. The reactionary policies of the previous reign had been abandoned, and Pius's determination to introduce reform was unquestioned; hence the Chancellor confined himself to expressions of support for reform, without seeking to hasten its coming.[86]

Metternich was also basically pleased—at least prior to the July Revolution—with the Papal attitude on the Sects, whose control was more necessary than ever in view of their growing strength. He urged upon Albani the same advice he had been giving since Consalvi's day: the Sects must be kept under close surveillance, those who actively conspired should be severely punished though always within the limits of the law, and the Papacy must cooperate closely with Austria against them.[87]

His advice fell on fertile ground: not only were Pius and Albani predisposed to accept Austrian guidance in general, but their attention had been dramatically called to the revolutionary danger by the discovery during the conclave of *Settarj* plots in Rome itself aimed at seizing power during the interregnum.[88] If even the traditional loyalty of Rome had begun to weaken, reports from the provinces revealed conditions far more serious, and the Romagna above all was a beehive of plots and assassinations which the Rivarola mission had stimulated rather than quieted.[89] Consequently, Pius was fully prepared to accept Metternich's advice and act upon it—or at least attempt to do so: his good will was undeniable, but, as so often with the Papal regime, performance was another story. Pius made his position clear by issuing a new condemnation of the Sects in the first weeks of his reign.[90] In view of the 1821 condemnation, this constituted only a declaration of principle. Of greater practical significance—and greater interest to Metternich[91]—Albani set up a special commission to investigate the revolutionary organization discovered at Rome during the conclave; efficiently organized with Austrian assistance, the commission had greater success than usual, managing to uncover most of the ramifications of the plot and sentence a number of its leaders.[92] At Metternich's request, the Austrian police were given full details of the commission's discoveries. Under Albani's prodding, some at least of the Legates introduced greater vigor into the campaign against the Sects: the more daring forms of *Settarj* violence tapered off, and a measure of calm returned to the Romagna. Yet this tranquility was superficial, Lützow realized: "the *Settarj* certainly have not renounced their criminal plans, and they seize every opportunity to nourish discontent." Such opportunities were plentiful, for the "deficiencies of the Roman government...feed this moral sickness which the enemies of Throne and Altar know how to use adroitly."[93]

The deficiencies of the regime hampered the anti-*Settarj* struggle in another way: Albani "can count on only a few devoted and reliable persons," Lützow reported. "Corruption is so general, and enemies of the government so widespread in all departments, that he risks confiding his secrets to some traitor, who will then dispose of them according to his political principles or his financial advantage."[94] As throughout the Restoration, a solution for the problem of the Sects could be attained only by a thorough reform of the regime. Until that was accomplished, even the most vigorous repression would have only superficial success; and Albani, now eighty, was increasingly demonstrating that he lacked the energy and determination necessary to carry out such reform. The Secretary of State was confident that the regime was in no real danger; but his confidence rested on an awareness not of Papal strength, but of Austrian protection: "he fears nothing so long as the attention of Austria is not distracted so that that Power remains in a position to defend this peninsula."[95]

This was to carry faith in Austria a bit farther than even Metternich wished, to the point where it prevented the Papacy from working energetically for its own salvation by reform and repression. By the end of 1829, he suspected that Albani's reliance upon Austria was leading him into just this sort of inaction; and the Chancellor was reluctantly coming to the conclusion that it might be necessary to work for his replacement as Secretary of State.[96]

Metternich could not deny that Albani's administration was a definite improvement over that of Leo XII, and that some progress was being made towards reform and more effective repression of the Sects; but he was alarmed by Albani's strange confidence as 1830 opened that "all is tranquil, and no-

where are there signs of discontent so great as to arouse fear of revolution."
Profoundly aware of the threatening European situation, Metternich found
little reassurance in Albani's claim that no serious trouble was to be feared
from the Italian Sects, for, reluctant to act on their own initiative, they would
await directions from revolutionary circles in France: "it is from France that
the signals for any blow to be struck must come."[97] Come they would in this
year of 1830, and sooner than Albani dreamed. Early in August, word reached
Rome that revolution had once again broken out at Paris. The crisis of the
Restoration order had begun.

3. The July Revolution

"The old Europe is at the beginning of its end"—so Metternich, with mel-
ancholy prescience, greeted the news of the July Revolution.[98] He saw at once
the deadly threat which it posed. Revolution had triumphed, not in some state
of the third rank as in 1820, but in a great Power—the same where the revolution of 1789 had led to a generation of upheaval. Would not a successful
French revolution once again set fire to all Europe? Even if France did not,
as he feared she might, embark upon a new crusade to spread the gospel of
liberty by the sword, her example would inevitably inspire a new revolutionary
surge throughout the continent. The obvious means to exorcise this threat
was an armed intervention, as in 1821; but though Metternich was not in
principle averse to this, he had to admit that it was impractical under existing
conditions. The European Alliance had disintegrated during the 1820s, and
the conservative Powers were divided among themselves; their armies were
unprepared for war and their finances in disorder. Moreover, unless it was
clearly provoked by French aggression, an intervention would receive little
support from European opinion, and would surely arouse strong French
resistance. Since intervention was impractical, the new regime would have to
be tolerated, and on September 8, Austria formally extended diplomatic
recognition.[99]

But if Metternich had to tolerate the revolution in France, he was resolved
to prevent its spread into Central Europe. Italy seemed in the greatest
danger, the point most vulnerable to French invasion or subversion. From
the beginning of the crisis Metternich paid careful attention to the peninsula,
for he felt that there revolution was "not merely possible, but probable," and
he was resolved to repress it, if necessary, by military intervention.[100] Danger
signals were not hard to find, above all in the Papal State, which, as Metternich had long known, was the Achilles' heel of the conservative order in Italy.
For years, only fear of Austria had held back the Italian Sects from revolt;
now that fear was balanced by the hope that protection would be forthcoming
from France. So reasoned Metternich; and as Summer turned to Fall and the
revolutionary wave spread into Belgium, as rumors of plots and agitation
multiplied throughout Europe, as the Paris radicals openly encouraged an
Italian revolution and the Paris government proclaimed its doctrine of non-

intervention, he watched with growing anxiety the course of events in the Papal State.

The reports that came from Lützow were not reassuring. If the July Revolution had produced consternation everywhere, the reaction at Rome was close to panic. "The pontifical government is overwhelmed by these events," Lützow reported; "utterly stupefied, it fears everything, without knowing what to do." Pius feared a repetition of the political and religious disasters of the 1790s. He foresaw "religion again overthrown" in France and throughout Europe. On a more immediate level, he feared that France would invade Italy again, or at least give dangerous encouragement to the Sects. Only two reflections brought him any comfort: first, the hope that his own popularity and his well-known interest in reform might undercut the appeal of the Sects; second, his confidence in Austria.[101] All might still be well if only "Austria does not lose sight of Italy and continues to protect it."[102]

Reports from the provinces confirmed the Pope's forebodings. Officials in the Legations and Marches unanimously agreed that a revolutionary situation was developing, inspired by the news from France as well as by economic distress resulting from the poor harvests of the last two years. At present, a superficial calm prevailed, because the Sects were awaiting some assurance that France would protect them against Austria. If such assurance was forthcoming, revolution would be inevitable, and the Legates had little hope of suppressing it with their own means.[103]

Neither Pius nor Albani seemed capable of the firm and decisive action necessary to meet the crisis. Even the most elementary precautions were neglected. Deprived of direction from its center, the machinery of government seemed paralyzed. "The uncertainty of the government is understandable," Lützow explained, "when one considers that the sovereign is an elderly man who has led an unworldly life and is in poor health," while Albani had already demonstrated that he lacked the "energy to act as the situation demands." Both seemed "plunged in apathy, . . . resigned to circumstances that seem unalterable," putting their trust in Divine Providence—and the Austrian army.[104]

Appalled by this inaction, Lützow exerted all his influence to stir Pius and Albani from their apathy. Accustomed as they were to following Austrian advice, they were easily induced to take the basic precautions which Lützow urged: vigilance over the Sects was stepped up, the army and police were reinforced, and food was purchased for those provinces worst hit by poor harvests.[105]

But the July Revolution had created problems for Rome not only in the Papal State, but in international affairs as well, and two of these were immediately pressing: whether to recognize the new French government, and whether Rome could rely upon Austrian military aid in the event of revolution.

Like other conservative states, the Papacy was reluctant to recognize the July Monarchy.[106] The recognition of a regime created by revolution and founded upon the principle of popular sovereignty would appear to give Papal approval to these dangerous concepts; repugnant as a matter of principle, this might also be dangerous in practice, since it would increase the self-confidence of the Sects. Moreover, there seemed good reason to hope that the Powers would soon unite to crush the new regime, thus eliminating any necessity for recognition. Consequently, Rome at first took a stand against recognition: in a circular of August 17, Albani declared that Rome would not recognize Louis Philippe except in the unlikely event that all the Powers did so.[107] He followed this with orders to local authorities that the French tricolor might not be displayed, nor the new French cockade worn, not even on French vessels; if necessary, force might be used to guarantee compliance with these orders.[108]

There were, however, strong arguments in favor of a less intransigent course, as Albani, among others, soon realized. Fundamental was the consideration that by the end of August the new regime was firmly in power and unlikely to collapse in the near future; nor did the Powers seem disposed to overthrow it. The Papacy would have to deal with the July Monarchy in some way, and an attitude of resolute nonrecognition would lead to major problems. Even if France was restrained from direct retaliation by fear of the Powers, she could do considerable damage to the Papacy by encouraging, or allowing her nationals to encourage, subversion in the Papal State. Difficulties would also arise for Papal commerce with France. Most serious of all, nonrecognition would surely strengthen the anticlericalism already potent in France, leading perhaps to new outbreaks of mob violence against the Church which the government would do little to check; indeed, the French government itself—which had already deposed the Catholic Church from its old status as the official state religion—might well retaliate by a wider assault on the rights and privileges of the Church, even to the point of schism.[109]

Impressed by these dangers, Albani revoked his prohibition against the new French flag and cockade on August 24.[110] Almost immediately thereafter came word that an ambassador from Louis Philippe would shortly come to Rome to announce his accession to the Pope. The moment of decision was at hand, yet those around the Pope were still not agreed as to the proper course to follow: the *Zelanti*, led by the Bourbonophile De Gregorio, argued vehemently against recognition, while Albani was increasingly inclined to favor it.[111] In this dilemma, Pius and Albani turned to the man from whom they had long since become accustomed to seek reliable guidance in the confusing affairs of this world. Since the beginning of the crisis, the Papal government had made discreet inquiries as to Metternich's intentions on the recognition question;[112] now its inquiries took on an almost frantic note of urgency. In theory, this appeal for advice was merely the reflection of the old Papal principle of awaiting the example of the Powers before recognizing a new government; but in reality, the Pope's only concern was: what would Austria do? "This will be decisive for us," Albani told the Nuncio; "we will closely imitate the example of the Imperial court."[113] Clearly, the tendency to look to Vienna for guidance, which had been growing at Rome since 1826, had been strengthened immensely by the July Revolution: with France liberal and anticlerical, Austria was left as the only officially Catholic Power and the only conservative Power that had an interest in Italy.

Questioned by the Nuncio, Metternich replied in mid-August that Austria had no intention of overthrowing the July Monarchy by force, and implied that Louis Philippe would probably receive recognition eventually.[114] He repeated this implication more clearly in a circular of August 22, which was to be communicated to the Italian courts.[115] Urged by Metternich to imitate the Austrian stand, Albani hereafter became a strong advocate of recognition. But opposition persisted among the Pope's other advisers, and at length Pius decided to "earnestly solicit" a precise statement of Austrian intentions; if the reply was definitely favorable to recognition, he would imitate the Austrian example.[116]

Pleased at this evidence of Papal faith in his guidance, Metternich willingly gave the precise information requested, and advised Pius to grant recognition.[117] At once all hesitation vanished; once definitely assured of Austrian policy, Pius hastened to imitate it.[118] The French ambassador was cordially received and presented with a letter of congratulation for Louis Philippe; soon afterwards, the Paris Nuncio was accredited to the new government.[119]

Thus the question of Papal recognition was settled; and—thanks to Metternich's advice and the Pope's willingness to follow it—settled in such a way as to prevent the further aggravation of international tension and of church-state hostility in France which would surely have resulted if the intransigence of the *Zelanti* had prevailed. Metternich's influence over the Papacy has been much criticized, and certainly it was not always exerted to the true benefit of Catholicism; but there can be little doubt that on this occasion he saved Rome from a blunder that would have had serious consequences.

The second question that preoccupied Pius concerned the extent to which he could rely upon Austria for protection against invasion or revolution. As we have seen, he had always regarded Austria as Rome's only hope of dealing with revolution; indeed, he had long hoped that the mere presence of an Austrian garrison in Lombardy would suffice to intimidate the Sects, but the ferment produced by the July Revolution made it unwise to count upon this any longer.[120] Hence, as soon as word came of the July Revolution, Albani instructed the Vienna Nuncio both to urge Austria to increase her forces in Italy and to discover whether she was disposed to act against an Italian revolution.[121] Metternich reassured the Nuncio: Austria and the other Powers were determined to protect the existing order in Europe against both aggression and revolution, and Austria was now reinforcing its army in Italy to be ready for either eventuality.[122]

Albani was temporarily calmed by this reply; but his disquiet revived at the end of August when the Belgian revolution broke out and France announced the principle of nonintervention. The obvious reluctance of the Powers to risk war with France by intervening in Belgium cast doubt upon Austria's willingness to intervene in Italy. Rumors spread that in the face of French threats, Austria had agreed that the principle of nonintervention applied to Italy; released from their main fear, the Sects stepped up their plotting.[123] In alarm, Albani on September 21 again directed the Nuncio to inquire whether the Powers, above all Austria, were truly resolved to aid the Italian states, or whether they had in fact accepted the principle of nonintervention.[124] After a lengthy interview with Metternich, Spinola reported that Austria and the other Powers firmly rejected the doctrine of nonintervention, and were resolved to aid any ruler who requested help against revolution. This was true in Italy above all, since "its tranquility directly concerns Austria, so that she cannot fail to react to agitation there," in contrast to Belgium where her interests were not directly involved.[125]

This was an accurate assessment of Metternich's position;[126] but it failed to satisfy Albani, who considered it too vague and would have preferred a formal promise of aid.[127] The Secretary of State was being unreasonable, of course, since thus far he had made only general inquiries at Vienna, and had not requested a formal Austrian commitment. To such general inquiries, Metternich—seeing no reason to offer a formal commitment which had not been requested—had returned assurances of a general nature, though sufficient to enlighten Spinola, if not Albani, as to Austrian intentions.

But the timorous Secretary of State was still unsatisfied, and in mid-October he decided to request a formal commitment; but before he could act, the Habsburg Duke of Modena, Francis IV, saw fit on his own initiative to offer Austrian military support to Pius VIII in the event of revolution.[128] The Duke's motives are unclear; but his action was certainly unauthorized by Vienna, and—contrary to contemporary suspicions—had not been instigated by Metternich.[129]

Pius VIII gladly accepted the offer. Bernetti, now Legate of Bologna, which was the chief trouble spot, was authorized to call upon General Frimont, commander of the garrison in Lombardy, to intervene in case of revolt.[130] Nonetheless, Pius was uneasy. Why should Vienna offer its aid through a third party? Many cardinals had definite misgivings at what seemed a rather suspicious Austrian eagerness to send troops into the State; could the old suspicion of Austria's annexationist ambitions have some foundation after all? Rumors began to circulate that Austria was intriguing to persuade the Pope to allow an occupation of the Papal State, and the French chargé, Bellocq—who had long been stirring up distrust with inaccurate reports of Austrian policies in Italy—performed another disservice to the cause of international understanding by reporting these rumors as facts, and charging that Austria was engaged in another attempt to annex the Legations.[131] Pius therefore accepted the Duke's offer with a certain diffidence, posing the condition that Austrian forces should not enter his state until he formally invited them. Albani too was puzzled by the "Austrian" offer, and in November he asked Metternich to clarify the situation by explaining Austrian policy.[132]

The Chancellor was astonished by Albani's inquiry, for he was completely unaware of the Duke's offer—and far from pleased to hear of it.[133] He had realized since the beginning of the crisis that intervention in Italy might be necessary, and with that possibility in mind he had reinforced the Lombard garrison. However, he hoped that intervention might be avoided, for its dangers were great: it would surely lead to a confrontation with France, whose old quest for predominance in Italy was now reinforced by the enthusiasm of the Left for the Italian cause. Such a confrontation might easily lead to war. Moreover, intervention in Italy would mean committing Austrian forces there, thus weakening her ability to react quickly if war should break out north of the Alps, or a revolution require action elsewhere in the Austrian orbit. Finally, intervention tended to arouse suspicion even among Italian conservatives that Austria intended to tighten her hold on the peninsula. Consequently, though Metternich was firmly resolved to intervene in Italy if that was necessary to prevent the triumph of revolution, he was equally determined not to intervene for any less critical reason. Although he frequently assured Albani and other Italian leaders that he would not tolerate revolution in the peninsula, he sought to avoid making specific commitments in advance, for he feared that a guarantee of Austrian aid might encourage them to call upon Vienna prematurely, to deal with uprisings which their own forces were sufficient to repress. Moreover, if such a commitment became known, France would regard it as a provocative move, and tension between the two Powers would be aggravated.[134]

But general assurances could not long satisfy those Italian states which felt most immediately threatened. Piedmont was the most uneasy, its memories of 1796 and 1821 having been revived by the spectacle of a revolutionized France once again on its border and by well-founded reports that Piedmontese exiles were planning an incursion to stir up revolt.[135] In September, 1830, Piedmont requested a formal Austrian promise to intervene in the event of revolution. Metternich had to agree, but he took care to impose conditions intended to prevent a premature or unnecessary intervention. He ordered General Frimont that if any Italian state should ask for the aid of his troops, he was to comply, provided three conditions were met: first, that a genuine revolt had taken place which the Italian government itself could not repress; second, that the government concerned had formally requested intervention; third, that Frimont was morally certain that his forces were strong enough to ensure success—an unsuccessful intervention under present circumstances would be a moral and military disaster for the conservative cause.[136]

Metternich communicated these instructions to Piedmont, but not to the other Italian states, which had not yet requested an Austrian commitment. He was thus surprised and annoyed to learn of the Duke of Modena's unauthorized offer and the confusion which it had produced. He at once dispatched to Rome a detailed explanation of his policy, assuring the Pope that Austria's aid would be forthcoming if genuinely needed and formally requested, but that otherwise she would never intervene in the Papal State.[137]

His explanation reached Rome on December 2, when the consequences of the Duke's meddling were becoming serious. Many conservative cardinals were advocating an immediate appeal for Austrian occupation of the Legations as the only way to forestall revolt, while Papal officials manifested a dangerous tendency to neglect essential precautions in the confidence that Austria could be relied upon to deal with whatever trouble might occur. Other cardinals, however, had been alarmed by Austria's apparent eagerness to intervene, and old suspicions had revived. Foreign diplomats too were suspicious, especially the French. Finally, the Sects, if somewhat intimidated by the threat of intervention, had nevertheless seized upon it for propaganda depicting Austria as an aggressive threat to Italy.[138]

Metternich's explanation cleared the air at once. The fears of the Papal government were dissipated, and foreign diplomats too were reassured.[139] Even the danger of revolt seemed to diminish: with Austrian intervention certain, the Sects could hardly hope to overthrow the government.[140]

But these developments came too late to gratify Pius VIII. Even as Metternich wrote, the Pope became seriously ill, and by November 28 his death was clearly at hand. Lützow analyzed for Metternich the likely results of this "imminent catastrophe."[141] Pius's death would have given Austria cause for regret at any time, given his sound principles and Austrophile views. But his death at this moment could have far more serious effects. Pius had to some extent been a guarantee against revolution. He was personally popular, and his interest in reform had revived hope that revolt might not be necessary to improve the regime. Moreover, the Sects knew that Pius had "the most intimate relations with Austria" and could rely upon her military aid. But with his death "all these considerations will vanish from the sight of the revolutionary league." Then too, his death would lead to a conclave at the worst possible moment. An interregnum was always a time of weak rule, of caretaker government by cardinals whose attention was fixed upon the election. Major decisions could not be taken, crises could be met only weakly and tardily, and the ordinary routine of the administration came to a virtual standstill. Such paralysis would be very dangerous in a potentially revolutionary situation; nor would the *Settarj* fail to point it out to illustrate the inherent deficiencies of the Papal regime, which only its overthrow would remedy. Since the Papal police would share in the general relaxation of the administration, the Sects could proceed more openly with their plots. The reins of government would be particularly loose in the area of greatest danger, the transapennine provinces, whose cardinal-legates would leave their posts to take part in the conclave. Moreover, the conclave itself—"a struggle of intrigue and treachery"—would display the least edifying side of the Papacy, to the benefit of anti-papal propaganda.

The danger of revolt would thus be great during the interregnum. Aggravating it further was the French doctrine of nonintervention, which was undermining the fear of Austrian intervention which had long restrained the Sects. Lützow concluded with the warning that agitation would grow throughout the interregnum; that if the conclave was prolonged, revolution was likely; and that if revolution took place only Austrian intervention could save the Temporal Power.

Lützow's analysis could not have been bettered. Pius died on November 30, 1830. The conclave, opening on December 14, dragged on for two months against a background of rising discontent; and in February, 1831, the Legations rose in revolt. The new revolutionary crisis, which Metternich had so long foreseen and the Papacy had done so little to prepare against, was upon them.

4. In Medias Res

As 1830 came to an end, Austro-Papal relations seemed to have settled into a mutually beneficial pattern of cordial cooperation in striking contrast to the situation which Metternich had found upon first taking office. As of 1809, the traditional entente between Rome and Vienna had long since ceased to exist. The religious policy of Joseph II had opened a yawning gap between his Empire and the Papacy, which was further widened during the 1790s by Austria's attempt to annex the Legations. Considering this split contrary to the political and religious interests of the Empire, Metternich resolved to heal it.

The first move in his campaign to win back Papal confidence was his attempt to secure the liberation of Pius VII, which, after initial failure, was finally successful in 1814. To build upon this promising beginning, he championed the restoration of the Papal State at the Congress of Vienna; his success did much to dissipate Papal resentment and distrust of Austria, and won him the confidence of Cardinal Consalvi, the only Papal statesman of the age with whom he enjoyed a genuine rapport. It was to Consalvi that he made his first overtures for Austro-Papal cooperation, which had now emerged as the prime objective of his Papal policy. Cooperation, he had come to feel, offered major advantages: a "Union of Throne and Altar" in which the Papacy would lend its moral authority to the defense of the Restoration order against revolution; the reinforcement of Austria's position in Italy by the support of the second-largest Italian state; the acquisition of influence at Rome which might persuade the Papacy to refrain from open assault on the Josephist system.

His overtures were favorably received by Consalvi, who could also see major advantages in cooperation: Austria could offer military protection against revolution or aggression, and diplomatic support for Papal interests in non-Catholic lands; Austrian backing for his reforms would be helpful against the *Zelanti*, while cooperation with her against the Sects would be mutually beneficial; finally, cooperation with Metternich offered the best hope of overthrowing the state church system.

The five years after the Congress saw successful cooperation between Metternich and Consalvi in political affairs; but this success was soon endangered by the revival of religious controversy. The immediate source of conflict lay in the attempt to extend Josephism into Austria's newly-acquired territories, especially Lombardy-Venetia; relations were severely strained, but Metternich's influence over the Emperor plus Consalvi's conciliatory policy enabled them to reach a satisfactory settlement of the points at issue.

Hardly had these disputes been settled when the outbreak of the Italian revolutions of 1820–1821 renewed political tension. Austria's equivocal conduct towards the Papacy during the Neapolitan crisis shook Papal confidence in her good faith. Fundamentally more serious, however, was Metternich's decision in 1821 that Austria must exert greater control over Italy if future revolutions were to be avoided. His reasoning was sound enough, but Consalvi could not tolerate an enhanced Austrian predominance that would undermine Papal independence, and at the Congress of Verona he took the lead in defeating Metternich's plans. The postal controversy brought further bitterness, and by 1823 Austro-Papal relations were colder than they had been since 1809.

Contrary to all expectation, the pontificate of Leo XII saw a dramatic reversal of this deterioration—the result not of that pontiff's intention, but of the changing religious and political circumstances of the period. The change in the Emperor's religious views which Metternich had brought about—gradual but by 1829 unmistakable—was eliminating what had long been the fundamental obstacle to Austro-Papal entente. As Josephism declined, Austrian religious policy became increasingly acceptable to Rome. Equally important, the political crisis in the Papal State—the decline of government authority and the rise of discontent and *Settarj* agitation produced by Leo's reactionary policies—led to a reversal of the Papal attitude towards Austrian power in Italy: it now seemed, not a threat to Papal independence, but a comforting assurance of protection against a revolution which Rome itself would be too weak to suppress. The newly favorable Papal attitude towards Vienna that resulted was particularly evident during the reign of Pius VIII, but it was clear that even a less Austrophile pope than he would have good reason to follow much the same policy of cooperation—especially after the July Revolution deprived Rome of its old option of turning to France rather than Austria for protection.

By 1830, then, Metternich had made notable progress towards the stable entente with Rome which he desired. Pitfalls might well lie ahead, of course: the old distrust of Austrian predominance in Italy, though presently in eclipse, was by no means dead at Rome, while as long as Josephism survived in the Empire the danger of new religious controversies could not be ignored. Yet, with skillful management, the Chancellor might reasonably hope to steer his policy of Austro-Papal cooperation safely past these dangers.

Certainly he was determined to make the effort, for by 1830 the benefits of Austro-Papal cooperation seemed to him self-evident. Austria had derived major gains: Papal participation in the struggle against revolution had strengthened the conservative cause; Papal acquiescence in Austria's hegemony in Italy had strengthened her position there; Papal moderation in religious affairs had averted dangerous confrontations over Josephism. Rome too had benefited, in particular by gaining the assurance of Austrian protection against revolution and by making considerable progress towards its otherwise unattainable goal of overthrowing the state church system. Apparently the entente was advancing the interests of both participants.

And yet, as early as 1830, a perceptive observer might have noted that Austro-Papal cooperation was not without its hazards. Metternich himself realized that Austria's protection of the Temporal Power involved serious risks: that revolution in the Papal State would involve her in a military intervention not only costly and distracting, but liable to lead to collision with a revolutionized France; that support of the Temporal Power would place Austria squarely in the path of the rising tide of Italian nationalism; that, unless Metternich could yet manage to secure genuine reform in the Papal State, Austria would be discredited before European opinion by its championing of what would increasingly be regarded as a reactionary and unpopular regime. And another danger loomed closer to home. By abandoning Josephism and supporting the revival of Papal authority and clerical influence in the Empire, Metternich had won Papal cooperation in the struggle against revolution. No doubt the support of the Church had strengthened the hold of the conservative order upon the devout masses. But what of the other classes in the Empire? Might not the gain in strengthened popular loyalty be outweighed if the educated minority was alienated by the clerical overtones of what was becoming known as the "Metternich System?"

For Rome too, cooperation held its dangers. True, the political cost—dependence upon Austria—seemed to many at Rome well justified, as the only hope of resisting the revolutionary challenge. But might not this protection be purchased at too high a price—the erosion of the only real justification for the Temporal Power, which was that it preserved Papal political and spiritual freedom of action? For as Papal reliance upon Austria grew, its independence must become increasingly illusory. And could Rome resist its protector's demand that it follow a strictly conservative policy, and instead give a fair hearing to those Catholics who wished to see it adopt a more progressive outlook?

But whether Austro-Papal relations would continue along the path of co-operation upon which they now seemed embarked; and whether the ultimate effects of this Union of Throne and Altar would be as beneficial for both as they had anticipated—these are questions whose answer we must defer until the conclusion of our study of Austria and the Papacy in the Age of Metternich.

Notes

Chapter I

1. Since there is no comprehensive study of Austro-Papal relations prior to the Metternich era, the subject is best studied in the relevant sections of such general works as: Ludwig von Pastor, *The History of the Popes from the close of the Middle Ages;* Augustin Fliche and Victor Martin, eds., *Histoire de l'Eglise depuis ses origines jusqu'à nos jours;* Ernst Tomek, *Kirchengeschichte Österreichs;* Josef Wodka, *Kirche in Österreichs;* and Alfons Huber and Oscar Redlich, *Geschichte Österreichs,* supplemented where possible by specialized studies such as Salvatore Pugliese, *Le prime strette dell'Austria in Italia;* Norbert Huber, *Österreich und der Heilige Stuhl vom Ende des spanischen Erbfolgekriegs bis zum Tode Klemens XI;* Hans Kramer, *Hapsburg und Rom in den Jahren 1708–1709;* Adam Wandruszka, *Österreich und Italien im 18. Jahrhundert;* S. von Bischoffshausen, *Papst Alexander VIII und der Wiener Hof.*

2. Note, e.g., the dispatch of Garampi, November 7, 1761, in Paolo Brezzi, *La diplomazia pontificia,* 242–244.

3. I am aware that "Josephism" was a wide-ranging phenomenon, whose manifestations went far beyond the religious sphere; but since in this work I deal only with its religious aspects, I intend for convenience's sake to use the term as if it applied only to religious policy.

4. On the Austrian attempt to annex the Legations, see: Ercole Cardinal Consalvi, *Memorie,* 138–144; Charles van Duerm, *Un peu plus de lumière sur le Conclave de Venise;* Guy Mollat, *La question romaine,* 51–80.

Pope Pius VII (1800–1823), born Barnabas Luigi Chiaramonti at Cesena, August 14, 1742; bishop of Tivoli, 1782; Cardinal, 1785; elected Pope at the conclave of Venice in 1800. See Jean Leflon, *Pie VII,* and Josef Schmidlin, *Histoire des Papes de l'epoque contemporaine,* vol. 1: *Pie VII.* For a survey of the literature on Pius VII and his pontificate, see Alan J. Reinerman, "Papacy and Papal State in the Restoration: Studies since 1939," *The Catholic Historical Review,* 44 (January, 1978): 36–46.

5. On religious affairs in 1800–1809, see the correspondence of the Vienna Nuncio, especially his reports of June 30, 1807 and August 18, 1808, in Archivio Segreto Vaticano (hereafter cited as AV); Archivio della Nunziatura di Vienna (hereafter ANV), 232; and Ferdinand Maass, *Der Josephinismus,* 4:48–100; Tomek 3:513–560; Consalvi, *Memorie,* 174–182. On political affairs, see Ludwig Graf von Lebzeltern, *Un collaborateur de Metternich: Mémoires et papiers de Lebzeltern* (hereafter cited as Lebzeltern), 6–67; Ilario Rinieri, *Napoleone e Pio VII,* 1:97–102; Alois Hudal, *Die österreichische Vatikanbotschaft, 1806–1918,* 1–14.

6. Lebzeltern, 10–61.

7. E.g., the report of Lebzeltern to Stadion, June 18, 1808, Haus-, Hof- und Staatsarchiv Vienna (hereafter cited as HHSA), Rom: Berichte, 1808. Unless otherwise stated, all HHSA documents in this study are from the Staatskanzlei: Auswärtiges Amt collection. On the quarrel between Napoleon and Pius VII, see Henri Wels-

chinger, *Le Pape et l'Empereur;* C. de Mayol de Lupe, *La captivité de Pie VII;* Rinieri, *Napoleone*; Consalvi, *Memorie.*

8. HHSA, Rom: Weisungen, Stadion to Lebzeltern, February 16, 1808. AV, ANV 232, Severoli to Pacca, February 13, February 20, 1808.

9. HHSA, Rom: Weisungen, Stadion to Lebzeltern, March 30, 1809. AV, ANV, Severoli to Pacca, May 21, 1809.

10. Lebzeltern to Metternich, October 16, 1809, in Lebzeltern, 68–87; also, Hudal, 14–16. Contrary to the charge made by Edouard Driault, *Napoleon en Italie*, 545–548, Pius VIII refused to take an active part in stirring up a religious war. His motives are explained in Bartolomeo Pacca, *Historical Memoirs*, 1:103–112.

11. Lebzeltern to Metternich, October 16, 1809, in Lebzeltern, 68–87. On the military background, see Piers Mackesy, *The War in the Mediterranean, 1803-1810*, 305–334.

12. Lebzeltern to Metternich, October 16, 1809, in Lebzeltern, 68–87.

13. See Mayol de Lupe, 104–221.

14. There seems to be no point in listing here the immense literature on Metternich, especially since those works pertinent to this study will be cited at appropriate places in the Notes and listed in the Bibliography. The standard biography is still Heinrich Ritter von Srbik, *Metternich, der Staatsmann und der Mensch*. For a survey of the recent literature, see the third volume of Srbik, and Paul W. Schroeder, "Metternich Studies since 1925," *Journal of Modern History*, 33 (1961): 237–260.

15. Lebzeltern to Metternich, October 16, 1809, in Lebzeltern, 68–87. On Metternich's attitude towards the Papacy at this time, see also AV, ANV 219, "De mea agendi ratione post initiam Vienna pacem in rebus politicis," "Conversazione col Conte di Metternich, 21 febbraio 1810," "Conversazione col Conte di Metternich, 15 marzo 1810;" and Fedor von Demelitsch, *Metternich und seine auswärtige Politik*, 89–93.

16. AV, ANV 219, "Mia conversazione col Conte di Metternich e Cav. Lebzeltern, 15 marzo 1810." Clemens Lothar Wenzel Fürst von Metternich, *Mémoires, documents et écrits divers laissés par le Prince de Metternich,* 1:304–306, Metternich to Francis I, August 10, 1809.

17. AV, ANV 219, "Conversazione col Conte di Metternich, 22 marzo 1810."

18. AV, ANV 219, "Reclamo per il mio titolo di nunzio dopo la pace di Vienna," "Conversazione col Ct. di Metternich, 22 marzo 1810," "Conversazione col Cav. Hudelist, 8 Aprile 1811;" Metternich's report to Francis I, October 21, 1809, in HHSA, Vorträge 270, 1809.

19. For Pius's firmly negative view, see Lebzeltern, 158–160; Consalvi, *Memorie*, 351–373; Rinieri, *Napoleone*, 2:38–45. On Metternich's role in the marriage, see Srbik, *Metternich*, 1:129–132; Metternich, *Mémoires*, 1:99–114; Demelitsch, *Metternich*, 146–219.

20. See Severoli's "De mea agendi ratione post initam Vienna Pacem in rebus politicis," "De Napoleon non vitendo de ejusque divortio," "Riflessioni sul matrimonio di Napoleone," and "Abboccamento col'Imperatore e coll'Arcivescovo, 22 febbraio 1810," in AV, ANV 219.

21. "It is incredible with what indifference Metternich welcomed my words," wrote the indignant Nuncio: AV, ANV 219, "De Napoleon non vitendo de ejusque divortio." From this point onwards, Severoli became increasingly critical of Metternich and the Imperial government, an attitude which led to his recall in 1816.

22. AV, ANV 219, "Avvertenze sugli affari ecclesiastici date al Ct. di Metternich prima di sua partenza, 22 marzo 1810," "Conversazione col Ct. di Metternich e Cav. di Lebzeltern, 15 marzo 1810," Metternich, *Mémoires*, 2:320–322. Demelitsch, *Metternich*, 181–183.

23. Louis Madelin, *Histoire du Consulat et de l'Empire*, 10:62-63; Demelitsch, *Metternich*, 182-183.

24. Metternich, *Mémoires*, 2:324-336, 349-353. AV, ANV 219, "Conversazione col Ct. di Metternich e Cav. di Lebzeltern, 15 marzo 1810." Lebzeltern, 142-152. Henri Chotard, *Le Pape Pie VII à Savone*, 57-65.

25. Metternich, *Mémoires*, 2:333-336.

26. *Ibid.*, 2:336-344.

27. *Ibid.*, 2:336-344; Lebzeltern, 148-152.

28. Lebzeltern, 148-152.

29. On Lebzeltern's mission, see Lebzeltern, 153-200; Metternich, *Mémoires*, 2:344-355; Chotard, 73-133; Demelitsch, *Metternich*, 184-200; Mayol de Lupe, 329-345; P. Feret, *Histoire diplomatique*, 1:232-235.

30. Lebzeltern, 158-163.

31. *Ibid.*, 163-178.

32. *Ibid.*, 178-182. Metternich, *Mémoires*, 2:349-354.

33. Metternich, *Mémoires*, 2:349-353.

34. Lebzeltern, 195-196.

35. *Ibid.*, 195-200; Metternich, *Mémoires*, 2:349-353; Demelitsch, *Metternich*, 198-200.

36. Lebzeltern, 160-168, 182-187; Metternich, *Mémoires*, 2:353-355.

37. E.g., Metternich to his wife, *Mémoires*, 3:195, and to Countess Lieven, *Lettres du Prince de Metternich à la Comtesse de Lieven*, 274-277.

38. Demelitsch, *Metternich*, 337-339. Ilario Rinieri, *Il Congresso di Vienna e la Santa Sede*, 27, n. 2.

39. AV, ANV 219, "Conversazioni col Cav. Hudelist e Ct. di Metternich, 8 Aprile 1811;" "Conversazione col Ambasciatore di Russia," undated, but 1811-1812.

40. Pacca, 2:244-253; Rinieri, *Congresso*, 34-36; Welschinger, *Le Pape*, 403-409. On the peace negotiations of 1813, see Albert Sorel, *Europe et la révolution française*, 8:111-180, and Charles Webster, *The Foreign Policy of Castlereagh, 1812-1815*, 135-153.

41. HHSA, Rom: Varia, Pius VII to Francis I, July 24, 1813.

42. AV, ANV 219, Severoli's memoires of August 20 and August 26, 1813, and undated, but July-August 1813, to Metternich, and "Miei reclami al Congresso di Praga;" also Pacca, 2:252-253, and Welschinger, *Le Pape*, 405-409, who, however, accepts the so-called Secret Treaty between Austria and England, supposedly signed in July, 1813, by which Austria was to annex part of the Papal State. It has long since been shown to be a fraud: e.g., Rinieri, *Congresso*, 35-43.

43. AV, ANV 219, Severoli's memoires of August 20 and August 26, 1813. Sorel, 8:112.

44. AV, Rubrica 254 (hereafter R254), Testaferrata to Pius VII, April 13, 1814. Public Record Office, London (hereafter cited PRO), Foreign Office 92 (hereafter FO 92), Castlereagh to Liverpool, March 5, 14, 1814. M. H. Weil, *Le Prince Eugene et Murat, 1813-1814*, 3:566-567. Robert Stewart, Viscount Castlereagh, *Memoirs and Correspondence*, 9:104-105, Aberdeen to Castlereagh, December 19, 1813.

45. Fedor von Demelitsch, *Actenstucke zur Geschichte der Coalition vom Jahre 1814*, 334, 345, 353-356, 446. August Fournier, *Der Congress von Chatillon*, 235, 358.

46. Welschinger, *Le Pape*, 423-427; Feret, 1:376-378.

47. Rinieri, *Congresso*, 13-22; Welschinger, *Le Pape*, 424-427; Mayol de Lupe, 697-703.

48. HHSA, Rom: Berichte, Lebzeltern to Metternich, April 25 #1, and April 28, 1814 #5.

49. Lebzeltern, 306-307.

50. *Ibid.*, 307, Metternich to Lebzeltern, April 7, 1814.

51. AV, R242, Consalvi to Pacca, June 13, 1814. HHSA, Rom: Berichte, Lebzeltern to Metternich, May 22, 1814 #12. Lebzeltern, 308-312.

52. E.g., Metternich to Mier, December 25, 1813, in Weil, *Prince Eugene,* 3: 566-567.

53. On this treaty and its background, see Weil, *Prince Eugene,* 3:245-525.

54. *Ibid.*, 3:612-613, Neipperg to Metternich, December 31, 1813.

55. Treaty printed in *Ibid., 3*:614-619.

56. See, e.g., Demelitsch, *Actenstucke,* 234-235, and Alfons Klinkowstrom, ed., *Österreichs Theilnahme an den Befreiungskreigen*, 616-618.

57. HHSA, Rom: Berichte, Lebzeltern to Metternich, April 25, #1 & 2, and April 29, 1814 #5.

58. HHSA, Rom: Varia, Pius VII to Francis I, April 1, 1814.

59. HHSA, Rom: Berichte, Lebzeltern to Metternich, April 28 #5, and April 29, 1814 #5.

60. HHSA, Rom: Berichte, Lebzeltern to Metternich, April 25 #1, April 29, 1814 #5, and May 2, 1814 #6 & 7. Rinieri, *Congresso,* 90-101.

61. HHSA, Rom: Berichte, Lebzeltern to Metternich, April 25, 1814 #1.

62. Lebzeltern to Mauri, April 30, 1814, in Rinieri, *Congresso,* 101.

63. HHSA, Rom: Berichte, Lebzeltern to Metternich, April 29 #5, and May 2, 1814 #6 & 7.

64. Pius VII to Francis I, April 29, 1814, HHSA, Rom: Varia, 1814.

65. *Ibid.,* Rom: Berichte, Lebzeltern to Metternich, May 6, 1814 #9. Annibale della Genga (1760-1829), Nuncio in Cologne, 1794-1799; Nuncio in Munich, 1802-1808; cardinal 1816; elected as Pope Leo XII in 1823; see Raffaele Colapietra, *La formazione diplomatica di Leone XII,* in which the mission to Paris is covered on pp. 193-214.

66. AV, R241, Instructions for Monsignor Della Genga, May 7, 1814.

67. Pius VII to Francis I, May 3, 1814, HHSA, Rom: Varia, 1814.

68. E.g., Pius VII to Francis I, May 19, 1814, May 20, 1814, HHSA, Rom: Varia, 1814.

69. HHSA, Rom: Berichte, Lebzeltern to Metternich, May 28, 1814 #13.

70. Lebzeltern, 322-330.

71. HHSA, Rom: Berichte, Lebzeltern to Metternich, April 23 #1, April 28 #5, May 28 #13, June 25 #18-A, and July 15, 1814 #21-A.

72. On Consalvi, the basic source is his own *Memorie,* which unfortunately ends in 1812. There is no adequate biography. The older works of Ernest Daudet, *Le Cardinal Consalvi* and Engelbert Fischer, *Cardinal Consalvi* are superficial and now obsolete; nor can the more recent biographies be recommended, since Richard Winterich, *Sein Schichsal war Napoleon* is a popularized and superficial treatment, while G. A. Angelucci, *Il grande Segretario di Stato della Santa Sede E. Consalvi,* is an uncritical panegyric. The brief essay which Leopold von Ranke wrote in the 1830s, "Cardinal Consalvi und seine Staatsverwaltung unter dem Pontificate Pius VII," *Historische-biographische Studien. Samtliche Werke, XL,* shows more insight than any of the above.

73. HHSA, Rom: Weisungen, Instructions for Kaunitz, May 31, 1817.

74. Note, e.g., Metternich's judgments on Consalvi, in HHSA, Rom: Weisungen, Instructions for Kaunitz, May 31, 1817, for Apponyi, September 16, 1820; and in *Mémoires,* 4:91.

75. Rinieri, *Congresso,* 655. Bartolomeo Pacca (1756-1844), Nuncio in Lisbon, 1801; Prosecretary of State, 1808-1809; imprisoned by Napoleon 1810-1814: see his *Memoirs,* as well as G. Brigante Colonna, *Bartolomeo Pacca.*

76. AV, R242, Instructions for Consalvi, May 20, 1814.

77. *Ibid.,* Consalvi to Pacca, June 6 and 8. The treaty is in Comte d'Angeberg (Leonard Chodzko), *Le Congrès de Vienne et les traités de 1815,* 1:161-205. This episode led to a bitter quarrel between Consalvi and Della Genga, which was to have major repercussions later; see Colapietra, 195-218.

78. AV, R242, Consalvi to Pacca, June 6 and June 8, 1814.

79. *Ibid.,* June 13, June 24, 1814. After Napoleon's invasion of the Papal State, the Papacy ceded the Legations to France by the Treaty of Tolentino of 1797.

80. HHSA, Rom: Weisungen, Metternich to Lebzeltern, August 21, 1815.

81. AV, R242, Consalvi to Pacca, 18-20 November 1814 #119.

82. HHSA, Rom: Weisungen, Metternich to Lebzeltern, July 22, 1815, Instructions for Kaunitz, May 31, 1817; Kongressakten, 14: Wiener Kongress, F. 25, Mémoire des Hofrats von Gentz, May 4, 1815. AV, R242, Consalvi to Pacca, June 13, 24, and 30, September 4 and 8, 1814. It is true that numerous historians have asserted that Metternich did plan to annex the Legations, and was only stopped by the opposition of France and Russia: e.g., Nicomede Bianchi, *Storia documentata della diplomazia europea in Italia dall'anno 1814 all'anno 1861,* 1:2-8, 134-137, et passim; Sorel, 8:365 et passim; M. H. Weil, *Joachim Murat, Roi de Naples,* 1:73-76, 91-92, 279-282; Guido Gigli, *Il Congresso di Vienna, 1814-1815,* 139-155. But none of these can present solid evidence to support the charge, basing it rather upon rumors, the gossip of non-Austrian diplomats, allusions to Austrian plans in 1800, and the famous but nonexistent Secret Treaty of Prague of 1813. Thus Bianchi cites the Secret Treaty and the rumors reported by Italian diplomats; Sorel does the same, except that the rumors were reported by French diplomats; and Gigli does not bother to cite evidence. Weil—whose error is the most surprising of all, since he alone had worked in HHSA and was usually free from the anti-Austrian prejudices of the Risorgimento era—bases his charges on the Secret Treaty and the reports of Severoli. Unfortunately, the Secret Treaty never existed, while Severoli was renowned for his hostility to Austria. It is significant that Weil can cite no evidence from HHSA to support his charge, despite his meticulous research there. I could find no hint in Metternich's correspondence that he planned to annex the Legations; in fact, he repeatedly denied any such plan, and Consalvi, a perceptive observer not given to overcredulity, came to believe his denials. And in the end, Austria did not annex the Legations, though certainly not because of Russian or French opposition—Russia would have allowed Austria to annex as much of Italy as she wished, while France was prepared to let Austria take the Legations if she would allow the Bourbons to control Parma: e.g., AV, R242, Consalvi to Pacca, 18 November 1814 #119. To sum up, it seems clear that Metternich had no sinister plan to annex the Legations and did not particularly want them, though there were circumstances which might conceivably have driven him to consider taking them. The charge merely reflects the suspicions of contemporary diplomats, which were given a certain plausibility by earlier Austrian designs on the Legations and were sustained in later years by the prejudices of the Risorgimento; the modern historian has no grounds for accepting it.

83. AV, R242, Consalvi to Pacca, September 8 and October 25, 1814 #91. Weil, *Joachim Murat,* 2:316, report of Schwartzenberg.

84. HHSA, Kongressakten, 14: Wiener Kongress, F. 25, Mémoire des Hofrats von Gentz, May 5, 1815. AV, R242, Consalvi to Pacca, June 13 and 24, September 4 and 8, 1814. PRO, F.O. 139, Project of Arrangements for Italy, November 5, 1814.

85. AV, R242, Consalvi to Pacca, June 13, 24, and 30, September 8, 1814. HHSA, Neapel: Weisungen, Metternich to Mier, August 22, 1814. Weil, *Joachim Murat,* 1, 271-276. Klinkowstrom, 616-618.

86. AV, R242, Consalvi to Pacca, June 13 and 24, September 8, 1814.

87. E.g., AV, R242, Consalvi to Pacca, June 13 and 24, September 4 and 8, 1814.

HHSA, Kongressakten, 14: Wiener Kongress, F. 25, Mémoire des Hofrats von Gentz, May 4, 1815.

88. AV, R242, Consalvi to Pacca, June 13, 1814.

89. *Ibid.*, June 30, 1814.

90. There is a vast literature dealing with the Congress of Vienna. Of the general studies, the best are those of Charles Webster, *The Congress of Vienna*, and Karl Griewank, *Der Wiener Kongress*. The basic collection of documents is D'Angeberg, *Le Congrès*. On Austrian policy, see Srbik, *Metternich*, 1:182-230, and Metternich, *Mémoires*, 2:474-513. Also useful are the various collections of documents of Friedrich von Gentz: *Depêches inédites aux Hospodars de Valachie*, *Briefe von Friedrich von Gentz an Pilat*, and *Tagebücher;* and the reports of the Austrian secret police, published by August Fournier, *Die Geheimpolizei auf dem Wiener Kongress*, and M. H. Weil, ed., *Les Dessous du Congrès de Vienne*. On Papal policy, see Adolfo Omodeo, "Il Cardinale Consalvi al Congresso di Vienna," *La Critica*, 36 (1938): 426-440, 37 (1939): 24-36; Rinieri, *Il Congresso*; and Alessandro Roveri, *La Santa Sede tra rivoluzione francese e restaurazione*. The correspondence between Consalvi and Pacca during the Congress has now been edited by Alessandro Roveri, *La missione Consalvi e il Congresso di Vienna*, which is superior to the earlier edition by Ilario Rinieri, *Correspondenza inedita dei cardinali Consalvi e Pacca nel tempo del Congresso di Vienna*. On Italian questions, see especially Bianchi, *Storia documentata*, vol. 1; Weil, *Joachim Murat*, vols. 2-4; Walter Maturi, "Il Congresso di Vienna e la Restaurazione dei Borboni a Napoli," *Rivista Storica Italiana*, 55 (1938): 32-72, and 56:1-61.

91. AV, R242, Consalvi to Pacca, September 4 and 8, 1814.

92. AV, R242, Consalvi to Pacca, September 8, 1814.

93. E.g., *ibid.*, September 10, 19, 26, October 1 and 19, 1814.

94. E.g., HHSA, Rom: Weisungen, Metternich to Lebzeltern, August 21, 1815, Instructions for Kaunitz, May 31, 1817, Instructions for Apponyi, September 16, 1820.

95. AV, R242, Consalvi to Pacca, December 3, 1814 #132; also, September 19 and 26, November 1, 1814 #97, in which his gradual growth of confidence in Metternich can be traced.

96. *Ibid.*, October 19, 1814 #85.

97. *Ibid.*, November 13, 1814.

98. *Ibid.*, November 16 #107, November 18-20 #119, 1814. In fact neither ex-ruler wanted the Legations, partly from religious scruples, partly from fear that the Pope would not leave their possessor in peace. Note, for example, the advice of Francis I to his daughter, *ibid.*, November 16, 1814 #107, and Maria Louisa's scruples, *ibid.*, November 25, 1814, #126. On the question of Parma, see Gigli, 149-151; Elena Nevola, "La questione di Parma al Congresso di Vienna e un memoriale del Neipperg," *Archivio storico per le provincie parmensi*, 3rd series, 3:111-125; Leny Montagna, *I ducati parmensi nella diplomazia, 1796-1815;* Weil, *Joachim Murat*, vol. 1; Metternich, *Mémoires*, 2:474-501; Klinkowstrom, 616-620. On Maria Louisa, see P. Marmottan, *Le royaume d'Etrurie*.

99. AV, R242, Consalvi to Pacca, November 16 #107, November 18-20 #119, 1814.

100. *Ibid.*, November 16, 1814 #107.

101. *Ibid.*, November 25, 1814 #126. Also, December 9 #138, December 17 #148, 1814; M. G. Pallain, ed., *Correspondance inédite du Prince Talleyrand et du Roi Louis XVIII pendant le Congrès de Vienne*, 152-158, 189-192; Klinkowstrom, 617-620.

102. AV, R242, Consalvi to Pacca, November 18-20 #119, 19 #113, 29 #129, December 3 #132, 7 #135, 9 #138, 17 #148, and 21 #149, 1814.

103. There seems no point in describing in detail the numerous talks which Consalvi had with Metternich on this subject, since all followed the same basic pattern—Consalvi expressing the points mentioned above and requesting support, Metternich

replying that support would be forthcoming but that the Congress could not reach a definite decision on the Legations until it had arranged other major questions: see *ibid.*, September 19, October 1, 19 #85, 25, 30, November 16 #107, 18–20 #119, 19 #113, 29 #129, December 3, #132, 7 #135, and December 17 #148, 1814.

104. E.g., *ibid.*, December 7 #135, 14 #142, and 17 #148, 1814.

105. *Ibid.*, December 7, 1814 #135.

106. *Ibid.*, November 15, 1814 #126.

107. *Ibid.*, November 18–20 #119. See also November 29 #129, December 3 #132, 9 #138, 14 #142, 17 #148, and 28 #155, 1814. Talleyrand's instructions—in Weil, *Joachim Murat*, 1:552–556—were to work for the return of the Legations to the Pope, and he assured Louis XVIII that he was acting in that sense—e.g., Pallain, 189–192. In reality, he wanted to take the Legations for Maria Louisa if she could not obtain Parma, or to give them to Marie Louise if this would obtain Parma for the ex-Queen of Etruria. On the difficult and unfriendly relationship between Consalvi and Talleyrand at the Congress, see Giuseppi Gallavresi, "Le Prince de Talleyrand et le Cardinal Consalvi," *Revue des questions historiques*, 77 (1905): 158–172.

108. AV, R242, Consalvi to Pacca, November 29 #132, December 14 #142 and 28, #155, 1814 and January 4, 1815 #171.

109. AV, R242, Consalvi to Pacca, November 18–20, 1814 #119.

110. *Ibid.*, December 9, 1814 #138. Note also Consalvi's contrast between the attitudes of Austria and France, to the latter's disadvantage, in his report to Pacca, February 11, 1815 #232, *ibid.*

111. *Ibid.*, January 11 #184, 14 #190, 21 #197, February 15 #239, 22 #249, 1815.

112. *Ibid.*, June 30, 1814.

113. *Ibid.*, June 13, 24, and 30, 1814. HHSA, Rom: Varia, Esterhazy to Metternich, September 4, 1814; Neapel: Weisungen, Metternich to Mier, August 22, 1814.

114. AV, R242, Consalvi to Pacca, July 12, 25, August 17 #29, and September 8, 1814. HHSA, Rom: Berichte, Lebzeltern to Metternich, June 25 #18-A, July 9 #20-A, July 16 #21-A, August 1 #24, and September 3 #30-A, 1814; Rom: Varia, Esterhazy to Metternich, September 4, 1814.

115. AV, R242, Consalvi to Pacca, September 4 and 8, 1814.

116. *Ibid.*, September 8, 17 #45, and 19 #47, 1814; Pacca to Consalvi, September 1, and 24 #19, 1814. HHSA, Neapel: Berichte, Mier to Metternich, August 31 #33, and September 9 #36, 1814.

117. HHSA, Rom: Weisungen, Metternich to Lebzeltern, November 29, 1814 #1; Rom: Varia, Metternich to Esterhazy, October 22, 1814. AV, Consalvi to Pacca, October 1 and 19, #85, 1814.

118. HHSA, Neapel: Berichte, Mier to Metternich, September 2, 1814 #53. To make assurance doubly sure, Talleyrand was also negotiating secretly with Ferdinand IV to secure the promise of Benevento in return for his support at the Congress: Weil, *Joachim Murat*, 1:266. On Talleyrand's acquisition and rule of Benevento, see A. M. P. Ingold, *Bénévent sous la domination de Talleyrand*. On the situation in Benevento during 1814–1815, see Alfredo Zazo, "L'occupazione napoletana e austriaca e i primordi della Restaurazione in Benevento," *Samnium*, 1956, 189–206, 1957, 1–26, 121–147.

119. HHSA, Rom: Weisungen, Metternich to Lebzeltern, November 29, 1814 #1. AV, R242, Consalvi to Pacca, October 19 #85 and 25 #91, 1814.

120. AV, R242, Consalvi to Pacca, October 25 #91, November 1 #97, 1814. HHSA, Rom: Weisungen, Metternich to Lebzeltern, November 29, 1814 #1.

121. AV, R242, Pacca to Consalvi, October 31, 1814; also, November 10 and 13, 1814.

122. *Ibid.*, Consalvi to Pacca, November 19, 1814 #113.

123. *Ibid.*, Pacca to Consalvi, December 5, 1814, Consalvi to Pacca, December 21, 1814 #149; also, December 17, 1814 #148.

124. HHSA, Rom: Weisungen, Metternich to Lebzeltern, November 29, 1814 #1.

125. *Ibid.*, November 29, 1814 #2.

126. AV, R242, Pacca to Consalvi, October 27, November 10, 26, December 3, 8, 12, 24, and 29, 1814. HHSA, Rom: Berichte, Lebzeltern to Metternich, December 10 #54, 15 #56-A & B, 17 #57-A & B, and 24 #60, 1814, and Lebzeltern to Mier, December 11 and 13, 1814.

127. HHSA, Neapel: Weisungen, Metternich to Mier, November 29, 1814.

128. HHSA, Neapel: Berichte, Mier to Metternich, December 13 #84, 16 #85, and 29 #87, 1814. AV, R242, Consalvi to Pacca, December 31, 1814 #168.

129. HHSA, Rom: Weisungen, Metternich to Lebzeltern, January 1, 1815.

130. AV, R242, Consalvi to Pacca, February 1, 1815.

131. *Ibid.*, January 21, 1815 #197; also, January 7 #175, January 11 #184, and January 14 #190, 1815.

132. On the evolution of Metternich's policy, his motives, and his negotiations with France, see Weil, *Joachim Murat,* 2:270–467, as well as his "Le révirement de la politique autrichienne à l'égard de Joachim Murat," *Biblioteca de storia italiana recente,* 2 (1909): 393–435.

133. AV, R242, Consalvi to Pacca, February 25, 1815 #250.

134. AV, R242, Consalvi to Pacca, March 8, 1815 #262; also, March 15, 1815 #272.

135. On Murat's decision, see Weil, *Joachim Murat,* 3; on the Proclamation of Rimini, see Domenico Spadoni, "Nel centenario del proclama di Rimini," *Rassegna storica del Risorgimento,* 2:329–363.

136. HHSA, Rom: Weisungen, Metternich to Lebzeltern, April 12, 1815.

137. AV, R242, Consalvi to Pacca, March 29, 1815 #290.

138. *Ibid.*

139. *Ibid.*, March 29 #290, and April 15 #293, 1815; Pacca to Consalvi, April 15, 1815.

140. HHSA, Rom: Weisungen, Metternich to Lebzeltern, April 12, 1815. AV, R242, Consalvi to Pacca, April 12 #288, and 15 #293, 1815; Metternich to Consalvi, April 13, 1815.

141. AV, R242, Pacca to Consalvi, March 28, 1815. HHSA, Rom: Berichte, Lebzeltern to Metternich, March 20 #85, 22 #86, and April 26 #102, 1815.

142. On Murat's defeat, see Weil, *Joachim Murat,* vols. 4–5.

143. AV, R242, Consalvi to Pacca, February 11 #232, 15 #239, April 12 #288, and May 9, 1815 #314. Maturi, "Il Congresso," 56:34–35.

144. AV, R242, Consalvi to Pacca, May 15, 1815 #319; also May 20, 1815 #321. HHSA, Rom: Weisungen, Metternich to Lebzeltern, May 17, 1815.

145. AV, R242, Consalvi to Pacca, April 12, 1815 #288; also, April 30 #309, May 15 #319, May 28 #327, 1815. HHSA, Rom: Weisungen, Metternich to Lebzeltern, May 17, 1815.

146. He was particularly aware of Consalvi's determination to resist because the Austrian police had intercepted the latter's correspondence with Pacca on this point: HHSA, Rom: Weisungen, Metternich to Lebzeltern, May 17, 1815.

147. Maturi, "Il Congresso," 56:52–61. Weil, *Joachim Murat,* 4:464–467.

148. AV, R242, Consalvi to Pacca, June 12, 1815 #332 & 336, Maturi, "Il Congresso," 56:57–58. Klinkowstrom, 563–564.

149. AV, R242, Consalvi to Pacca, May 28, 1815 #327.

150. *Ibid.*, May 20 #321, 28 #327, June 2 #331, and 12 #332 & 336, 1815. HHSA, Rom: Weisungen, Metternich to Lebzeltern, May 17, 1815.

151. AV, R242, Consalvi to Pacca, May 15 #319, June 2 #331, and June 12 #336, 1815.

152. *Ibid.*, March 8 #212, and May 15 #319, 1815.
153. HHSA, Rom: Weisungen, Metternich to Lebzeltern, May 17, and July 22, 1815. AV, R242, Consalvi to Pacca, May 15 #319, and 28 #327, 1815.
154. AV, R242, Consalvi to Pacca, May 28 #327, 1815.
155. *Ibid.*, June 2 #331, and 12 #332 & 336, 1815. HHSA, Rom: Weisungen, Metternich to Lebzeltern, June 22, 1815. The treaty is printed in Leopold Neumann, *Recueil des traités et conventions conclus par l'Autriche*, 3:21-22.
156. AV, R242, Consalvi to Pacca, June 12 #332, 1815.
157. *Ibid.*, June 12 #336, 1815.

Chapter II

1. Metternich expressed this intention frequently in his correspondence throughout the 1815-1848 period: e.g., HHSA, Rom: Weisungen, Metternich to Lebzeltern, January 20, 1815, Instructions for Kaunitz, May 31, 1817, Instructions for Apponyi, September 16, 1820, Metternich to Wittgenstein, May 26, 1838, copy with Metternich to Lutzow, June 5, 1838; Rom: Varia, Metternich to Consalvi, July 3, 1816, November 22 and December 13, 1820, Instructions for Lebzeltern, December 12, 1820; Toskana: Weisungen, Instructions for Apponyi, April 1816. AV, R247, Leardi to Consalvi, February 22, 1818, January 18 and May 8, 1821.
2. HHSA, Rom: Weisungen, Metternich to Wittgenstein, May 26, 1838, copy with Metternich to Lützow, June 5, 1838.
3. *Ibid.*, Toskana: Weisungen, Instructions for Apponyi, May 22, 1816.
4. AV, R247, Leardi to Consalvi, May 8, 1821.
5. *Ibid.*, Leardi to Consalvi, February 22, 1818.
6. E.g., HHSA, Rom: Weisungen, Metternich to Apponyi, September 16, 1820, and June 20, 1823. Metternich, *Mémoires*, 3:57-61, Metternich to Nesselrode, August 20, 1817.
7. On Metternich's Italian policy during this period, see Srbik, 1:182-229, 556-599; Paul W. Schroeder, *Metternich's Diplomacy at its Zenith, 1820-1823;* Arthur G. Haas, *Metternich, Reorganization and Nationality 1813-1818;* Karl Grossman, "Metternichs Plan eines italienischen Bundes," *Historische Blätter,* 4 (1931): 37-76; Antonio Maria Bettanini, "Un disegno di confederazione italiana," *Studi di storia dei trattati e politica internazionale;* Guillaume de Bertier de Sauvigny, *Metternich et la France,* 1:117-147, 229-232, 2:316-581; Narciso Nada, *Le relazioni diplomatiche fra l'Austria e il Regno di Sardegna, 1814-1830.*
8. HHSA, Rom: Weisungen, Instructions for Kaunitz, May 31, 1817.
9. Note, e.g., his remarks to Apponyi, September 16, 1820, and to Wittgenstein, May 26, 1838, in HHSA, Rom: Weisungen, and to Nesselrode, August 20, 1817, *Mémoires,* 3:57.
10. AV, R242, Consalvi to Pacca, February 11 #232, 22 #245, 1815. Archivio della S. Congregazione De Propaganda Fide, Fondo Consalvi (hereafter ACPFFC), N. 34, Consalvi to Spina, July 2, 1818. HHSA, Rom: Berichte, Lebzeltern to Metternich, July 29 #135, August 12 #142, September 7 #156, November 11, 1815 #189, April 27 #95, 30 #96, 1816, and Lebzeltern to Hudelist, August 26, 1815.
11. Part of this correspondence has been printed in Charles van Duerm, ed., *Correspondance du Cardinal Hercule Consalvi avec le Prince Clément de Metternich.* The originals are in HHSA, Rom: Varia, 1814-1823.
12. E.g., HHSA, Rom: Weisungen, Metternich to Lebzeltern, July 22, August 21,

1815; Instructions for Kaunitz, May 31, 1817; Instructions for Apponyi, September 16, 1820; Toskana: Weisungen, Instructions for Apponyi, May 22, 1816.

13. E.g., *Ibid.*, Rom: Varia, Metternich to Consalvi, August 28 and October 7, 1815, April 23 and July 3, 1816.

14. At least, after the Austrophobe Severoli had been replaced in 1816 at Metternich's request because of his violent criticism of Austria and his hostility to Austro-Papal cooperation: HHSA, Rom: Weisungen, Metternich to Lebzeltern, July 22, 1815. His successor, Monsignor Paolo Leardi, was known for his "ties of affection with Austria" and was a close friend of Lebzeltern; he was chosen by Consalvi primarily because of his commitment to the policy of cooperation; Rom: Berichte, Lebzeltern to Metternich, January 22, 1816.

15. On the general religious situation of the Papacy during the Restoration, see Schmidlin, *Histoire des Papes* and Jean Leflon, *La Crise révolutionnaire,* 321-375.

16. E.g., HHSA, Rom: Varia, Metternich to Consalvi, July 3, 1816.

17. See below, 80-81.

18. E.g., AV, R260, Gennotte to Consalvi, July 11, 1819. HHSA, Rom: Weisungen, Metternich to Lebzeltern, May 22, 1816.

19. "It is certain...that if Austria wants them, she will have them without opposition": Consalvi to Pacca, June 13, 1814, AV, R242.

20. The reality of Austrian designs on the Legations after 1815 has been generally accepted, not only by the many historians writing in the spirit of the Risorgimento, from Bianchi, *op. cit.* 1:221-223, to Gellio Cassi, *Il Cardinale Consalvi ed i primi anni della restaurazione pontificia,* 189-193, but also by such generally unbiased modern historians as Raffaele Colapietra, *La chiesa tra Metternich e Lamennais,* 79-84; but none can offer evidence other than the rumors current a century ago. My own research in HHSA uncovered no evidence of Austrian designs on the Legations after 1815. All the evidence points the other way. Metternich categorically denied these rumors, not only to Consalvi, but to his own subordinates, and with every appearance of sincerity: e.g., HHSA, Rom: Weisungen, to Lebzeltern, May 22, 1816, or to Kaunitz, October 15, 1817—the latter, in fact, reveals that when Naples suggested a joint occupation of the State at Pius's death, Metternich rejected it. No doubt, as Metternich believed, these rumors were spread by Austria's rivals, France and Russia, to stir up Italian distrust of her: HHSA, Grossbritannien: Weisungen, Metternich to Esterhazy, July 9, 1819, secret. It is worth noting, too, that the more perceptive French diplomats did not credit these rumors: e.g., Bertier de Sauvigny, *op. cit.,* 233-234. As for the faction in the Legations that sought annexation by Austria, Metternich distrusted rather than encouraged it: Van Duerm, 175. The most that can be said is that some subordinate Austrian officials may have encouraged the agitation on their own initiative: HHSA, Rom: Berichte, Lebzeltern to Metternich, November 17, 1815.

21. Austrian ambassadors had frequent occasion to complain of the wide acceptance of this belief at Rome, which handicapped their efforts to win Papal cooperation: e.g., HHSA, Rom: Berichte, Lebzeltern to Metternich, September 7 #156, 14 #158, 1815.

22. AV, R242, Instructions for Cardinal Spina, October 19, 1822.

23. *Ibid.,* "Quesiti che si propongono," 1822. Also R248, Consalvi to Macchi, December 2, 1822.

24. HHSA, Rom: Berichte, Lebzeltern to Metternich, April 25, 1814 #1. Metternich frequently expressed this assumption in his correspondence, e.g., HHSA, Rom: Weisungen, Instructions for Apponyi, September 16, 1820.

25. On Metternich's plans for a Confederation, see Bettanini; Grossmann; Srbik, *Metternich,* 1:206-217; Haas, 65-73.

26. Which provided that "Italy, except the states to be returned to Austria, will be composed of sovereign states;" D'Angeberg, *Congrès,* 1:165.

27. AV, R242, Consalvi to Pacca, September 8, October 29 #92, November 1 #97, 1814.

28. *Ibid.,* December 29 #158, 1814.

29. Archivio di Stato, Florence (hereafter cited as ASF), Filza 1930, Corsini to Ferdinand III, May 9, 1815, AV, R242, Consalvi to Pacca, March 21 #280, 1815.

30. E.g., AV, R242, Consalvi to Pacca, May 20 #321, 1815.

31. *Ibid.,* March 21 #280, 1815.

32. Text in Comte d'Angeberg, *Recueil des traités,* 197–203. See Metternich to Francis I, June 20, 1815, Vorträge 292, HHSA, and Maturi, "Il Congresso," on the background.

33. Grossmann, Bettanini, and Nada, *Relazioni diplomatiche,* vol. 1.

34. E.g., AV, R260, Lebzeltern to Consalvi, April 16, May 4, July 1, 1816; Metternich to Consalvi, July 3, 1816. R247, Severoli to Consalvi, July 21, 1816.

35. E.g., AV, R242, Instructions for Spina, October 19, 1822.

36. *Ibid.,* Consalvi to Pacca, January 18 #197, 1815.

37. Giuseppi Berti, *Russia e stati italiani nel Risorgimento,* 114–117.

38. On the German princes, AV, R247, Severoli to Consalvi, April 12, 1817, Leardi to Consalvi, July 4, 1818, January 16, October 16, November 6, 1819, and January 5, 1820; on Turkish persecutions, AV, ANV 242, Hudelist to Severoli, May 25, 1816, Consalvi to Metternich, July 4, 1818, Metternich to Leardi, December 22, 1818; R247, Leardi to Consalvi, October 20, 1819, and June 8, 1822.

39. As it was in fact withdrawn in the controversy with the German princes when in 1818 Austria was irritated by Rome's refusal to grant various religious concessions. The Vienna Nuncio was told bluntly that Austria "could easily extinguish this conflagration," but saw no reason to do so in view of the Papal attitude: AV, ANV 246, Leardi to Consalvi, May 25, 1818.

40. ACPFFC, 34, Consalvi to Spina, July 1818.

41. A motive of which Metternich was well aware: HHSA, Rom: Weisungen, Instructions for Kaunitz, May 31, 1817.

42. As Joseph de Maistre complained: *Correspondance diplomatique,* 2:93.

43. Austrian representatives at Rome frequently attested to the sincerity of Consalvi's cooperation against the Sects: e.g., HHSA, Rom: Berichte, Lebzeltern to Metternich, July 29, August 12, September 7, October 7, 1815, April 27, June 12, 1816; Apponyi to Metternich, August 15, 1816, April 5 and 30, 1817.

44. HHSA, Rom: Varia, Consalvi to Metternich, June 11, 1815, October 1, 1818; Berichte, Apponyi to Metternich, August 15, 1816 #6-C.

45. *Ibid.,* Varia, Consalvi to Metternich, June 11, 1816; also October 1, 1818; Berichte, Lebzeltern to Metternich, October 7, 1815 and April 27, 1816.

46. *Ibid.,* Russland: Weisungen, Metternich to Lebzeltern, November 5, 1816.

47. Much has been written on the Sects, yet their origin and development remain obscure. A good introduction to the subject is Carlo Francovich, "L'azione rivoluzionaria risorgimentale," in *Nuove questioni di storia del Risorgimento e dell'Unità d'Italia,* 1:457–512. Much useful information on the Sects in the Papal State can be found in AV, R165, "Unioni e società segrete," and in the reports of the Austrian diplomats and agents in HHSA, Rom: Berichte and Varia.

48. AV, R165, Gazzoli to Consalvi, June 12, 1817, Delegate of Forli to Consalvi, April 17, 1819, Spina to Consalvi, August 12, 1820. HHSA, Rom: Berichte, Lebzeltern to Metternich, May 21, #112-A & B, 1816; Weisungen, Instructions for Kaunitz, May 31, 1817, with annex.

49. This account of Metternich's policy towards the Sects is based primarily upon his own writings, especially HHSA, Rom: Weisungen, Instructions for Kaunitz, May 31, 1817, with annexes, Instructions for Apponyi, September 16, 1820, Metternich to Apponyi, May 22, July 21, and September 8, 1816; Grossbritannien: Weis-

ungen, Metternich to Esterhazy, July 9, 1819. See also: Donald E. Emerson, *Metternich and the Political Police,* 57–99, and Haas, 102–112.

50. HHSA, Rom: Weisungen, Instructions for Kaunitz, May 31, 1817. On the C.B.A., see Haas, 102–112.

51. In 1816, for example, Austrian agents were taken in by reports of a vast "Guelf" conspiracy, organized by England and supported by Consalvi among others, to drive Austria from Italy; the "plot" caused great alarm at Vienna, but proved to be the invention of an adventurer who hoped to obtain money for his revelations. See R. John Rath, "La costituzione Guelfa e i servizi segreti austriaci," *Rassegna storica del Risorgimento,* 50 (1963): 346–376, Haas, 106–109, and Alessandro Cutolo, *Il Duca di Brindisi, 12–49.*

52. AV, R242, Consalvi to Pacca, September 8, 1814, November 23 #136, 1814, February 1 and 11, 1815; "Osservazioni sul progetto della Commissione Politica," 1822; Instructions for Spina, October 19, 1822.

53. HHSA, Rom: Weisungen, Instructions for Kaunitz, May 31, 1817.

54. *Ibid.,* Metternich to Lebzeltern, May 22 #3, July 7 #3, 1816; Varia, Metternich to Consalvi, April 23 and May 22, 1816; Berichte, Lebzeltern to Metternich, March 28, 1816.

55. AV, R260, Lebzeltern to Consalvi, May 4, 1816.

56. HHSA, Rom: Weisungen, Metternich to Apponyi, July 7 #3, 1816.

57. AV, R260, Lebzeltern to Consalvi, May 4, 1816.

58. HHSA, Rom: Weisungen, Instructions for Kaunitz, May 31, 1817.

59. E.g., AV, R242, Consalvi to Pacca, January 18 #197, 1815.

60. See the reports of the Legates of Bologna and Ravenna in AV, R165, as well as those of the Austrian ministers in Rome, who at Metternich's insistence carefully studied the internal situation of the State: e.g., Lebzeltern to Metternich, May 21 #112-A & B, 1816. See also Massimo Petrocchi, *La restaurazione romana* and *La restaurazione, il Cardinale Consalvi, e la riforma del 1816,* for a general survey. On conditions in Rome, see Domenico Spadoni, "Roma segreta all' indomani della Restaurazione," *Rassegna storica del Risorgimento,* 9:927–953; in the Marches, Aldo Berselli, "La restaurazione e le società segrete nelle Marche," in *L'apporto delle Marche al Risorgimento nazionale,* 67–106, and Mario Natelucci, *Il contributo delle Marche al Risorgimento;* on the Legations, a good survey of the literature is Luigi Lotti, "Le Legazioni, *Bibliografia dell'età del Risorgimento,* 2:273–290. That the Legations became the chief trouble spot in the State suggests that Consalvi won a Pyrrhic victory in regaining them—but it must be remembered that their revenue was essential for the financial stability of the State, and that Consalvi's reforms, if implemented, would have reduced discontent there.

61. AV, R242, Consalvi to Pacca, June 12 #336, 1815.

62. HHSA, Rom: Berichte, Lebzeltern to Metternich, May 21 #112-A & B, 1816, Apponyi to Metternich, August 2 #4-B, 1816. Also, Petrocchi, *Restaurazione romana,* 94–106.

63. HHSA, Rom: Varia, Consalvi to Metternich, June 11, June 22, August 23, 1816; Berichte, Lebzeltern to Metternich, May 21 #112-A & B, May 31, #130, 1816, Apponyi to Metternich, June 21 #4, August 15 #6-A, 1816; Weisungen, Instructions for Kaunitz, May 31, 1817.

64. AV, R260, Metternich to Consalvi, July 3, 1816. Much of the information which Consalvi passed on to Austria may be found in "Serie II—Polizensachen," a special file in HHSA, Rom: Berichte, begun in July, 1817.

65. HHSA, Rom: Weisungen, Metternich to Apponyi, July 21, 1816, Instructions for Kaunitz, May 31, 1817, Metternich to Gennotte, May 24 #2, 1820; Grossbritannien: Weisungen, Metternich to Esterhazy, July 9, 1819. In a sense, of course, this belief

was a serious miscalculation, since the Sects did carry out a revolution in Naples in 1820; yet it must be remembered that this revolution, and the others of the period, were easily put down by Austrian forces. When Austria was finally driven from Italy it was only with the aid of a great Power—France—as Metternich had predicted. On the Russian diplomatic offensive in Italy during 1815–1820, see Alan J. Reinerman, "Metternich, Alexander I, and the Russian Challenge in Italy, 1815–1820," *Journal of Modern History,* 46 (1974): 262–276.

66. HHSA, Rom: Weisungen, Metternich to Kaunitz, July 10, 1817; also, Metternich to Apponyi, July 7 #3, 1816, Instructions for Kaunitz, May 31, 1817, Metternich to Kaunitz, October 15 #5, 1817.

67. Made, for example, by F. A. Gualterio, *Gli ultimi rivolgimenti italiani,* 1:286–287, and repeated by more recent historians, e.g., Petrocchi, *Restaurazione romana,* 87.

68. HHSA, Rom: Weisungen, Metternich to Kaunitz, October 15 #5, 1817.

69. *Ibid.,* Metternich to Apponyi, July 7, 1816.

70. He had only planned to exile from Rome three or four of the most prominent foreign agitators: *Ibid.,* Rom: Varia, Consalvi to Metternich, August 23, 1816.

71. AV, R165, Consalvi to the Legate of Forli, March 13, 1821.

72. *Ibid.,* Consalvi to the Legate of Forli, July 15, 1820, March 13, 1821; to the Delegate of Perugia, July 31, 1820; to the Legate of Bologna, July 3, 1816; to the Legate of Ferrara, July 5, 1820.

73. *Ibid.,* Consalvi to the Legate of Forli, July 15, 1820, March 13 and July 8, 1821; to the Delegate of Perugia, July 31, 1820; to the Legate of Bologna, June 28, 1820; to the Governor of Rome, July 17, 1820; to the Delegate of Ascoli, March 31, 1821.

74. E.g., *Ibid.,* Consalvi to the Legate of Ferrara, July 5, 1821; to the Legate of Forli, March 13, 1821.

75. See below, Section 3.

76. *Ibid.,* Consalvi to Spina, March 31, 1821, to the Legate of Ferrara, July 5, 1821, to the Legate of Forli, March 13, 1821; R247, Leardi to Consalvi, March 10 and June 30, 1821. HHSA, Rom: Varia, Apponyi to Metternich, July 27, 1821. It was the severity of such subordinates, in particular the Legates of Forli and Ferrara in 1821, which led to the charge that Consalvi had given in to Austrian pressure for harsh treatment of the Sects. The truth was that in early 1821, Metternich had advised Consalvi to take advantage of the temporary discouragement of the Sects produced by the suppression of the Neapolitan revolution to deal with those who were actively conspiring against the Papal government: HHSA, Rom: Varia, Metternich to Consalvi, April 11, 1821. However, Consalvi had already decided this for himself and given orders to arrest active conspirators: e.g., AV, R165, Consalvi to the Legate of Forli, March 13, 1821. Unfortunately, the authorities in Forli, Ferrara, and Ravenna carried out his orders with arbitrary severity, prosecuting suspects without regard for legal process and imposing unduly harsh penalties. Metternich, far from demanding such proceedings, was appalled by them, and hastily advised Consalvi to suspend the prosecutions until the injustices of his subordinates could be corrected: HHSA, Rom: Varia, Metternich to Apponyi, July 17, 1821. But Consalvi had already reached the same conclusion and rebuked those responsible: AV, R165, Consalvi to the Legate of Forli, July 15, 1821, to the Legate of Ravenna, July 15, 1821. The campaign against the Sects was then placed on a moderate and legal course, but not before considerable harm had been done to the reputation of the Papal regime. The incident is typical of the difficulties Consalvi experienced in securing the proper execution of his policies.

77. E.g., HHSA, Rom: Varia, Metternich to Consalvi, August 2, 1820, April 11, 1821. AV, R247, Leardi to Consalvi, March 10, June 30 and July 10, 1821.

78. Haas, 159, and P. Pedrotti, "I rapporti di Tito Manzi col Governo Austriaco in alcuni documenti viennesi," *Rassegna storica del Risorgimento,* 29 (1942): 3–45.

Another reason for the system's dissolution was that its operations had become too widely known. The Emperor formally decreed the dissolution on March 13, 1820, less than four months before the Neapolitan revolution. However, the exchange of information between Rome and Vienna continued. In 1821, a new institution was set up to take the system's place: the notorious Milan Investigation Commission, which was to prosecute Confalonieri.

79. HHSA, Rom: Varia, Metternich to Consalvi, August 2, 1820, April 11, 1821, Consalvi to Metternich, August 12, 13, 19, and September 22, 1820; Rom: Weisungen, Metternich to Gennotte, August 2, 1820, Instructions for Apponyi, September 16, 1820, Metternich to Apponyi, April 11, 1821. AV, R165, Consalvi to the Legate of Forli, December 16, 1820, to Spina, August 19, 1820.

80. E.g., AV, R165, Consalvi to the Legate of Ferrara, October 25, 1820. HHSA, Rom: Berichte, Apponyi to Metternich, October 28 #15-B, 1820; Rom: Weisungen, Metternich to Apponyi, October 6 and 7, 1820.

81. AV, R242, Consalvi to Pacca, June 12 #336, 1815.

82. E.g., Franco Venturi, "Elementi e tentativi di riforme nello Stato Pontificio del Settecento," *Rivista storica italiana,* 71 (1963): 778–817, Vittorio E. Giuntella, "La capitale e i problemi dello Stato," *Studi romani,* 14 (1966): 269–291; and Luigi del Pane, *Lo Stato pontificio e il movimento riformatore del Settecento.*

83. AV, R242, *Consalvi to Pacca,* June 12 #336, 1815.

84. AV, R247, Consalvi to Severoli, January 23, 1817. The attempt of Cassi, to present him as sharing the convictions of the liberals can hardly be taken seriously; upon being told that a Swiss journal had praised his reforms as "liberal," Consalvi rejected this description and stated his opposition to the principles of contemporary liberalism: AV, R257, Consalvi to Valenti, February 10, 1817. See also, ANV 125, Consalvi to Severoli, December 14, 1816.

85. AV, ANV 244, Consalvi to Leardi, September 9, 1820; see also, R242, Consalvi to Pacca, March 20, 1815, Consalvi to Spina, February 8, 1821, Instructions for Spina, October 19, 1822.

86. Cf. Leopold von Ranke, *Samtliche Werke,* 40:57: "er war mehr geschmeidig und vielseitig, als kraftvoll und von schöpferischem Genius." Also Petrocchi, *Restaurazione romana,* 31–35.

87. AV, R247, Consalvi to Severoli, September 14, 1816.

88. *Ibid.,* R242, Consalvi to Pacca, June 12 #336, 1815.

89. *Ibid.,* December 28 #155, 1814.

90. On Consalvi's earlier interest in reform, see his *Memorie,* 145–161.

91. The *Zelanti* have never been the subject of a systematic study; useful insights may be found in: Colapietra, *La chiesa,* especially ch. 1, and *La formazione;* Vittorio E. Giuntella, "Profilio di uno Zelante," *Rassegna storica del Risorgimento,* 63(1956): 413–418; and a "view from within" in Pacca, *Memoirs.*

92. AV, R25, Bernetti to Consalvi, November 4, 1815. "Idea veramente signolare!" was Consalvi's comments on this sentiment. See also Pacca's account of his second ministry, appendix in Antonio Quacquarelli, *La ricostruzione dello Stato Pontificio,* a vivid expression of the incomprehension which even an intelligent *Zelante* felt at Consalvi's reform plans.

93. See Pacca's account of his ministry, in Quacquarelli, *La ricostruzione.*

94. Omodeo, "Il Cardinale Consalvi," 84; Giuntella, "Profilio di uno Zelante," 417–418.

95. Narciso Nada, *Metternich e le riforme nello Stato Pontificio: la missione Sebregondi a Roma, 1832–1836,* 93–104; Domenico Demarco, *Il tramonto dello Stato Pontificio: il pontificato di Gregorio XVI,* ch. 1.

96. On *Zelanti* policy during the first year of the Restoration, see Quacquarelli, *La ricostruzione;* Maria Moscarini, *La restaurazione pontificia nelle provincie di prima*

ricupera; Petrocchi, *Restaurazione romana,* ch. 3. Another valuable source, not yet exploited, consists of the reports sent by Lebzeltern during 1814-1815, in HHSA, Rom: Berichte.

97. AV, R25, Memoriale of Dr. Guarmani, October 18, 1815.

98. It is thus not surprising that laymen removed from the government were perhaps the most numerous group in the Papal *Settarj:* HHSA, Rom: Berichte, Lebzeltern to Metternich, May 21 #112-A & B, 1816, Rom: Weisungen, "Mémoire sur les societés secretes en Italie," May 1817.

99. AV, R247, Severoli to Pacca, July 25, July 30, August 6, 1814, R242, Consalvi to Pacca, June 13 and August 17, 1814.

100. *Ibid.*, R165, Gazzola to Consalvi, August 16, 1815, Spina to Consalvi, August 12, 1816. HHSA, Rom: Berichte, Lebzeltern to Metternich, May 21 # 112-A & B, 1816.

101. AV, R242, Consalvi to Pacca, September 8, 1814, December 26 #155, 1814.

102. E.g., HHSA, Lebzeltern to Metternich, July 9 #20-B, 1814, September 3 #30-B, 1814, June 21 #123, 1815.

103. On Metternich's interest in reform, see Srbik, *Metternich,* 1:429-464, which, however, ignores his interest in the reform of other states, as do R. W. Seton-Watson, "Metternich and Internal Austrian Policy," *Slavonic Review,* 17 (1939): 539-555, 18 (1939): 129-141, and Egon Radvany, *Metternich's Projects for Reform in Austria;* Haas is more useful than these. Metternich's efforts to reform other states are touched upon in such works as Schroeder, *Metternich's Diplomacy;* Angelo Filipuzzi, "La Restaurazione nel regno delle Due Sicilie dopo il Congresso di Lubiana," *Annali Triestini di diritto, economia e politica,* 11 (1940): 161-206, 230-282; and Ruggero Moscati, *Il regno delle Due Sicilie e l'Austria 1821-1830,* though none of these takes his interest in reform very seriously. More perceptive are the works of Narciso Nada, *L'Austria e la questione romana dalla Rivoluzione di Luglio alla fine della Conferenza diplomatica romana 1830-1831,* and *Metternich.* An overview of his efforts at reform in the Papal State and their implications for his policy is given in Alan J. Reinerman, "Metternich and Reform: The Case of the Papal State, 1814-1848," *The Journal of Modern History,* 42 (December, 1970): 524-548.

104. HHSA, Frankreich: Weisungen, Metternich to Apponyi, December 4, 1846.

105. See e.g., HHSA, Rom: Weisungen, Instructions for Apponyi, September 16, 1820, "Mémoire sur les societés secretes en Italie, May 1817; Kongressakten: Laybach, "Circulaire aux missions en Italie, May 14, 1821, "Aperçu sur les affaires d'Italie," May 15, 1821.

106. This description of Metternich's ideas on reform is based mainly on his recommendations for the Papal State, as described below, and the documents cited there, and partly on the works cited in note 103, above, especially Haas, Srbik, and Nada.

107. Little has been done on Metternich's efforts to reform the Italian state, aside from the Papal State; a little information may be found in Schroeder, *Metternich's Diplomacy,* Filipuzzi, "La Restaurazione," and Moscati, *Il regno,* but much work remains to be done.

108. In contrast to most historians—Nada seems to be the only exception—who depict Metternich as the archfoe of reform in the papal State: e.g., Bianchi, *Storia documentata,* 1:221, Cassi, 189-192, Pietro Silva, *La Monarchie di Luglio e l'Italia,* 133. At the root of this misunderstanding lies a combination of the anti-Austrian bias of the Risorgimento, and a failure to distinguish between political reform in the sense of parliamentary or constitutional government—which Metternich indeed opposed— and nonpolitical reforms compatible with absolutism, which he favored.

109. HHSA, Rom: Weisungen, Instructions for Kaunitz, May 31, 1817, Instructions for Apponyi, September 16, 1820, Mettrnich to Lebzeltern, July 22, 1815, Metternich to Apponyi, November 22, 1820 and April 12, 1821.

110. *Ibid.,* Rom: Berichte, e.g., Lebzeltern to Metternich, July 9 #20-B, September 3 #30-B, 1814.

111. E.g., AV, R242, Consalvi to Pacca, July 18, August 17 #26, September 4, October 10 #82, November 18–20 #119, 29 #129, December 28 #155, 1814.

112. E.g., *Ibid.,* Pacca to Consalvi, July 22, August 4, September 19 #89, 20, and November 3, 1814.

113. The account of these discussions is based on AV, R242, Consalvi to Pacca, September 8, December 28 #155, 1814, May 20 #321, 28 #327, and June 12 #336, 1815. HHSA, Rom: Weisungen, Metternich to Lebzeltern, July 22, 1815, Instructions for Kaunitz, May 31, 1817; Varia, Apponyi to Metternich, July 27, 1816. APFFC, 35, "Osservazioni di S. A. sulle istituzioni dello Stato Pontificio," 1815.

114. On the administration of Lombardy-Venetia, which did not prove as satisfactory as Metternich had hoped, see R. John Rath, *The Provisional Austrian Regime in Lombardy-Venetia 1814–1815,* A. Sandona, *Il regno Lombardo-Veneto 1814–1859,* and Haas.

115. HHSA, Rom: Weisungen, Metternich to Lebzeltern, July 22, 1815; Varia, Apponyi to Metternich, July 27, 1816. ACPFFC, 34, Consalvi to Spina, July, 1818.

116. HHSA, Rom: Weisungen, Metternich to Lebzeltern, July 22, 1815.

117. Edicts of July 5 and 14, 1815, in AV, R242, 1815.

118. HHSA, Rom: Berichte, Lebzeltern to Metternich, July 29 #135, 1815.

119. This campaign had so great an effect on Pius that Consalvi felt obliged to counter it with a formal defense of his policies as early as July 14, 1815: "Promemoriale presentata a N.S. dal Card. Decano à di 14 luglio 1815," ACPFFC, 33.

120. Petrocchi, *Cardinale,* chs. 2–3; Omodeo, "Cardinale Consalvi," ch. 1; Colapietra, *La chiesa,* ch. 1. A source not previously used for this struggle, but of great value, is the reports of the Austrian ambassadors, who were deeply involved: HHSA, Rom: Berichte, 1815–1823.

121. HHSA, Rom: Berichte, Lebzeltern to Metternich, August 12 #142, 1815, April 30 #96, 1816.

122. *Ibid.,* July 29 #135, 1815.

123. *Ibid.,* November 17 #202, 1815, February 29 #63 and April 30 #96, 1816. See also Franz Grosse-Wietfeld, *Justizreformen im Kirchenstaat 1815–1816.*

124. HHSA, Rom: Berichte, Lebzeltern to Metternich, September 30 #166, and December 14 #202, 1815, May 21 #113, 1816.

125. *Ibid.,* August 26 #148, 1815, April 30 #96, 1816.

126. *Ibid.,* December 14 #202, 1815, April 30 #96, 1816. Palazzo Venezia, formerly the Venetian embassy, became the Austrian embassy after 1797.

127. *Ibid.,* September 30 #166, 1815, November 17 #191, 1815, December 14 #202, 1815, April 30 #96, 1816, May 21 #113, 1816.

128. *Ibid.,* May 21 #113, 1816.

129. *Ibid.,* August 12 #142, 1815, April 30 #96 and May 21 #113, 1816.

130. *Ibid.,* May 21 #113, 1816.

131. *Ibid.,* Varia, Apponyi to Metternich, July 27, 1816. Note APFFC, 35, Rivarola to Consalvi, April 18, 1817, in which the writer, a *Zelante,* declared that Consalvi's reforms had been adopted only because of Austrian pressure on the Pope.

132. In Andreas Barberi, ed., *Bullarii Romani Continuatio,* 14:47–196.

133. HHSA, Rom: Berichte, Apponyi to Metternich, July 27 #1 :816; a similar defense in AV, R247, Consalvi to Severoli, September 14, 1816.

134. HHSA, Rom: Weisungen, Instructions for Kaunitz, May 31, 1817.

135. AV, R260, Lebzeltern to Consalvi, July 1, 1816, Metternich to Consalvi, July 3, 1816.

136. Cf. Spadoni, *Una trama,* ch. 1, and Pierino Carraroli, "Le Marche non insorsero nei moti del 1820–1821," *L'Apporto delle Marche al Risorgimento nazionale,* 107–113.

137. On his later reforms, see Alberto Aquarone, "La restaurazione nello Stato Pontificio ed i suoi indirizzi legislativi," *Archivio della Società Romana di Storia Patria,* 78 (1955): 119–189; Petrocchi, *Restaurazione romana,* ch. 1; Grosse-Wietfeld; Colapietra, *La chiesa,* ch. 1; and Giuseppi Forchielli, "Un progetto di codice civile del 1818 nello Stato Pontificio," *Scritti della Facoltà Giuridica di Bologna in onore di Umberto Borsi,* 89–164.

138. E.g., HHSA, Rom: Berichte, Kaunitz to Metternich, November 30 #36-J, 1817, Gennotte to Metternich, July 10 #70-B and September 15 #84-A, 1818, July 28 #143-A, and December 4 #109-A, 1819, April 17, 1820. Archivio Arcivescovile di Bologna (hereafter AAB), Carte Oppizzoni, Consalvi to Oppizzone, August 13, 1823.

139. HHSA, Rom: Berichte, Kaunitz to Metternich, November 23 #34-H, 1817, Gennotte to Metternich, May 10 #18-A and July 29 #40, 1820. The Delegate of Fermo, who declared publicly that he "had never read the *Motu-proprio* and hoped to die without ever having done so," differed from most of his colleagues only in bluntness: AV, R26, Consalvi to the Delegate of Fermo, July 5, 1817.

140. Note Metternich's judgment when, after the revolutions of 1831, the question of reforming the Papal administration was again being considered, that "if Cardinal Consalvi, who was without contradiction the man most distinguished for talent and ability of any in the Papal government...nonetheless could not overcome...the opposition of the vast majority of the Sacred College," his lesser successors had no hope of so doing: HHSA, Rom: Weisungen, Metternich to Lützow, January 25 #1, 1833.

141. *Ibid.,* Berichte, Apponyi to Metternich, July 27 #1, 1816.

142. ACPFFC, 34, Consalvi to Spina, July 1818.

143. HHSA, Rom: Weisungen, Instructions for Kaunitz, May 31, 1817.

144. Lebzeltern, 345–349.

145. HHSA, Rom: Weisungen, Instructions for Kaunitz, May 31, 1817, Metternich to Kaunitz, October 18 #1 & 2, 1818, Instructions for Apponyi, September 16, 1820; Toskana: Weisungen, Instructions for Apponyi, May 22, 1816. Anton Count Apponyi, Minister June 1816–March 1817, Ambassador 1820–1826; Alois Prince Kaunitz-Rietberg, Ambassador 1817–1820. Another figure at Palazzo Venezia was Wilhelm Freiherr von Gennotte, Secretary of the Embassy, who usually handled routine matters, but was at times charged with important affairs in the absence of the ambassador.

146. HHSA, Rom: Weisungen, Metternich to Kaunitz, October 18 #2, 1818.

147. AV, ANV 125, Consalvi to Severoli, July 10, 1815; ANV 233, Severoli to Consalvi, July 1 and 5, 1815. HHSA, Rom: Berichte, Lebzeltern to Metternich, July 29 #132, 1815. On the occupation, see Weil, *Joachim Murat,* 5:42–56, 267–271, et passim.

148. Convention of June 12, 1815, in AV, R242. R260, Pacca to Lebzeltern, July 1, 1815, Lebzeltern to Consalvi, July 7, 1815. HHSA, Rom: Berichte, Lebzeltern to Saurau, July 3 #1, 1815, with annexes, Lebzeltern to Metternich, July 3 #125, 13 #129, and 29 #132, 1815.

149. HHSA, Rom: Varia, Consalvi to Metternich, July 10, 1815, Metternich to Consalvi, August 28 #1, 1815; Berichte, Lebzeltern to Metternich, July 3 #129, and 29 #132, 1815.

150. As claimed, for example, in Nicomede Bianchi, *Storia della politica austriaca rispetto ai sovrani ed ai governi italiani,* 344–345.

151. AV, ANV 125, Consalvi to Severoli, July 10, July 27, 1815, Severoli to Consalvi, July 26, August 12, 1815. HHSA, Rom: Varia, Metternich to Consalvi, July 27, August 28, 1815.

152. HHSA, Rom: Varia, Consalvi to Metternich, August 12, 1815.

153. AV, R260, Consalvi to Lebzeltern, September 23, 1815. HHSA, Rom: Berichte, Lebzeltern to Metternich, September 30 #164 and December 2 #199, 1815.

154. HHSA, Rom: Berichte, Lebzeltern to Metternich, December 2 #199, and 21 #208, 1815. AV, R260, Consalvi to Lebzeltern, January 14, 1816.

155. HHSA, Rom: Berichte, Lebzeltern to Metternich, June 10 #136, 1816.

156. *Ibid.*, Rom: Varia, Consalvi to Metternich, June 11, 1816.
157. AV, ANV 233, Severoli to Consalvi, September 16 and October 7, 1815.
158. HHSA, Rom: Berichte, Lebzeltern to Metternich, November 11 #189, 1815, November 30 #196, December 21 #205, 1815, and February 22, 1816; Varia, Consalvi to Metternich, August 12, 1815, January 1 and 18, 1816. AV, ANV 233, Severoli to Consalvi, December 6, 1815.
159. HHSA, Rom: Berichte, Lebzeltern to Metternich, November 11 #189, 1815.
160. *Ibid.*, Varia, Consalvi to Metternich, August 12, 1815, January 1 and 18, 1816; Pius VII to Francis I, December 2, 1815.
161. AV, ANV 233, Severoli to Consalvi, December 6, 1815.
162. *Ibid.*, December 27, 1815.
163. *Ibid.*, Varia, Metternich to Lebzeltern, January 6, 1816.
164. *Ibid.*, Metternich to Consalvi, February 16, 1816, Francis I to Pius VII, March 11, 1816; Weisungen, Metternich to Lebzeltern, February 14 and 16, 1816.
165. *Ibid.*, Berichte, Lebzeltern to Metternich, February 22 #54, 24 #60, and March 11 #79, 1816.
166. *Ibid.*, Varia, Metternich to Consalvi, February 16 and March 12, 1816.
167. *Ibid.*, March 12, April 23 and June 7, 1816; Berichte, Lebzeltern to Metternich, April 27 #95, 1816. AV, ANV 233, Severoli to Consalvi, March 25, April 2 and 10, 1816.
168. HHSA, Rom: Varia, Consalvi to Metternich, January 1 and 18, 1816; Berichte, Lebzeltern to Metternich, February 14, 24 #60, and March 11 #79, 1816.
169. HHSA, Rom: Berichte, Lebzeltern to Metternich, April 27 #95, 30 #96, and June 12 #140, 1816, Apponyi to Metternich, August 15 #6-A & C, 1816; Varia, Consalvi to Metternich, February 24 and June 11, 1816. Lebzeltern, 322-357.
170. HHSA, Rom: Varia, Metternich to Consalvi, March 12, 1816, Consalvi to Metternich, February 14, 1816.
171. As a French diplomat described him: Bertier de Sauvigny, *Metternich et la France,* 1:121.
172. His instructions, dated May 22, 1816, are in HHSA, Toskana: Weisungen, 1816.
173. His instructions, dated May 31, 1817, are in HHSA, Rom: Weisungen, 1817.
174. *Ibid.*, Metternich to Gennotte, December 28, 1818; Berichte, Gennotte to Metternich, January 14 and February 9 #109-A, 1819. Hudal, 48-60.
175. On French policy at Rome in 1815-1829, see Bertier de Sauvigny, *Metternich et la France,* 1:120-125; Henry Contamine, *Diplomatie et diplomates sous la Restauration,* 323-325; Feret, 2:61-260.
176. Cf. Metternich's sour comments on the "extraordinary and quite unexpected condescension" of the French: *Mémoires,* 3:99.
177. Cf. HHSA, Rom: Berichte, Kaunitz to Metternich, December 13 #38-A, 1817.
178. ACPFFC, 34, Consalvi to Spina, July 1818.
179. Austrian and French diplomacy at Rome was not always in conflict, since both did have certain common interests—for example, in particular, neither wished to see an intransigent *Zelante* become Pope. Cooperation thus sometimes took place, for example, in 1817 when Pius VII was seriously ill and a conclave was expected, Metternich secured the promise of French cooperation to prevent the election of a *Zelante*; the Pope's recovery rendered the plan unnecessary.
180. E.g., HHSA, Rom: Berichte, Kaunitz to Metternich, November 6 #32-A, 1817. See Jeronimo Becker, *Relaciones Diplomaticas entre España y la Santa Sede durante el Siglo XIX,* 34-52.
181. E.g., HHSA, Grossbritannien: Weisungen, Metternich to Esterhazy, April 19, 1817.

182. On the Russian campaign, see Reinerman, "Metternich, Alexander I."

183. ACPFFC, 34, Consalvi to Spina, July 1818. Note his wish that "Austria must exercise a profound influence" at Rome to counterbalance that of France, Spain, and Russia: HHSA, Berichte, Apponyi to Metternich, April 5, 1817.

184. HHSA, Rom: Berichte, Apponyi to Metternich, April 5, 1817.

185. *Ibid.*, Grossbritannien: Weisungen, Metternich to Esterhazy, July 5, 1819.

Chapter III

1. Eduard Winter, *Der Josefinismus*, is the most persuasive statement of the thesis that Josephism was the product of a far-reaching intellectual movement aimed at spiritual reform and modernization. Fritz Valjavec offers similar interpretation in *Der Josephinismus* (Munich, 1945). The most authoritative statement of the opposing view—that Josephism was primarily a means of reinforcing state power—is Maass, *Der Josephinismus*; Herbert Rieser reaches the same conclusion in *Der Geist des Josephinismus und sein Fortleben*. Franco Valsecchi, *L'assolutismo illuminato in Austria e in Lombardia* skillfully places the religious policy of Joseph II within the context of his general policy. On the intellectual currents associated with Josephism in Austria, see Robert A. Kann, *A Study in Austrian Intellectual History*, and Eduard Winter, *Romantismus, Restauration, und Frühliberalismus im österreichischen Vormärz*. See also Paul P. Bernard, "The Origins of Josephism," *Colorado College Studies* No. 7 (1964), Heinrich Benedikt, "Der Josephinismus vor Joseph II," in *Österreich und Europa*, 183–201, and Erick Zollner, "Bemerkungen zum Problem der Beziehungen zwischen Aufklärung und Josephinismus," *Ibid.*, 203–219.

2. See, e.g., the opinion of Severoli to Consalvi, July 15, 1815, AV, ANV 233, and Eduard Hosp, *Kirche Österreichs im Vörmarz*, 191–198.

3. AV, ANV 219, "De miserando Ecclesiae statu in Austria" and "De mea Agendi Ratione in rebus ecclesiae," both by Severoli, 1814. Maass, *Der Josephinismus*, 4:52–97. Hubert Bastgen, *Die Neuerrichtung der Bistümer im Österreich nach der Säkularisation*, 1–26. Franz Schnable, *Storia religiosa della Germania nell'ottocento*, trans. M. Bendiscioli, 6–42. Ignaz Beidtel, *Geschichte der österreichischen Staatsverwaltung*, 2:156–172.

4. AV, ANV, 233, Severoli to Pacca, August 29, 1814.

5. Such somber descriptions of Austrian religious conditions are frequent in the reports of the Nuncios: e.g., AV, ANV 233, Severoli to Pacca, August 29, November 19, 1814, to Consalvi, July 15, 1815; ANV 246, Leardi to Consalvi, August 29, December 28, 1817. Doubtless the Nuncios were not the most impartial observers of the Josephist system; still, their descriptions of its pernicious effects are too frequent and too detailed to be disregarded completely. Moreover, a similar picture emerges from such works as Rudolf Till, *Hofbauer und sein Kreis*, and Eduard Hosp, *Zwischen Aufklärung und katholischer Reform: Jakob Frint*.

6. AV, ANV 233, Severoli to Pacca, August 29, 1814.

7. HHSA, Rom: Berichte, Lebzeltern to Metternich, April 4 #96, 1816.

8. This firm confidence in divine protection was an essential factor in their outlook, explaining much that would otherwise seem rash and inexplicable in their policies. For examples of this confidence and the contempt it often bred for mere worldly realities, see the correspondence between the *Zelante* Rivarola and Consalvi, in APFFC, Busta 35, March–April 1817, or the correspondence of the *Zelante* prelate Monsignor Bona-

ventura Gazzola with Marchese Spreti, in Busta 197, Museo Centrale del Risorgimento, Rome (hereafter cited as MCR).

9. On the political and religious impact of Romanticism, see A. Joussain, *Romantisme et politique*; C. Schmitt, *Politische Romantik;* A. Gerbi, *La politica del Romanticismo;* Georges Goyau, *L'Allemagne religieuse. Le Catholicisme,* 1:161–312; Winter, *Romantismus.*

10. AV, R247, Leardi to Consalvi, May 8, 1821. Joseph de Maistre was of course the most prominent spokesman for this viewpoint, especially in his *Du Pape,* which first appeared in 1819; see Camille Latreille, *Joseph de Maistre et la Papauté,* and Robert Triomphe, *Joseph de Maistre: Étude sur la vie et la doctrine d'un matérialiste mystique.*

11. HHSA, Rom: Varia, Francis I to Pius VII, April 12, 1821.

12. AV, R260, "Obbligo dei nominati," 1817.

13. During his tenure as Prosecretary of State in 1814–1815, Pacca drew up such a bull, directed not merely against Austria, but against all the Catholic monarchies of Europe; fortunately, the return of Consalvi prevented its publication: Quacquarelli, *La ricostruzione dello Stato Pontificio,* 163. The project was soon revived, specifically against Austria, by the *Zelanti,* who in 1818–1819 were so far successful as to win the approval of Pius VII for a bull condemning the Josephist system; only the tenacious opposition of Consalvi defeated the project: HHSA, Rom: Berichte, Gennotte to Metternich, August 19 #78-B, 1818, July 12 #142-B, 1819, February 5 #2-A and July 8 #32-D, 1820, and reports of Altieri to Metternich, July 10 and August 16, 1818.

14. Cf. Omodeo, "Il Cardinale Consalvi al Congresso di Vienna," 179, who—disapprovingly—credits him with having "given the decisive impetus to the triumph of Papal absolutism and the elimination of the state-churches."

15. AV, R242, Consalvi to Pacca, September 8, 1814.

16. HHSA, Rom: Berichte, Khevenhüller to Colloredo, January 26, 1805.

17. APFFC, Busta 35, Consalvi to Rivarola, April 8, 1817.

18. AV, R247, Consalvi to Leardi, February 27, 1818.

19. *Ibid.,* ANV 243, Consalvi to Leardi, August 11, 1817; R260, "Quesito da esaminarsi," 1817.

20. *Ibid.,* R242, Consalvi to Pacca, September 17, 1814.

21. HHSA, Rom: Berichte, Gennotte to Metternich, July 10 #70-B, August 19 #78-B, and September 15 #84-A, 1818, and July 21 #142-B, 1819.

22. On the organization and composition of this congregation, made up entirely of *Zelanti,* see Pacca's account in Quacquarelli, *La ricostruzione,* 160–162, and Lajos Pásztor, "La Congregazione degli Affari Ecclesiastici Straordinari tra il 1814 e il 1850," *Archivum Historiae Pontificiae,* 6 (1968): 191–307. On its intransigence and hostility to Consalvi, see HHSA, Rom: Berichte, Gennotte to Metternich, August 19 #78-B, 1818, and the reports of Altieri, July 10 and August 16, 1818.

23. On Consalvi's religious diplomacy, see Hubert Bastgen, "Die Konkordatsära unter Consalvi," *Nel I centenario dalla morte del Card. Ercole Consalvi,* 31–42; Schmidlin, 1:53–88, 221–381; Leflon, *La crise révolutionnaire,* 321–365; Walter Maturi, *Il concordato del 1818 tra la Santa Sede e le Due Sicilie,* which gives a most perceptive analysis of Consalvi's diplomacy and the obstacles it met from both regalists and *Zelanti.*

24. Down to 1816, Consalvi anticipated that the religious affairs of Germany as a whole would be regulated by a general concordat with all the states, Austria included—a plan that Metternich strongly favored as a means of strengthening Austrian influence over the German Confederation. However, the middle-sized states rejected this plan, partly from distrust of Austria, partly in the hope of securing more favorable terms through individual negotiations with Rome. Consequently, Consalvi had to

embark upon the course of negotiating concordats with the individual states, and thus with Austria. See: AV, R242, Consalvi to Pacca, November 16 #107, 1814, January 4 and 18 #194, 1815; Ernst Ruck, *Die römische Kurie und die deutsch Kirchenfrage auf dem Wiener Kongress;* L. König, *Pius VII, die Säkularisation und das Riechskonkordat;* Schnabel, *Storia religiosa,* 6-42; Schmidlin, 1:256-279; Goyau, 1:83-139.

25. This account of Metternich's fight against Josephism is based upon the documents cited and upon: Maass, *Der Josephinismus,* 4:98-143; Metternich, *Mémoires,* 3:1-7, 101; Bastgen, *Die Neuerrichtung,* 132-278; A. Beer, "Kirchliche Angelegenheiten in Österreich 1816-1842," *Mitteilungen des Instituts für österreichische Geschichtsforschung,* 18 (1897): 493-575; Srbik, *Metternich,* 1:523-524; Andreas Posch, "Die kirchenpolitische Einstellung Metternichs," *Religion, Wissenschaft, Kultur,* 13 (1962): 119-127.

26. HHSA, Rom: Weisungen, Instructions for Kaunitz, May 31, 1817, Metternich to Kaunitz, October 18 #1 & 2, 1818, Instructions for Apponyi, September 16, 1820, Metternich to Wittgenstein, May 26, 1838. AV, R247, Leardi to Consalvi, February 22, 1818.

27. To the point where some seem to have organized an anti-Austrian secret society: *Carte segrete,* 1:129-131.

28. E.g., *Ibid.,* Metternich to Lebzeltern, August 21, 1815, to Kaunitz, October 18 #1 & 2, 1818. AV, R247, Leardi to Consalvi, February 22, 1818.

29. Metternich, *Mémoires,* 7:34.

30. *Ibid.,* 3:3-5n. Cf. the opinions, expressed in almost the same words, of the Neapolitan Ambassador, Ruffo to Medici, undated but June-July, 1818, ASN, AB, 657, and of the Nuncio, Goyau, 2:407, note 2.

31. E.g., AV, R247, Leardi to Consalvi, February 22, 1818, April 6 and May 8, 1821.

32. *Ibid.,* R242, Consalvi to Pacca, September 8 #39, 10, 17 #45, 19 #47, October 3 #59, 19 #85, 22, 1814, Pacca to Consalvi, September 19 #62, October 1, 6, November 5, 13, 1814. HHSA, Rom: Weisungen, Metternich to Lebzeltern, September 10, 1814; Berichte, Lebzeltern to Metternich, October 1, 1814. On the background of this situation, see G. Rizzardo, "Il Patriarchato di Venezia durante il regno napoleonico 1806-1814," *Nuovo archivio veneto,* 27 (1914): 1-19, and Giovanni Mantese, "Corrispondenza inedita di Papa Pio VII, Card. Ercole Consalvi, e Mauro Cappellari con G. M. Peruzzi, vescovo di Chioggia e amministratore apostolico di Venezia," *Archivum historiae pontificiae,* 4 (1966): 260-280. Count Prokop Lazansky (1771-1823), President of the Zentralorganisierungs Hofkommission, and a fervent Josephist, often in conflict with Metternich.

33. AV, R242, Consalvi to Pacca, September 10, 17 #45, October 4 #62, 19 #78, 1814, Pacca to Consalvi, December 15, 1814. Maass, *Der Josephinismus,* 4:479-482.

34. HHSA, Rom: Weisungen, Metternich to Lebzeltern, November 26, 1814. Maass, *Der Josephinismus,* 4:102-107. Bastgen, *Die Neuerrichtung,* 301-344.

35. Maass, *Der Josephinismus,* 4:491-505.

36. AV, ANV 233, Consalvi to Leardi, June 14, 1817.

37. HHSA, Rom: Berichte, Kaunitz to Metternich, July 1 #6-A, 1817.

38. Text of the agreement in Angelo Mercati, ed., *Raccolta di concordati,* 1:514-515. On its background, see Hans Schlitter, *Pius VI und Joseph II 1782-1784.* Napoleon had prohibited the *Romreise,* thus contributing to the strained relations between himself and Rome: Melchiorre Roberti, "La legislazione ecclesiastica nel perioda napoleonica," *Chiesa e stato,* 1:255-332.

39. Maass, *Der Josephinismus,* 4:505, Francis I to Metternich, February 27, 1816. HHSA, Rom: Weisungen, Metternich to Lebzeltern, April 3, 1816.

40. Maass, *Der Josephinismus,* 4:536, Lorenz to Francis I, July 30, 1816.

41. AV, R260, Consalvi to Apponyi, August 30, 1816. HHSA, Rom: Weisungen,

Metternich to Lebzeltern, May 8, 1816; Berichte, Apponyi to Metternich, August 3 #4-D, 1816, with annex.

42. *Ibid.* Also, HHSA, Rom: Berichte, Apponyi to Metternich, August 4 #4-E, September 21 #14-D, 1816.

43. The Papal objections to the marriage laws are summarized in AV, R260, "Innovazioni della Corte Austriaca," 1819.

44. HHSA, Rom: Berichte, Lebzeltern to Metternich, April 4 #92, 1816.

45. *Ibid.*, Lebzeltern to Metternich, April 4 #92, 30 #96, and June 10 #133, 1816; Apponyi to Metternich, August 3 #4-D & E, 1816.

46. *Ibid.*, Lebzeltern to Metternich, June 11 #137, 1816.

47. *Ibid.*, Lebzeltern to Metternich, March 8 #69, April 4 #92, April 30 #96, June 10 #133, 1816; Apponyi to Metternich, August 3 #4-D & E, 1816. Maass, *Der Josephinismus*, 4:510, Metternich to Francis I, April 3, 1816. On Gruber, see K. Pleyer, "Augustin Gruber (1763-1835)," *Unsere Heimat*, 34 (1963): 95-105, and Hosp, *Kirche*, 25-42.

48. AV, R260, Lebzeltern to Consalvi, July 3, 1816; Metternich to Consalvi, July 4, 1816; Consalvi to Metternich, August 23, 1816.

49. HHSA, Rom: Berichte, Apponyi to Metternich, August 15 #6-D, 1816; Vorträge, 201, Metternich to Francis I, August 4, 1816.

50. AV, R260, Consalvi to Apponyi, August 2, 1816.

51. Maass, *Der Josephinismus*, 4:510, Metternich to Francis I, April 3, 1816; 4:511, Staatskanzlei to Z. O. Hofkommission, April 3, 1816.

52. *Ibid.*, Lazansky to Francis I, April 11, 1816; 4:519, Lazansky to Francis I, April 12, 1816; Lorenz to Francis I, April 22, 1816.

53. *Ibid.*, 4:534, Metternich to Francis I, July 24, 1816; Lorenz to Francis I, July 30, 1816; 4:545, Metternich to Francis I, August 26, 1816.

54. *Ibid.*, 4:551, Francis I to Wallis, October 18, 1816; 4:552, Wallis to Francis I, October 28, 1816; 4:557, Wallis to Francis I, January 30, 1817.

55. *Ibid.*, 4:571, Metternich to Francis I, February 1817.

56. *Ibid.*, 4:124-125. Joseph Alois Jüstel, Councillor (Hofrat) and spiritual adviser to the Zentralorganisierungs Hofkommission, was among the most influential Josephists around the Emperor: see Andreas Posch, "Staatsrat Josef Jüstel," *Zeitschrift des historischen Vereins für Steirmark*, 44 (1953): 99-109; Hosp, *Kirche*, 238-247.

57. HHSA, Rom: Weisungen, Instructions for Kaunitz, May 31, 1817.

58. AV, ANV 246, Leardi to Consalvi, May 21 #1 & 2, and June 4, 1817.

59. *Ibid.*, June 7, 1817.

60. AV, ANV 243, Consalvi to Leardi, June 14 and August 11, 1817; R260, Consalvi to Litta, Di Pietro, Pacca, Fontana, June 21, 1817. HHSA, Rom: Berichte, Kaunitz to Metternich, June 17 and July 1, 1817; Varia, Consalvi to Metternich, June 23, 1817.

61. AV, ANV 243, Consalvi to Leardi, June 14, 1817.

62. The following account of the 1817 negotiations is based on HHSA, Rom: Berichte, Kaunitz to Metternich, June 16 #1, 17 #2-B, 20 #3-A & B, 23 #4-A & E, 26 #5, July 1 #6-A, 4 #7-J, 13 #9-A, and 25 #13-A, 1817; Jüstel to Metternich, July 15, 1817; Weisungen, Metternich to Kaunitz, June 24, 27, July 4, 8, 1817; Varia, Consalvi to Metternich, June 23, 1817. AV, ANV 243, Consalvi to Leardi, August 11, 1817; Vorträge, 208, Metternich to Francis I, July 19, 1817.

63. AV, ANV 243, Consalvi to Leardi, August 11, 1817.

64. HHSA, Rom: Berichte, Kaunitz to Metternich, July 1 #6-A, 1817.

65. *Ibid.*, Weisungen, Metternich to Kaunitz, June 27, 1817.

66. Maass, *Der Josephinismus*, 4:603, Jüstel to Metternich, July 15, 1817.

67. HHSA, Rom: Berichte, Kaunitz to Metternich, July 13 #9-A, 1817. During the negotiations two minor disputes were settled. A new ceremonial and oath for the in-

stallation of bishops that had been introduced into Lombardy-Venetia in 1816, and against which the Pope had protested, were now accepted by him after certain changes had been made. He also agreed to confirm the Imperial nominees to the sees of Brünn and Munkatsch. He had refused to do this in 1816 because he thought they had taken this oath; when Kaunitz explained that they had not, Pius dropped his objections: *ibid.*, Kaunitz to Metternich, July 29 #14-A, 1817. Another dispute was discussed but not settled: the Pope's refusal to confirm the Imperial nominee to the see of Mantua, Monsignor Morandi, because of the latter's alleged bad character. The Pope refused to yield, and the Emperor eventually dropped the nomination. *Ibid.*, Gennotte to Metternich, June 10, 1817; Kaunitz to Metternich, December 7 #37-K, 1817.

68. *Ibid.*, Rom: Varia, Consalvi to Metternich, July 14, 1817. On these negotiations, Maturi, *Il Concordato;* Feret, vol. 2; H. Bastgen, *Bayern und der Heilige Stuhl in der ersten Hälfe des 19. Jahrhundert* , vol. 1. In fact, as noted earlier, the concordat with France was not ratified by the Chamber.

69. AV, ANV 243, Consalvi to Leardi, August 11, 1817.

70. HHSA, Vorträge, 208, Metternich to Francis I, July 19, 1817.

71. *Ibid.*, Imperial resolution of August 5, 1817.

72. *Ibid.*, Rom: Berichte, Kaunitz to Metternich, September 16 #25-C, 30 #27-A, October 13 #30-A, and December 7 #37-K, 1817; January 17 #43-A, and February 7 #47-B, -C, -D, 1818.

73. AV, R247, Leardi to Consalvi, December 28, 1817.

74. On the Salzburg question before 1815, see Bastgen, *Die Neuerrichtung,* 17–79; Maass, *Der Josephinismus,* vol. 4, ch. 4; Tomek, 3:93–101, 178–189, 318–321, 493–501. On Salzburg under the Prince-Bishops, see Hans Widmann, *Geschichte Salzburgs.* On Salzburg during the Restoration, see Bastgen, *Die Neuerrichtung,* 132–278, and Hosp, *Kirche,* 21–43.

75. AV, R247, Consalvi to Leardi, June 17, 1818.

76. *Ibid.*, Leardi to Consalvi, December 28, 1817.

77. *Ibid.*, Consalvi to Leardi, April 2 and June 17, 1818; R260, Consalvi to Kaunitz, July 28, 1817 and June 1, 1818.

78. Bastgen, *Die Neuerrichtung,* 147–160.

79. HHSA, Rom: Weisungen, Instructions for Kaunitz, May 31, 1817.

80. *Ibid.*, Berichte, Kaunitz to Metternich, July 25 #13-A, and 29, #14-A, 1817.

81. *Ibid.*, Kaunitz to Metternich, November 22 #35-A, 1817.

82. *Ibid.*, Weisungen, Metternich to Kaunitz, March 10, 1818; Berichte, Kaunitz to Metternich, March 30 #54-C, 1818. AV, R247, Consalvi to Leardi, April 3, and June 17, 1818.

83. AV, ANV 246, Leardi to Consalvi, August 8, 1818.

84. *Ibid.*, Leardi to Consalvi, May 25, 1818.

85. HHSA, Rom: Berichte, Gennotte to Metternich, August 19 #78-B, 1818.

86. APFFC, Consalvi to Spina, July 1818.

87. AV, R247, Consalvi to Leardi, April 2 and June 17, 1818.

88. AV, ANV 246, Leardi to Consalvi, August 18 and September 1, 1818.

89. HHSA, Rom: Varia, Consalvi to Metternich, October 1, 1818.

90. Francis I himself was not eager to discuss religious issues with the Pope, and gave orders that all points in dispute should be settled before his arrival: HHSA, Rom: Weisungen, Metternich to Kaunitz, February 24, 1819. Metternich, on the other hand, had long intended that such discussions should take place, as a means of breaking down the Emperor's Josephist convictions: see, e.g., his comments in his *Mémoires,* 3:5n. On the function of the Italian trip in strengthening Austrian influence against the attacks of Russia, see Alan J. Reinerman, "Metternich, Alexander I, and the Russian Challenge."

91. HHSA, Rom: Varia, Metternich to Consalvi, October 17, 1818.

92. *Ibid.,* Consalvi to Metternich, November 10, 1818.

93. AV, ANV 244, Consalvi to Leardi, February 20, 1818.

94. HHSA, Rom: Weisungen, Metternich to Kaunitz, February 14 #1, 1819.

95. *Ibid.,* February 24 #2, 1819.

96. *Ibid.,* Berichte, Gennotte to Metternich, March 11 #115-A, 13 #116, and 16 #117-A, -B, 1819. AV, ANV 244, Consalvi to Muzi, April 2, 1819; R260 Consalvi to Kaunitz, March 15, 1819.

97. HHSA, Rom: Weisungen, Metternich to Gennotte, March 20, 1819; Vorträge, Metternich to Francis I, July 11, 1819.

98. HHSA, Rom: Varia, Metternich to Consalvi, October 17 #1 & 2, 1818, Consalvi to Metternich, November 10, 1818; Weisungen, Metternich to Kaunitz, February 24, 1819. Little has been done on the visit to Rome, or the Italian tour of which it formed a part; the only studies on the latter, Nino Cortese, "Il principe di Metternich a Napoli nel 1819," *Il Mezzogiorno ed il Risorgimento italiano* (Naples, 1964), 378–388, and Karl Glossy, "Kaiser Franz Reise nach Italien im Jahr 1819," *Jahrbuch der Grillparzer Gesellschaft,* 14 (1904): 149–169, are too slight to be of much use, while the section in Metternich's *Mémoires,* 3:190–220, consists mainly of reflections on art and history. Hence, information on the trip must be pieced together from the relevant files in HHSA; of particular value is Grossbritannien: Weisungen, especially Metternich to Esterhazy, April 4, April 23, July 5 and 9, secret, and to Neumann, November 1, 1819.

99. Maass, *Der Josephinismus,* 4:142–143, and 5:1–15, holds that this change began only after the visit to Rome, of which it was a consequence. It seems, however, that the change had begun earlier, as revealed by the steps described above. Maass considers the reforms in the religious orders as significant evidence of the Emperor's change of heart after visiting Pius VII; however, the Emperor had already decided upon these reforms before visiting Rome: AV, R260, Leardi to Consalvi, February 5, 1819. See also the report of Altieri, April 8, 1819, in HHSA, Rom: Berichte.

100. Political affairs were also discussed by Metternich and Consalvi, notably the need for continued cooperation against the Sects and continued Austrian support for Consalvi's reforms; here too no records were kept, and we know what was said only in very general terms. However, Metternich emerged from these talks fully satisfied with Consalvi's policies and his attitude towards Austria, and convinced that Austro-Papal cooperation was solidly established: HHSA, Grossbritannien: Wiesungen, Metternich to Esterhazy, July 5 and 9, 1819, secret. There is no hint that Metternich revived his old plan for a Confederation, as French diplomats suspected; while their fears that the visit was a sort of reconnaissance to prepare for the annexation of the Legations were quite unfounded. In fact, Pius and Consalvi were left fully satisfied that Rome had nothing to fear from Austria in the political sphere: HHSA, Rom: Berichte, report of Altieri, April 8, 1819.

101. I was no more successful than Maass, *Der Josephinismus,* 4:142–143, or Beer, 531, in finding such records, either in AV, or in HHSA.

102. These documents may be found in AV, R260, 1819 Fascio 1.

103. *Ibid.,* "Innovazioni della Corte Austriaca, della quali il S. P. non puo dispensarsi dal chiederne la revoca," 1819.

104. HHSA, Rom: Berichte, report of Altieri, April 8, 1819.

105. *Ibid.,* reports of Altieri, April 8, May 4, 1819. Metternich, *Mémoires,* 3:3–5n.

106. Maass, *Der Josephinismus,* 4:143.

107. Metternich, *Mémoires,* 3:3–5, n.

108. HHSA, Grossbritannien: Weisungen, Metternich to Esterhazy, July 5, 1819; also July 9, 1819, secret.

109. Maass, *Der Josephinismus,* 5:7-8.

110. On the return of the Jesuits and its significance, see Alan J. Reinerman, "The Return of the Jesuits to the Austrian Empire and the Decline of Josephinism," *Catholic Historical Review,* 52 (1966): 372-390.

111. AV, ANV 244, Leardi to Consalvi, March 11, 1820.

112. *Ibid.,* R247, Leardi to Consalvi, April 29, 1820.

113. *Ibid.,* Leardi to Consalvi, October 17, 1820.

114. HHSA, Rom: Berichte, Gennotte to Metternich, February 5, 1820.

115. Maass, *Der Josephinismus,* 5:52-58.

116. HHSA, Rom: Weisungen, Instructions for Apponyi, September 16, 1820.

117. Only a partial copy—printed in Maass, *Der Josephinismus,* 4:631—has survived, but this is sufficient to indicate that the *memoire* was essentially a restatement of the basic Papal complaints against the state church system as set down in such documents as "Innovazioni della Corte Austriaca...," AV, R260, 1819.

118. HHSA, Rom: Varia, Apponyi to Metternich, October 14, 1820.

119. Note his warning to Metternich on this point just after the latter's departure from Rome: HHSA, Rom: Varia, Consalvi to Metternich, August 7, 1819.

120. Maass, *Der Josephinismus,* 5:14-16.

121. *Ibid.,* 16-17. Bishop Jacob Frint (1766-1834), appointed Hof- und Burgpfarrer in 1810, he was a strong promoter of the Catholic revival in Austria; see Hosp, *Zwischen Aufklarung.*

122. AV, ANV 247, Leardi to Consalvi, September 21, 1820.

123. *Ibid.,* ANV 244, Consalvi to Leardi, December 20, 1820.

124. *Ibid.,* Leardi to Consalvi, March 6, April 17 and 27, 1822.

125. Maass, *Der Josephinismus,* 5:213, Lorenz to Francis I, July 3, 1823.

126. Cf. Maass, *Der Josephinismus,* 4:142-143; Schmidlin, 1:344-345.

127. See, e.g., his pessimistic comments to Leardi, December 20, 1820, in AV, ANV 244, or to Blacas, August 2, 1822, in APFFC, Busta 34.

Chapter IV

1. On the Neapolitan revolution, see Aurelio Lepre, *La rivoluzione napoletana del 1820-1821;* George T. Romani, *The Neapolitan Revolution of 1820-1821;* and Annibale Alberti, ed., *Atti del Parlimento delle Due Sicilie.*

2. E.g., HHSA, Grossbritannien: Weisungen, Metternich to Esterhazy, July 17, 1820; Rom: Weisungen, Instructions for Apponyi, September 16, 1820.

3. On Metternich's policy during the Neapolitan crisis, see Schroeder, *Metternich's Diplomacy,* 25-128; Alberti, vol. 4; Srbik, *Metternich,* 1:600-608; Maurice Bourquin, *Histoire de la Sainte Alliance,* 259-287; Henry A. Kissinger, *A World Restored: Metternich, Castlereagh and the Problems of Peace, 1812-1822,* Chapters 14-15.

4. On Papal policy towards the Neapolitan revolution, see Joseph H. Brady, *Rome and the Neapolitan Revolution of 1820-1821: A Study in Papal Neutrality.*

5. Brady, 17-51. HHSA Rom: Varia, Consalvi to Metternich, July 8, August 12 and 13, 1820; Berichte, Gennotte to Metternich, July 8 #32-A, 12 #33, 1820.

6. AV, R247, Leardi to Consalvi, July 27, 1820.

7. HHSA, Rom: Varia, Metternich to Consalvi, August 2, 1820.

8. *Ibid.,* Consalvi to Metternich, August 12 and 23, 1820, January 6, 1821.

9. APFFC, Busta 34, Consalvi to Blacas, August 2, 1822.

10. HHSA, Rom: Varia, Metternich to Consalvi, August 2, September 2, 15, and November 22, 1822; Weisungen, Instructions for Apponyi, September 16, 1820, Metternich to Apponyi, November 22, 1820.

11. HHSA, Rom: Varia, Metternich to Consalvi, November 22, 1820; Weisungen, Metternich to Apponyi, November 22, 1820.

12. *Ibid.*, Varia, Metternich to Consalvi, August 2, 1820.

13. E.g., *ibid.*, September 5, 1820; Cf. the stress he placed upon allaying Consalvi's suspicions in his instructions for Apponyi, September 16, 1820, in Weisungen, *ibid.*

14. *Ibid.*, Varia, Consalvi to Metternich, August 23, 1820.

15. *Ibid.;* also August 12, 1820.

16. *Ibid.*, Metternich to Consalvi, September 2 and 15, 1820; Weisungen, Instructions for Apponyi, September 16, 1820.

17. Examples of such requests and their fulfillments, too numerous to cite individually, may be found in HHSA, Rom: Varia and Berichte, for August 1820-February 1821.

18. Országos Széchényi Könyvtar, Budapest (hereafter cited as OSK), Fonds Apponyi (hereafter FA), Metternich to Apponyi, September 16, 1820. AV, R242, Spina to Consalvi, October 7, 1820.

19. HHSA, Rom: Berichte, Apponyi to Metternich, October 7, 1820.

20. Schroeder, *Metternich's Diplomacy,* 60–103; Srbik, *Metternich,* 1:603–605; Bourquin, 259–283.

21. HHSA, Rom: Varia, Metternich to Consalvi, November 22, 1820; Weisungen, Metternich to Apponyi, November 22, 1820.

22. AV, Archivio della Nunziatura di Parigi (hereafter ANP), VIII, Consalvi to Macchi, November 1, 1820.

23. HHSA, Rom: Berichte, Apponyi to Metternich, December 4 #25-K, 1820.

24. This last had been a sore point for some time. Rome had furnished numerous supplies, against promise of prompt repayment, to the Austrian troops in transit through the State in 1815, but it was not until 1818 that the Austrian Finance Ministry even began to consider repayment, and then it rejected most of the Papal claim on the grounds that the Papal records were inaccurate. This question dragged on throughout Consalvi's ministry, and was never settled to Rome's satisfaction. It is covered in great detail in AV, ANV for 1815–1823, but to follow it here seems pointless. Austria's ungenerous behavior in this affair certainly annoyed Consalvi greatly, but Metternich's claim that it was chiefly responsible for the Cardinal's alienation from Austria was a vast exaggeration, as the Prince no doubt knew: AV, R247, Leardi to Consalvi, June 30, 1821.

25. MCR, Busta 208, Consalvi to Sanseverino, November 22, 1820.

26. HHSA, Rom: Varia, Metternich to Apponyi, December 13, 1820.

27. *Ibid.*, Weisungen, Metternich to Apponyi, first annex to #1 of November 22, 1820.

28. *Ibid.*, Varia, Metternich to Consalvi, December 13, 1820.

29. *Ibid.*, Berichte, Apponyi to Metternich, January 9 #34-D, 1821.

30. *Ibid.*, Metternich to Consalvi, December 13 #1 & 2, 1820; Francis I to Pius VII, December 12, 1820.

31. AV, R244, Pius VII to Ferdinand I, December 3, 1820.

32. HHSA, Rom: Varia, Instructions for Lebzeltern, December 12, 1820; Kongressakten, Troppau, "Opinion du Cabinet de Russie sur les moyens de conciliation...," December 6, 1820, "Réponse du Cabinet autrichien," December 10, 1820. OSK, FA, Metternich to Apponyi, December 13, 1820. On the background of this proposal and the reasons for Capodistrias's hostility to the intervention, see Schroeder, *Metternich's Diplomacy,* ch. 3.

33. HHSA, Rom: Varia, Lebzeltern to Metternich, January 6 and February 1, 1821, Metternich to Consalvi, January 18, 1821; Berichte, Apponyi to Metternich, January 4 #33-A, 1821.

34. *Ibid.*, Varia, Instructions for Lebzeltern, December 12, 1820; Berichte, Apponyi to Metternich, January 3 #33-G, and January 9 #34-D, 1821, with annexes.

35. Note the report of an Austrian agent in Rome that "The Secretary of State's attitude towards our Court has become one of extreme suspicion. . . . This distrust has grown as a result of the mission of Baron Lebzeltern, whose requests he seems to regard as only a means to increase our supremacy in Italy": APFFC, Busta 27, unsigned report to the Governor of Milan, January 12, 1821. This report is one of several which Consalvi was able to intercept, and of which copies are in this file. His acquaintance with these reports no doubt increased his distrust of Austria, since they revealed the continued desire of the Austrian military and the Milan government to garrison Papal cities as a means of keeping the Sects in check. See especially the report of August 28, 1821, unsigned but apparently from the Governor of Milan, containing a detailed plan for the surprise garrisoning of seventeen Papal cities, from Rome downwards. Though this plan, which apparently originated in the Milanese Gubernium, never received Imperial approval, its discovery could not help but confirm Consalvi's suspicions of Austria.

36. HHSA, Rom: Berichte, Apponyi to Metternich, January 3 #33-G, 1821.

37. E.g., his "Coup d'oeil impartiel sur l'attitude actuelle du cabinet romain," January 1821, APFFC, Busta 35, a long and eloquent defense of Austrian policy culminating in an appeal to Consalvi to return to his former policy of trust and cooperation.

38. HHSA, Rom: Varia, Consalvi to Metternich, January 6, 1821.

39. AV, R165, Consalvi to Blacas, January 6, 1821.

40. "The Secretary of State now seems to put his trust entirely in Count Blacas and the French Court . . ., which he has called upon for aid against our Court at the Congress of Laybach," as the unnamed Austrian agent in Rome reported to the Governor of Milan, January 10, 1821, APFFC, Busta 35. On the role of Blacas in the Neapolitan crisis and the general ineffectiveness of French diplomacy at this time, see Bertier de Sauvigny, *Metternich et la France*, 2:315-473, and Vladimiro Sperber, "Intorno alla politica napoletana della Francia," *Rassegna storica del Risorgimento*, 17 (1968): 167-212.

41. HHSA, Rom: Varia, Metternich to Consalvi, January 18, 1821.

42. *Ibid.*, Weisungen, Metternich to Apponyi, January 18 #2 & 3, 1821. AV, R242, Consalvi to Spina, February 8, 1821.

43. AV, R242, Consalvi to Spina, January 16, 1821.

44. *Ibid.*, Spina to Consalvi, January 26 and 30, 1821.

45. AAB, Governo di Bologna, Consalvi to Oppizzoni, January 24, 1821.

46. On the Congress of Laybach, see Schroeder, *Metternich's Diplomacy*, 104-128; Bourquin, 283-288; Kissinger, 270-285; Webster, *Castlereagh 1815-1822*, 312-345; Maria Avetta, "Al Congresso di Lubiana coi ministri del Re Vittorio Emanuele I," *Il Risorgimento italiano*, 16 (1923): 1-50, and 17 (1924): 212-250; Bertier de Sauvigny, *Metternich et la France*, 2:417-473.

47. AV, R242, Apponyi to Consalvi, January 6, 1821, Consalvi to Apponyi, January 7, 1821, Consalvi to Metternich, January 6, 1821. Giuseppi Spina (1756-1828), Consalvi's most able and trusted subordinate; as Legate of Bologna after 1818 he won general approval for the moderation and skill with which he governed this most difficult of Papal provinces.

48. *Ibid.*, Instructions for Spina, January 10, 1821.

49. *Ibid.*, Spina to Consalvi, January 24 #3, 1821.

50. Copy of the statement in *ibid.*, 1821. This account of the meeting of January 26

is based on: *Ibid.,* Spina to Consalvi, January 28, 1821; HHSA, Kongressakten, Laybach, Journal des Conferences, January 26 and 28, 1821; Rom: Weisungen, Metternich to Apponyi, January 30 #1, 1821; Archivio di Stato, Turin (hereafter AST), I Sezione, Congresso di Lubiana, San Marzano's report of Jaunary 28, 1821; Bertier de Sauvigny, *Metternich et la France,* 2:448–449.

51. HHSA, Rom: Weisungen, Metternich to Apponyi, January 30 #1, 1821.

52. *Ibid.* The point is worth stressing, since historians from Bianchi—*Storia documentata,* 2:143–144—onward have tended to depict Spina's declaration as a bold defiance of Metternich.

53. Copy of Spina's statement and of the plan for Naples in AV, R242, 1821.

54. *Ibid.,* Spina to Consalvi, February 27, 1821; Consalvi to Spina, May 2, 1821.

55. Brady, 104–110.

56. Copy in AV, R242, 1821.

57. *Ibid.,* R210, Consalvi to all Delegates and Legates, January 27, 1821.

58. HHSA, Rom: Berichte, Apponyi to Metternich, February 28 #48-B, and March 3, # 49-A, 1821.

59. AV, R210, Amat to Consalvi, February 10, 1821, Consalvi to Amat, February 17, 1821, Consalvi to Delegate of Perugia, February 14, 1821. The Vice-Legate was in charge at Bologna during Spina's absence at the Congress of Laybach.

60. *Ibid.,* Consalvi to Amat, February 14, 1821; to all Delegates and Legates, February 17, 24, and March 7, 1821.

61. *Ibid.,* Consalvi to all Delegates and Legates, March 10, 1821.

62. *Ibid.,* Oppizzoni to Consalvi, February 12 and 13, 1821; Amat to Consalvi, February 14, 1821.

63. *Ibid.,* R242, Spina to Consalvi, February 15 and 17, 1821.

64. *Ibid.,* Spina to Consalvi, February 17 and 22, 1821. Metternich was confident of Blacas's support: OSK, Metternich to Apponyi, December 13, 1820, and January 18, 1821; HHSA, Rom: Varia, Blacas to Metternich, December 26, 1820.

65. AV, R165, Consalvi to Delegate of Ancona, February 12, 1821.

66. *Ibid.,* Delegate of Ancona to Consalvi, February 15 #1 & 2, 1821. This seems to be the same incident that Bianchi, *Storia documentata,* 2:73–75, incorrectly describes as taking place in August, 1820, six months before any Austrian troops entered the Papal State.

67. AV, R210, Delegate of Perugia to Consalvi, February 22, 1821; Delegate of Spoleto to Consalvi, March 10, 1821; R242, Consalvi to Spina, February 21, 1821.

68. On the Piedmontese revolt and the Austrian reaction, see C. Torta, *La rivoluzione piemontese del 1821;* Schroeder, *Metternich's Diplomacy,* 115–123; Cesare Spellanzon, *Storia del Risorgimento e dell'Unità d'Italia,* 1:842–62.

69. HHSA, Rom: Weisungen, Metternich to Apponyi, March 15 #2, 1821.

70. AV, R247, Consalvi to Leardi, March 31, 1821. HHSA, Rom: Berichte, Apponyi to Metternich, March 27 #55-B, 31 #57-B, 1821; Weisungen, Metternich to Apponyi, April 12 #1 & 2, 1821.

71. *Ibid.,* Metternich to Apponyi, May 20 #1, 1821; Vorträge 226, June 7, 1821.

72. AV, R165, Consalvi to Apponyi, June 4, 1821.

73. If the correspondence in Van Duerm, *Correspondance,* is joined with that in HHSA, Rom: it can be seen that more letters were exchanged in the Fall of 1820 than in all the years since 1816 put together.

74. HHSA, Frankreich: Weisungen, Metternich to Vincent, December 16, 1820.

75. AV, R247, Leardi to Consalvi, April 17, 1821; also, April 26, May 31, and June 30, 1821.

76. *Ibid.,* Consalvi to Leardi, May 19, 1821, offers an indignant defense of his policy.

77. Payment in full was completed by the end of 1821, in contrast to the interminable delays and unsatisfactory settlement of the 1815 claims: Brady, 164–166.

78. HHSA, Rom: Weisungen, Metternich to Apponyi, February 16 #2, 1822.

79. E.g., *Ibid.*, April 12, July 4, 17, and August 21, 1821. AV, R247, Leardi to Consalvi, May 24, 31, and June 30, 1821.

80. E.g., HHSA, Kongressakten, Laybach, "Points à arrêter relativement à la conduite à suivre vis-à-vis les princes d'Italie," May, 1821.

Chapter V

1. HHSA, Rom: Varia, Metternich to Consalvi, November 22, 1820.

2. *Ibid.;* also, Weisungen, Metternich to Apponyi, November 22, 1820, and April 19, 1821.

3. *Ibid.*, Varia, Metternich to Consalvi, November 22, 1820.

4. *Ibid.*, Berichte, Apponyi to Metternich, April 14 #61-A, 1821.

5. AV, R242, Consalvi to Metternich, December 5, 1820.

6. HHSA, Rom: Berichte, Apponyi to Metternich, January 9 #34-D, 1821. AV, R242, Spina to Consalvi, January 26, 1821.

7. HHSA, Rom: Weisungen, Metternich to Apponyi, April 19, 1821; also April 12, 1821.

8. *Ibid.*, Varia, Metternich to Consalvi, April 12, 1821.

9. *Ibid.*, Francis I to Pius VII, April 12, 1821.

10. *Ibid.*, Berichte, Apponyi to Metternich, April 6 #59-A, 12 #60, 14 #61-A, and May 4 #65-F, 1821.

11. *Ibid.*, Kongressakten, Laybach, "Resultats de ma conference avec S. M. Alexandre," January 13, 1821; Kongressakten, Florenz-Rom-Neapel, Procès-verbal of the ministerial conference of April 21, 1821; Rom: Berichte, Apponyi to Metternich, May 4 #65-F, 1821.

12. *Ibid.*, Rom: Berichte, Apponyi to Metternich, May 4 #65-F, 1821.

13. *Ibid.* This ritual resembles those described in R. John Rath, The *Carbonari*: Their Origins, Aims and Initiation Rites," 359-365.

14. HHSA, Rom: Berichte, Apponyi to Metternich, May 4 #65-F, 1821.

15. *Ibid.*, May 9 #66-B, 15 #67-A, 21 #69-C, June 7 #70-K, 23 #73-A, 1821.

16. Rath, "The *Carbonari*," 362.

17. HHSA, Rom: Berichte, Apponyi to Metternich, May 9 #66-B, 15 #67-A, 1821.

18. *Ibid.*, May 9 #66-B, 1821.

19. *Ibid.*, Weisungen, Metternich to Apponyi, May 20 #2, 1821.

20. *Ibid.*, Berichte, Apponyi to Metternich, July 9 #75-A, 1821.

21. *Ibid.*, Varia, Apponyi to Metternich, July 27, 1821; Metternich to Consalvi, August 2, 1821; Berichte, Apponyi to Metternich, September 20 #2-A, 1821.

22. *Ibid.*, Berichte, Apponyi to Metternich, July 9 #75-A, 22 #76-B, and September 1 #82-A, 1821.

23. *Ibid.*, Weisungen, Metternich to Apponyi, August 12 #1, 1821.

24. Barberi, *Bullarii romani continuatio,* 15:446-448.

25. AV, R247, Leardi to Consalvi, September 27 and November 26, 1821.

26. HHSA, Rom: Berichte, Apponyi to Metternich, September 14 #84-A and 17 #87-C, 1821.

27. *Ibid.*, September 1 #82-A, and 14 #84-A, 1821; Weisungen, Metternich to Apponyi, July 21 #1 and August 21 #1, 1821. AV, R247, Leardi to Consalvi, November 26, 1821.

28. HHSA, Rom: Weisungen, Metternich to Apponyi, April 19, 1821; also, August 21, 1821.

29. Andrea Ostoja, "La Carboneria e le sette segrete in Dalmazia e Istria," *Atti e memorie della societa dalmata di storia patria,* 2 (1970): 5–224.

30. ASN, AB, 278, Intonti to the King, October 9, 1821. Denials of the edict's efficacy by Abbe de Pradt, *Europe and America in 1821,* 2:207–209, and Alberto Aquarone, "La restaurazione nello Stato Pontificio," *Archivio della societa romana di storia patria,* 78 (1955): 119–189, as well as by the *Carbonari* themselves, "Rimonstranza della societa de'Carbonari al sommo pontifice Pio VII," ASN, AB, Libri ed opuscoli #1972.

31. This description of Metternich's policy in 1821 is based primarily on HHSA, Kongressakten, Laybach, "Points à arrêter relativement à la conduite à suivre vis-à-vis les princes d'Italie," May 1821, "Circulaire aux Missions autrichiennes en Italie," May 12, 1821, "Aperçu sur les affaires d'Italie et sur quelques remèdes à employer," May 15, 1821; Rom: Weisungen, Metternich to Apponyi, July 4 and August 21 #2 & 3, 1821; Russland: Weisungen, Metternich to Lebzeltern, July 18 #3, 1821.

32. E.g., AV, R242, Instructions for Spina, October 19, 1822. There is, however, no hint in Metternich's correspondence that these suspicions were justified; instead, we find repeated denials—not only to foreign statesmen, but to his own most trusted subordinates—of any ambitious or aggressive intent: e.g., HHSA, Russland: Weisungen, Metternich to Lebzeltern, June 23, 1821, or Rom: Weisungen, to Apponyi, July 4, 1821. There can be little doubt that he was sincere in claiming that his plans were intended only to defend the Restoration Order in Italy—with, of course, the Austrian predominance which this implied.

33. Unlike the Confederation, the Commission has been little studied. Moreover, I have been unable to find a clear statement by Metternich as to the exact nature he envisaged for it; most of the details of my account of the Commission have been supplied by the accounts of the Italian diplomats to whom he described his plans: AV, R242, Instructions for Spina, October 19, 1822, Consalvi to Macchi, December 2, 1822, "Osservazioni sul progetto della Commissione Politica," 1822; AST, Sezione II, "Istruzioni reali al Conte della Torre," October 23, 1822. Additional light is shed by a comparison with the body on which the Commission was modeled, the Zentral Untersuchungs Kommission, established at Mainz in 1819 at Metternich's instigation: see P.A.G. von Mayer, ed., *Corpus Juris Confoederationis Germanicae,* 2:99–100.

34. HHSA, Kongressakten: Laybach, Journal des Conférences, February 26, 1821. Originally to be held in Florence, the Congress was moved to Verona because better security could be maintained on Austrian soil.

35. HHSA, Kongressakten: Laybach, "Circulaire du Cabinet de Berlin aux Missions prussiennes en Italie," May 26, 1822.

36. The arguments he advanced to win over the Tsar are summarized in HHSA, Kongressakten: Laybach, "Points à arrêter relativement à la conduite à suivre vis-à-vis les princes d'Italie," May 1821, and "Aperçu sur les affaires d'Italie et quelques remèdes à employer," May 15, 1821; and in Státní Ústředni Archiv, Prague (hereafter cited: SUA), Fonds Plasy Acta Clementina (all SUA materials cited are from this collection), C 30, Memoranda IV, "Mémoire secret sur la tendance, le travail, et les moyens des sectes révolutionnaires en Europe pour S.M.I. de Toutes les Russies," 1822.

37. On Metternich's plans for the reform of the Neapolitan government, see *ibid.,* Troppau, "Points," November 15, 1820, and Angelo Filipuzzi, "La restaurazione nel Regno delle Due Sicilie."

38. *Ibid.,* Laybach, "Points à arrêter...," May 1821.

39. *Ibid.,* "Circulaire aux ministres de l'Empereur en Italie," May 12, 1821. On the Tsar's attitude towards Austria and the Italian states, see Reinerman, "Metternich, Alexander I, and the Russian Challenge," and Berti, *Russia e stati italiani,* 453–498.

40. On the difficult situation created for Metternich by the Greek crisis, see Schroeder, *Metternich's Diplomacy,* 164–194; Kissinger, 286–311; Srbik, *Metternich,* 1:609–614. The impact of this crisis on his Italian policy has been generally ignored.

41. HHSA, Frankreich: Weisungen, Metternich to Vincent, June 30 #2, 1821; Rom: Weisungen, Metternich to Apponyi, July 17, 1821.

42. *Ibid.,* Kongressakten: Laybach, "Circulaire aux Missions autrichiennes en Italie."

43. Copies in *ibid.*

44. Archivio di Stato, Parma (hereafter ASP), Casa e corte di Maria Luigia d'Austria, Neipperg to Metternich, June 8, 1821. Bianchi, *Storia documentata,* 2:77.

45. Bianchi, *Storia documentata,* 2:87. Schroeder, *Metternich's Diplomacy,* 153.

46. AST, Sezione II, "Istruzioni reali al Conte Pralormo," January 12, 1822.

47. ASF, Ordine 2392, Serie 1931, Fossombroni to Corsini, November 29, 1822, Corsini to Fossombroni, November 24, 1822.

48. HHSA, Rom: Berichte, Apponyi to Metternich, June 30 #73-A, 1821; also June 2, #70-J, 1821.

49. E.g., HHSA, Rom: Weisungen, Metternich to Apponyi, July 4 #1, 17, August 21 #2 & 3, 1821, and February 16, 1822. AV, R247, Leardi to Consalvi, June 30 and July 10, 1821.

50. HHSA, Rom: Berichte, Apponyi to Metternich, September 1 #82-C and December 20 #10, 1821, September 11 #63-C, 1822.

51. AV, R242, Consalvi to Leardi, May 1, 1822, to Spina, November 28, 1822, December 4, 1822, "Osservazioni sul progetto di una Commissione...," 1822.

52. Bianchi, *Storia documentata,* 2:87–88, 370–375.

53. APFFC, Busta 34, Consalvi to Blacas, August 2, 1822.

54. AV, R242, Consalvi to Spina, November 28 and December 4, 1822.

55. Bianchi, *Storia documentata,* 2:371–372.

56. AV, R242, "Quesiti che si propongono...," 1822.

57. APFFC, Busta 34, Consalvi to Blacas, August 2, 1822. AV, R242, Consalvi to Spina, November 28, 1822.

58. APFFC, Busta 34, Blacas to Consalvi, August 18, 1822. AAB, Carte Oppizzoni, Consalvi to Oppizzoni, August 28, August 31, 1822.

59. Jean Baptiste Comte de Villèle, *Mémoires et correspondance,* 3:55–59, 170–177.

60. *Ibid.,* 55–59, 170–174. AV, R248, Macchi to Consalvi, October 29, 1822.

61. AV, R248, Macchi to Consalvi, October 29, 1822.

62. On the Congress of Verona and its background, see Irby C. Nichols, *The European Pentarchy and the Congress of Verona;* Bertier de Sauvigny, *Metternich et la France,* 2:609–661; Schroeder, *Metternich's Diplomacy,* 195–236; Srbik, *Metternich,* 614–618; Villèle, vol. 3; Bourquin, 315–348; Harold Temperley, *The Foreign Policy of Canning;* François Vicomte de Chateaubriand, *Le Congrès de Verone.* These general works give relatively little attention to Italian affairs, which have, naturally, received greater attention from Italian historians, beginning with Bianchi, *Storia documentata,* 2:82–145. But if Bianchi describes certain aspects of Austrian policy, he fails completely to discern the overall pattern, to realize that these are not isolated incidents but part of a comprehensive plan devised by Metternich to strengthen Austrian hegemony. Later Italian historians have inherited this limited vision, e.g., Spellanzon, and Giorgio Candeloro, *Storia dell'Italia moderna,* 2:121–124, as have the

authors of the two studies of Papal policy at the Congress, Furlani, "La Santa Sede," and Angelo Tamborra, "I Congressi della Santa Alleanza di Lubiana e di Verona e la politica della Santa Sede," *Archivio storico italiano,* 118 (1960): 190–211.

63. On the Spanish crisis and Metternich's reaction to it, see Nichols; Schroeder, *Metternich's Diplomacy,* 195–223; Bertier de Sauvigny, *Metternich et la France,* 2:305–311, 593–803.

64. HHSA, Rom: Berichte, Apponyi to Metternich, September 11 #63-C, 1822.

65. AV, R242, Consalvi to Leardi, September 17, 1822; to Metternich, October 20, 1822. Some weeks earlier, the Duke of Modena had accused Spina of favoring the Sects while Legate of Bologna. Furlani, "La Santa Sede," 474–484, argues that this was an attempt by Metternich to prevent the appointment of Spina, who had allegedly earned his dislike by his defence of Papal interests at Laybach. I have been unable to find any indication in Metternich's correspondence in HHSA or elsewhere that this was the case, nor was Metternich dissatisfied with Spina's conduct at Laybach: HHSA, Rom: Weisungen, Metternich to Apponyi, January 30 #1, 1821.

66. AV, R242, Instructions for Spina, October 19, 1822.

67. *Ibid.,* Spina to Consalvi, December 2, 1822. The Neapolitans wanted the army reduced in size for reasons of economy, but they were determined that it should not be evacuated completely.

68. "Parma today can only be considered an Austrian province": HHSA, Grossbritannien: Weisungen, Metternich to Esterhazy, July 5, 1819. ASP, Neipperg to Metternich, June 8, 1821. AV, R242, Spina to Consalvi, December 2, 1822.

69. ASF, Corsini to Fossombroni, November 24, December 2, 1822.

70. Archivio di Stato, Lucca (hereafter ASL), R. Intima Segretaria de Gabinetto, Filza 470, Mansi to Maria Louisa, December 4, 1822.

71. AST, Sezione II, "Istruzioni reali al Conte della Torre per la sua missione al Congresso di Verona," October 23, 1822.

72. AV, R242, "Rapporto dell'Udienza particolare," November 7, 1822.

73. Villèle, 3:177–182, 198–205, 224–239, 263–265.

74. *Ibid.,* 224–239, 263–265. AV, R242, Consalvi to Macchi, December 2, 1822.

75. ASF, Corsini to Fossombroni, November 14, 1822. AV, R242, Spina to Consalvi, November 23, 1822.

76. AV, R242, Spina to Consalvi, November 20, 1822; also November 23, 1822, and ASF, Corsini to Fossombroni, November 24, 1822.

77. AV, R242, Consalvi to Spina, November 28 and 30, 1822.

78. ASF, Corsini to Fossombroni, November 23 and 24, 1822; Fossombroni to Corsini, November 29, 1822.

79. *Ibid.,* Corsini to Fossombroni, December 2, 6, and 8, 1822. AV, R242, Spina to Consalvi December 2 and 5, 1822. ASL, Mansi to Maria Louisa, December 4, 1822.

80. AV, R242, Spina to Consalvi, December 2, 1822.

81. *Ibid.,* Consalvi to Spina, December 4, 1822; also December 7, 1822.

82. ASF, Corsini to Fossombroni, December 8, 1822.

83. OSF, FA, Metternich to Apponyi, December 22, 1822. ASF, Corsini to Fossombroni, December 8, 9, and 10, 1822. AV, R242, Spina to Consalvi, December 9, 11, and 17, 1822.

84. AV, R242, Spina to Consalvi, December 9, 1822. Also ASF, Corsini to Fossombroni, December 10, 1822.

85. AV, R242, Spina to Consalvi, December 9, 1822.

86. OSF, FA, Metternich to Apponyi, December 22, 1822. ASF, Corsini to Fossombroni, December 8, 1822.

87. AV, R242, Consalvi to Macchi, December 2, 1822; Spina to Consalvi, December 9, 1822. ASF, Corsini to Fossombroni, November 2 and 3, 1822.

88. AV, R242, Consalvi to Macchi, December 2, 1822.

89. *Ibid.*, Spina to Consalvi, December 12, 1822.

90. OSF, FA, Metternich to Apponyi, December 22, 1822. HHSA, Rom: Varia, Metternich to Apponyi, February 22, 1823.

91. Copy of the declaration in HHSA, Kongressakten: Verona.

92. Copy of Spina's declaration in AV, R242, 1822.

93. *Ibid.*, Spina to Consalvi, December 14, 17, and 28, 1822. ASF, Corsini to Fossombroni, December 15, with copy of his declaration. HHSA, Kongressakten: Verona, Procès—verbal of December 13, 1822.

94. AV, R242, Spina to Consalvi, December 17, 1822.

95. OSF, FA, Metternich to Apponyi, December 22, 1822. Also, HHSA, Rom: Varia, Metternich to Apponyi, February 12, 1823.

96. In a sense, Consalvi must be absolved from this implied criticism, since for him the problem had other dimensions. In the last analysis, his motive was religious, not political: the preservation of the Papal State's independence was sought not for its own sake, but as essential for the Papacy's freedom to carry out the spiritual functions which were its reason for existing. Not even to avert the triumph of revolution could he acquiesce in the transformation of the State into an Austrian satellite; better, from his point of view, that the State itself should be overthrown than that it should survive under foreign control—the Papacy's spiritual freedom and reputation for impartiality would survive the first calamity more easily than the second.

97. On Austrian postal policy, see Josef Karl Mayr, *Metternichs Geheimer Briefdienst.* Little else has been written on this subject, except Silvio Furlani, "La convenzione austro-pontificia del 1815," *Archivio della Deputazione romana di storia patria,* 69 (1946): 23–58, and "La questione postale italiana al Congresso di Verona," *Nuova rivista storica,* 32 (1948): 36–49.

98. On the 1815 negotiations, see HHSA, Rom: Berichte, Lebzeltern to Metternich, July 29, August 26, September 4, 20, and October 7, 1815, and Furlani, "La convenzione."

99. HHSA, Rom: Berichte, Lebzeltern to Metternich, September 4, 1815.

100. His objections to the draft are explained in AV, R117, "Osservazioni sul progetto del Sig. Baron Lilien," 1815.

101. Unless, as often happened, some other state offered the use of its courier, or a trustworthy private traveller was willing to carry Papal dispatches. Code could be used, of course, but the skill of the Austrian cryptographers made this an insecure refuge. This explains why Consalvi's correspondence with the Vienna Nuncio or with Spina at Laybach and Verona was so guarded in tone: it was written in the knowledge that it would soon become known to Metternich.

102. Copy in AV, R117, 1815, of the drafts of Lilien and Consalvi, and of the Convention.

103. HHSA, Rom: Berichte, Lebzeltern to Metternich, September 20 and October 7, 1815.

104. *Ibid.*, Weisungen, Metternich to Lebzeltern, August 21, October 5 and 14, 1815.

105. Mayr, *Briefdienst,* 61.

106. *Ibid.*, 67–68.

107. *Ibid.*, 61–72. On Piedmontese postal policy, see Giulio Guderzo, *Vie e mezzi di communicazione in Piemonte,* 334–430.

108. The Austrian chargé at Turin, Daiser, went so far as to argue that the 1820 revolutions could have been avoided had Austria been in full control of the Italian posts: HHSA, Sardinien: Berichte, January 30. 1823.

109. ASF, Trattati Internazional, CXLIV, Convenzione postale, September 4, 1822.

110. AV, R261, Blacas to Consalvi, October 28, 1822; R248, Macchi to Consalvi, October 29, 1822. Villèle, 3:170–174.

111. AV, R248, Macchi to Consalvi, October 29, 1822. On Consalvi and Piedmont, see Anna Costa, "Giuseppi Barberoux, 1816–1824," *Bollettino storico-bibliografico subalpino,* 66 (1968): 465–521.

112. AST, Sezione II, Istruzioni agli agenti all'estero, "Istruzioni reali al Conte della Torre per la sua Missione al Congresso di Verona," October 23, 1822.

113. AV, R117, Spina to Consalvi, November 27, 1822. Also AST, Sezione II, Carte Politiche: Congresso di Verona, Della Torre to Collegno, November 23 #8, 27 #19 & 20, 1822 and ASL, Mansi to Maria Luisa, December 4, 1822.

114. AST, Della Torre to Collegno, November 16, 23 #17 & 18, and 27 #19 & 20, 1822.

115. ASF, Corsini to Fossombroni, November 28, December 7, 8, and 10, 1822. AST, Della Torre to Collegno, November 28 #22, December 7 #31, and 14 #37, 1822.

116. See Bertier de Sauvigny, Metternich et la France, 2:663–829.

117. AV, R117, Macchi to Consalvi, January 9, March 17, April 22, May 20, and August 2, 1823.

118. *Ibid.,* Consalvi to Barberoux, January 29, 1823.

119. *Ibid.,* Tosti to Consalvi, February 19, 1823.

120. *Ibid.,* Consalvi to Tosti, February 10, 1823.

121. *Ibid.,* Apponyi to Consalvi, December 10, 1822; Consalvi to Apponyi, December 19, 1822.

122. HHSA, Rom: Berichte, Apponyi to Metternich, December 30 #15-A, 1822.

123. AV, R117, Consalvi to Macchi, February 8, 1823; ANV 250, Consalvi to Leardi, April 12, 1823.

124. AV, ANV 250, April 13, 1823. Copy of the Convention in R117, 1823.

125. *Ibid.,* R117, Macchi to Consalvi, April 22, 1822.

126. AV, ANV 250, Consalvi to Apponyi, March 29, 1823; to Leardi, June 28 and August 13, 1823; R117, Apponyi to Consalvi, June 19, 1823. HHSA, Vorträge 234, May 13, 1823.

127. This account of the postal negotiations is based on AV, ANV 250, Consalvi to Leardi, August 13, 1823; R117, Consalvi to Macchi, August 4, 9, and 14, 1823; and HHSA, Rom: Berichte, Apponyi to Metternich, August 19 #64-B, 1823.

128. Convention of August 19, 1823, in AV, R117, 1823.

Chapter VI

1. HHSA, Rom: Weisungen, Instructions for Kaunitz, May 31, 1817; Instructions for Apponyi, September 16, 1820; Metternich to Apponyi, November 28, 1822, and June 20, 1823. The conclave of 1823 has been frequently studied. The most reliable accounts are Raffaele Colapietra, "Il Diario Brunelli del conclave del 1823," *Archivio storico italiano,* 120 (1962): 76–146, and Charles Terlinden, "Le Conclave de Leon XII," *Revue d'histoire ecclesiastique,* 8 (1913): 272–303. Earlier studies are unreliable, marked by bias and factual error: Mario Rossi, "Il Conclave di Leone XII," *Bollettino della R. Deputazione di storia patria per l'Umbria,* 33 (1935): 135–215; Ugo Oxilla, "Tre Conclavi," *Rassegna storica del Risorgimento,* 20 (1933): 564–584, and "Il Conclave di Papa Leone XII," *ibid.,* 8 (1921): 611–616; Artaud de Montour, *Storia del Papa Leone XII,* 31–60; Eugenio Cipoletta, *Memorie politiche sui conclavi,* 91–153;

F. Petruccelli della Gattina, *Histoire diplomatique des conclaves,* 4:331-345; Bianchi, *Storia documentata,* 2:154-163. On the French role, Bertier de Sauvigny, *Metternich et la France,* 2:830-844, is far superior to Feret, 2:267-283. Becker, *Relaciones diplomatices,* is the only work to cover the role of Spain.

2. HHSA, Rom: Weisungen, Metternich to Kaunitz, October 15, 1817; Grossbritannien: Weisungen, Metternich to Esterhazy, April 19, 1817: Vorträge, Metternich to Francis I, June 14, 1817.

3. HHSA, Rom: Berichte, Kaunitz to Metternich, November 6 #32-A & F, 1817.

4. *Ibid.,* Weisungen, Metternich to Kaunitz, November 6, 1817. Bertier de Sauvigny, *Metternich et la France,* 1:122-124.

5. HHSA, Rom: Weisungen, Metternich to Kaunitz, October 15, 1817; Petruccelli della Gattina, 4:321-322; Becker, 64-65.

6. E.g., HHSA, Rom: Weisungen, Instructions for Apponyi, September 16, 1820.

7. *Ibid.,* Berichte, Apponyi to Metternich, November 6 #1, 1822.

8. *Ibid.,* Weisungen, Metternich to Apponyi, November 28, 1822.

9. *Ibid.,* Russland: Weisungen, Metternich to Lebzeltern, June 28 #7, 1823; Vorträge 234, June 13, 1823.

10. *Ibid.,* Berichte, Apponyi to Metternich, January 6, 1823. Giuseppi Albani (1750-1834), several of whose ancestors had represented Austria at earlier conclaves, attained great influence at Rome despite his dubious reputation: Chateaubriand described him as "rich and excessively avaricious, he is involved in all sorts of dubious enterprises.... I am not sure he believes in God...." Archives du Ministère des Affaires Êtrangeres, Paris (hereafter AAEP), Correspondance Politique, Rome, Chateaubriand to Portalis, April 2, 1829. On the office of Protector, see Richard Blaas, "Das Kardinalprotektorat der deutschen und österreichischen Nation im 18. und 19. Jahrhundert," *Mitteilungen des Österreichischen Staatsarchivs,* 10 (1957): 148-185.

11. HHSA, Vorträge 234, June 13, 1823.

12. *Ibid.,* June 16 and July 9, 1823.

13. *Ibid.,* Rom: Weisungen, Metternich to Apponyi, June 20, 1823. Note that the version of these instructions in Metternich, *Mémoires,* 4:57-62, is unreliable, having apparently been edited to remove anything detrimental to the reputation of Metternich, Austria, or the Papacy. Thus, much of the original has been eliminated—often without any indication being given—including several key points. Historians who rely solely upon it as a guide to Metternich's policy may be led astray, e.g., Colapietra, "Diario."

14. In this account of Metternich's tactics, his instructions of June 20 are supplemented with those of September 12, 1823, *Ibid.,* but all quotations are from the former.

15. On the exclusive, see Ludwig Wahrmund, *Das Ausschliessungsrecht der katholischen Staaten bei den Papstwahlen;* Alexander Eisler, *Das Veto der katholischen Staaten bei der Papstwahl;* Silvio Pivano, "Il Veto od Exclusiva nell'elezione del Pontefice," *Scritti minori di storia e storia del diritto* (Turin, 1965), 333-391, and the bibliography there cited.

16. See, e.g., Guillaume de Bertier de Sauvigny, "Sainte-Alliance et Alliance dans les conceptions de Metternich," *Revue historique,* 223 (1960): 249-274.

17. HHSA, Rom: Weisungen, Metternich to Apponyi, September 12, 1823.

18. *Ibid.,* Frankreich: Berichte, Vincent to Metternich, July 18 #113, 1823. On earlier French rivalry with Austria, see Louis Dollot, "Conclaves et diplomatie française au XVIII siècle," *Revue d'histoire diplomatique,* 75 (1961): 124-135.

19. Bianchi, *Storia documentata,* 2:379, Instructions for Cardinal Ruffo.

20. Geheimes Staatsarchiv, Munich (hereafter GSM), Päpstlicher Stuhl 736, Rechberg to Haefflin, September 20, 1823. HHSA, Rom: Weisungen, Metternich to Apponyi, September 12, 1823.

21. HHSA, Rom: Weisungen, Metternich to Apponyi, September 12, 1823. On the altered Piedmontese attitude towards Austria, see AST, Sezioni II, Istruzioni agli agenti all'estero, Instructions for Count Pralormo, January 12, 1822.

22. The liberal Spanish regime had drawn up instructions for the conclave which were very anti-Austrian in tone: Ministerio de Asuntos Exteriores, Madrid, Archivo General (hereafter MAE), Embajada cerca de la Santa Sede (unless otherwise stated, all MAE materials are from this source), Legajo 692, Reales Ordenes, "Instrucliones reservadas para el caso de conclave," April 1822. Ferdinand VII on his restoration replaced them with a new set, ultrareactionary and so favorable to the *Zelanti,* which, however, were delayed and so did not reach Rome until the conclave had ended: *ibid.,* Leg. 693, "Sentimento por la muerte del Papa Pio VII y recomendacion para el conclave," September, 1823.

23. HHSA, Rom: Weisungen, Metternich to Apponyi, September 12, 1823.

24. *Ibid.,* Berichte, Apponyi to Metternich, July 11 #54-B, and August 28 #67-B, 1823.

25. *Ibid.,* Weisungen, Metternich to Apponyi, June 20, 1823.

26. *Ibid.,* Berichte, Apponyi to Metternich, August 21, 1823.

27. *Ibid.,* September 1, 1823, continuation of #67-B. Francesco Cavalchini (1755-1828), of a harsh and violent character, won unpopularity by his severity as Governor of Rome in 1801-1808. Tommaso Arezzo (1756-1833) performed important diplomatic missions during Consalvi's first ministry, and as Legate of Ferrara after 1816 he proved a wise and moderate governor of a difficult province. Fabrizio Turiozzi (1755-1826) was of mediocre ability and in poor health, but sympathetic to Consalvi's principles.

28. HHSA, Rom: Berichte, Apponyi to Metternich, September 2, 1823, continuation of #67-B. Francesco Saverio Castiglione (1761-1830) had made his reputation as an expert in canon law; he wavered between the moderates and the *Zelanti,* but was on good terms with Consalvi; he eventually moved definitely into the moderate camp and was elected Pope Pius VIII in 1829: see Odo Fusi-Pecci, *La vita del Papa Pio VIII.* Carlo Oppizzoni (1769-1855) won praise from liberals and conservatives alike during his long term as Archbishop of Bologna (1804-1855); though inclined to the *Zelanti* position in religious affairs, he was politically moderate and a friend of Consalvi, whom he supported at the conclave.

29. HHSA, Rom: Berichte, Apponyi to Metternich, August 30, 1823, continuation of #67-B.

30. *Ibid.,* Apponyi to Metternich, August 27 #66-E, 1823.

31. *Ibid.*

32. *Ibid.,* Weisungen, Metternich to Apponyi, September 12, 1823.

33. *Ibid.*

34. AAEP, vol. 956, Chateaubriand to Laval, July 18, 1823.

35. *Ibid.,* August 27, 1823.

36. AST, Lettere ministri, Parigi, Alfieri to Della Torre, August 28, 1823. Becker, 67-69.

37. Petruccelli della Gattina, 4:336; Bianchi, *Storia documentata,* 2:184.

38. HHSA, Rom: Berichte, Apponyi to Metternich, August 28 #67-B, 1823.

39. E.g., the Piedmontese ambassador in Rome calculated that only one of the six Piedmontese cardinals was reliable; the others would "follow the dictates of their consciences" and vote for the *Zelanti,* regardless of royal orders: *ibid.* The religious revival of this period has been frequently studied; a good introduction, with bibliography, is in Leflon, *La crise révolutionnaire,* esp. 357-371.

40. GSM, Rechberg to Haefflin, September 20, 1823. Bianchi, *Storia documentata,* 2:379-384.

41. HHSA, Rom: Berichte, Apponyi to Metternich, August 28 #67-B, 1823, and

December 26 #8-B, 1823. Note the comment of the Neapolitan cardinals who, criticized by their court for having supported the *Zelanti*, retorted that in electing a pope the cardinals "must be guided only by the inspiration of the Holy Spirit"—a sentiment which would have seemed absurd to the court cardinals of an earlier generation.

42. GSM, Haefflin, to Rechberg, October 1, October 4, 1823.

43. HHSA, Rom: Berichte, Lebzeltern to Metternich, April 30 #96, 1816.

44. Significantly, in the satires circulated during the conclave, the aspect of Consalvi most criticized was his "despotism": Biblioteca Nazionale, Rome (hereafter BNR), MS. 918, "Satire per il conclave del 1823."

45. HHSA, Rom: Berichte, Apponyi to Metternich, October 6 #79-A, 1823.

46. *Ibid.*, October 6 #79-A, 11 #80-C, 1823. When in December, 1823, the illness of Leo XII made a new conclave seem likely, Apponyi decided to ask Consalvi not to take part, as his support would only weaken the court party: December 26 #8-B, 1823.

47. *Ibid.*, "Extrait de la correspondance chiffrée de S.E. le Card. Albani," September 7-12, 1823. The willingness of the *Zelanti* to await the French cardinals was the result of Laval's careful cultivation of their good will: AAEP, vol. 957, Laval to Chateaubriand, September 15 #9, 1823.

48. HHSA, Rom: Berichte, Apponyi to Metternich, September 13 #70-C, and September 17 #70-E, 1823.

49. *Ibid.*, "Suite de la correspondance," September 17-19, 1823. For the French side of the story, see AAEP, vol. 957, Laval to Chateaubriand, September 15, 1823. The French were willing to cooperate with Albani, but planned to avoid too close identification with him and to cultivate the *Zelanti* as well, hoping in the end to impose Castiglione as a compromise on both factions.

50. HHSA, Rom: Berichte, "Suite de la Correspondance," September 18-19, 1823.

51. *Ibid.*, "Extrait de la correspondance," September 21, 1823, postscript.

52. *Ibid.*, "Extrait de la correspondance," September 21, 1823.

53. GSM, Haefflin to Rechberg, October 1, 1823.

54. *Ibid.*

55. HHSA, Rom: Berichte, Apponyi to Metternich, October 11 #80-C, 1823. The leading *Zelanti* candidates were Della Genga, De Gregorio, and Cavalchini.

56. *Ibid.*, Weisungen, Metternich to Apponyi, November 5, 1823. GSM, Haefflin to Rechberg, October 4, 1823, reveals that the *Zelanti* had won over Haefflin with the argument that Della Genga's election was in the best interests of the Church and therefore also in those of the monarchical order, despite the King's orders to the contrary.

57. HHSA, Rom: Berichte, "Suite de la correspondance," September 27-28, 1823.

58. *Ibid.* See also AAEP, vol. 957, De la Fare to Laval, September 27 and 28, 1823. It will be remembered that Chateaubriand was by no means as hostile to the *Zelanti* as was Metternich, and preferred a moderate of that faction. Since Della Genga was reasonably moderate in his religious views—his political opinions being a matter of indifference—Laval regarded him as quite acceptable—Laval to Chateaubriand, September 28, 1823—as did Chateaubriand himself: Chateaubriand to Laval, October 8 #32, 1823.

59. HHSA, Rom: Berichte, Apponyi to Metternich, September 28 #77, 1823. The conclave of 1823 marked the beginning of the end of the Powers' influence upon Papal elections, which would decline until 1918 when the collapse of the Habsburg Empire removed the last state to claim the right of exclusion. This decline has not been studied *per se*, and must be traced through such works as Schmidlin, *Histoire des papes,* Leflon, *La crise révolutionnaire*, and Friedrich Engel-Janosi, *Österreich und der Vatikan, 1846-1918.*

60. HHSA, Rom: Berichte, Apponyi to Metternich, October 2 #78-C, 1823. On the relationship between Consalvi and Della Genga, see Raffaele Colapietra, *La forma-*

zione diplomatica di Leone XII and *La chiesa tra Metternich e Lamennais,* 136–144. It is true that, as Colapietra, *La chiesa,* 142–144, and Artaud de Montor, *Leone XII,* 130–134, point out, a partial reconciliation took place between them: Leo, realizing that Consalvi's talents were too valuable to be cast aside, appointed him in January, 1824, to head the Propaganda Fide. This appointment itself, however, indicated the limits of the reconciliation: the Propaganda was a major post, where Consalvi could use his abilities to the benefit of the Church; but it was also a position which would allow him no influence upon the government of the Papal State or upon Papal relations with the Catholic Powers.

61. HHSA, Rom: Berichte, Apponyi to Metternich, October 6 #79-A, and December 16 #7-C, 1823, January 15 #12-A, and 26 #14-B, 1823.

62. E.g., Metternich, *Memoires,* 4:91.

63. As Metternich had come to realize by 1833. HHSA, Rom: Weisungen, Metternich to Lutzow, January 25 #1, 1833.

64. On Leo's earlier career, see Colapietra, *La formazione*.

65. HHSA, Rom: Berichte, Apponyi to Metternich, October 11 #80-C, 1823.

66. *Ibid.,* Weisungen, Metternich to Apponyi, April 3, 1824.

67. *Ibid.,* Berichte, Apponyi to Metternich, October 1 #78, 6 #79-A, October 11 #80-C, 1823. Bertier de Sauvigny, *Metternich et la France,* 2:843–844.

68. HHSA, Rom: Berichte, Apponyi to Metternich, October 29 #82, 1823. Colapietra, *La chiesa,* 176–177, 379–382. Bertier de Sauvigny, *Metternich et la France,* 3:993–1014.

69. HHSA, Rom: Berichte, Gennotte to Metternich, August 17 #45, 1824, Metternich to Gennotte, September 7, 1824. Bertier de Sauvigny, *Metternich et la France,* 3:1004–1007.

70. HHSA, Rom: Weisungen, Metternich to Apponyi, April 3, 1824.

71. *Ibid.,* Berichte, Apponyi to Metternich, October 11 #80-G, 1823. Colapietra, *La chiesa,* 176–181.

72. HHSA, Rom: Berichte, Apponyi to Metternich, November 2 #1, 1823; also October 29 #82, and November 24 #50-A, 1823.

73. On Leo's domestic policy, see Colapietra, *La chiesa,* ch. 2, Schmidlin, 2:13–23, Alberto Aquarone, "La restaurazione nello Stato Pontificio," 165–185. As usual, the reports of the Austrian ambassadors are a useful source of information on Papal domestic policy.

74. In Andreas Barberi, ed., *Bullarii romani continuatio,* 16:128–245.

75. In practice, few nobles responded, apparently realizing that feudal institutions could not be usefully maintained under modern conditions: Giuseppe La Farina, *Storia d'Italia dal 1851 al 1860,* 1:356.

76. HHSA, Rom: Berichte, Apponyi to Metternich, April 24 #26-A, 1824. Worth noting is Severoli's justification for the suppression of chairs in the sciences: the troubles of Europe had begun "precisely when the number of chairs in the sciences began to multiply," and accordingly it was "necessary to return to the time when studies were simpler."

77. This celebrated edict forbade the wearing of any "scandalous or immodest clothing," including "those women who, though seeming at first glance covered, wear clothing so tight-fitting as to offer most cunningly a lascivious show": *Diario di Roma,* December 15, 1824, in HHSA, Rom: Berichte, 1824.

78. *Ibid.,* Apponyi to Metternich, April 2 #26-A, 1824.

79. The older interpretation—based on partisan contemporary works such as Domenico Antonio Farini, *La Romagna dal 1796 al 1828* and Luigi Carlo Farini, *The Roman State from 1815 to 1850*—that the terrorism of the Sects was essentially a defensive reaction to government persecution, has yielded to the realization—more easily perceived in an age when the theory and practice of terrorism have become uncomfort-

ably more familiar than in Victorian times—that it was in fact an offensive action aimed at demoralizing and discrediting the government and terrifying its supporters into quiescence, thus preparing the way for an eventual seizure of power. See Colapietra, *La chiesa*, 122-136, 189-199, and "Un carteggio del Cardinale Consalvi," *Rassegna di politica e di storia*, 8 (1962): 21-32.

80. HHSA, Rom: Berichte, Apponyi to Metternich, April 16 #28, 21 #30-A, May 2 #31-A, 1824, Gennotte to Metternich, May 26 #34-A, 1824. Colapietra, *La chiesa*, 199-201.

81. On the Rivarola mission, see Colapietra, *La chiesa*, 189-199, 256-72, and "Lettere del Cardinale Rivarola durante la Restaurazione," *Rassegna di politica e di storia*, 12 (1966): 57-64; L.C. Farini, 1:21-23; M. Perlini, *I processi politici del Cardinale Rivarola;* D.A. Farini, 104-130; Ugo Oxilla, "Il Cardinale Rivarola e l'attentato del 1826," *Rassegna storica del Risorgimento*, 13 (1926): 273-309, as well as the reports of Apponyi to Metternich in Rom: Berichte, HHSA, April 16 #28, 21 #30-A, May 2 #31-A, 26 #34-A, August 17 #45-C, December 11 #5-A, and 31 #7-B, 1824. On the Pallotta mission, see *ibid.*, April 16 #28, 21 #31-A, May 16 #32-C, 21 #33-C, and June 21 #38, 1824; Colapietra, *La chiesa*, 199-214; Elio Lodolini, "Il brigantaggio nel Lazio meridionale dopo la Restaurazione, 1814-1825," *Archivio della Societa romana di Storia patria*, 83 (1960), 189-268.

82. HHSA, Rom: Berichte, Apponyi to Metternich, April 20 #26-A, 1824.

83. *Ibid.*, April 16 #28, 1824.

84. Such warnings are numerous in the reports of the Austrian embassy during this period: e.g., *Ibid.*, March 15 #23-A, April 2 #26-A, 16 #28, and May 2 #31-A, 1824.

85. *Ibid.*, Weisungen, Metternich to Apponyi, April 3, 1824.

86. *Ibid.*, Metternich to Gennotte, July 14 #1 & 2, 1824.

87. *Ibid.*, January 3, 1825.

88. Lodolini, 189-268; Colapietra, *La chiesa*, 278-287.

89. HHSA, Rom: Weisungen, Metternich to Apponyi, April 3, 1824.

90. *Ibid.*, Berichte, Apponyi to Metternich, April 21 #30-A, and May 15 #32-A, 1824; Gennotte to Metternich, May 21 #33-A, 1824.

91. *Ibid.*, Weisungen, Metternich to Gennotte, September 7, 1824. Apponyi was absent from Rome during much of 1824-1825 on various special missions for Metternich.

92. *Ibid.*, Berichte, Gennotte to Metternich, October 16 #51-A, 1824; also November 17 #1-A, 1824.

93. *Ibid.*, December 11 #5-A, 1824.

94. *Ibid.*, January 11 #2-A, 1826.

95. *Ibid.*, April 2 #18, August 21 #32-A, and November 9 #51-A, 1825. In fact, Metternich had no such plan in mind at the time, but the dragon's teeth he had sown at Verona were now sprouting luxuriantly, in the form of suspicions that would long outlive the plans which had given them birth.

96. E.g., *Ibid.*, Weisungen, Metternich to Apponyi, September 16, 1820, and June 20, 1823.

97. AV, ANV 254, Della Somaglia to Ostini, May 11, 23, June 13, and September 30, 1824; ANV 255, Ostini to Della Somaglia, January 14 #53, 28 #59, April 29 #92 & 93, May 1 #95, 5 #97, 22 #101, 26 #102, 31 #103 & 104, and December 8 #156, 1824, January 3 #161, March 5 #183, 1825.

98. *Ibid.*, ANV 255, Della Somaglia to Ostini, November 12 #150, 1824, March 2 #181, December 3 #271, 1825. Maass, *Der Josephinismus*, 5:85-9. Metternich, *Mémoires*, 4:235-242.

99. AV, ANV, 255, Ostini to Della Somaglia, November 12 #150, 1824, March 2 #181, May 10 #201, June 23 #216, July 18 #224, December 3 #271, 1825.

100. *Ibid.*, December 3 #271, 1825.

101. *Ibid.*, ANV 254, Della Somaglia to Ostini, March 21, 1826. Colapietra, *La chiesa,* 444–448.

102. The literature on Lamennais is immense: see F. Duine, *Essaie de bibliographie de Félicité Robert de la Mennais* (Paris, 1923); later works are listed in such recent biographies as Peter N. Stearns, *Priest and Revolutionary: Lamennais and the Dilemma of French Catholicism* and Guido Verucci, *Felicite Lamennais.*

103. See, e.g., Félicité Lamennais, *Oeuvres complètes,* 8:301–307, "De l'opposition," and 308–315, "Quelques réflections," both dating from 1823.

104. A balanced view of the state of the French church during the Restoration, its relations with the monarchy, and its reaction to Lamennais, is presented in Guillaume de Bertier de Sauvigny, *The Bourbon Restoration,* 300–327.

105. On the spread of Lamennais's ideas in Italy and the development of the ultramontane movement which they inspired there, the most thorough study is Sandro Fontana, *La controrivoluzione cattolica in Italia 1820–1830,* superior to G. Zadei, *L'Abate Lamennais e gli italiani del suo tempo.* See also Giuseppi Pignatelli, *Aspetti della propaganda cattolica a Roma da Pio VI a Leone XII,* valuable for setting the movement in its historical context; Gabriele de Rosa, *Storia del Movimento Cattolico in Italia,* 1:24–40; the articles published anonymously by P. Pirri in *Civilta Cattolica,* "La fortuna del La Mennais in Italia," 81 (1930), pt. 3:193–212, pt. 4:3–19, and "Il movimento Lamennaisiano in Italia," 83 (1932), pt. 3:313–327, 567–583; Walter Maturi, *Il Principe di Canosa*; Angiolo Gambaro, *Sulle orme del Lamennais in Italia,* and "La fortuna di Lamennais in Italia," *Studi francesi,* 2 (1958): 189–219; Guido Verucci, "Per una storia del cattolicismo intransigente in Italia dal 1815 al 1848," *Rassegna storica toscana,* 4:251–285. The name "ultramontane" is perhaps inappropriate for an Italian movement, but its use is sanctioned by the practice both of contemporaries and of such later historians as Fontana and Colapietra; if technically incorrect, the name is symbolically appropriate since, if the name was borrowed from France, so were the ideas of the Italian movement.

106. On Ventura and ultramontanism at Naples, see Charles Remusat, *Il P. Ventura e la filosofia*; E. Montasio, *Gioacchino Ventura;* A. Rastoul, *Le. P. Ventura;* P. Rizzo, *Teocrazio e neo-cattolicismo nel Risorgimento: pensiero politico del Ventura;* de Rosa, 1:39–42; Fontana, 72–79; Maturi, *Il Principe di Canosa*; Francesco Andreu, "Il Padre Ventura," *Regnum Dei,* 17 (1961): 11–16. On Turin, see C. Bona, *Le Amicizie: società segrete e rinascita religiosa* and Gambaro, *Sulle orme.* On Modena, see Graziano Manni, *La polemica cattolica nel Ducato di Modena 1815–1861,* and Fontana, 79–83.

107. Maturi, *Canosa,* 195–200; de Rosa, 1:39–40; Fontana, 87–105.

108. On Ventura's activities at Rome, see Colapietra, *La chiesa,* 237–248, et passim, and "L'insegnamento del Padre Ventura alla Sapienza," *Regnum Dei,* 18 (1962): 230–259.

109. Colapietra, *La chiesa,* 220–225.

110. On the Holy Year, see the reports of Apponyi to Metternich in HHSA, Rom: Berichte, especially March 28 #23-B, April 2 #26-B, 21 #30-A, May 2 #31-A, 15 #32-A and 21 #33-A, 1824; Egidio Fortini, *Memorie storiche dell'universale Giubileo celebrato nell'anno 1825;* and Geoffroy de Grandmaison, *Le jubilé de 1825.*

111. Nicholas Cardinal Wiseman, *Recollections of the Last Four Popes,* 335–227; P. Dudon, "Lettres inédites de Lamennais a Abbé Baraldi," *Documents d'histoire,* 9 (March 1911): 146–148; A. Gambaro, "Carteggi inediti del Lamennais coi Italiani," *Giornale critico della filosofia italiana,* 9 (1928): 184–204, and *Sulle orme,* ch. 3; P. Pirri, "Lamennais en Italie," *Études,* February 20, 1933, 422–442; AAEP, Vol. 958, Artaud to Damas, September 14, 1824.

112. Colapietra, *La chiesa,* 244–252. Actually, this was a refounding of the *Gior-*

nale, which had existed in the eighteenth century as a vehicle for Papal counterattacks on the Enlightenment and Revolution: on this background, see Pignatelli.

113. HHSA, Rom: Berichte, Apponyi to Metternich, March 15 #23-A, 1824.

114. *Ibid.,* Gennotte to Metternich, September 18 #48-A, 1824. Lamennais apparently failed to attract Metternich's attention prior to 1824; I could find no mention of his name in Metternich's papers before that year. The early stage of Metternich's relationship with Lamennais, prior to 1830, remains largely unexplored. Though most works on Lamennais refer to this relationship, they invariably begin with Metternich's opposition to Lamennais in his post-1830 liberal phase. The same is true of those works specifically dedicated to this relationship, notably Jean-Rene Derré, *Metternich et Lamennais;* Andreas Posch, "Lamennais und Metternich," *Mitteilungen des Instituts für österreichische Geschichtsforschung,* 62 (1954): 490–516; and Liselotte Ahrens, *Lamennais und Deutschland.* All ignore developments prior to 1830, and none mentions the ultramontane crisis of 1824–1826. Colapietra, *La chiesa,* discusses this crisis, but his failure to use Austrian sources limits his understanding of Metternich's position.

115. Srbik, *Metternich,* 1:306–315.

116. HHSA, Rom: Weisungen, Metternich to Apponyi, April 3, 1824.

117. *Ibid.,* Metternich to Gennotte, September 7 #1, 1824, January 3 #5, 1825.

118. *Ibid.,* Berichte, Gennotte to Metternich, May 2 #21, 1825.

119. See, e.g., his comments in AV, ANV 255, Ostini to Della Somaglia, May 23, 1826.

120. *Ibid.,* April 4 #330, May 23 #366, and 27 #370, 1826.

121. This is a point that tends to be overlooked by those who, like Colapietra or Fontana, criticize Metternich for his assault on ultramontanism at Rome. His intervention was well justified in terms of Austrian interests, and it could be argued that only his success prevented the duplication of the French sequence of events elsewhere in Europe. On the religious controversy in France and its effects on the decline of the Resotration order there, see Bertier de Sauvigny, *Restoration,* 365–456.

122. AV, R165, Albani to Della Somaglia, May 30, 1825.

123. *Ibid.,* Della Somaglia to Albani, June 5, 1825.

124. *Ibid.,* Della Somaglia to Albani, June 26, 1825.

125. *Ibid.,* R257, Tosti to Della Somaglia, June 20, 1825. On Metternich's visit to France, see Bertier de Sauvigny, *Metternich et la France,* 3:953–988. Luigi Lambruschini (1776–1854), Archbishop of Genoa 1819–1826, Paris Nuncio 1827–1831, cardinal 1831, Secretary of State 1836–1846: see Luigi M. Manzini, *Il Cardinale Luigi Lambruschini.*

126. Verucci, *Lamennais,* 127–151; Bertier de Sauvigny, *Restoration,* 300–325, 365–392.

127. E.g., HHSA, Rom: Berichte, Gennotte to Metternich, October 30 #48-A, November 9 #51-A, and December 1 #56-C, 1825, January 11 #2-A, and May 11 #23-A, 1826.

128. HHSA, Rom: Berichte, Gennotte to Metternich, May 2 #21, November 9 #51-A, reserved, and December 1 #56-C, 1825.

129. AV, ANV 255, Ostini to Della Somaglia, November 29 #268, 1825. Pietro Ostini, appointed Internuncio after Leardi's death in December 1823, and served in that capacity until 1827; returned as Nuncio, 1832–1836.

130. *Ibid.,* December 3 #271, 1825.

131. *Ibid.,* ANV 254, Della Somaglia to Ostini, January 8, 1826.

132. Colapietra, *La chiesa,* 290–293.

133. HHSA, Rom: Berichte, Gennotte to Metternich, May 2 #21, 1825.

134. AV, R248, Macchi to Della Somaglia, April 14, 17, and 24, 1826; Della Somaglia to Macchi, April 30, 1826.

135. HHSA, Rom: Berichte, Gennotte to Metternich, May 2 #21, November 9 #51-A, 1825. Colapietra, *La chiesa,* 417–421.

136. HHSA, Rom: Berichte, Gennotte to Metternich, January 17 #10-D, April 2 #18, and May 2 #21, 1825. Colapietra, *La chiesa,* 252–254.

137. AV, ANV 255, Ostini to Della Somaglia, April 4 #330, 1826.

138. HHSA, Rom: Berichte, Gennotte to Metternich, May 11 #23-A, 1826.

139. AV, ANP, VIII, Macchi to Della Somaglia, April 1 #1056, 3 #1059, 12 #1064, 17 #1069, 26 #1074, and June 1 #1092, 1826.

140. AAEP, 960, Laval to Damas, April 26, 1826.

141. HHSA, Rom: Berichte, Gennotte to Metternich, May 11 #23-A, and June 6 #28-B, 1826.

142. *Ibid.*, May 11 #23-A, 1826.

143. AV, ANV 255, Ostini to Della Somaglia, May 23 #366, 1826.

144. HHSA, Rom: Varia, Metternich to Gennotte, May 23, 1826.

145. On the decisive importance of Metternich's intervention, see *ibid.*, Gennotte to Metternich, June 12, 1826; AV, R247, Della Somaglia to Ostini, June 4, 1826; Colapietra, *La chiesa,* 443–448, and Pignatelli, 306.

146. HHSA, Rom: Berichte, Gennotte to Metternich, June 6 #28-B, 1826. AV, ANV 254, Della Somaglia to Ostini, June 4 and 15, 1826. Colapietra, *La chiesa,* 447–448.

147. ANV. Della Somaglia to Ostini, June 4, 1826.

148. AV, ANV 255, Ostini to Della Somaglia, June 15 #380, 1826.

149. HHSA, Rom: Berichte, Gennotte to Metternich, June 6 #28-B, 1826.

150. *Ibid.*, Varia, Leo XII to Francis I, June 13, 1826. On Bernetti's mission, see also Colapietra, *La chiesa,* 448–458, and Adriano Sorbelli, "L'ambasceria della Santa Sede in Russia nel 1826," *Memorie dell'Accademia delle Scienze dell'Istituto di Bologna,* 1943–1944, 29–61, though neither offers much on Bernetti's stay in Vienna.

151. It is worth pointing out that Lamennais's proclamation of liberal Catholicism after 1830 found little sympathy among liberals, most of whom remained as hostile to liberal Catholicism as to the conservative variety.

152. E.g., Colapietra, "L'insegnamento," 245; Jean-Rene Derré, *Lamennais, ses amis, et la mouvement des idées à l'époque romantique,* 391–392.

153. E.g., Dudon; Gambaro, *Sulle orme,* 164. The condemnation of Lamennais by Gregory XVI and Metternich's role in it will be discussed in the second volume of this study.

154. Colapietra, *La chiesa,* 666, and "L'insegnamento;" Fontana, 301–313.

155. AV, ANV 255, Ostini to Della Somaglia, June 20 #382, October 12 #454, November 13 #466, November 25 #477, December 14 #483 & 484, and 26, #489, 1826.

156. HHSA, Rom: Berichte, Lützow to Metternich, February 27 #24-B, August 2 #49-A, September 13 #52-B, 1828. On the religious crisis in France and its impact on Franco-Papal relations, see Bertier de Sauvigny, *Restoration,* 365–418; Colapietra, *La chiesa,* 413–442; Feret, 2: 347–393.

157. E.g., HHSA, Rom: Berichte, Lützow to Metternich, October 18 #13, 1827, and May 10 #34-A, 1828. ANV 255, Della Somaglia to Spinola, October 13 and December 13, 1827.

158. E.g., AV, ANV 256, Spinola to Della Somaglia, November 24 #134, and 28 #137, 1827. ANV 257, Della Somaglia to Spinola, October 13, November 10, and December 13, 1827. HHSA, Rom: Berichte, Lützow to Metternich, October 18 #13, and November 24 #17-A, 1827, and May 10 #34-A, 1828; Weisungen, Metternich to Lützow, October 26, 1827, February 9, 29, 1828. On Metternich's role in shaping the Papal attitude to the Greek revolution, see Alan J. Reinerman, "Metternich, the Papacy, and the Greek Revolution," *East European Quarterly,* 12 (1978): 177–188.

159. AV, ANV 256, Spinola to Della Somaglia, November 23 #132, 1827; ANV 257,

Della Somaglia to Spinola, October 13, 1827, January 31, February 23, March 11, and June 5, 1828. HHSA, Rom: Berichte, Lützow to Metternich, May 10 #34-A, 1828; Weisungen, Metternich to Lützow, October 26, 1827. See also Patrizia Ugolini, "La politica estera del card. Tommaso Bernetti Segretario di Stato di Leone XII," *Archivio della Società romana di storia patria,* 92 (1969): 213–320.

160. On Chateaubriand's Roman embassy, see Marie Jeanne Durry *L'ambassade romaine de Chateaubriand;* Emmanuel Beau de Lomenie, *La carrière politique de Chateaubriand,* 2:268–321; Bertier de Sauvigny, *Metternich et la France,* 3:1181– 1191. Chateaubriand felt—or at least reported to his government—that he was making great progress in winning Papal good will; but his accounts seem much exaggerated. For example, early in 1829 he had a lengthy audience with Leo, in which he expounded his ideas on a wide range of subjects; Leo allegedly replied in the most flattering fashion, indicating agreement on all points. Chateaubriand jubilantly reported that he had established a personal relationship of special confidence with the Pope— AAEP, vol. 965, Chateaubriand to La Ferronays, January 12, 1829—and historians have tended to accept his report at face value, e.g., Colapietra, *La chiesa,* 521–524, Durry, 52–55, Beau de Lomenie, 2:285. However, Leo, describing the same interview to Lützow, complained bitterly that Chateaubriand, after "insistently demanding an audience,...had absolutely nothing to say." HHSA, Rom: Berichte, Lützow to Metternich, January 17 #64-A, 1829.

161. Rudolf Count Lützow had been sent to Rome in the Summer of 1827 to fill the vacancy left by Apponyi's transfer to Paris. Metternich had first intended to return Lebzeltern, whose career had been wrecked by his innocent involvement in the Decembrist Movement; but the hostility of the *Zelanti,* who had never forgiven Lebzeltern for his support of Consalvi's reforms, defeated the plan: AV, ANV 255, Ostini to Della Somaglia, August 7, 1826; Lebzeltern, 466–474. Metternich eventually gave in and appointed Lützow, who proved competent if not brilliant, and remained as Ambassador until 1848; the description of his embassy by one of his subordinates, edited by Angelo Filipuzzi, *Pio IX e la politica austriaca in Italia dal 1815 al 1848,* 3–36, is too harsh in its criticism.

162. AV, ANV 256, Spinola to Della Somaglia, February #191, 1828.

163. *Ibid.,* January 4 #483, 1829.

164. *Ibid.,* November 6 #116, 1827.

165. *Ibid.,* September 13 #87, 1827.

166. *Ibid.,* November 24 #131, 1827. Ugo Pietro Spinola, Nuncio in Vienna, 1827–1832.

167. AV, ANV 256, Spinola to Della Somaglia, February 21 #193, 1828.

168. HHSA, Rom: Varia, Leo XII to Francis I, December 8, 1827.

169. *Ibid.,* Francis I to Leo XII, March 16, 1828.

170. AV, ANV 256, Spinola to Della Somaglia, August 28 #357, 1828; also April 26 #240, 1828.

171. *Ibid.,* Spinola to Bernetti, October 24 #441, 1828, and January 4 #483, 1829.

172. *Ibid.,* June 12 #284, June 17 #293, and October 24 #441, 1828. ANV 257, Bernetti to Spinola, June 12, July 3, and December 20, 1828.

173. AV, ANV 256-A, Spinola to Bernetti, January 4 #483, 1829.

174. *Ibid.,* ANV 258, Bernetti to Della Somaglia, January 17, 1829.

175. HHSA, Rom: Berichte, Lützow to Metternich, February #24-B, 1828.

176. On the reaction to these events in the Papal State, see *ibid.,* October 18 #13, November 24 #17-A, and December 8 #18-B, 1827; February 27 #24-B, August 2 #49-A, and September 13 #52-B, 1828.

177. *Ibid.,* December 8 #18-B, 1827.

178. *Ibid.,* December 22 #19-B, 1827.

179. *Ibid.*, Gennotte to Metternich, July 29 #36, and August 11 #38, 1826; Perlini, 115–121; Oxilla, "Rivarola.

180. HHSA, Rom: Berichte, Gennotte to Metternich, April 1 #8, 1827, Lützow to Metternich, July 23 #3-B, and December 8 #18-B, 1827; Colapietra, *La chiesa*, 306–323; Perlini, 122–146.

181. Colapietra, *La chiesa*, 275.

182. HHSA, Rom: Berichte, Gennotte to Metternich, December 1 #56-D, 1825. See also Nazzareno Trovanelli, *La decapitazione di Montanari e di Targhini*.

183. HHSA, Rom: Berichte, Gennotte to Metternich, January 11 #2-A, 1826.

184. *Ibid.*, December 21 #53-B, 1826. AV, ANV 254, Della Somaglia to Ostini, June 7, 1824.

185. HHSA, Rom: Berichte, Gennotte to Metternich, April 1 #8, 1827; also March 16 #5-B, 1827, and Feret, 2:307–310.

186. HHSA, Rom: Berichte, Lützow to Metternich, July 23 #3-B, 1827.

187. In fact, most of the few *Settarj* leaders whom Invernizzi managed to bring to trial were caught for him by the Austrians: *ibid.*, July 23 #3-B, 1827.

188. Colapietra, *La chiesa*, 329–333.

189. HHSA, Rom: Berichte, Lützow to Metternich, August 2 #49-A and September 13 #52-B, 1828; Weisungen, Metternich to Lützow, July 5, 1828.

190. The further evolution, or devolution, of this situation will be described in the second volume of this study.

191. HHSA, Rom: Weisungen, Metternich to Lützow, July 5, 1828.

192. *Ibid.*, April 11 #2, 1827.

193. *Ibid.*, Berichte, Lützow to Metternich, February 10 #68-A, 1829. Worth noting, as a measure of the change which had taken place in Austro-Papal relations during Leo's last years, is the contrast between Lützow's sincere regret at Leo's death in 1829 and the ill-concealed satisfaction with which Apponyi had anticipated the Pope's demise during his illness in 1823: Apponyi to Metternich, December 24 #80-A, and 26 #8-B, 1823.

194. *Ibid.*, Lützow to Metternich, February 10 #68-A, 1829. See the examples in Emilio del Cerro *Roma che ride*, 200–209.

195. HHSA, Rom: Berichte, Lützow to Metternich, December 8 #18-B, 1827, and February 10 #68-A, 1829.

Chapter VII

1. HHSA, Rom: Weisungen, Metternich to Lützow, February 21 #1 & 2, March 4, 12, 1829. Part of section 1 originally appeared, in different form, as "Metternich vs. Chateaubriand: Austria, France, and the Conclave of 1829," in *The Austrian History Yearbook*, vol. 12. On the conclave of 1829, see Raffaele Colapietra, "Il Diario del conclave del 1829," *Critica storica*, 1 (1962), 517–541, 636–661, the best account of the inner workings of the conclave, but one which uses only Italian sources and is unreliable on the international aspects, and his "Gaetano Moroni nel conclave del 1829," *Rassegna di politica e di storia*, 9 (1963): 13–17; also, Joseph Schmidlin, *Histoire des Papes*, 2:138–146. Earlier accounts are inferior, marked by bias and factual errors: Ugo Oxilla, "Tre conclavi"; Artaud de Montor, *Histoire de Pape Pie VIII*, 16–45; Eugenio Cipoletta, *Memorie politiche sui conclavi*; F. Petruccelli della Gattina, *Histoire diplomatique des conclaves*, 4:366–386; Nicomede Bianchi, *Storia documentata,*

2:217–222, 422–431; Odo Fusi-Pecci, *La vita del Papa Pio VIII*, 175–188; Pietro Dardano, *Diario dei conclavi del 1829 e 1831*, 28–47 and endpiece, "Tabella." All these mention the role played by Austria, but none offers a thorough and reliable account. The documentation in Metternich, *Mémoires*, 4:587, is too brief to be very useful, while of the numerous modern studies of Metternich, only Guillaume de Bertier de Sauvigny, *Metternich et la France*, 3:1266–1273, discusses his role at this conclave. The role of France has attracted greater attention, mainly because Chateaubriand happened to be the French ambassador, but these studies tend to be superficial on the political aspects of the conclave and to accept Chateaubriand's own inflated account of his role as presented in *Mémoires d'outre-tomb*, 106–121; the most reliable is Marie Jeanne Durry, *L'Ambassade romaine de Chateaubriand*. Also useful is Louis Thomas, ed., *Journal d'un conclave*. On the role of Spain, see Jeronimo Becker, *Relaciones diplomaticas*, 74–77; on that of Naples, Ruggero Moscati, "Il governo napoletano e il conclave di Pio VIII," *Rassegna storica del Risorgimento*, 20 (1933): 257–274.

2. HHSA, Rom: Berichte, Lützow to Metternich, February 14 #70-C, 1829; also, February 28 #75-A, March 10 #78-C, and March 20 #81-A, 1829.

3. *Ibid.*, February 14 #70-C, 1829.

4. *Ibid.* Cf. the identical opinion 4: of the Bavarian minister: GAM, 752, Malzen to the King, March 5 #8, 1829.

5. HHSA, Rom: Berichte, Lützow to Metternich, February 14 #70-C, 19 #72, 1829, with "Liste des cardinaux." Mauro Cappellari (1765–1846), of an aristocratic family of Belluno, attracted attention by his books defending the Papacy against revolutionary criticism; Cardinal in 1826; elected Pope Gregory XVI at the conclave of 1831. See D. Federici, *Gregorio XVI tra favola e realtà*. Emmanuele de Gregorio (1758–1834), Prefect of the Congregation of the Council, a prominent leader among the moderate *Zelanti*, linked by family ties to the Bourbon.

6. HHSA, Rom: Weisungen, Metternich to Lützow, February 21 #1, March 4, 1829.

7. *Ibid.*, March 4, 1829.

8. *Ibid.*

9. *Ibid.*, March 5 #1, 1829.

10. *Ibid.*, March 12, 1829.

11. "Instructions pour les cardinaux français," February 21, 1829, AAEP, vol. 965. The instructions of the Foreign Minister to Chateaubriand were similar, though less detailed: Portalis to Chateaubriand, February 21 #11, 22, #12, and 24 #13, 1829.

12. *Ibid.*, Chateaubriand to Portalis, February 17, 1829.

13. On Chateaubriand's policy, see his reports to Portalis, AAEP, vols. 965–966, for February–March 1829, which, however, do not always tell the whole truth about his activities. For a corrective, if somewhat jaundiced, view of Chateaubriand, see the reports of Lützow in Rom: Berichte, especially February 14 #70-D, 19 #72, March 10 #78-C, 11, #79-D, 14 #80, 20 #81-B, 21 #82-A, 31 #84-B, and April 10 #87-B, 1829. Also useful in this sense are the reports of the Bavarian minister—GAM, Malzen to the King, March 14 #9, 21 #10, and April 2 #13, 1829—and those of the Piedmontese minister—AST, Crosa to de la Tour, February 24, March 7, 10, 12, 19, 24, 28, and April 1, 4, 25, 1829.

14. HHSA, Rom: Berichte, February 24, 1829, Lützow to Metternich.

15. On the opening weeks of the conclave, see *ibid.*, February 24 #74, 28 #75-A, March 5 #76-B, and 7 #77, 1829; AAEP, vol. 965, Chateaubriand to Portalis, February 23 #20, 28 #21, March 3 #22, 6 #23, and 10 #24, 1829; AST, Crosa to De la Tour, February 24, 26, March 3, 7, 1829; Colapietra, "Il Diario del conclave," 536–541, 636–643; Dardano, 24–26, and tabella; Thomas, 3–20.

16. AST, Crosa to De la Tour, March 7, 1829.

17. HHSA, Rom: Berichte, Lützow to Metternich, March 10 #78-B, 1829; also,

March 5 #76-B, April 10 #87, October 24 #111-A, 1829; Colapietra, "Il Diario del conclave," 643–647 et passim; Thomas, 19–23, et passim.

18. HHSA, Rom: Berichte, March 10 #78-B, 1829. Gaetano Count Gaystruck (1770–1846), Archbishop of Milan, 1818; Cardinal, 1824.

19. Thomas, 19.

20. Dardano, 36.

21. HHSA, Rom: Varia, Albani to Metternich, April 21, 1829; Berichte, Lützow to Metternich, March 10 #78-C, 20 #81-A, 21 #82-A, and 29 #83-A, 1829; Colapietra, "Il Diario del conclave;" Thomas, 19–55.

22. Thomas, 71.

23. Copy in HHSA, Rom: Varia, 1829.

24. In AAEP, vol. 965, 1829.

25. Fusi-Pecci, 257–258.

26. See, e.g., Chateaubriand's *Mémoires d'outre-tombe,* 112–113.

27. HHSA, Rom: Weisungen, Metternich to Lützow, March 25, 1829.

28. Colapietra, "Moroni," 14–15, and "Il Diario del conclave," 530–532, 646–647; Durry, 108–111.

29. Dardano, tabella.

30. HHSA, Rom: Varia, Albani to Metternich, April 21, 1829.

31. Colapietra, "Moroni," 16.

32. HHSA, Rom: Varia, Albani to Metternich, April 21, 1829.

33. Colapietra, "Moroni," 16, and "Il Diario del conclave," 533–534.

34. Much of Albani's final report to Metternich on the conclave—April 21, 1829, Rom: Varia, HHSA—is obviously intended to excuse this opposition to a highly acceptable candidate. It is impossible to say whether Albani sincerely considered Bernetti's plan as a feint and opposed it as such, as he told Metternich, or whether this was merely an excuse for an opposition motivated by his ambition to become Secretary of State, which only Castiglione's victory would make possible.

35. Dardano, tabella.

36. Thomas, 93.

37. HHSA, Rom: Varia, Albani to Metternich, April 21, 1829; Berichte, Lützow to Metternich, March 31 #84-A, -B, April 4 #85, and 10 #87-B, 1829. Durry, 84–86. Colapietra, "Moroni."

38. HHSA, Rom: Berichte, Lützow to Metternich, March 31 #84-B, 1829. Cf. the judgment of the Piedmontese ambassador: "without him, De Gregorio or Cappellari would surely be pope; it was he alone who elected this pontiff." AST, Crosa to De La Tour, April 1, 1829.

39. HHSA, Rom: Berichte, Lützow to Metternich, March 31 #84-B, 1829.

40. *Ibid.,* April 4 #85, 1829.

41. AAEP, vol. 965, Chateaubriand to Portalis, April 28 #34, 1829.

42. HHSA, Rom: Berichte, Lützow to Metternich, April 4 #85, 1829.

43. *Ibid.,* April 10 #87-A, 1829.

44. *Ibid.,* Weisungen, Metternich to Lützow, April 9 #1, 1829.

45. Emmanuel Beau de Loménie, ed., *Lettres de Chateaubriand à Madame Recamier,* 114–115.

46. AAEP, vol. 965, Chateaubriand to Portalis, March 31 #30, 1829.

47. *Ibid.*

48. *Ibid.,* Portalis to Chateaubriand, April 8, 1829.

49. E.g., *ibid.,* Chateaubriand to Portalis, April 2 #31, 16 #33, 28 #34, and vol. 966, May 4 #36, 1829. As part of the same effort, Chateaubriand sent to France the *Journal du conclave* later published by Thomas.

50. AAEP, vol. 965, Chateaubriand to Portalis, April 28 #34, 1829.

51. AAEP, vol. 965, Portalis to Chateaubriand, April 25, 1829. Actually, the French defeat in 1829 did no great harm to French interests. Pius was careful to maintain good relations with Paris, and his attitude towards its religious problems was as understanding as could have been expected. If he remained favorable to Austrian predominance in Italy, this cost France nothing that it had not long since lost.

52. Chateaubriand, *Mémoires*, 205.

53. *Ibid.*, 205-208; Durry, 101-104.

54. HHSA, Rom: Weisungen, Metternich to Lützow, April 9 #1 & 2, 1829; Varia, Metternich to Albani, May 24, 1829.

55. *Ibid.*, Berichte, Lützow to Metternich, May 2 #91-A, 1829.

56. AV, ANV, 256-B, Spinola to Albani, February 14, 1830; also, June 13, August 11, 1829, and April 3, 1830; ANV 258, Albani to Spinoli, July 4, October 31, and December 24, 1829. HHSA, Rom: Weisungen, Metternich to Lützow, February 14, 1830. Anton von Prokesch-Osten, *Geschichte des Abfalls der Griechen*, 6:189-191, 196-201. On this question, see Donat Vernier, *Histoire du Patriarcat Armenien Catholique*.

57. AV, ANV 258, Albani to Spinola, July 14 and 21, 1829; ANV 256-A, Spinola to Albani, August 11 and December 1, 1829.

58. *Ibid.*, ANV 258-A, Albani to Spinola, April 1, 1830; also, ANV 256-B, Spinola to Albani, March 20, April #1049, and May 8, 1830.

59. *Ibid.*, ANV 258-A, Albani to Spinola, April 24, July 25, August 8, September 12, October 20, November 10, and December 5, 1829; ANV 256-A, Spinola to Albani, November 21 and December 17, 1829, May 1 and 8, 1830.

60. *Ibid.*, ANV 258-A, Albani to Spinola, April 24, 1830.

61. *Ibid.*, January 14, 1830.

62. *Ibid.*, February 25, 1830.

63. HHSA, Rom: Berichte, Lützow to Metternich, April 24 #130-A, 1830. Even Gennotte, in contrast to his usual suspicion of Roman motives, praised Pius's religious policy wholeheartedly: to Metternich, May 22 #134-B, 1830.

64. AV, ANV 258-A, Albani to Spinola, January 26, 1830.

65. HHSA, Rom: Berichte, Lützow to Metternich, January 30 #121-A, 1830.

66. *Ibid.*, Gennotte to Metternich, May 22 #134-B, 1830. Apparently this offer had no sequel, probably because of the distraction produced by the outbreak of the July Revolution and the death of Pius VIII.

67. On Lamennais's activities and relations with Rome during this period, see: Fusi-Pecci, 207-209; Guido Verucci, *Felicite Lamennais*, 141-151; Jean-René Derré, *Lamennais et ses amis*, 392-407; Luigi Lambruschini, *La mia nunziatura in Francia*, which should be amplified and corrected by consulting the Nuncio's original reports in AV, R248 and ANP, 1829-1830.

68. AV, ANV 256-A, Spinola to Albani, May 29, 1829; also April 1, 1829.

69. *Ibid.*, May 19, 1830. See also Wagner's comments on the mémoire, in Ferdinand Maass, *Der Josephinismus*, 5:277-373. John Michael Wagner (1788-1842), Court Chaplain, 1818-1828; had great influence over Francis I, whose confessor he was; anti-Josephist, he was to play a leading role in the attack on the state church, usually in alliance with Metternich.

70. These later negotiations will be covered in the second volume.

71. AV, ANV 258-A, Albani to Spinola, August 10, 1830.

72. HHSA, Rom: Berichte, Lützow to Metternich, August 20 #148-B, 1830.

73. A good example is Chateaubriand's report of April 23, 1829 in which he bitterly denounced Albani and suggested that Pius should be forced to replace him: *ibid.*, Metternich to Lützow, May 22, 1829, secret, with copy of Chateaubriand to Portalis, April 23, 1829. As Metternich had anticipated, Albani was "highly shocked" by this

revelation, embittered towards France, and duly grateful to Austria: Berichte, Lützow to Metternich, June 6 #96, 1829. Pius too was irritated: *ibid.,* June 13 #97-B, 1829. After Chateaubriand's departure, the Austrian police provided Metternich with equally effective ammunition, a long series of reports from the French chargé, Bellocq, vigorously denouncing Papal policy: Weisungen, Metternich to Lützow, June 23, October 9, 23 #1 & 2, November 6 #1, and December 4, 1829, with annexed copies. Only the arrival of the new French ambassador at the end of 1829 put an end to these reports, which had done great harm to Franco-Papal relations: Berichte, Lützow to Metternich, July 4 #100-A, 18 #101-A, October 24 #111-A, and December 5 #116-A, 1829.

74. *Ibid.,* Berichte, Lützow to Metternich, April 10 #87-A, 1820. For an example of these complaints, and an illustration of the sort of reform which would still have satisfied moderate opinion at this period, see the anonymous petition to the 1829 conclave, in *Carte segrete e atti ufficiali della polizia austriaca in Italia,* 1:393–396: it called for modernization of the administration, elimination of confusion and arbitrary practices in the legal system, the rule of law, a sound financial system, and admission of laymen into the administration—in essence, the same reforms for which Metternich had been pressing since 1815.

75. HHSA, Rom: Berichte, Lützow to Metternich, April 4 #85, April 10 #87-A, 1829, and April 24 #130-A, 1830.

76. *Ibid.,* April 4 #130-A, 1830.

77. *Ibid.,* April 24 #130-A, 1830.

78. *Ibid.,* April 4 #85, 10 #87-A, 1829, and April 24 #130-A, 1830.

79. *Ibid.,* April 25 #90-B, 1829.

80. *Ibid.,* April 24 #130-A, 1830.

81. *Ibid.,* April 10 #87-A, 1829.

82. E.g., *ibid.,* August 14 #145-B, 1830.

83. *Ibid.,* April 24 #130-A, 1830.

84. *Ibid.* AV, ANV 258, Albani to Spinola, August 13, 1829. Schmidlin, 2:149–150.

85. HHSA, Rom: Berichte, Lützow to Metternich, April 24 #130-A, 1830.

86. E.g., *Ibid.* Varia, Metternich to Albani, May 24, 1829.

87. *Ibid.* Also Weisungen, Metternich to Lützow, April 9 #2, October 23 #1, and December 18 #3, 1829.

88. *Ibid.,* Berichte, Lützow to Metternich, February 21 #73-B, and March 20 #81-E, 1829; Weisungen, Metternich to Lützow, March 5 #2, 1829. Fusi-Pecci, 223–226.

89. See the numerous alarming reports from the Legates, especially those at Bologna and Ravenna, in AV R165, for 1829–1830.

90. In Fusi-Pecci, 259–264.

91. The contemporary suspicion—e.g., *Carte segrete,* 1:417—that this condemnation was instigated by Metternich seems unfounded; I could find no evidence in HHSA or AV that he had instigated it, and when the condemnation was reported to him, he failed even to comment upon it. Probably he regarded it as superfluous in view of the condemnation of 1821.

92. HHSA, Rom: Berichte, Lützow to Metternich, October #110, 1829.

93. *Ibid.,* April 24 #130-A, 1830.

94. *Ibid.,* December 5 #116-A, 1829.

95. *Ibid.,* August 15 #105, 1829.

96. *Ibid.,* Weisungen, Metternich to Lützow, December 18 #3, 1829; also October 23 #1, 1829, and Varia, Metternich to Albani, January 7, 1830.

97. *Ibid.,* Berichte, Lützow to Metternich, January 2 #118-D, 1830.

98. Metternich, *Mémoires,* 5:23; cf. his judgment of 1847 that "the revolution of

1830 was the point from which the illness first gathered the strength which is growing still and can only grow more": to Apponyi, January 31, 1847, SUA, C 5, Extrait III. On the July Revolution's effect on international affairs, see Vicomte de Guichen, *La révolution de juillet et l'Europe;* Alfred Stern, *Geschichte Europas von 1830 bis 1848,* vol. 1; Gustav Huber, *Kriegsgefahr über Europa 1831-1832;* Werner Näf, *Abrustungsverhandlungen im Jahre 1831;* Kurt Hoffmann, *Preussen und die Julimonarchie;* Pierre Renouvin, *Histoire des relations internationales,* vol. 5; Srbik, *Metternich,* 1:645-684; Metternich, *Mémoires,* vol. 5.

99. See Metternich's explanations: HHSA, Preussen, Metternich to Werner, August 23 #1, 1830; AST, Lettere Ministri: Vienna, Pralormo to De la Tour, August 12, 1830; and Fritz L. Hoffmann, "Metternich and the July Revolution," *East European Quarterly,* 12 (1967): 143-154. On the question of recognition, see A. Masure, "La reconnaissance de la Monarchie de Juillet," *Annales de l'École Libre des Sciences Politiques,* 1892, 698-721, 1893, 72-117. Metternich originally wanted the Powers to make their recognition contingent upon an explicit French promise to respect the 1815 settlement, but English and Prussian reluctance defeated him: HHSA, Grossbritannien: Weisungen, Metternich to Esterhazy, August 14, 1830; Berichte, Esterhazy to Metternich, August 30 #46-B, 1830; Preussen; Berichte, Werner to Metternich, August 19 #64-A, 1830.

100. Metternich, *Mémoires,* 5:46; also, 5:60, 71; and AST, Lettere Ministri: Vienna, Pralormo to De la Tour, August 12, 1830. On the impact of the July Revolution on Italy, see Pietro Silva, *La Monarchie di Luglio e l'Italia,* the standard work, but unreliable on Austrian policy, as is also César Vidal, *Louis Philippe, Metternich et la crise italienne 1831-1832;* Francesco Salata, *Maria Luigia e i moti del trentuno;* Moscati, *Il Regno,* vol. 2; Bianchi, *Storia documentata;* R. del Piano, *Roma e la rivoluzione del 1831;* Giuliano Procacci, éd., *Le relazioni diplomatiche fra lo Stato Pontificio e la Francia, 1830-1848,* vol. 1.

101. HHSA, Rom: Berichte, Lützow to Metternich, August 14 #145-B, 1830; also August 20 #148-B, 28 #151-B, September 11 #155-A, and November 28 #170-A, 1830.

102. *Ibid.,* August 28 #151-B, 1830.

103. A sizable body of such reports is found in AV, R149; a number were published in Hubert Bastgen, "Provvidenze del Governo Pontificio dopo la rivoluzione francese del luglio 1830," *Rassegna storica del Risorgimento,* 15 (1928): 321-361.

104. HHSA, Rom: Berichte, Lützow to Metternich, August 14 #145-B, 1830; also, AV, ANV 258-A, Albani to Spinola, August 19 and September 7, 1830.

105. HHSA, Rom: Berichte, Lützow to Metternich, August 14 #145-B, August 20 #148-B, September 11 #155-A & B, and November 6 #162-A, 1830. AV, ANV, 258-A, Albani to Spinola, August 19 and September 7, 1830.

106. On this question, see Sante Celli, "Il riconoscimento di Luigi Filippo da parte della Sante Sede," 67-104.

107. AV, R242, "Circolare ai Nunzi sulla proclamazione di Luigi Filippo," August 17, 1830.

108. *Ibid.,* Circular of August 21, 1830.

109. On the religious situation in France after the revolution, see Enzo Piscitelli, *Stato e chiesa sotto la Monarchia di Luglio,* and Procacci, 1:110. AV, R242, Circular of August 24, 1830.

111. *Ibid.,* ANV 258-A, Albani to Spinola, August 17, 1830. HHSA, Rom: Berichte, Lützow to Metternich, August 28 #151-B, 1830.

112. E.g., AV, ANV 258-A, Albani to Spinola, August 10, 17, and 19, 1830. HHSA Rom: Berichte, Lützow to Metternich, August 14 #145-B, 1830.

113. AV, ANV 258-A, Albani to Spinola, August 31, 1830.

114. *Ibid.,* ANV 256-B, Spinola to Albani, August 17 #1178, and 19 #1186, 1830.

115. In HHSA, Toskana: Weisungen.

116. *Ibid.,* Rom: Berichte, Lützow to Metternich, September 11 #155-A, 1830. Also, AV, ANV 258-A, Albani to Spinola, August 31 and September 7, 1830.

117. AV, ANV 256-B, Spinola to Albani, August 28 and September 9, 1830.

118. AV, ANP XXVI, Albani to Lambruschini, September 16, 1830.

119. *Ibid.,* September 25 and 27, 1830.

120. HHSA, Rom: Berichte, Lützow to Metternich, August 20 #148-B, 1830.

121. AV, ANV 258-A, Albani to Spinola, August 10, 1830.

122. ANV 256-B, Spinola to Albani, August 19, 21, 28, and September 9, 1830. See also SUA, C 5, Metternich to Apponyi, November 9, 1830.

123. HHSA, Rom: Berichte, Lützow to Metternich, November 28 #170-A, 1830. AV, R242, Albani to Spinola, September 21, 1830.

124. AV, R242, Albani to Spinola, September 21, 1830.

125. *Ibid.,* ANV 256-B, Spinola to Albani, October 2, 1830.

126. See the works cited in note 100, above, and, on Metternich's attitude to the principle of nonintervention, HHSA, Rom: Varia, "Le principe de la non-intervention," 1831, and "Précis historique sur les mouvements....," February 14, 1831.

127. AV, ANV 258-A, Albani to Spinola, October 16, 1830; R242, Albani to the Chargé in Turin, October 16, 1830.

128. AV, ANV 258-A, Albani to Spinola, November 13, 1830. The Duke's letter is printed in Lajos Pasztor, "I Cardinali Albani e Bernetti e l'intervento austriaco nel 1831."

129. Such suspicions were voiced, e.g., by Bellocq—December 2, 5, and 9, 1830, AAEP—and have been accepted by such historians as Silva, and Vidal. But the charge is implausible: not only is there no evidence in HHSA to support it, but it goes contrary to Metternich's policy, which aimed at avoiding intervention in Italy if possible. The most plausible explanation lies in the Duke's fear of revolution; note his earlier announcement to Metternich that, in the hope of intimidating the Sects, he was spreading rumors that Austrian troops would enter Modena at the first sign of revolution: HHSA, Modena: Varia, Francis I to Metternich, October 22, 1830. Perhaps, fearing an outbreak of revolution in the Papal State which would then spread to Modena, he made his offer in the hope that it would give rise to rumors that Austria was ready to intervene in the State, which might frighten the *Settarj* there into quiescence—certainly, it did in fact soon give rise to such rumors: Rom: Berichte, Lützow to Metternich, December 4 #172-A, 1830.

130. AV, ANV 258-A, Albani to Spinola, November 13, 1830. HHSA, Rom: Berichte, Lützow to Metternich, November 28 #170-A, 1830.

131. See his reports of October 11, 19, November 2, and December 9, 1830, in AAEP. These charges too are unfounded, though they have been accepted by such historians as Silva, 48–49, Vidal, 33–34, Feret, 2:438–439, and B. Gamberale, "Gli inizi del pontificato di Gregorio XVI," *Rassegna storica del Risorgimento,* 14 (1927): 657-715.

132. AV, ANV 258-A, Albani to Spinola, November 13, 1830.

133. HHSA, Rom: Weisungen, Metternich to Lützow, November 24, 1830.

134. For Metternich's views on intervention in Italy, see HHSA, Rom: Weisungen, Metternich to Lützow, November 24, 1830.

135. On the situation in Piedmont, see Francesco Lemmi, *La politica estera di Carlo Alberto,* 1–46; Antonio Monti, *Un drammatico decennio di storia piemontese,* 156–184; Narciso Nada, *Le relazioni diplomatiche fra l'Austria e il Regno di Sardegna, 1830–1848,* vol. 1.

136. HHSA, Sardinien: Weisungen, Metternich to Senfft, September 29, 1830. Lemmi, 24-34.

137. *Ibid.*, Rom: Weisungen, Metternich to Lützow, November 24, 1830.

138. *Ibid.*, Berichte, Lützow to Metternich, December 4 #172-A, 1830.

139. Bellocq continued to send alarming reports to Paris, but the French ambassador to Naples, Latour-Marburg, reported authoritatively that they were unfounded: AAEP, CP, Naples, vol. 154, to Sebastiani, December 12 #5, 1830.

140. HHSA, Rom: Berichte, Lützow to Metternich, December 4 #172-A, 1830.

141. *Ibid.*, November 28 #170-A, 1830.

Bibliography

I. A Note on the Archival Sources

Since this study is based primarily upon archival materials, some description of the relevant archives and their holdings seems in order.

I. On the Austrian side, the chief source has been the *Haus-, Hof-, und Staatsarchiv,* Vienna (HHSA), where Metternich's official papers are to be found. The most useful collection was the *Staatskanzlei: Auswärtiges Amt* section, from which I consulted the following groups:

Frankreich: Weisungen, Berichte, Varia.
Friedensakten.
Grossbritannien: Weisungen, Berichte.
Kongressakten: Vienna, Troppau, Florenz-Rom-Neapel, Verona.
Modena: Weisungen, Berichte, Varia.
Neapel: Weisungen, Berichte, Varia.
Preussen: Weisungen, Berichte, Varia.
Rom: Weisungen, Berichte, Varia.
Russland: Weisungen, Berichte.
Sardinien: Weisungen, Berichte, Varia.
Toskana: Weisungen, Berichte, Varia.
Vorträge.

Also of use are the *Gesandtschaftarchiven,* the archives from embassies abroad now returned to Vienna, because materials in G.A. and St. K. are not always duplicates— some materials are found only in one or the other, hence both must be consulted for completeness; also, since G.A. contains the originals of Metternich's dispatches and the rough drafts of the ambassadors' reports to him, while St. K. contains the reverse, the student may save both time and eyestrain by using the final clear copies of both rather than the often illegible rough drafts of either. I consulted the G.A. for each of the states listed above under St. K.

For further information on HHSA, see Ludwig Bittner, *Gesamtinventar des Wiener Haus-, Hof- und Staatsarchiv* (5 vols.; Vienna, 1936–1940).

II. In the *Státní Ústredni Archiv* (SUA: Central State Archive) in Prague, *Fonds Plasy, Acta Clementina* contains Metternich's personal and family papers. This proved to have only a limited value for my study, since a large part of the material deals only with private affairs, while of that which deals with public affairs, much has been printed in the *Mémoires*—though often incompletely—or duplicates material in HHSA.

III. The private papers of Count Apponyi are in the *Országos Széchényi Könyvtar* (OSK: National Széchényi Library), Budapest; those documents relative to his mission to Rome are in Fond II/450. Though many of these are duplicates of HHSA papers, others including some of considerable importance are not found elsewhere.

IV. On the Papal side, the most valuable source is the *Archivio Segreto Vaticano* (AV: Vatican Secret Archives). I have made most use of the *Segretariato di Stato* collection, *Fondo Moderno*; it is subdivided into two general categories, *Interno* and

Estero, and these in turn into *Rubriche.* The following *Rubriche* were used for my study:

Interno:	R25: Pubblica amministrazione
	R117: Affari postali
	R155: Rapporti politici
	R165: Unioni e società sospette
	R166: Delitti contro la sicurezza pubblica
	R210: Passagio di truppe
Estero:	R241: Circolari ai Nunzi
	R242: Questioni di alta diplomazia
	R243: Concordati
	R244: Lettere di Sua Santità
	R245: Lettere di sovrani
	R247: Nunzii in Vienna
	R248: Nunzii in Parigi
	R252: Nunzii in Napoli
	R253: Nunzii in Firenze
	R254: Nunzii in Lucerna
	R257: Incaricato di affari in Torino
	R258: Console generale in Milano
	R260: Austria ambasciatore
	R261: Francia ambasciatore
	R265: Napoli ministero
	R267: Sardegna ministero
	R268: Russia ministero
	R269: Prussia ministero
	R272: Toscana incaricato

Of the other Vatican collections, the *Archivi rientrati,* the archives of the various Papal nunciatures now brought back to Rome, have been most useful, in particular the *Archivio della Nunziatura di Vienna* (ANV) and the *Archivio della Nunziatura di Parigi* (ANP). They correspond to the Gesandtschaftarchiv in HHSA, and are useful in a similar way.

A more detailed account of the AV collections may be found in: Karl A. Fink, *Das vatikanische Archiv* (2nd ed.; Rome, 1951).

V. The *Archivio della S. Congregazione De Propaganda Fide* (APFFC) contains, in its *Fondo Consalvi,* most of the Cardinal's private papers—others are in the Carte Consalvi, Spogli dei cardinali collection in AV, but these contained nothing of use for my study. This *Fondo* is divided into *buste,* of which numbers 27, 30, 31, 34, and 35 contained relevant material. Historians have thus far made little use of this valuable source.

VI. The *Archivio Generale Arcivescovile di Bologna* contains, in the *Carte Oppizzoni,* Cartone 2, Consalvi's correspondence with the Archbishop of Bologna, Cardinal Oppizzoni, one of his closest allies; this is a useful source for Consalvi's policies as well as for conditions in the Legations, but has been little used.

VII. The *Museo Centrale* of the Instituto per la Storia del Risorgimento Italiano, Rome (MCR), contains a wide variety of documentary holdings, of which I have used the following:

Buste 10/16, *Carte del Card. Luigi Amat.*
Busta 197, *Carte del Marchese Camillo Spreti.*
Busta 208, *Carteggio Consalvi-Sanseverino.*
Busta 336, N. 89, *Minuto Pacca-Consalvi.*

VIII. The Biblioteca Nazionale, Rome (BNR) holds extensive manuscript collections, of which I consulted MS. 918, "Satire per il conclave del 1823."

Many of the Italian State Archives offered useful materials for my study:

IX. *Archivio di Stato, Florence* (ASF):
    Affari Esteri, Serie 1929/1930: Congresso di Vienna
                        1931: Rivoluzioni di Napoli, Spagna, e Portogallo
                        1973: Legazione in Roma
                        1990: Legazione in Vienna
                        Trattati Internazionali, CXLIV.

X. *Archivio di Stato, Turin* (AST):
    Sezione II, Affari Esteri: Istruzioni agli agenti all'estero
                      Carte politiche, Congresso di Verona
                      Trattati nazionali ed esteri, Mazzo d'addizione #7:
                      Congressi di Troppau e Laybach.
                      Lettere Ministri: Roma
                                        Vienna
                                        Parigi

XI. *Archivio di Stato, Naples:* (ASN):
    Archivio Borbone: 3. Carte del re Ferdinando IV (I)
                    4. Carte del re Francesco I
                    5. Carte del re Ferdinando II
(The A.B. consists of the papers retained by the Bourbons after their expulsion from Naples in 1860, and recently acquired by ASN; they are of particular value since many of the ASN files were destroyed during World War II).

XII. *Archivio di Stato, Lucca* (ASL):
    R. Intima Segretaria di Gabinetto: Filza 470, Rapporti diretti alla Sovranità
                                        dai Dicastri.

XIII. *Archivio di Stato, Parma* (ASP):
    Casa e Corte di Maria Luigia d'Austria, 709/718, Copialettere della corrispondenza Neipperg.
                            732/747, Copialettere della corrispondenza Neipperg-Metternich.
    Segretaria di Stato e di Gabinetto, 384/388, Carteggio Neipperg.
                          777/779, Corrispondenza varia del Neipperg.

Of the major archives outside Italy and the former Austrian Empire, the following were consulted:

XIV. *Archives du Ministère des Affaires Étrangeres, Paris* (AAEP). Here the most useful collections were:
    Correspondance Politique: Rome
                                  Vienne

XV. *Archivo General, Ministerio de Asuntos Exteriores, Madrid* (MAE):
    Archivo de la Embajada de España cerca de la Santa Sede:
        Legajo 690, Reales Ordenes 1820
        Legajo 692, Reales Ordenes 1822
        Legajo 693, Reales Ordenes 1823
        Legajo 750/752, Oficios de la Embajada, 1820/23.

XVI. *Deutsches Zentralarchiv, Historische Abteilung II, Merseburg,* D.D.R. (DZM):
    Auswärtigen Angelegenheiten: Rom. Correspondance avec le mission du roi.
    Gesandtschaft Rom: Politische Berichte.

XVII. *Geheimes Staatsarchiv, Munich* (GSM): *Päpstlicher Stuhl,* 735/759.

XVIII. *Public Record Office, London* (PRO):

F.O. 7: Austria, General Correspondence.
F.O. 43: Italian States, General Correspondence.
F.O. 92: Continent, Conferences.
F.O. 120: Embassy and Consular Archives, Austria.
F.O. 139: Archives of Conferences.
XIX. *Archives of the Foreign Ministry of the Soviet Union.* The documents that were communicated to me from this source originated in the Russian embassy in Rome, but proved to concern only routine administrative affairs and trivia.

II. Published Primary Sources

Alberti, Annibale Alberti (ed.). *Atti del Parlimento delle Due Sicilie.* Bologna, 1926.
Bandini, G. *Giornali e scritti politici clandestini della Carbonaria romagnola 1819–1821.* Rome, 1908.
Barberi, Andreas (ed.). *Bullarii romani continuatio.* 16 vols.; Rome, 1835-1855.
Beau de Loménie, Emmanuel (ed.). *Lettres de Chateaubriand à Madame Recamier.* Paris, 1929.
Carte segrete e atti ufficiali della polizia austriaca in Italia. 3 vols.; Capolago, 1851.
Castlereagh, Robert Stewart, Viscount. *Memoirs and Correspondence of Viscount Castlereagh,* ed. Charles Vane. 12 vols.; London, 1850-1853.
Cerro, Emilio del. *Roma che ride.* Turin, 1904.
Chateaubriand, François Vicomte de. *Le Congrès de Vérone.* Paris, 1838.
————. *Mémoires d'outre-tombe,* eds. Edmond Biré and Pierre Moreau. Paris, N.d.
Chodzko, J.L.B. ("Comte d'Angeberg"). *Le Congrès de Vienne et les traités de 1815.* 4 vols.; Paris, 1863-1864.
————. *Recueil des traités, conventions, et actes diplomatiques concernant l'Autriche et l'Italie.* Paris, 1859.
Consalvi, Ercole. *Memorie,* ed. Mario Nasalli Rocca di Corneliano. Rome, 1950.
Dallolio, Alberto (ed.). *I moti del 1820-1821 nelle carte bolognesi.* Bologna, 1923.
Dardano, Pietro. *Diario dei conclavi del 1829 e 1831,* ed. D. Silvagni. Florence, 1879.
Demelitsch, Fedor von. (ed.) *Actenstücke zur Geschichte der Coalition vom Jahre 1814,* vol. 49:2 in *Fontes Rerum Austriacarum.* Vienna, 1899.
Diario di Roma. Rome, 1815-1830.
Duerm, Charles van (ed.). *Correspondance du Cardinal Hercule Consalvi avec le Prince Clément de Metternich.* Louvain, 1899.
Engel-Janosi, Friedrich (ed.). *Die politische Korrespondenz der Päpste mit den österreichischen Kaisern, 1804-1918.* Vienna, 1964.
Farini, Domenico Antonio. *La Romagna dal 1796 al 1828,* ed. Luigi Rava. Rome, 1899.
Filipuzzi, Angelo (ed.). *Pio IX e la politica austriaca in Italia dal 1815 al 1848 nella relazione di Riccardo Weiss di Starkenfels.* Florence, 1958.
Gentz, Friedrich von. *Briefe von Friedrich von Gentz an Fiiat.* 2 vols.; Leipzig, 1868.
————. *Briefe von und an Friedrich von Gentz,* eds. F.C. Wittichen and Ernst Salzer. 3 vols.; Munich, 1909-1913.
————. *Dépêches inédites aux Hospodars de Valachie,* ed. Prokesch von Osten. 3 vols.; Paris, 1876-1877.
————. *Tagebücher,* ed. Ludmilla Assing. 4 vols.; Leipzig, 1873-1874.
Klinkowstrom, Alfons (ed.). *Österreichs Theilnahme an den Befreiungskriegen.* Vienna, 1887.
Lambruschini, Luigi. *La mia nunziatura in Francia,* ed. P. Pirri. Bologna, 1934.

Lamennais, Félicité Robert de. *Oeuvres complètes.* 12 vols.; Paris, 1836–1837.
Lebzeltern, Ludwig Graf von. *Un collaborateur de Metternich: Mémoires et papiers de Lebzeltern,* ed. Emmanuel de Lévis-Mirepoix, Prince de Robech. Paris, 1949.
_____. *Les rapports de Lebzeltern, ministre d'Autriche à la cour de Russie, 1816–1826,* ed. Grand Duke Nicholas Mikhailowitch. St. Petersburg, 1913.
Maistre, Joseph de. *Correspondance diplomatique, 1811–1817,* ed. A. Blanc. Paris, 1861.
Mayer, P. A. G. von (ed.). *Corpus Juris Confoederationis Germanicae.* Frankfurt-am-Main, 1859.
Metternich-Winneburg, Clemens Lothar Wenzel Fürst von. *Mémoires, documents et écrits divers laissés par le Prince de Metternich,* ed. Prince Richard von Metternich-Winneburg. 8 vols.; Paris, 1880–1884.
_____. *Lettres du Prince de Metternich à la Comtesse de Lieven,* ed. Jean Hanoteau. Paris, 1909.
Moscati, Ruggero, *Il Regno delle Due Sicilie e l'Austria. Documenti dal marzo 1821 al novembre 1830.* 2 vols.; Naples, 1937.
Nada, Narciso (ed.). *Le relazioni diplomatiche fra l'Austria e il Regno di Sardegna, 1814–1830.* 3 vols.; Rome, 1964–1970.
_____. *Le relazioni diplomatiche fra l'Austria e il Regno di Sardegna, 1830–1848.* Rome, 1972—.
Neumann, Leopold (ed.). *Recueil des traités et conventions conclus par l'Autriche.* 5 vols.; Leipzig, 1857.
Pacca, Bartolomeo. *Historical Memoirs,* trans. George Head. 2 vols.; London, 1850.
Pallain, M.G. (ed.). *Correspondance inédite du Prince Talleyrand et du Roi Louis XVIII pendant le Congrès de Vienne.* Paris, 1881.
Pasquier, Étienne Dennis Duc de. *Histoire de mon temps. Mémoires du Chancelier Pasquier.* 6 vols.; Paris, 1893–1895.
Pradt, Abbé de. *Europe and America in 1821,* trans. J.D. Williams. 2 vols.; London, 1822.
Procacci, Giuliano (ed.). *Le relazioni diplomatiche fra lo Stato Pontificio e la Francia,* Series II, 1830–1848. Fonti per la Storia d'Italia. Rome, 1962—.
Rinieri, Ilario. *Corrispondenza inedita dei cardinali Consalvi e Pacca nel tempo del Congresso di Vienna.* Turin, 1903.
Robich, Prince Emmanuel de (ed.). *Un collaborateur de Metternich: Mémoires et papiers de Lebzeltern.* Paris, 1949.
Roveri, Alessandro (ed.). *La missione Consalvi e il Congresso di Vienna. Fonti per la Storia d'Italia.* 3 vols.; Rome, 1970–1973.
Sala, G.A. *Piano di riforma umiliato a Pio VII.* Rome, 1888.
Thomas, Louis (ed.). *Journal d'un conclave.* Paris, 1913.
Villèle, Jean Baptiste Comte de. *Mémoires et correspondance.* 5 vols.; Paris, 1889.
Weil, M.H. (ed.). *Les dessous du Congrès de Vienne.* 2 vols.; Paris, 1917.
Wiseman, Nicholas Cardinal. *Recollections of the Last Four Popes.* London, 1858.

III. Secondary Sources: Books

General works—whether on the Restoration, the Risorgimento, or on Austrian, Papal, or Italian history—are not listed unless they have been of particular value or have been cited in the footnotes. Nor has any attempt been made to list all the books on Metternich's career, particularly those of a derivative or popular nature; for a survey of the literature, see the article by Schroeder cited below or the third volume of Srbik's biography.

Ahrens, Liselotte. *Lamennais und Deutschland.* Munster, 1930.

Alberti, Annibale. *I Congressi che preparono il Risorgimento: da Vienna a Lubiana.* Rome, 1936.

Angelucci, G.A. *Il grande Segretario di Stato della Santa Sede E. Consalvi.* Rome, 1924.

Artaud de Montor, Alexis François. *Histoire du Pape Pie VII.* 3 vols.; 2nd ed.; Paris, 1837.

————. *Storia del Papa Leone XII.* Milan, 1843.

————. *Histoire du Pape Pie VIII.* Paris, 1844.

Bastgen, S. *Bayern und der Heilige Stuhl in der ersten Hälfe des 19. Jahrhundert.* 2 vols.; Munich, 1940.

Bastgen, Hubert. *Die Neuerrichtung der Bistümer im Österreich nach der Säkulrisation* Vienna, 1914.

Beau de Lomenie, Emmanuel de. *La carrière politique de Chateaubriand.* 2 vols.; Paris, 1929.

Becker, Jeronimo. *Relaciones diplomaticas entre España y la S. Sede durante el Siglo XIX.* Madrid, 1909.

Beidtel, Ignaz. *Geschichte der österreichischen Staatsverwaltung 1740–1848.* 2 vols.; Innsbruck, 1896-1898.

Berti, Giuseppi. *Russia e stati italiani nel Risorgimento.* Rome, 1957.

Bertier de Sauvigny, Guillaume de. *France and the European Alliance.* Notre Dame, 1958.

————. *Metternich and his Times,* trans. Peter Ryde. London, 1962.

————. *The Bourbon Restoration,* ed. Lynn Case. Philadelphia, 1966.

————. *Metternich et la France après le Congrès de Vienne.* 3 vols.; Paris, 1968-1971.

Beyle, Henri ("Stendhal"). *Promenades en Rome.* Paris, 1926.

————. *Rome, Naples, et Florence en 1817.* Paris, 1818.

Bianchi, Nicomede. *Storia della politica austriaca ai sovrani ed ai governi d'Italia.* Savona, 1857.

————. *Storia documentata della diplomazia europea in Italia dall'anno 1814 all' anno 1861.* 8 vols.; Turin, 1865-1872.

Bischoffshausen, S. von. *Papst Alexander VIII und der Wiener Hof.* Stuttgart, 1900.

Bona, Candido. *Le amicizie: società segrete e rinascita religiosa.* Turin, 1962.

Bourquin, Maurice. *Histoire de la Sainte Alliance.* Geneva, 1954.

Brady, Joseph H. *Rome and the Neapolitan Revolution of 1820–1821. A Study in Papal Neutrality.* New York, 1937.

Breycha-Vauthier, Arthur. *Aus Diplomatie und Leben. Maximen des Fürsten Metternich.* Graz, 1961.

Brezzi, Paolo. *La diplomazia pontificia.* Milan, 1942.

Brigante Colonna, G. *Bartolomeo Pacca.* Bologna, 1931.

Brosch, Moritz. *Geschichte des Kirchenstaats.* 2 vols.; Gotha, 1882.

Candeloro, Giorgio. *Storia dell'Italia moderna.* Milan, 1956—.

Cassi, Gellio. *Il Cardinal Consalvi ed i primi anni della restaurazione pontificia.* Milan, 1931.

Chotard, Henri. *Le Pape Pie VII à Savone.* Paris, 1887.

Cipoletta, Eugenio. *Memorie politiche sui conclavi.* Milan, 1863.

Colapietra, Raffaele. *La chiesa tra Metternich e Lamennais. Il pontificato di Leone XII.* Brescia, 1963.

_____. *La formazione diplomatica di Leone XII.* Rome, 1966.

_____. *La politica economica della Restaurazione romana.* Naples, 1966.

Contamine, Henry. *Diplomatie et diplomates sous la Restauration, 1814–1830.* Paris, 1970.

Corti, Egon Cäsar. *Metternich und die Frauen.* 2 vols.; Zurich, 1948.

Cutolo, Alessandro. *Il Duca di Brindisi.* Milan, 1960.

Daudet, Ernest. *Le Cardinal Consalvi.* Paris, 1866.

Demarco, Domenico. *Il tramonto dello Stato Pontificio. Il Papato di Gregorio XVI.* Turin, 1949.

Demelitsch, Fedor von. *Metternich und seine auswärtige Politik.* Stuttgart, 1898.

Derré, Jean-René. *Lamennais, ses amis, et la mouvement des idées à l'époque romantique.* Paris, 1962.

Derré, Jean-René. *Metternich et Lamennais.* Paris, 1963.

Dito, Oreste. *Massoneria, Carboneria, ed altre società segrete del Risorgimento italiano.* Turin, 1905.

Driault, Edouard. *Le grand empire.* Paris, 1924.

_____. *Napoleon en Italie.* Paris, 1906.

Droz, Jacques. *L'Europe centrale: Evolution historique de l'idée de Mitteileuropa.*

Duerm, Charles van. *Un peu plus de lumière sur le conclave de Venise.* Louvain, 1896.

Duine, F. *Essaie de bibliographie de Félicité Robert de La Mennais.* Paris, 1923.

Durry, Marie Jeanne. *L'Ambassade romaine de Chateaubriand.* Paris, 1927.

Eisler, Alexander. *Das Veto der katholischen Staaten bei der Papstwahl.* Vienna, 1907.

Emerson, Donald E. *Metternich and the Political Police.* The Hague, 1968.

Engel-Janosi, Friedrich. *Österreich und der Vatikan 1846–1918.* 2 vols.; Graz, 1958.

Farini, Luigi Carlo. *The Roman State from 1815 to 1850,* trans. by W.E. Gladstone. 4 vols.; London, 1851.

Federici, D. *Gregorio XVI tra favola e realtà.* Rovigo, 1947.

Feret, P. *Histoire diplomatique. La France et la Saint-Siège sous le Premier Empire, la Restauration, et la Monarchie de Juillet.* 2 vols.; Paris, 1911.

Fischer, Engelbert. *Cardinal Consalvi.* Mainz, 1899.

Fliche, Augustin, and Victor Martin (eds.), *Histoire de l'Église depuis ses origines jùsqu'à nos jours.* 24 vols.; Paris, 1945-1958.

Fontana, Sandro. *La controrivoluzione cattolica in Italia 1820–1830.* Brescia, 1968.

Fortini, Egidio. *Memorie storiche dell'universale giubileo celebrato nell'anno 1825.* Rome, 1901.

Fournier, August. *Der Congress von Chatillon.* Leipzig, 1900.

_____. *Die Geheimpolitzei auf dem Wiener Kongress.* Vienna, 1913.

Fusi-Pecci, Odo. *La vita del Papa Pio VIII.* Rome, 1965.

Gambaro, Angiolo. *Sulle orme del Lamennais in Italia.* Turin, 1958.

Gerbi, A. *La politica del Romanticismo.* Bari, 1932.

Ghisalberti, Alberto M. *Cospirazioni del Risorgimento.* Palermo, 1938.

Gigli, Guido. *Il Congresso di Vienna, 1814–1815.* Florence, 1938.

Goyau, Georges. *L'Allemagne religieuse. Le Catholicisme (1800–1846).* 2 vols.; Paris, 1906.

Grandmaison, Geoffroy de. *Le jubilé de 1825.* Paris, 1902.

Griewank, Karl. *Der Wiener Kongress.* 2nd ed.; Leipzig, 1954.

Grosse-Wietfeld, F. *Justizreformen im Kirchenstaat in den ersten Jahren der Restauration* Paderborn, 1932.

Gualterio, G.A. *Gli ultimi rivolgimenti italiani.* 5 vols.; Florence, 1852.

Guderzo, Giulio. *Vie e mezzi di comunicazioni in Piemonte.* Turin, 1961.

Guichen, Vicomte de. *La révolution de juillet et l'Europe.* Paris, 1916.

238   *Austria and the Papacy*

Haas, Arthur G. Metternich. *Reorganization and Nationality, 1813–1818. A Story of Foresight and Frustration in the Rebuilding of the Austrian Empire.* Wiesbaden, 1963.

Hayward, Ferdinand. *Le dernier siècle de la Rome pontificale.* 2 vols.; Paris, 1927–1928.

Hoffmann, Kurt M. *Preussen und die Julimonarchie 1830–1834.* Berlin, 1936.

Hosp, Eduard. *Kirche Österreichs im Vormärz.* Vienna, 1971.

————. *Zwischen Aufklärung und katholischer Reform: Jakob Frint.* Vienna, 1962.

Huber, Alfons, and Oscar Redlich. *Geschichte Österreichs.* 7 vols.; Vienna, 1885–1938.

Huber, Gustav. *Kriegsgefahr über Europa 1830–1832.* Berlin, 1932.

Huber, Norbert. *Österreich und der Heilige Stuhl vom Ende des spanischen Erbfolgekriegs bis zum Tode Klemens XI. Archif fürösterreichische Geschichte, XI.* Vienna, 1937.

Hudal, Alois. *Die österreichische Vatikanbotschaft, 1806–1918.* Munich, 1952.

Ingold, A.M.P. *Bénévent sous la domination de Talleyrand.* Paris, 1916.

Joussain, A. *Romantisme et politique.* Paris, 1924.

Kann, Robert A. *A Study in Austrian Intellectual History.* New York, 1960.

Kissinger, Henry. *A World Restored: Metternich, Castlereagh, and the Problems of Peace 1812–1822.* Boston, 1957.

König, L. *Pius VII, die Säkularisation und das Reichskonkordat.* Innsbruck, 1904.

Kraehe, Enno E. *Metternich's German Policy.* Princeton, 1963—.

Kramer, Hans. *Hapsburg und Rom in den Jahren 1708–1709.* Innsbruck, 1936.

————. *Österreich und das Risorgimento.* Vienna, 1963.

La Farina, Giuseppe. *Storia d'Italia dal 1815 al 1860.* 2 vols.; Turin, 1860.

Lauber, Emil. *Metternichs Kampf um die europäische Mitte.* Vienna, 1939.

Leflon, Jean. *Pie VII. Des abbayes Bénédictines à la Papauté.* Paris, 1958.

————. *La crise révolutionnaire 1789–1846.* Vol. XX of *Histoire de l'Église* eds. Fliche and Martin. Paris, 1949.

Lemmi, Francesco. *La politica estera di Carlo Alberto.* Florence, 1928.

Lepre, Aurelio. *La rivoluzione napoletana del 1820–1821.* Rome, 1967.

Luzio, A. *Il processo Pellico-Maroncelli.* Milan, 1903.

Maass, Ferdinand. *Der Josephinismus: Quellen zu seiner Geschichte in Österreich.* 5 vols.; Vienna, 1951–1961.

————. *Der Frühjosephinismus.* Vienna, 1969.

Mackesy, Piers. *The War in the Mediterranean, 1803–1810.* Cambridge, Mass., 1957.

Madelin, Louis. *Histoire du Consulat et de l'Empire.* 16 vols.; Paris, 1937-1954.

————. *La Rome de Napoleon.* 2nd ed.; Paris, 1906.

Maistre, Joseph de. *Du Pape,* ed. J. Louie. Geneva, 1966.

Manni, Graziano. *La polemica cattolica nel Ducato di Modena 1815–1861.* Modena, 1968.

Manzini, Luigi M. *Il Cardinale Luigi Lambruschini.* Vatican City, 1960.

Marmottan, P. *Le royaume d'Étrurie.* Paris, 1895.

Maturi, Walter. *Il concordato del 1818 tra la Santa Sede e le Due Sicilie.* Florence, 1929.

————. *Il Principe di Canosa.* Florence, 1944.

Mayol de Lupe, C. de. *La captivité de Pie VII.* Paris, 1912.

Mayr, Josef Karl. *Metternichs Geheimer Briefdienst: Postlagen und Postkurse.* Vienna, 1935.

Mollat, Guy. *La question romaine de Pie VII à Pie XI.* Paris, 1932.

Montagna, Leny. *I ducati parmensi nella diplomazia 1796–1815.* Parma, 1907.

Montasio, E. *Gioacchino Ventura.* Turin, 1862.

Monti, Antonio. *Un drammatico decennio di storia piemontese.* Milan, 1943.

Moscarini, Maria. *La restaurazione pontificia nelle provincie di prima ricupera.* Rome, 1933.

Nada, Narciso. *Austria e la questione romana dalla rivoluzione di luglio alla fine della conferenza diplomatica romana.* Turin, 1953.

―――. *Metternich e le riforme nello lo Stato Pontificio. La missione Sebregondi 1832–1836.* Turin, 1957.

Näf, Werner. *Abrustungsverhandlungen im Jahre 1831.* Bern, 1931.

Natelucci, Mario. *Il contributo delle Marche al Risorgimento nazionale.* Città di Castello, 1962.

Nichols, Irby C. *The European Pentarchy and the Congress of Verona, 1822.* The Hague, 1971.

Nuove questioni di storia del Risorgimento e dell'unità d'Italia. 2 vols.

Ottolini, A. *La carboneria dalle origini ai primi moti insurrezionali.* Modena, 1936.

Pane, Luigi del. *Lo Stato Pontificio e il movimento riformatore del settecento.*

Pastor, Ludwig von. *History of the Popes from the Close of the Middle Ages.* 40 vols.; St. Louis, 1891–1954.

Perlini, M. *I processi politici del Cardinale Rivarola.* Mantova, 1910.

Petrocchi, Massimo. *La restaurazione, il Cardinale Consalvi, e la riforma del 1816.* Florence, 1941.

―――. *La restaurazione romana, 1815–1823.* Florence, 1943.

Petruccelli della Gattina, F. *Histoire diplomatique des conclaves.* 4 vols.; Brussels, 1866.

Piano, R. del. *Roma e la rivoluzione del 1831.* Imola, 1931.

Pierantoni, A. *I Carbonari dello Stato Pontificio ricercati dalle inquisizioni austriache nel Regno Lombardo-Veneto 1817–1825.* 2 vols.; Rome, 1910.

Pignatelli, Giuseppi. *Aspetti della propaganda cattolica a Roma da Pio VI a Leone XII.* Rome, 1974.

Pirenne, Jacques-Henri. *La Sainte-Alliance.* 2 vols.; Neuchâtel, 1946–1949.

Piscitelli, Enzo. *Stato e chiesa sotto la Monarchia di Luglio.* Rome, 1950.

Polisensky, Josef. *Opavský kongres roku 1820 a evropská politika let 1820–1822.* Ostrava, 1962.

Prokesch-Osten, Anton Graf von. *Geschichte des Abfalls der Griechen und der Gründung des hellenischen Königreiches.* 6 vols.; Vienna, 1867.

Pugliese, Salvatore. *Le prime strette dell'Austria in Italia.* Milan, 1932.

Quacquarelli, Antonio. *La crisi del potere temporale del Papato nel Risorgimento.* Bari, 1940.

―――. *La ricostruzione dello Stato Pontificio.* Florence, 1945.

Radvany, Egon. *Metternich's Projects for Reform in Austria.* The Hague, 1971.

Rath, R. John. *The Provisional Austrian Regime in Lombardy-Venetia, 1814–1815.* Austin, 1969.

Remusat, Charles. *Il P. Ventura e la filosofia.* Milan, 1953.

Rieser, Herbert. *Der Geist des Josephinismus und sein Fortleben.* Vienna, 1962.

Rinieri, Ilario. *Il Congresso di Vienna e la Santa Sede.* Rome, 1904.

―――. *Napoleone e Pio VII.* 2 vols.; Turin, 1906.

Rizzo, P. *Teocrazia e neo-cattolicismo nel Risorgimento: pensiero politico del Ventura.* Palermo, 1938.

Rohden, Peter Richard. *Die klassische Diplomatie von Kaunitz bis Metternich.* Leipzig, 1939.

Romani, George T. *The Neapolitan Revolution of 1820–1821.* Evanston, 1950.

Rosa, Gabriele de. *Storia del movimento cattolico in Italia.* 2 vols.; Bari, 1966.

Roveri, Alessandro. *La Santa Sede tra rivoluzione francese e restaurazione.* Florence, 1974.

Ruck, Ernst. *Die römische Kurie und die deutsch Kirchenfrage auf dem Wiener Kongress.* Basel, 1917.

Salata, Francesco. *Maria Luigia e i moti del Trentuno.* Parma, 1932.

Sandona, A. *Il regno lombardo-veneto 1814–1859; la costituzione e l'amministrazione.* Milan, 1912.

Schenk, Hans G. *The Aftermath of the Napoleonic Wars. The Concert of Europe—an Experiment.* New York, 1947.

Schlitter, Hans. *Pius VI und Joseph II 1782-1784.* Vienna, 1894.

Schmidlin, Josef. *Histoire des papes de l'epoque contemporaine,* trans. L. Marchal. 2 vols.; Paris, 1938-1940.

Schmitt, C. *Politische Romantik.* Munich, 1925.

Schnabel, Franz. *Storia religiosa della Germania nell'ottocento,* trans. M. Bendiscioli Brescia, 1944.

Schroeder, Paul W. *Metternich's Diplomacy at its Zenith, 1820-1823.* Austin, 1962.

Schwarz, Wilhelm. *Die Heilige Allianz. Tragic eines europäischen Friedensbundes.* Stuttgart, 1935.

Silva, Pietro. *La Monarchi di Luglio e l'Italia.* Turin, 1917.

Silvagni, David. *La corte e la società romana nei secoli XVIII e XIX.* 3 vols.; Rome, 1883.

Spadoni, Domenico. *La cospirazione di Macerata nel 1817.* Macerata, 1895.

―――――. *Per la prima guerra d'independenza italiana nel 1815.* Pavia, 1929.

―――――. *Sette, cospirazioni e cospiratori nello Stato Pontificio.* Turin, 1904.

―――――. *Una trama e un tentativo rivoluzionario dello Stato Romano nel 1820-1821.* Rome, 1910.

Spellanzoni, Cesar. *Storia del Risorgimento e dell'Unità d'Italia.* 5 vols.; Milan, 1933-49.

Sorel, Albert. *Europe et la révolution française.* 10th ed.; 8 vols.; Paris, 1917.

Srbik, Heinrich Ritter von. *Metternich: der Staatsmann und der Mensch.* 3 vols.; Munich, 1925-1954.

―――――. *Mitteleuropa: das Problem und die Versuche seiner Lösung in der deutsch Geschichte.* Weimar, 1937.

Stearns, Peter. *Priest and Revolutionary: Lamennais and the Dilemma of French Catholicism.* New York, 1967.

Stern, Alfred. *Geschichte Europas seit den Verträgen von 1815 bis zum Frankfurter Frieden von 1871.* 10 vols.; Stuttgart, 1894-1924.

Straus, Hannah Alice. *The Attitude of the Congress of Vienna toward Nationalism in Germany, Italy, and Poland.* New York, 1949.

Temperley, Harold. *The Foreign Policy of Canning, 1822-1827.* London, 1925.

Till, Rudolf. *Hofbauer und sein Kreis.* Vienna, 1952.

Tivaroni, Carlo. *Storia criticia del risorgimento.* 9 vols.; Turin, 1888-1897.

Tomek, Ernst. *Kirchengeschichte Österreichs.* 3 vols.; Innsbruck, 1949.

Torta, C. *La rivoluzione piemontese del 1821.* Rome, 1908.

Trovanelli, Nazzareno. *La decapitazione di Montanari e di Targhini.* Cesena, 1890.

Valente, Angela. *Gioacchino Murat e l'Italia meridionale.* 2nd ed.; Turin, 1965.

Valjavec, Fritz. *Der Josephinismus: zur geistigen Entwicklung Österreichs im XVIII und XIX Jahrhundert.* Munich, 1945.

Valsecchi, Franco. *L'assolutismo illuminato in Austria e Lombardia.* 2 vols.; Bologna, 1931.

Ventrone, Alfonso. *L'amministrazione dello Stato Pontificio.* Rome, 1942.

Vernier, Donat. *Histoire du Patriarcat armenien catholique.* Lyons, 1891.

Verucci, Guido. *Felicite Lamennais.* Naples, 1963.

Vidal, César. *Louis Philippe, Metternich, et la crise italienne 1831-1832.* Paris, 1932.

Wahrmund, Ludwig. *Das Ausschliessungsrecht der katholischen Staaten bei den Papstwahlen.* Vienna, 1888.

Wandruszka, Adam. *Österreich und Italien im 18. Jahrhundert.* Vienna, 1963.

Webster, Charles. *The Foreign Policy of Castlereagh, 1812-1815.* London, 1931.

―――――. *The Foreign Policy of Castlereagh, 1815-1822.* London, 1925.

_____. *The Congress of Vienna.* 2nd ed.; London, 1934.

Weil, M.H. *Joachim Murat, Roi de Naples: La dernière année de Règne.* 5 vols.; Paris, 1909-1910.

_____. *Le Prince Eugene et Murat, 1813-1814.* Paris, 1902.

Weinzierl-Fischer, Erika. *Die österreichischen Konkordate von 1855 und 1933.* Vienna, 1960.

Welschinger, Henri. *Le divorce de Napoleon.* Paris, 1889.

_____. *Le Pape et l'Empéreur.* Paris, 1905.

Widmann, Hans. *Geschichte Salzburgs.* 3 vols.; Gotha, 1914.

Winter, Eduard. *Der Josefinismus: die Geschichte des österreichischen Reformkatholizmus.* 2nd ed.; Berlin, 1962.

_____. *Romantismus, Restauration, und Frühliberalismus im österreichischen Vormärz.* Vienna, 1968.

Winterich, Richard. *Sein Schicksal war Napoleon. Leben und Zeit des Kardinalstaatsekretärs E. Consalvi.* Heidelberg, 1951.

Wodka, Josef. *Kirche in österreichs.* Vienna, 1959.

Zadei, Guido. *L'Abate Lamennais e gli italiani del suo tempo.* Turin, 1929.

IV. Secondary Sources: Articles

Andreu, Francesco. "Chateaubriand ambasciatore a Roma e il P. Ventura," *Regnum Dei,* 4 (1948): 307-342.

_____. "Il padre Ventura," *Regnum Dei,* 17 (1961): 11-16.

Aquarone, Alberto. "La restaurazione nello Stato Pontificio ed i suoi indirizzi legislativi," *Archivio della societa romana di storia patria,* 78 (1955): 119-189.

Artom, Eugene. "Italia e Francia nell'età della Restaurazione," *Rassegna storica toscana* 8 (1962): 103-124.

Avetta, Maria. "Al Congresso di Lubiana coi ministri del Re Vittorio Emmanuele I," *Il Risorgimento italiano,* 16 (1923): 1-50, 17 (1924): 212-250.

Bastgen, Hubert. "Un promemoria sopra le cause della rivoluzione nello Stato Pontificio nel 1831," *Rassegna storica del Risorgimento,* 11 (1924): 435-463.

_____. "Provvidenze del Governo Pontificio dopo la rivoluzione francese di luglio 1830." *Rassegna storica del Risorgimento,* 15 (1928): 321-361.

Beer, A. "Kirchliche Angelegenheiten in Österreich 1816-1842," *Mitteilungen des Instituts für österreichische Geschichtsforschung,* 18 (1897): 493-575.

Benedikt, Heinrich, "Der Josephinismus vor Joseph II," *Österreich und Europa. Festgabe für Hugo Hantsch,* Graz, 1965, 183-201.

_____. "Kirchenstaat: Kirche-Staat," *Österreiches Archiv für Kirchenrecht,* 11 (1960): 1-16.

Bernard, Paul P. "The Origins of Josephinism: Two Studies," *Colorado College Studies* No. 7, 1964.

Berselli, Aldo. "Movimenti politici a Bologna dal 1815 al 1859," *Bollettino del Museo del Risorgimento,* 5 (1960): 201-254.

Bertier de Sauvigny, Guillaume de. "Sainte-Alliance et Alliance dans les conceptions de Metternich," *Revue historique,* 223 (1960): 249-274.

Bettanini, Antonio Maria. "Un disegno di confederazione italiana nella politica internazionale della Restaurazione," *Studi di storia dei trattati e politica internazionale.* Padova, 1939, 3-50.

Blaas, Richard. "Das Kardinalprotektorat der deutschen und österreichen Nation im 18. und 19. Jahrhundert," *Mitteilungen des Österreichischen Staatsarchivs,* 10 (1957): 148-185.

Brusatti, Alois. "Graf Philipp Stadion als Finanzminister," *Osterreich und Europa. Festgabe für Hugo Hantsch.* Graz, 1965, 281-294.

Carraroli, Pierino. "Le Marche non insorsero nei moti del 1820-1821," *L'apporto delle Marche al Risorgimento nazionale.* Ancona, 1961.

Celli, Sante. "Il riconoscimento di Luigi Filippo da parte della Santa Sede," *Chiesa e Stato nell'ottocento,* ed. R. Aubert. Padova, 1962, 67-104.

Colapietra, Raffaele. "Amministrazione e burocrazia nello Stato Pontificio della Restaurazione," *Rassegna di politica e di storia,* 12 (1966): 142-145.

_____. "Un carteggio del Cardinale Consalvi," *Rassegna di politica e di storia,* 8 (1962): 21-32.

_____. "Un carteggio del Cardinale Spina," *Rassegna di politica e di storia,* 9 (1963): 7-12.

_____. "Il Diario Brunelli del conclave del 1823," *Archivio storico italiano,* 120 (1962): 76-146.

_____. "Il diario del conclave del 1829," *Critica storica,* 1 (1962): 517-541, 636-661.

_____. "Gaetano Moroni nel conclave del 1829," *Rassegna di politica e di storia,* 9 (1963): 13-17.

_____. "L'insegnamento del Padre Ventura alla Sapienza," *Regnum Dei,* 10 (1962): 230-259.

_____. "Le lettere del Cardinale Rivarola durante la Restaurazione," *Rassegna di politica e di storia,* 12 (1966): 57-62.

Contamine, Henry. "Il rêve du système féderatif français et l'Italie," *Rassegna storica toscana,* 8 (1962): 187-200.

_____. "La grande tentative d'expansion de la Charte et L'Italie," *Atti del XXXVII Congresso del Risorgimento italiano,* Rome, 1961, 60-68.

Cortese, Nino. "Il Principe di Metternich a Napoli nel 1819," *Il Mezzogiorno ed il Risorgimento italiano,* Naples, 1964, 378-388.

Costa, Anna. "Giuseppi Barbaroux, ambasciatore presso la Santa Sede 1816-1824," *Bollettino storic-bibliografico subalpino,* 66 (1968): 465-521.

Dollot, Louis, "Conclaves et diplomatie française au XVIII siècle," *Revue d'histoire diplomatique,* 75 (1961): 124-135.

Dudon, P. "Lettres inédites de Lamennais à Abbé Baraldi," *Documents d'histoire,* 9 (March, 1911): 146-148.

Filipuzzi, Angelo. "La restaurazione nel Regno delle Due Sicilie dopo il Congresso di Lubiana," *Annali Triestini di diritto, economia e politica,* 11 (1940): 161-206, 230-282.

Fulani, Silvio. "L'abolizione del corriere toscana di Roma nei primi anni della Restaurazione," *Archivio storico italiano,* 104 (1947): 74-85.

_____. "La convenzione postale austro-pontificia del 1815," *Archivio della deputazione romana di storia patria,* 69 (1946): 23-58.

_____. "La questione postale italiana al Congresso di Verona," *Nuova rivista storica,* 32 (1948): 36-49.

_____. "La Santa Sede e il Congresso di Verona," *Nuova rivista storica,* 39 (1955): 465-491, 40 (1956): 14-47.

Gallavresi, Giuseppi. "Le Prince de Talleyrand et le Cardinal Consalvi," *Revue des questions historiques,* 77 (1905): 158-172.

Gamberale, Bice. "Gli inizi del pontificato di Gregorio XVI," *Rassegna storica del Risorgimento,* 14 (1927): 657-715.

Gambaro, Angiolo. "Carteggi inediti del Lamennais coi Italiani," *Giornale critico della filosofia italiana,* 9 (1928): 184-204.

_____. "La fortuna di Lamennais in Italia," *Studi francesi,* 2 (1958): 189-219.

Giuntella, Vittorio. "La capitale e i problemi dello Stato," *Studi romani,* 14 (1966): 269-291.

_____. "Profilio di uno 'Zelante' Mons Bonaventura Gazzola," *Rassegna storica del Risorgimento,* 43 (1956): 413-418.

Glossy, Karl. "Kaiser Franz Reise nach Italien in Jahr 1819," *Jahrbuch der Grillparzer Gesellschaft,* 14 (1904): 149-418.

Grossman, Karl. "Metternichs Plan eines italienischen Bundes," *Historische Blätter,* 4 (1931): 37-76.

Hoffmann, Fritz L. "Metternich and the July Revolution," *East European Quarterly,* 12 (1967): 143-154.

Lodolini, Elio. "Il brigantaggiow nel Lazio meridionale dopo la Restaurazione, 1814-1825," *Archivio della società romana di storia patria,* 83 (1960): 189-268.

Lotti, Luigi. "Le Legazioni," *Bibliografia dell'età del Risorgimento,* 2 vols.; Florence, 1972. 2:273-290.

Maass, Ferdinand. "Der Wiener Nuntius Severoli und der Spätjosephinismus," *Mitteilungen des Instituts für österreichische Geschichtsforschung,* 63 (1955): 484-499.

Mantese, Giovanni. "Corrispondenza inedita di Papa Pio VII, del Card. Consalvi, e di Mauro Cappellari, poi Gregorio XVI, con G.M. Peruzzi, Vescovo di Chioggia e amministratore apostolico de Venezia," *Archivum Historiae pontificiae,* 4 (1966): 260-280.

Masure, A. "La reconnaissance de la Monarchie de Juillet," *Annales de l'École Libre des sciences politiques,* 1892:698-721, 1893:72-117.

Maturi, Walter. "Il Congresso di Vienna e la restaurazione dei Borboni a Napoli," *Rivista storica italiana,* 55 (1938): 32-72, 56:1-61.

Moscati, Ruggero. "Il governo napoletano e il conclave di Pio VIII," *Rassegna storica del Risorgimento,* 20 (1933): 257-274.

Nevola, Elena. "La questione di Parma al Congresso di Vienna e un memoriale del Neipperg," *Archivio storico per le provincie parmensi,* 3rd series, 3 (1938): 111-125.

Omodeo, Adolfo. "Il Cardinale Consalvi al Congresso di Vienna," *La Critica,* 36: (1938): 426-440, 37 (1939): 24-36.

Oxilla, Ugo. "Il Cardinale Rivarola e l'attentato del 1826," *Rassegna storica del Risorgimento,* 13 (1926): 273-309.

_____. "Il conclave di Papa Leone XII," *Rassegna storica del Risorgimento,* 8 (1921): 611-616.

_____. "Tre conclavi," *Rassegna storica del Risorgimento,* 20 (1933): 564-584.

Pasztor, Lajos. "La Congregazione degli Affari Ecclesiastici Straordinari tra il 1814 e il 1850," *Archivum Historiae Pontificiae,* 6 (1968): 191-307.

_____. "I Cardinali Albani e Bernetti e l'intervento austriaco nel 1831," *Rivista di storia della Chiesa in Italia,* 7 (1954): 95-115.

_____. "Ercole Consalvi Prosegretario del Conclave di Venezia," *Archivio della società romana di storia patria,* 83 (1960): 99-187.

Pedrotti, P. "I rapporti di Tito Manzi col governo austriaco," *Rassegna storica del Risorgimento,* 29 (1942): 3-45.

Piola Caselli, Elisabetta. "Un ministro toscano al Congresso di Vienna," *Rassegna nazionale,* 194 (1913): 487-509, 195 (1914): 48-70, 184-208, 326-362, 196 (1914): 39-70.

Pirri, P. "La fortuna del La Mennais in Italia," *Civiltà Cattolica,* 81 (1930): Part 3, 193-212, Part 4, 3-19.

_____. "Lamennais en Italie," *Études,* February 20, 1933, 422-442.

_____. "Il movimento Lamennaisiano in Italia," *Civiltà Cattolica,* 83 (1932): Part 3, 313-327, 567-583.

Pivano, Silvio. "Il veto od exclusiva nell'elezione del pontefice," *Scritti minori di storia e storia del diritto,* Turin, 1965, 333-391.

Pleyer, K. "Augustin Gruber 1763-1835," *Unsere Heimat,* 34 (1963): 95-105.

Polisênsky, Josef. "Il Congresso di Opava (Troppau) e la politica europea degli annis 1820-1822 nei fondi degli archivi cechi," *Studi storici,* 4 (1963): 293-301.

Posch, Andreas. "Die kirchenpolitische Einstellung Metternichs," *Religion, Wissenschaft, Kultur,* 13 (1962): 119-127.

————. "Lamennais und Metternich," *Mitteilungen des Institutes für österreichische Geschichtsforschung,* 62 (1954): 490-516.

————. "Straatsrat Josef Jüstel," *Zeitschrift des historischen Vereins für Steirmark* 44 (1953): 99-110.

Quacquarelli, Antonio. "Crisi economica dello Stato Pontificio nell'età della restaurazione," *Rivista italiana di scienze economiche,* 11 (1940): 1103-1110.

Ranke, Leopold von. "Cardinal Consalvi und seine Staatsverwaltung unter dem Pontificat Pius VII," *Historische-biographische Studien. Samtliche Werke,* 40. Leipzig, 1877.

Rath, R. John. "The *Carbonari*: their Origins, Initiation Rites, and Aims," *American Historical Review,* 49 (1964): 353-370.

————. "La costituzione guelfa e i servizi segreti austriaci," *Rassegna storica del Risorgimento,* 50 (1963): 346-376.

Reinerman, Alan J. "Metternich, Alexander I, and the Russian Challenge in Italy, 1815-1820," *Journal of Modern History,* 46 (1974): 262-276.

————. "Metternich, the Papacy, and the Greek Revolution," *East European Quarterly,* 12 (1978): 177-188.

————. "Metternich and Reform: The Case of the Papal State, 1814-1848," *Journal of Modern History,* 42 (1970): 524-548.

————. "Papacy and Papal State in the Restoration (1814-1846): Studies since 1939," *The Catholic Historical Review,* 64 (1978): 36-46.

Rinieri, Ilario. "Le sette in Italia dopo la restaurazione del 1815," *Il Risorgimento italiano,* 19 (1926): 1-23.

Rizzardo, G. "Il Patriarchato di Venezia durante il regno napoleonico, 1806-1814," *Nuovo archivio veneto,* new series, 28 (1914): 1-19.

Roberti, Melchiorre. "La legislazione ecclesiastica nel periodo napoleonico," *Chiesa e stato.* 2 vols.; Milan, 1939. 1:255-332.

Rosi, Mario. "Un plebescito repubblicano al tempo del Congresso di Vienna," *Rivista d'Italia,* February 1905, 256-281.

Rossi, Mario. "Il conclave di Leone XII," *Bollettino della R. Deputazione di storia patria per l'Umbria,* 33 (1935): 135-215.

Schroeder, Paul W. "Metternich Studies since 1925," *Journal of Modern History,* 33 (1961): 237-260.

Seton-Watson, R.W. "Metternich and internal Austrian Policy," *Slavonic and East European Review,* 17 (1939): 539-555, 18 (1940): 129-141.

Sorbelli, Adriano. "L'ambasceria della Santa Sede in Russia nel 1826," *Memorie dell' Accademia delle Scienze dell'Istituto di Bologna,* 1943-1944, 29-61.

Spadoni, Domenico. "Nel centenario del proclama di Rimini," *Rassegna storica del Risorgimento,* 2 (1915): 329-363.

————. "Roma segreta all'indomani della restaurazione," *Rassegna storica del Risorgimento,* 9 (1922): 80-93.

Sperber, Vladimer. "Intorno alla politica napoletana della Francia nel 1820-1821," *Rassegna storica del Risorgimento,* 57 (1968): 167-212.

Tamborra, Angelo. "I congressi della Santa Alleanza di Lubiana e di Verona e la politica della Santa Sede," *Archivio storico italiano,* 118 (1960): 190-211.

Terlinden, Charles. "Le conclave de Léon XII," *Revue d'histoire ecclesiastique,* 8 (1913): 272-303.

Toth, Lucio. "Gli ordinamenti territoriali e l'organizzazione perifica dello Stato Pontificio," *Studi in occasione del centenario.* 2 vols.; Milan, 1970. 1:95-148.

Ugolino, Patrizia. "La politica estera del card. Tommaso Bernetti Segretario di Stato di Leone XII," *Archivio della società romana di storia patria,* 92 (1969): 213-320.

Venturi, Franco. "Elementi e tentativi di riforme nello Stato Pontificio del settecento," *Rivista storica italiana,* 71 (1963): 778-837.

Verucci, Guido. "Per una storia del cattolicismo intransigente in Italia dal 1815 al 1848," *Rassegna storica toscana,* 4 (1958): 251-285.

Weil, M.H. "Le révirement de la politique autrichienne à l'égard de Joachim Murat," *Biblioteca di storia italiana recente,* 2 (1909): 393-435.

Zazo, Alfredo. "L'occupazione napoletana e austriaca e i primordi della Restaurazione in Benevento," *Samnium,* 29 (1956): 189-206, 30 (1957): 1-26, 121-147.

Zöllner, Erich. "Bemerkungen zum Problem der Beziehungen zwischen Aufklärung und Josephinismus," *Österreich und Europa. Festgabe für Hugo Hantsch.* Graz, 1965.

INDEX

N.B. Pages in italics refer to biographical footnotes.